STRATEGIC PLANNING

Clark Holloway

Nelson-Hall nh Chicago

Library of Congress Cataloging-in-Publication Data

Holloway, Clark.
    Strategic planning.

    Bibliography: p.
    Includes index.
    1. Strategic planning.   I. Title
HD30.28.H67   1986   658.4'012   85-25837
ISBN 0-8304-1070-8

Manufactured in the United States of America

10 9 8 7 6 5 4 3 2 1

The paper in this book is pH neutral (acid-free).

Contents

Preface

This book, by definition, is about strategic planning. The meaning of the term may at first seem self-evident. Over the years business people have talked about long-range planning, comprehensive planning, top-management planning, business planning, and undoubtedly other types of planning as well. One of the first things this book does is to attempt to clarify all these terms and tell why the name *Strategic Planning* is appropriate, what it means, and how such planning differs from other types of planning.

There is another dimension of possible confusion. It is now fashionable to talk of strategic management. We explore the distinctions in this direction also. Strategic planning overlaps and draws help from many disciplines: business policy, organizational theory, and the various other quantitative and qualitative fields. While we would not attempt to draw a rigorous dividing line between strategic management and strategic planning, on the one hand, the former tends toward "blue sky" issues and to answer questions regarding What is to be done? On the other hand, strategic planning tends to relate more to the "nuts and bolts" of the strategy process and to answer questions regarding How is it to be done? The common ground that the two share is more important: both require the ability to think strategically, to aim at the "big picture," and to be undistracted by less important details.

The target of this book is not only the professional planner, but instead, all of those who do planning or who wish to do planning. We allude here to the fact that the chief executive officer (CEO) and other line executives are the planners, while the "professional planners" in fact are engaged in facilitating planning, reporting planning, and perhaps guiding planning.

v

One usually thinks of strategic planning as it applies to organizations and particularly to businesses. Again, we can expand the precepts of strategic planning in two directions. First, an individual would do well to plan his or her own life in the strategic manner. Think ahead, plan ahead, know what your objectives are for some years in the future, so that you can take appropriate steps to achieve them. Second, the precepts apply equally well to nonprofit organizations. No organization exists unless it has objectives, and the way to make sure those objectives reach fulfillment is to follow a strategic planning road map. While the book often refers specifically to a business situation, the more universal application should always be kept in mind.

Even in the business sphere, it is sometimes thought that strategic planning is only useful to the very large corporation. This is not true. We feel that strategic planning is beneficial to all organizations, of all sizes. Large businesses are often emphasized in discussions of planning because their complexity and wide range of activities make more interesting examples and provide a wide range of role models. Certain planning activities occur in small companies either not at all or only at a very simplified level. However, the reader should not infer that strategic planning is unimportant in the small business; indeed we feel that quite the reverse is the situation.

This leads to a discussion of the contingency aspects of strategic planning. What specific techniques are appropriate in one large multinational corporation (MNC) may not be appropriate in another large MNC. By the same token, what is appropriate in a particular MNC may not be appropriate in a small business, in planning for personal life, or in a nonprofit organization. In an overall philosophic sense, strategic planning is truly indispensable, and has been proven so, to organizations of all types and all sizes. The level at which planning is done also has contingency aspects. Strategic planning can, of course, be done in any part of an organization, but the planning that counts most and that exerts the most influence is done at the top of the organizational hierarchy. Each organization has its own planning systems, and the ways in which the extremely important feedback principle is introduced, the interrelationships between corporate and functional planning, and the relationships between planning and control, will all have contingency aspects.

From his own background, the author brings to bear four disparate views on the subject of strategic planning: first, long industrial experience, culminating with hands-on planning effort in a major corporation; second, formalized academic study in the field; third, consulting work in strategic planning; and fourth, application of these principles to nonprofit organizations in the course of this consulting work.

We believe in a number of precepts that will be emphasized throughout the book.

- The presence of various hierarchies is important to recognize. In addition to the usual organizational hierarchy, there are a hierarchy of objectives, a hierarchy of strategies, and a hierarchy of plans. These range from the overall corporate strategic plan to the functional or divisional strategic plans, and further to the various tactical or operating plans.

- The feedback principle encourages an organization to cycle upwards and downwards over its various hierarchies in order to achieve consistent and properly interrelated elements.

- Analyses of strengths, weaknesses, opportunities, and threats (called SWOT analyses) are imperative. An organization must be able to identify these factors in order to plot its course and to choose its strategy. Data bases and information handling come into this effort to an important degree.

- Computer models and computerized analyses, for a large majority of organizations, are becoming increasingly needed and increasingly accepted.

As far as pedagogy is concerned, we believe that the best way to learn a subject is to engage in activity related to the subject. The best way to learn strategic planning is to plan. It is suggested that, as students progress through this book, they simultaneously engage themselves in preparing a strategic plan for either a real or a hypothetical organization. The exercise at the end of each chapter is intended to guide the student, first, in finding a suitable organization, and second, in progressing through the various aspects of planning that need to be considered. A reader who is a practitioner rather than an MBA student can treat the exercises as a step-by-step list of what needs to be considered in preparing a strategic plan for his or her own organization. We also include case histories showing how good strategic planning has been done in two corporations.

There is no question but that planning pays off and that an organization is stronger and more profitable through planning. The experts and the literature, much of which is cited in this book, overwhelmingly agree on this. Nevertheless, an event such as a nuclear blast might negate government planning. Such an event in the corporate arena was the world's largest takeover of the Gulf Oil Corporation by Chevron. The planning principles illustrated in the book by Gulf examples remain viable and unchanged by the "nuclear blast."

Sincere thanks are due to many associates in the Gulf Oil Corporation in London, Pittsburgh, Houston, and elsewhere. At the University of Pittsburgh, discussions with John Grant, Bill King, and Ed Sussna have been most beneficial. And last but not least, the collegial and supportive atmosphere at the University of South Carolina, including discussions with Alan Bauerschmidt, Carl Clamp, Greg Dess, Herb Hand, John Logan, Jack Pearce, Richard Robinson, Robert Rosen, Joe Ullman, and Ron Wilder, has greatly encouraged the writing of this book. The support of Deans Jim Hilton and Jim Kane has also been much appreciated.

Chapter 1

Introduction
and Overview

"Strategic management" is a phrase currently in favor, having supplanted the phrase "business policy" or the single word "management." The new term emphasizes allowance for contingencies: it is implied that a cookbook recipe cannot be used in all situations.

Strategic management has a flavor of success about it, perhaps because of its distinguishing characteristics:

1. *Establish mission.* The managers and executives of the organization have a clear idea of its purpose and why it exists.
2. *Select objectives.* There is a set of one or more objectives—the desired results to be achieved in the long-term future.
3. *Set goals.* Short-term objectives are assigned specific calendar dates for achievement.
4. *Analyze strengths and weaknesses.* The organization is scrutinized and analyzed for its strengths and weaknesses.
5. *Study threats and opportunities.* The environment is studied from the standpoint of threats to the organization and opportunities for the organization.
6. *Prepare planning documents.* The managers and executives of the organization engage in strategic planning. All of the above items are quantified and consolidated into documents showing what is to be accomplished, when, and by whom. Typically these documents include both financial and volume projections and extend five to ten years into the future.
7. *Ensure implementability.* Members of the organization implement

the plans and monitor the successful delivery of the organization's products or services.

It is apparent that the elements of strategic management are not repetitive—they cannot be programmed into a "standing plan" procedure. Although not included in the above list, Chandler's (1962) concept—that it may be necessary to revise organizational structure in order to accomplish desired strategic results—is pertinent.

STRATEGIC PLANNING

The difference between strategic planning and strategic management is nebulous at best. In order to plan intelligently, one must certainly consider the elements in the preceding list. One might expect to pay particular attention to item 6, preparation of planning documents. For item 7, the major emphasis would be on assuring that the plans are possible of implementation rather than on implementation itself, which is not a planning function. With these reservations, we will use the list as a program for strategic planning, as summarized in figure 1.1. Note that an additional item has been added to figure 1.1:8. Review the process. Feedback is essential in strategic planning. Planning may be done continuously, irregularly, or on a fixed time schedule (often annually), but it must be recognized that each of the elements of figure 1.1 is subject to repeated evaluation and change.

Planning is a top-level activity, involving complex and interrelated business decisions. Each of the entries in figure 1.1 must and will be discussed at greater length in later chapters. The procedure will be to develop a conceptual basis for each step and in so doing to arrive at a conceptual framework for the entire strategic planning process.

Why Plan?

It has been said that if we fail to plan, we plan to fail. Yet can we really know what we should be planning for? Executives are rightly concerned about monitoring change, and many companies maintain some form of early warning system. How successful such systems can be may be questioned, that is, if they are based on the assumption of a continuation of present trends in consumption, economic growth, employment, or other factors. One wonders whether sharp breaks in such trends can be predicted and, even more difficult, whether the direction of such breaks can be predicted.

In spite of such doubts, major contributors to the planning literature, such as Steiner (1979), Ansoff (1965), Drucker (1973), and King and Cleland (1978), agree that a formal planning system is an important factor lead-

FIGURE 1.1 Strategic Planning Program

1. Establish mission
2. Select objectives
3. Set goals
4. Analyze strengths and weaknesses
5. Study threats and opportunities
6. Prepare planning documents
7. Ensure implementability
8. Review the process

ing to corporate success. The value of strategic planning is that it both simulates and stimulates.

The strategic planning process permits one to *simulate* the future on paper. If the planner is not pleased with the projection, the process can be modified and then repeated. Such planning encourages the creation and evaluation of a significant number of alternate courses of action. Strategic planning is a systems approach that guides the planner through the steps shown in figures 1.2 and 1.4. The available information sources, data banks, and computer models not only facilitate the study of alternatives, but they remind the planner that the task is to promote the entire organization rather than to suboptimize individual departments.

Strategic planning *stimulates* an executive to discharge responsibilities effectively. Every organization needs a hierarchy including mission, objectives, and goals. It has been rightly said that if you don't know where you are going, any road will get you there. Planning provides a framework for decision making throughout the organization, both preventing off-the-cuff decisions and encouraging and permitting the testing of value judgments with fellow executives. It is thus valuable as a communication device. All levels and segments of management can see and understand the desired interrelationship of effort within the organization.

Research to quantify the association between formal planning and organizational performance has been summarized by Leontiades and Tezel (1980). Results are mixed. About half the studies cited found a positive correlation between formal planning and superior organizational performance, while others found a weak link or no link. Such research is difficult. It is difficult or impossible to find comparable companies that operate with and without planning. One is therefore faced with the need to rank the quality of the planning effort of a company. It is not clear how this can be done independently and objectively by the researcher. Leontiades and Tezel, for example, rely on each corporate planner and corporate executive to rank his or her own system.

FIGURE 1.2   The Strategic Planning Process

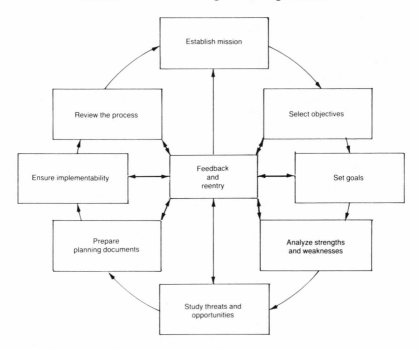

The Systematic Approach

Earlier in this century most chief executives knew with confidence the objectives of their organizations and how to achieve them. By the sixties, however, many factors (discussed below) were arising to undermine this confidence. Planning has been found to be a way of coping with these factors. Since managers and executives are always under time pressure, following systematic schedules of planning activities is obviously imperative.

One of the factors that has led to systematic strategic planning is the growing public concern with objectives of organizations, particularly where the organization is a corporation. These objectives have been scrutinized by various segments of the public—protest groups, the media, politicians, and the man on the street. Formalized strategic planning provides a basis for rational dialogue with these challengers.

Another factor is the increasing size and complexity of organizations. As companies grow larger, the effects of decisions become more widespread and longer lasting. With growth, it also becomes increasingly important (and difficult) to monitor and control the activities of subdivisions. Increasing variety of products or services is another important aspect of complexity. The pressure for short-term results is best countered by systematic strategic planning.

The third factor is the increasing rate of change in the modern world, so well detailed by Toffler (1972). Technologies and social patterns appear and disappear quickly. Consequently, the decision maker has less confidence that a decision valid today will remain valid for even the near future. It is therefore necessary to spend more time on planning and the consideration of alternatives. Better decisions must result when one follows a systematic schedule, as suggested by figure 1.1.

Feedback, or recycling, is an important concept in strategic planning, which is not apparent from figure 1.1. Consideration of any item in the figure may suggest modifications that need to be made in earlier items. The feedback concept is illustrated in figure 1.2.

An organization beginning the planning process for the first time would enter the diagram at the top by formulating its mission. It is possible that this and most of the other blocks in figure 1.2 may be dealt with only in the mind of the executive, but this is not recommended. For many reasons that will be detailed in later chapters, it is strongly suggested that all the blocks in figure 1.2 should result in explicit written statements and documents. The planning sequence proceeds clockwise around the circle. Once the first cycle has been completed, some of the items, particularly mission and objectives, may not need revision. An organization with an ongoing planning effort will repeatedly touch all bases on the diagram, even though some of the items may not be altered.

At any point, the study of a particular item may suggest needed changes in a preceding item. For example, a study of threats and opportunities may indicate that one or more of the organization's objectives must be modified. This is shown on the diagram by following the arrow into the center block, with reentry made back into the "Objectives" block. Having reentered a block, we proceed around the outer circle. In the example cited, if we modify objectives, it is necessary to reexamine goals and the other following items.

A System of Plans

Particularly where an organization has divisions, one finds it convenient to draw up a plan for each of these spheres of interest. A set of plans results, somewhat as is illustrated in figure 1.3.

The feedback concept as discussed above is relevant here also. One can not necessarily prepare a strategic plan and then develop product, market-

FIGURE 1.3 A System of Plans

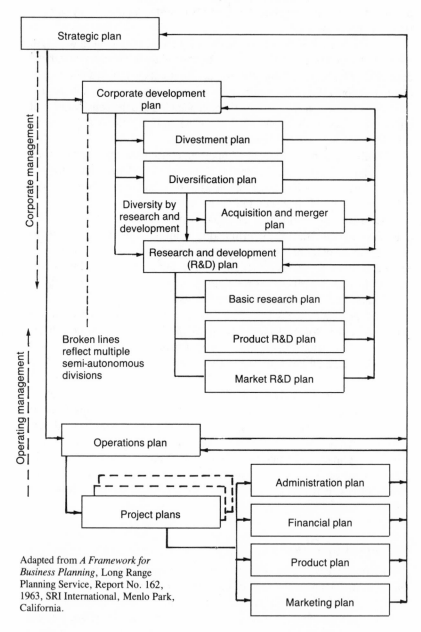

Adapted from *A Framework for Business Planning*, Long Range Planning Service, Report No. 162, 1963, SRI International, Menlo Park, California.

ing, financial, and administration plans to fit. Conversely, one cannot assume that the functional plans can be prepared first, with routine assembly into a strategic plan. To a large extent, one must prepare the strategic plan and the functional plans in parallel, using feedback to ensure compatability as the work proceeds. Further discussion on the functional versus the generalist viewpoint may be found below.

We can also visualize a system of plans from the standpoint of calendar time as depicted in figure 1.4. Plan 01 is made in year 0 for year 1, and so forth. The figure assumes that planning is being done for a period five years into the future, a common basis for the planning effort. Obviously, Plan 03 must relate closely to both Plan 02 and Plan 04; it would not be realistic to have facilities, products, or services appear and disappear in the span of a single year. Plan 01 is identical to the budget.

In the next planning year, Plan 01 is dropped and Plan 16 is created. As shown by the diagonal arrows, Plan 02 is revised and updated to become Plan 12, Plan 03 becomes Plan 13, etc. The decreasing block size as the planner considers years farther into the future is intended to suggest that less detail is provided for such future years. Note that as the plan for each future year is updated in the new planning year, the block size increases, that is, more detail and more specifics are provided.

Steiner (1969) gives data to indicate that a large fraction of the chief executive's time is used to make plans for the organization for the period three to five years in the future. In terms of figure 1.4, the CEO's input is thus into the construction of Plan 05, Plan 16, and so on.

The Top Management Role

All authorities agree that strategic planning must be done by the chief executive officer (CEO), and that the major responsibility of the CEO is to carry out strategic planning. Note that in the above sentence, the first phrase does not guarantee the second phrase; the two are independent. In order for the CEO to accomplish planning as well as other important duties, two prerogatives are necessary: staff and delegation. The situation can be depicted by abstracting figure 1.5 from a typical organization chart such as is given in a later chapter (figure 3.2). Solid lines show the authority relationship while dotted lines indicate the flow of data, tentative plans, directives, and other communications. For simplicity, only one set of dotted lines is given, but actually they would be replicated for each business unit president.

In cooperation with the group of business unit executives (BUE), mission, objectives, strategies, and policies are agreed on. The corporate planning staff is responsible for preparing economic forecasts, making assump-

FIGURE 1.4   The Time Sequence of Plans

Date of
planning

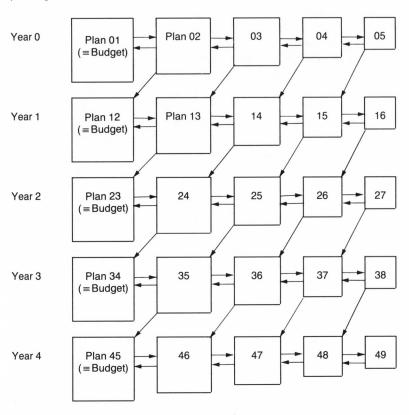

tions of various types, and developing guidelines on such things as time periods and the amount of detail required. Under the broad directive of the
CEO, these elements are also passed to the business unit executive. For each
unit, the BUE prepares the strategic plan, assisted by the unit staff. The corporate staff receives the plans from all BUEs, and reviews, analyzes, and
consolidates them into the strategic plan for the entire organization. The review process includes the CEO, and again we encounter the feedback principle, since if, for one reason or another, the corporate plan is not acceptable, revised inputs are given to the BUEs for reworking of their plans. The

FIGURE 1.5   The Basic Organization Chart for Planning

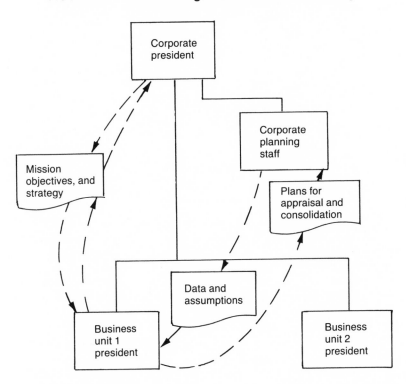

feedback continues until the detail plans and the overall strategic plan are simultaneously acceptable.

As shown in figure 1.6, the concept expands into a "cascade" system, where executives at each of several levels have staff to assist them in coordinating the planning of their subordinates. Note that the dotted lines in figure 1.6 represent the same material discussed above for figure 1.5, and also note that the two-way arrows suggest communication and discussion in both directions.

To a large extent, the question of functional versus generalist viewpoint is a matter of level within the organization. Thus, the BUE in figure 1.6 may appear as a generalist to the unit's line managers, since the BUE coordinates their possibly quite different activities. To the CEO, however, this same BUE could be considered as either a marketing or a manufacturing specialist, as the case might be.

FIGURE 1.6   The Cascade Planning Process

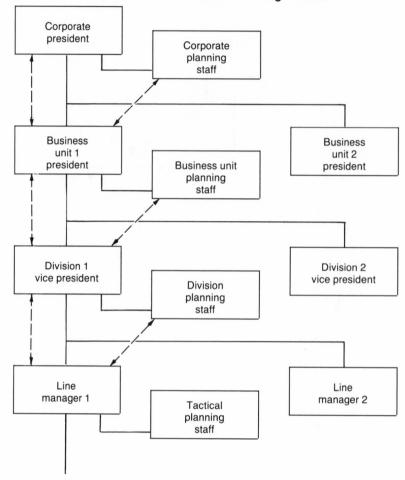

Strategic Planning Is Generalist Planning

It is well to restate and emphasize the thought of the previous section, that plans from all of an organization's functional units must be coordinated into, and perhaps subordinated to, the overall strategic plan. Usually, little formal training in management is available to the CEO, who must avoid retaining any functional biases from previous positions.

The generalist is responsible for the continuing health and prosperity of the organization. Short-term activities like supervision of operations, coordination of current functions, and tactical planning must not be allowed to subvert this strategic planning role. It is important to be "pro-active," to so influence the climate and the environment that decisions made in the present are effective in the future.

The Time Factor

There should be no dividing line between strategic planning (often regarded as synonymous with long range) and tactical planning (sometimes thought of as short range). The latter must be a subset of the former and must include more operational details. The time dimension is flexible. The border between tactical and strategic depends on many things, chief of which is undoubtedly the industry within which the company operates.

This desirable state of affairs is not always found in practice. Sometimes different plans are "owned" by different company departments. Figure 1.4 shows that the plan for each year within the planning horizon should be directly and intimately related to the preceding and following years. We may watch the plan for a particular year over a number of planning cycles. Initially, the broad concepts are just a gleam in the CEO's eye. Each year more details are added, as that particular year's plan approaches the present. Finally the present is reached, all details have been added, and at that point the plan is identical to the budget. We know of an industrial corporation where the budget is "owned" by the comptroller. Long-range plans are "owned" by the corporate planning group. Every year there is an intensive (and acrimonious) effort to "reconcile" the budget and the plans.

Our use of the word *budgeting* is perhaps an extension of its usual definition. Other terms that are sometimes used are responsibility budgeting, zero-based budgeting, and action planning. All these terms imply the concept that strategic plans start in the future and trace a smooth continuum to the present, so that in a given year specific guidance is provided, yet all concerned are assured that they are taking proper steps toward their future objectives.

Strategy has a military connotation, and rightly so. Each enterprise seeks out its competitor's weak points and attacks with its strengths. Some companies mistakenly conclude, therefore, that their strategies must be kept secret, even from their own functional managers, in order to prevent passing intelligence to their competitors.

It should be apparent from consideration of figure 1.6 and the feedback principle that such a course is folly. The operating manager cannot develop strategy in isolation. This manager must have the guidance of knowing strategy at corporate level and at the intervening levels so that the necessary vertical and horizontal integration can be accomplished.

The Strategic Planning System

Having described the strategic planning process (figure 1.2), several viewpoints of the system of plans (figures 1.3 and 1.4), as well a the CEO's role in strategic planning (figures 1.5 and 1.6), we now put these elements together into a strategic planning system. This is shown in figure 1.7, where previous figures are combined and some new elements are added.

At the left of the diagram is a decision subsystem. Plans are useless unless they result in action. After decisions have been made and results observed, these become input for a new planning cycle. The system of plans is indicated in the decisions subsystem blocks, since the plans are the starting point for action. Note that as one moves down the management hierarchy, decisions tend to change in character, from strategic to tactical to operating; however, there is much overlap. CEO's sometimes make tactical decisions, and often business unit executives make strategic decisions. Figure 1.7 is thus the "cascade" organization chart of figure 1.6 with the strategic planning process of figure 1.2 superimposed.

Planning failures can be caused by a lack of proper and pertinent information, and this in turn can lead to business failure. The need for a management information system is shown in figure 1.7. The corporate financial reporting system is typically one part of this, supplemented by a variety of specialized data bases. Some sort of formal intelligence gathering and organizing system is visualized, including methods of gaining information on competitors as well as current and future economic, technological, social, political, and legal trends. Such information usually enters the planning process via the planning staff.

Figure 1.7 also suggests the presence of a set of corporate computer models. These can be used as decision models to evaluate and explore the effects of alternate strategies and programs, or they can be used as planning models to set up the details of a multiyear strategic plan and to facilitate all the needed feedback and recycling in the preparation of such a plan.

STRATEGIC PLANNING CONSIDERATIONS

A number of ancillary factors must be taken into account in the strategic planning context. One of these is the human factor. Planning is aimed at specifying actions for the future. Sales objectives, for example, may be set years in advance, whereas the individual salesperson's motivation is based

FIGURE 1.7 The Strategic Planning System

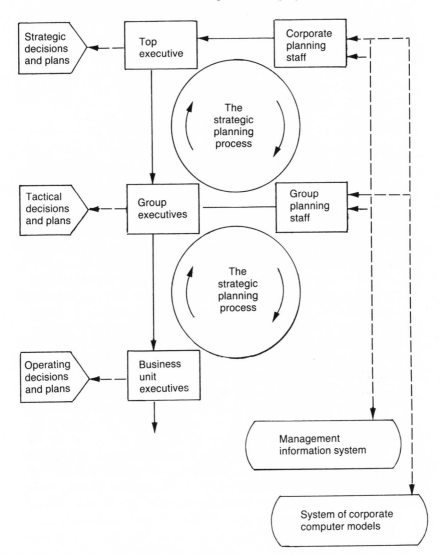

on performance week by week. The sales executive thus has the human problem of translating and coordinating these potentially divergent objectives.

As Chandler (1962) has noted, structure follows strategy. Having created plans (that is, strategy), we may now have the human problem of changing the structure—possibly disbanding a division, organizing a new division, or making massive personnel transfers.

Satisficing, Optimizing, and Adaptivizing

Ackoff (1970) has made a most significant contribution to planning in his discussion of three types of planning: satisficing, optimizing, and adaptivizing. To a large extent the differences among the terms reflect differences in executive attitude. The systems and approaches discussed and described in this book can be molded by the executive to follow any one, or a combination, of these philosophies.

The satisficing planner sets aims and objectives at a level that is good enough but makes no effort to achieve the best. To some extent, this attitude is conditioned by cost-benefits thinking. Increased benefits from a sophisticated plan may not justify the increase in planning costs compared to the price of making a "quick and dirty" plan. The satisficing planner tries to avoid departing from current operations, making large requests for resources, or proposing organizational changes. This philosophy is economical of planning time, money, and skill. Largely for this reason it is the most prevalent type of planning done today. It would certainly be recommended as the starting point for an organization just beginning its planning.

The executive who optimizes aims at the highest possible level of achievement and searches for the best way of attaining objectives, not merely a satisfactory way. This approach is made possible largely by management science and the availability of computer models of the organization. A corporate model set up in mathematical programming format contains the explicit notion of optimization. A simulation model can achieve optimization by trial-and-error usage of the model.

In many cases, a planner cannot express all goals in the quantitative terms required by a model. However, it is usually possible to come at least part of the way. In any case, the planner has acquired a valuable byproduct: a more intimate understanding of the organization. Someone has said, "The value of planning is in the process, not in the resulting plans."

Optimization in some areas, such as personnel and organizational structure, is imperfectly understood. It may therefore be wise to combine optimizing and satisficing. The planner can optimize the quantitative aspects of the business and merge these results with a satisficing treatment of the remaining areas.

Statistics recognizes two opposing errors: (1) rejecting a true hypothesis and (2) accepting a false hypothesis. Mitroff and Featheringham (1974) have proposed a third kind of error: solving the wrong problem. The adaptivizing planner operates in this area. Rather than optimize an existing situation, this planner examines whether the situation can be transformed into another, more promising, situation. A simple example would be in the planning related to a highly cyclical product. The optimizing planner would look at the details of raw-material procurement, manufacturing, and distribution. The adaptivizing planner, however, would search for a highly countercyclical product that could use the same facilities. Adaptive thinking is perhaps not new, but integrating it into the planning process is.

Here also, we encounter the contingency concept. Adaptivizing or optimizing will not be possible or desirable in all organizations. The executive, with the advice of the planner, must study the organization, its mission, and its objectives and then specify the planning style for the organization. This style, of course, need not be frozen for all time. Part of the strategic plan might include a strategy for improving the planning process.

ALTERNATIVE APPROACHES TO STRATEGIC PLANNING*

The sophisticated executive who is dissatisfied with a current planning system often turns to a consultant or reads a new book and sees promises of a "better way." Yet, to choose to make major changes in an existing planning system or to institute a formal planning structure to replace a less formal one on this basis, may merely be trading one set of problems and inadequacies for another. Similarly, an executive who is bringing formal planning into an organization for the first time may be uncertain of the validity of the advice received.

How then may one sift through the mass of conflicting recommendations to select an approach to strategic planning which is best for the organization?

The first step in answering the question lies in the question itself. In recognizing that any given approach to planning, however good, may not be

---

*This section is adapted from Clark Holloway and William R. King, "Evaluating Alternative Approaches to Strategic Planning," *Long Range Planning,* August 1979, p. 74, by permission of Pergamon Press Ltd.

good for a particular organization, the executive has implicity recognized that no single approach is universally valid.

Planning has developed as a pragmatic field; its theory base is thin. Much of the planning literature is anecdotal—reporting on single-company planning successes. Books and consulting firms generally present approaches based on a wider range of anecdotal evidence, but no consulting firm or author has adequate experience or evidence to put forth a universally valid planning system. The body of scholarly research involving comparative evaluations is so sparse and inadequate that some might question whether planning per se has demonstrable value to a firm. For instance, see Gerstner (1972), Ansoff, et al. (1970), and Thune and House (1976).

If a competent executive implements a planning system that is unnecessary or wrong for the organization, the results are bound to be unsatisfactory. Conversely, with a basic understanding of the philosophy of strategic planning, even a relatively inexperienced executive can select a logically sound and consistent planning system and can expect to achieve useful results.

The second step in a systematic process of evaluating alternative planning approaches is making certain that at least some of these approaches in fact deal with a broad concept of planning consistent with what the executive believes to be needed. Planning is a field that can be characterized as a "semantics jungle" in which words are used to mean one thing by some planners and another thing by others. The various definitions and interpretations of such basic planning terms as "strategy," "objective," and "policy" are illustrative of this.

Thus, the executive who makes a broad preliminary assessment of the substantive content of planning may avoid the grief that can result from taking a planning approach that does not really do what was expected or desired. One who wishes to concentrate on planning for new products may find the more comprehensive approaches too ambitious. So too will one who is primarily concerned with pricing strategy. A firm that cannot effectively implement a highly analytic approach to the planning process or one that cannot reasonably adopt a leadership role in its industry will find certain other approaches also misdirected.

The Substance of Strategic Planning

Strategic planning is, simply put, the process of positioning an organization so that it can prosper in the future. There are several implications that flow from this definition. First, it is about decision making. As Drucker (1973) has said, it deals, not with future decisions, but with the futurity of present decisions. Then, there are long-range connotations. Third, strategic planning deals with important topics. Next, it has to do with the inevitable obsolescence of existing products or processes and the provision for new ones to take their places. Finally, it deals with choices related to the organization itself as opposed to personal choices.

More specifically, the substance of planning is the choices that are made through a planning process. These elements of choice in planning are described in table 1.1. Not all of the terms there are employed in the same way by all authors and planners, but we believe them to represent a consensus of best contemporary usage. These decision elements by no means exhaust all synonyms and near-synonyms found in the literature. We make no attempt to interpret the various shades of meaning in alternate terms, since this has been done by King and Cleland (1978) and Steiner (1969). We group terms like "purpose," "basic socioeconomic purposes," and "values of managers" into the term "mission." Policy is a slippery concept that sometimes means strategy, objectives, or mission. It sometimes means all three. The term "strategic planning" is preferred in current usage over its many competitors: long-range planning, corporate planning, total planning, overall planning, or comprehensive planning.

The degree of permanence of the table 1.1 entries increases with their generality. The mission of an organization may not change in decades, but the chief executive must always be alert for the desirability of making a change. At the other end of the scale, projects could come and go in a matter of a few years or even months.

TABLE 1.1 Definitions

Term	Definition
Mission	A statement of what an organization is, why it exists, and the unique contribution it can make.
Objective	A desired or needed result to be achieved in the long-run future.
Strategy	A set of decision rules and guidelines to assist orderly progression toward an organization's objectives.
Goal	A specific, time-based point of measurement that the organization intends to meet in the pursuit of its broad objectives.
Program	A time-phased action sequence used to guide and coordinate operations in the pursuit of a goal.
Project	The implementation of a program or part of a program by identifiable activities and resources, and leading toward the attainment of specific goals.

A General Strategy for Evaluating Planning Approaches

Planning is a mental activity. When we say that planning is a process of positioning the organization to prosper in the future, we mean a mental "positioning." In this view, implementing the planning does not form part of planning per se, although some authors, for instance King and Cleland (1978), have treated the development of an implementation strategy as part of strategic planning.

Since mental activity does not occur in a disembodied spirit, planning requires at least one person. Planning may result in plans, and these plans may exist only in the mind of the planner, or they may be displayed as documents of one kind or another. It is useful to consider that these documents are generated by a planning system. In the simplest case, the system consists only of the planner dictating to a secretary. In a sophisticated situation, the system may include an elaborate input-data network, computer models, report generators, and feedback from operating centers to planning headquarters.

There are thus three important facets to planning that bear on the evaluation of alternative planning approaches—the conceptual, the organizational, and the systems orientation. Different organizations may employ different mixes of the three as their preferred planning style, and an organization may evolve from one mix to another as its planning matures. It seems axiomatic that planning in an organization must originate as purely conceptual in type. In the beginning some executive must say, "We need to do some planning." Subsequently the company can become systems oriented, organization oriented, or conceptual oriented, or it can achieve a balanced outlook with all facets playing a part.

In figure 1.8, each apex of the triangle represents one of the facets in its "pure" form. A company where all planning is done in the head of the chief executive and where the plans are retained there would be shown at point A. Next, it is possible to conceptualize an almost pure "systems" approach, in which a computer produces voluminous "planning" reports (financial forecasts, analyses of economic trends, etc.). This would be shown at point B. Then, a system that emphasizes a staff planning unit charged with producing similar reports and forecasts could illustrate point C, the pure "organization" facet. The circle D, exactly in the middle of the triangle, represents a blend of all components. We do not mean to imply that it is possible to precisely calculate such a point (by estimating the exact relative importance of each facet), nor do we imply that point D is the most desirable mix of components. It seems reasonable, however, to suggest that many companies

FIGURE 1.8   The Components of Planning

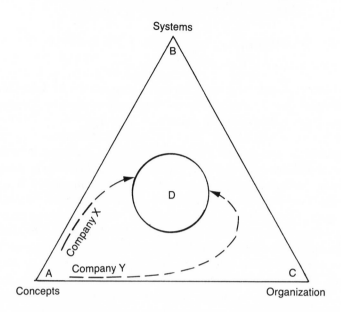

would be well advised to seek a posture within the central circle of figure 1.8.

Although planning in a firm will most often start at point A, two companies might evolve toward a desired "mature" position by very different routes. For example, Company X in the figure might conceive of the need for planning, buy an off-the-shelf interactive planning system, and then set up the needed organization to operate it. Company Y, on the other hand, might first study and implement the organizational requirements for planning, and then buy or develop the required systems.

Thus, figure 1.8 describes a framework that may be used to specify, in very general terms:

1. The "mix" of the three planning components needed for a particular organization.
2. The optimum "trajectory," or path, for arriving at the desired mix.

Taken together, the mix and trajectory represent a general strategy that can form the basis on which the executive may tentatively choose both the firm's planning objective and the path to achieve it. Companies X and Y in figure 1.8 have chosen to begin with a highly conceptual approach and to seek an objective in the center circle (which represents a relatively homogeneous blend of the three components). However, they might have chosen very different paths to follow in pursuing this objective.

Assessing Planning Approaches for Organizational Congruence

However useful the general strategy concept of figure 1.8 may be, it is not adequate for detailed evaluation of alternative planning approaches. Such an evaluation requires an assessment in specific terms and then in the more general terms of figure 1.8 of the degree of congruence between the organization's planning needs and the benefits offered by each contemplated approach to planning. This may be done in terms of the issues which constitute the underpinnings of each alternative planning approach.

Planning issues are topics about which it is possible and easy to have differences of opinion. For example, some planning authors go into great detail about the analysis and information aspects of planning. They feel that it is not possible to talk meaningfully about strategic planning unless these elements are important parts of the planning process. Others do not even mention these subjects. In contrast, the decision elements of planning (defined in table 1.1) are agreed on by almost all authorities. For instance, everyone agrees that a company must decide on its mission, even though not all use the name "mission." Examples of critical planning issues are given in table 1.2. This, of course, is not an exhaustive list.

Alternative planning approaches may be judged readily in terms of the degree to which they address various planning issues critical to a particular organization. This assessment of congruence may be done as a two-step process: (1) assessing the planning approach on an issue-by-issue basis, and (2) comparing the treatment given the array of issues by each approach with an array of organizational planning needs.

To illustrate how different planning approaches relate to these critical issues, we have repeated the table 1.2 issues in table 1.3. The body of table 1.3 shows an assessment of a selected set of current planning books in terms of their treatment of the various planning issues. These books are used as illustrations of alternative planning approaches from which the executive might wish to choose. An entry of 1 in the table indicates that the issue plays a major role in the planning approach prescribed in the book. Entries of 2 or 3 indicate successively weaker roles for the issue in the approach.

It should be noted that the importance of the various issues varies greatly according to this set of planning approaches. This confirms our premise that the approaches are quite different and that they are differentially applicable to various organizations.

TABLE 1.2   Critical Planning Issues

Analysis and information	The value of formalized data bases and statistical analyses versus the importance of creativity and the evils of stereotyped planning reports.
Assessing strengths and weaknesses	Importance of building on current strengths versus opportunity to be creative and innovative.
Nonfinancial objectives	Focus on financial performance measures versus emphasis on other intrinsic objectives such as social responsibility.
Role of chief executive	Chief executive as a decider or as facilitator and motivator of planning and strategic decision making.
The time dimension	The proper time span for plans and the planning process—e.g., annual versus continuous.
Creativity	The degree to which the fostering of creativity is a part of planning.
Role of planning staff	Staff as recommenders of strategy or as managers of the planning process.
Constraints and unsolved problems	The degree to which a planning approach may be inappropriate for a particular firm because of special needs, unresolved problems, etc.

Once an assessment of alternative planning approaches has been made in terms such as those shown in table 1.2, it may be compared with the planning needs of the organization. A chief executive who does not relish the role of salesperson for planning and facilitator of a participative planning process may wish to avoid an approach that stresses this role. If the firm is one that has not had extensive experience in the formal analysis of decisions and the development of decision-support information, an approach that stresses this may not be desired. In any case, a format such as table 1.2 may be used to rate both planning approaches and organizational planning needs as a basis for matching the two.

TABLE 1.3 Treatment of Issues

	Ackoff 1970	Andrews 1971	Ansoff 1965	Argenti 1974	Drucker 1973	Hussey 1974(a)	King and Cleland 1978	Newman and Logan 1971	Steiner 1969	Uyterhoeven 1973
Analysis and information	1			1		2	1		1	
Assessing strengths and weaknesses		1	1			1	1			
Nonfinancial objectives		1	2	1	1	1	1		2	2
Role of the chief executive		1			3		2		1	2
The time dimension	3				3		3	3	1	
Creativity			1						1	1
Role of staff	1	3		2			1	3	1	
Unsolved planning problems									3	

Code for authors' treatment:
   1 = major discussion
   2 = very important
   3 = important
 Blank = casual mention or not mentioned

Source: Clark Holloway and William R. King, "Evaluating Alternative Approaches to Strategic Planning," *Long Range Planning* (Aug. 1979).

Table 1.3 has been provided to illustrate that differences in approaches actually exist in the literature. It is the intention in this book to discuss the components of planning strategies so that the practitioner and the executive can select reasonable strategies for their own organizations.

Finalizing the Evaluation of Planning Approaches

Once the congruence of organizational needs and various planning approaches has been assessed, it is necessary to return to the broad strategy shown in figure 1.8. This step is necessary because the more detailed congruence assessment is likely to be performed in terms of or be biased in favor of current organizational needs.

Figure 1.8 stresses that a general strategy is made up of a future objective for the organization's planning approach as well as a trajectory for approaching the objective. If the issue-oriented congruence assessment has been done in terms that relate to both the objective and the trajectory, a consistency check in the more general terms of figure 1.8 should confirm the tentative selection of the best planning approach. If, as is more usually the case, the issue-oriented congruence assessment reflects primarily present planning needs or if it reflects only future needs with no consideration of the planning trajectory, the problem will be revealed at this stage.

Figure 1.9 shows how the issue-oriented evaluation of table 1.2 may be summarized in terms of the more general framework described in figure 1.8. Each of the alternative planning approaches has been evaluated on a summary basis that reflects the issue-by-issue analysis and then located on the triangle. The Andrews (1971) approach is evaluated to be closest to "pure" organizational and the Ansoff (1965) and Uyterhoeven (1973) approaches are the most highly conceptual, although they have different degrees of the "systems" and "organizational" dimensions.

Using this set of overall evaluations, an organization that had decided its strategy should be similar to that of company X in figure 1.8 might confirm its issue-by-issue congruence assessment that the King and Cleland (1978) or Steiner (1969) approach best reflects its future needs. It might use this assessment to advantage by noting that the Ansoff (1965) and Ackoff (1970) approaches appear to represent steps on the way toward the objective on the trajectory that they have previously chosen. In other words, if the company is just about to institute formal planning and is therefore currently "located" near the "conceptual" apex of the triangle, it might consider a sequential trajectory of the form Ansoff (1965), then Ackoff (1970), and finally, King and Cleland (1978) and Steiner (1969).

On the other hand, if the firm had decided in its preliminary assessment that it wished to have a highly "organizational" approach and had determined that the approach of Hussey (1974) appeared to be best on an issue-by-issue congruence basis, figure 1.9 might lead to a reassessment of Andrews (1971) as potentially better for its needs.

Summary of the Planning Approach Evaluation Method

Evaluating alternative planning approaches takes the important issue of which general approach is best out of the realm of happenstance and serendipity and into that of the systematic comparison of alternatives. Although highly subjective in nature, the methodology involves the following explicit steps:

FIGURE 1.9 Different Planning Philosophies

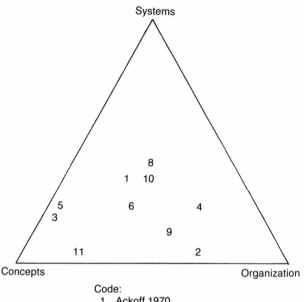

Code:
1 Ackoff 1970
2 Andrews 1971
3 Ansoff 1965
4 Argenti 1974
5 Drucker 1973
6 Hussey 1974(a)
8 King & Cleland 1978
9 Newman & Logan 1971
10 Steiner 1969
11 Uyterhoeven 1973

Source: Clark Holloway and William R. King, "Evaluating Alternative Approaches to Strategic Planning," *Long Range Planning* (Aug. 1979).

1. Selecting a planning strategy in terms of objectives and desired "trajectory."
2. Evaluating alternative planning approaches on the basis of detailed planning issues.
3. Matching planning approaches and organizational planning needs on an issue-by-issue basis.
4. Checking issue-by-issue congruence results for consistency with the planning strategy.

EXERCISE 1

We learn best by doing. To implement this philosophy, each student will prepare a business plan to cover the past year, the current year, and five forecast years.

This should be a significant study based on the student's selection of a real corporation or business or on a hypothetical organization. Size of the business is not a consideration. The average owner of a small business does too little systematic forward planning. If the student wishes to use private data, strict confidentiality can be guaranteed. If this is the case, mark the report CONFIDENTIAL.

Data for various corporations can be used as the starting point if a student wishes to create a dummy company; however, it will be necessary for the student to expand this starting point by postulating the planning problems, the breakdown of data into divisional levels, and other matters, to result in an interesting case study.

Two typed copies of the final research project will be required, each to include all charts and tables. One copy will be graded and returned to the student, while the other will remain in the files.

For this first exercise, select an organization, decide how you will acquire the necessary data (published material, write to the company), and prepare a one-page typed report outlining your program.

References

Ackoff, R. L. *A Concept of Corporate Planning*. New York: Wiley, 1970.

Andrews, K. R. *The Concept of Corporate Strategy*. Homewood, Ill.: Dow-Jones Irwin, 1971.

Ansoff, H. I. *Corporate Strategy*. New York: McGraw-Hill, 1965.

Ansoff, H. I., et al. "Does Planning Pay?" *Long Range Planning* (Dec. 1970).

Argenti, John. *Systematic Corporate Planning*. New York: Wiley, 1974.

Chandler, Alfred D., Jr. *Strategy and Structure*. Cambridge, Mass.: M.I.T. Press. 1962.

Drucker, Peter. *Management: Tasks, Responsibilities, Practices*. New York: Harper and Row, 1973.

Gerstner, L. V. "Can Strategic Planning Pay Off?" *Business Horizons* 15 (Dec. 1972), pp. 5–16.

Holloway, Clark, and King, William R. "Evaluating Alternative Approaches to Strategic Planning." *Long Range Planning* (Aug. 1979), p. 74.

Hussey, D. E., *Corporate Planning: Theory and Practice*. New York: Pergamon Press, 1974.

Hussey, D. E., ed. *The Corporate Planner's Yearbook, 1974-1975*. New York: Pergamon Press, 1974.

King, W. R. and Cleland, D. I. *Strategic Planning and Policy*. New York: Van Nostrand Reinhold, 1978.

Leontiades, M., and Tezel, A. "Planning Perceptions and Planning Results." *Strategic Management Journal* 1 (1980), pp. 65-76.

Mitroff, I. I., and Featheringham, T. R. "On Systematic Problem Solving and the Error of the Third Kind." *Behavioral Science* 19 (1974), pp. 383-93.

Newman, W. H., and Logan, J. P. *Strategy, Policy and Central Management*. Cincinnati, Ohio: South-Western Pub. Co., 1971.

Steiner, G. A. *Top Management Planning*. New York: Macmillan, 1969.

Thune, S. S., and House, R. S. "Where Long Range Planning Pays Off." *Business Horizons* (Aug. 1976), pp. 72-84.

Toffler, Alvin. *The Futurists*. New York: Random House, 1972. Pp. 164-89.

Uyterhoeven, H. E. R.: Ackerman, R. W.; Rosenblum, J. W. *Strategy and Organization*. Homewood, Ill.: Irwin, 1973.

Chapter 2

Conceptual Foundations of Strategy and Planning

Strategic planning is a pragmatic discipline. Its theory base is almost nonexistent. This chapter will summarize some of the published opinions of expert practitioners and theorists and, in so doing, will attempt to present an overall conceptual, normative model of the field of strategic planning. This will be done by outlining the limits along various "dimensions," within which strategic planning should fall. The chapter will describe in general what strategic planning should be, and it will not talk about any particular system in actual use.

This approach will be an extension of the ideas of Steiner (1969, p.12). Eight potential dimensions are proposed, but only the first five will be explored for some of the many implications and interactions possible. The dimensions are:

- Phase
- Time*
- Organization*
- Technique
- The introspective dimension
- Elements*
- Status
- Other "minor" dimensions

Steiner proposed five dimensions, three of which (*) are duplicated in the above list. Each of these dimensions will be defined, and the first five will be developed by citing literature to show how they are regarded, either inferentially or specifically. Because of the great wealth of literature on strategic planning, only the recent years have been covered (with the exception of a few classic works).

There are bound to be semantic difficulties. First, the milestones along each dimension are "fuzzy." In the time dimension, for example, what would be long-range planning to a fashion firm would be operational planning to a mining concern. Second, some of the dimensions themselves tend to merge into one another. For example, any of the following might be used to describe the same category:

- Complex versus simple
- Qualitative versus quantitative
- Written versus mental
- Formal versus informal

Finally, a problem in semantics might arise from the different levels of abstraction that are used in the literature. At the abstract end of the scale, Ackoff (1975) says long-range planning is a process directed to producing a desired future; at the other end, Grinyer and Wooller (1975) become very specific when they discuss computer models for long-range planning.

Each literature reference cited is covered in the discussion of the dimension to which it gives its major attention. This might cause some difficulty, for most papers treat of several related topics; hence, this classification must not be regarded as absolute. Further, it is sometimes a matter of opinion whether the form of forecasting *techniques* is the prime interest, or whether it is the *phase* of forecasting.

We begin with a brief orientation to the meaning of each dimension.

Phase

Most corporations do not have a separate department to carry out "futures research"; in such case it must be done by the corporate planning group, since strategic planning is impossible without it. Other phases (not necessarily in logical order) might be forecasting, analysis, choosing objectives, formulating strategy, managing strategy, evaluating strategy, evaluating results, and computer modeling.

Time

"Long-range planning" is a common synonym for strategic planning. Differences among tactical planning, strategic planning, and futures research can partly be explained by the time dimension shown in figure 2.1. It should be obvious, as the figure emphasizes, that there can be considerable overlap in terminology.

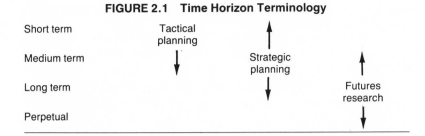

FIGURE 2.1   Time Horizon Terminology

Organization

Another synonym for strategic planning is "corporate planning"; this term implies that planning is done for the whole rather than for one of the parts. Nevertheless, it is possible to think in strategic terms for smaller and smaller units: corporation, subsidiary, functional group, division, department, product or project group. In this dimension we might also think in terms bigger than the corporation to bring in the environment as represented by government, geography, suppliers, or competitors. "Functional group" might be taken out of the size continuum to stand on its own as a subject of strategic planning in terms of production, research, new-product development, finance, marketing, acquisitions, plant and facility, or manpower.

Technique

The literature has proposed any number of management science or operations research techniques to expedite strategic planning: linear programming, simulation, statistical decision theory, Delphi, imaginative scenarios, projections, forecasts, technological assessments, predictions, prophecies, and revelations. It is likely that each technique is best suited for use with only a few other dimensions. For example, linear programming may be most appropriate to support short-term planning.

The Introspective Dimension

Strategic planning is an outgoing activity concerned with determining what an organization wishes to be in the future and with shaping that organization in the present so that it will improve its likelihood of attaining its desired goals in the future. From a practical as well as an academic standpoint, however, it is beneficial for strategic planning to look inward to see how its processes might better be carried out. This area is the concern of this book and of other works that discuss the theories and concepts of strategic planning or of those research methods that can be used to understand and improve strategic planning.

Elements

There is increasing abstraction as one proceeds along this dimension: environmental or other restrictions, rules, procedures, budgets, programs, policies, strategies, goals, objectives, purposes, creeds, charters. There is further semantic difficulty in that various authors use these words differently. One person's objective may be another's charter. The point was made earlier that dimensions may blur into one another. Should environmental restrictions be considered here or as a supraorganization in the organization dimension?

Status

Here we consider such things as whether strategic planning is an art or a science, along with the maturity of its development in a particular organization. What are the points of agreement among authors, and what are the points of disagreement? This would lead naturally into a discussion of the unresolved issues of strategic planning and the need and opportunity for research in the field. We do not explore this topic in this book.

Other "Minor" Dimensions

Anyone with a good imagination can propose new dimensions ad infinitum. After the major dimensions have been suggested, there is more and more overlap among dimensions as more are suggested. Other ways in which strategic planning might be classified are:

Complex–simple	Written–mental
Comprehensive–narrow	Formal–informal
Major importance–minor importance	Hard to implement–easy to implement
Qualitative–quantitative	Rational–irrational
Strategic–tactical	Flexible–inflexible
Confidential–public	Cheap–costly

These minor dimensions are not discussed in this book.

Each of the dimensions to be discussed in the following section has a number of subdivisions, and the ordering or importance of these is usually not obvious. In the phase dimension, one might consider treating futures research before goal setting, but in certain situations, it is only after setting goals that it becomes obvious that research on the future is imperative. The order in which subtopics are presented is felt to have some logic, but that order is by no means mandatory.

In a concluding section are a number of questions that remain open and questions for research that would be of significant benefit to workers in the field. There are undoubtedly major interactions among the dimensions of these questions; thus certain organizations tend to use certain techniques and to emphasize certain elements of the strategic planning process. The phases of futures research and strategy formulation have different implications with regard to the time dimension.

THE PHASE DIMENSION AND THE TIME DIMENSION

In chapter 1 and elsewhere we have proposed logical relationships among some of the phases of strategic planning. Here we will list other phases that may not have been considered.

Futurism, Futures Research

I summed up my thinking about futures research in a 1978 article:

> Futures research (FR) is an integral part of strategic planning. It is necessary to propose alternate futures before one can speculate about what a corporation must do to survive and prosper in such futures. One might suggest that FR is the "pure" part of long-range planning, while strategic planning is the "applied" part. The incentive for underwriting FR would be based on its necessity for supporting strategic planning. There are corporations which do not have an atmosphere within the company conducive to the beneficial application of strategic planning, and these companies would almost certainly not have FR either. If a corporation is attempting to use strategic planning, futures research must play an important, indispensible, integrated part.

Futurism is often concerned with doomsday or catastrophe, and so we have titles like *The Titanic Effect: Planning for the Unthinkable* (Watt 1974). Time is subjective in the FR context. In 1949, when George Orwell wrote *1984*, he was peering far ahead. When Martin and Mason (1976) wrote "Leisure 1980 and Beyond," they were only looking ahead four years. Both were dealing with futurism. Similarly, the same technique may be used in FR or elsewhere. Trend extrapolation via regression, for example, is certainly used by futurists, but it also finds application in short-term sales forecasting. Several other techniques, such as Delphi or envelope curves, usually imply futurism as well.

Forecasting

This term could easily overlap into FR. There are any number of papers considering the various techniques of forecasting, but these will be considered in a later section. Under phase, we are concerned more with why than how. Since one could forecast without planning, one must consider the relationship of forecasting to planning and, of course, it is a prelude to planning, as Tersine pointed out (1975). The design of a forecasting model must consider the purpose of the user; what is useful in sales forecasting might not apply elsewhere. Even in sales forecasting, a variety of approaches could be considered.

Technological forecasting, assessment, or change. In planning that involves new technology, the progression is something like this: technology forecast, technology feasibility study, economic feasibility study, market feasibility study, technology assessment. In lay language, this would be a series of questions: What is possible? Is it likely? Is it affordable? Will it sell? Will it hurt anything? Humphries (1976) discusses these questions.

Environmental scanning, forecasting, analysis, or appraisal. Utterbach (1979) has said that a corporation takes its planning style from its environment. Thomas (1974) says the environment is the key in any planning system. There are strong interactions between an organization and its environment, and so the environment might well have a different impact on a nonprofit organization than on a marketing organization. Considering the energy crisis, the hullabaloo about North Sea oil, and other current questions, environmental issues are apt to become an increasingly important factor. Waller (1975) wonders whether we may not become overly protective of our environment.

Policy

There may be some question as to whether policy formulation is an art or science, but most authorities would come down in favor of it as an art. There are large blank areas in any classification of research that has been done or attempted. While we are anxious for a comprehensive theory, it is not yet available. Duncan (1979) for example, discusses qualitative methods, while Hatten (1979) discusses quantitative methods.

Setting goals. There is much discussion in the literature on the respective merits of the "top down" versus the "bottom up" approaches. Dobbie (1974) correlates these with company size and previous goal-setting experience.

Strengths and weaknesses. Defining strengths and weaknesses and integrating them into strategic planning efforts is a major part of planning, as well pointed out by Stevenson (1976).

Strategy. Developing appropriate strategies is crucial to a corporation. The problem is to select strategy to meet corporate objectives while remaining within those corporate constraints set by the environment and the nature of the company. At the same time the strategy must be kept flexible and realistic (Weir 1974). Increasingly, it will be necessary to include social and nonprofit business needs in the list of constraints (Wilson 1972).

Strategy formulation and evaluation. Grant and King (1979) point out that the literature on formulation is scanty and merges into evaluation. There is considerable confounding with organizational level. This paper and others give extensive discussion to analytic models. The question arises whether strategy can be formulated by a model or, more probably, whether the formulation is the stroke of genius that occurs in between the runs of a model. Another viewpoint, from Cohen and Cyert (1973), is that formulation is a cyclic process involving bargaining between the components of an organization and its headquarters.

Control and Monitoring

The problem is that planning is an annual exercise, so that a five- or eight-year plan is modified each year, with the old year dropped off and a new year added. The company is (rightly) continually altering its plan and changing its targets. It therefore becomes difficult to say whether or not a plan has been successful. Nevertheless, the question is from time to time addressed, and one study by Holmberg (1974) has collected voluminous statistics from the utility industry.

Time

Here and there in the preceding material, the interaction of time with other variables has been discussed. It was also noted that the perception of time is subjective. Planning time or horizon time has also been considered as an explicit variable by several authors (Friedman and Segev 1976; Lee and Orr 1977; McClain and Thomas 1977).

THE ORGANIZATION DIMENSION

Type

Planning has been reported in a wide variety of organizations: not for profit (Wortman 1979); government (Duncombe 1976; East 1972; Michael and Carlisle 1976); academic (Massey 1976; Walters, Mangold, and Haran 1976), multimission or multinational (Berg and Pitts 1979; Lorange 1976; and Vancil and Lorange 1975); small business (Cooper 1979; Forbes 1974; and Shuman 1975); and large business (Dobbie 1975). Unfortunately, most authors do not theorize on the translation of their results to other organization forms.

Galbraith and Nathanson (1979) feel that organizational structure is a result of strategy (usually, but this can be reversed) and trace changes as a company develops from unifunctional to functional to multidivisional. Conflict and delay arise because the strategy formulator and the organizational innovator in the company are invariably different people. Berg and Pitts (1979) note that single-mission and multimission businesses differ not only in structure but also in interactions among the manager, the organization, and the environment. Cooper (1979) and Dobbie (1975) take steps toward generalizing the impact of business type on organization, while East (1972) compares planning in corporations and government. Lorange (1976) discusses planning as a function of organizational level in multinationals.

Function

There is no dearth of publications on planning within specific functions, and it is always acknowledged that such plans must be integrated with the corporate plan. To cite a few examples, there are cases of planning for finance (Power 1975), research and development (R & D) (Kahalas 1975), product development (Canning 1975), and production (Goodman 1974). Leyshon (1976) tells how market planning relates to corporate planning, while Hobbs and Heany (1977) give advice on coupling strategy to operating plans (which are usually functional). There is further discussion on integrating functional plans in the next section.

Organizational Theory in Planning

The organization dimension has to do with the organization for which plans are made. In contrast, Ackoff (1970) is interested in organization for planning, that is, the structuring of a corporate planning group. King and

Cleland (1978) discuss the relationships between these two types of organization.

The literature in this category is in rather good agreement. First, it is recognized that the whole business is the item of concern, and while functions must be considered, they are subordinate to the whole. This is often called the systems viewpoint: everything depends on everything else. Ansoff (1965) uses the term "synergy" to suggest that a group of independent divisions may gain (or lose) effectiveness by being banded together in a single company. In such a case, divisional objectives are certain to be in conflict with each other or with the corporation (Rasmusen 1974), and a cyclic process is needed to resolve these conflicts. Taylor (1975), Perry (1975), Rhenman (1972), and Wilson (1972) all speak of interrelationships between planning and organization and how to effect change in the organization when it is needed.

THE TECHNIQUE DIMENSION

Survey and Philosophy of Models

What is the use of models? Ackoff (1970) addresses this question and concludes they are useful to help routinize decisions, assist comparisons, and answer "what if" questions. King and Cleland (1978) and Steiner (1969) provide voluminous descriptions of different models, their integration, and the merits of the systems approach. More recently, Naylor and Schauland (1976a, 1976b), Rue (1974), and Grinyer and Wooller (1975) have also surveyed the corporate modeling situation.

It is unfortunately true that models have been built, often at great cost, only to be abandoned or used inefficiently. How to prevent this is of concern to long-range and strategic planning in general. The political questions of how to gain and maintain corporate support have been investigated by Naylor (1975) and by Hammond (1974).

Computer models. It is a rare planning model these days that does not use the computer. Nevertheless, many authors specifically emphasize that the computer is in the picture. Grinyer and Wooller (1975) have surveyed the field and identify these computer-based planning models, tell how they are obtained, describe their use, and discuss their costs and payoffs. Sometimes the computer tag denotes a system of independent but interrelated models (Holloway 1976).

Simulation models. Simulation is one of the major algorithms that can be used in modeling. Definition of the word is arbitrary, since in the broadest sense any model is a representation, or simulation, of reality. We suggest that a simulation model is one in which a computer considers a sequence of events and makes decisions that in turn lead to a new event. Naylor and Schauland (1976a) give a survey of simulation models.

Linear Programming (LP).   Culhan et al. (1975) provide an elementary exposition of linear programming (LP), together with a case example. LP is usually thought of as a tactical or short-range tool, but this is not necessarily the case (Holloway 1974). Noonan and Giglio (1977), Scherer and Joe (1977), and McNamara (1976) have written articles on long-range planning in the electric utilities using LP. Its application in multiperiod capital budgeting is, of course, well known.

Data Bases

Management Information Systems (MIS).   There is an entire spectrum of data bases or information bases to be included here under MIS. Much has been written on how to design appropriate systems (Hayes and Radosevich 1974; King and Cleland 1978; and Tipgos 1975). Lesko (1977) and King and Cleland (1974) discuss how to get information and what to do with it. Specific data bases are also outlined (Schoeffler 1976). More recently, artificial intelligence and expert systems are coming into the picture (Holloway 1983).

Inputs

Forecasting. Here we discuss the how of forecasting. A number of researchers have found that corporations are not getting their money's worth out of forecasting, but the reasons for this problem are not clear. Perhaps responsibilities and approaches have not been properly defined. The available methods are not fulfilling their promise in anticipating future change (Dory and Lord 1970). Thurston (1971) gives nine findings on the difficulties of technological forecasting. Any number of reviews of available methods have been published, but only two will be cited: Khalhaturov (1976) and Lanford and Immundo (1974). The question of where to get data to use in forecasting is also of interest (Nutt et al. 1976).

Environmental Assessment.   How the environment affects planning is discussed by Kahalas and Bjorklund (1976), Neubauer (1977), and Schendel et al. (1976).

Delphi.   Of the consensus methods of forecasting, this is the unquestioned leader. Delphi depends on polling a group of knowledgeable people with feedback, that is, allowing opinions to change after initial results are made known to all. Several critiques have been written (Linstone and Turoff 1975; Sackman 1975), and there is at least one record of a failure of the technique to yield significant results (Stander and Richards 1975).

Financial techniques. Methods developed under the aegis of financial analysis but applied in planning are mainly portfolio theory and risk considerations (Ansoff and Leontiades 1976; Channon 1979; Gup 1977; Pekar 1976; and Wacht 1976).

Other techniques. Any management science technique, or in fact any technique, could be used in strategic planning, limited only by the ingenuity of the planner. Baer (1976) has coined the term "counterfactual analysis" to denote the use of past events to explore future implications of policy. A sampling of infrequently used methods includes input-output analysis (Gols 1976), cluster analysis (Van Dam 1975), game theory (Armstrong and Hobson 1972)—even astrology (Kaye 1975) and extrasensory perception (Van Over 1975).

THE INTROSPECTION DIMENSION

The Failure Syndrome

Although the vast bulk of all publications is favorable to strategic planning, the opinion is not unanimous. Steiner (1969) in his early work listed planning pitfalls to be avoided. More recently, Pennington (1972) made the dogmatic statement that planning has failed. Koontz (1976) has given seven reasons why strategic planning is ineffective.

Uncertainty

This topic could perhaps have been discussed as a risk consideration associated with financial techniques. We will adopt the common definitions of risk and uncertainty: risk implies that a probability distribution can be specified, while uncertainty implies that nothing can be stated regarding probability. Four illustrative references (Boulding 1975; Harrison 1976; Kami 1976; and LaLonde and Zinszer 1975) all discuss planning in uncertain times, or planning in an age of discontinuity.

Procedures

Litschert and Nicholson (1974) propose that there are three types of corporate planning groups: capital budgeting, project development, and "think tanks." Rosen (1974) has thoughts on the entire scope of strategic planning: style versus organization; planners versus doers; use of models; communication; the plan; goals; risks; and the evolution of planning within a corporation.

Concepts

Locander (1976) outlines a model for conceptualizing the planning process, aimed particularly at new-product introductions. Steiner (1979) feels that contingency theories are midway between a statement of universal principles and the situation where each organization is a unique case. Complete theories are not apt to come soon, he feels, but will have four bases: case studies, organization-environment interactions, empirical evidence such as the Profit Impact of Market Strategies (PIMS) data base (Schoeffler 1976), and conceptualization. Ansoff (1979) notes that concepts of strategy will change as we move into postindustrial society and gives interesting time charts to support his observations. His recommended solution is to resolve future turbulent mismatches by procedures involving multidirectional flows and feedbacks.

SUMMARY OF "DIMENSIONS" DISCUSSION AND NEEDED RESEARCH

The discussion in this chapter should help serious planners recognize their problems and solve them. For the most part, the necessary attack has been suggested in these pages, but further help may be gained by additional study of the references cited for the points remaining questionable. In this course of action, the planner will actually be carrying out applied research.

It will be apparent to strategic planning scholars that this chapter has outlined voluminous research in what can and should be done if one is to understand strategic planning properly. First, the points along each dimension must be clarified; perhaps each dimension can be simplified by combining or redefining the points. Is this the case, perhaps, with strategy formulation, setting, and evaluation? Second, more attention needs to be given to separating the qualities of the dimensions themselves. For example, boundaries can be fuzzy between forecasting as a phase and as a technique, particularly if the question of introspection or nonintrospection is introduced. Third, the literature review should be extended in time and breadth beyond that given here, and the implications of each reference should be sought. Finally, the list of dimensions given earlier should be considered for logic and completeness, and the analysis extended to include those deemed important.

The dimensions discussed here do not exist in isolation; rather, they interact with each other. Suppose we wish to study the simultaneous effects of changes in organization, strategic planning phase, and strategic planning techniques.

Sometimes a graphical presentation helps to clarify a discussion, and up to three dimensions can be considered simultaneously. Figure 2.2 suggests that a great number of cells would have to be considered to complete all possible entries in the phase-technique-organization matrix. Points A, B, C, and D might represent:

A: Strategy formulation using linear programming in a multinational corporation

B: Forecasting using linear programming in a multinational corporation

C: Strategy formulation using simulation in a multinational corporation

D: Strategy formulation using linear programming in government

The figure could first be considered from an applications or nonintrospective standpoint—what might be the desiderata or problems over the three-dimensional space. The introspective, or how to set up the planning for the matrix, would also be of interest.

The graphical approach is limited to three dimensions, as we have said. The time, status, and minor dimensions not discussed above perhaps could be handled by editorial remarks inserted at appropriate points in the analysis. The only remaining dimension is elements (unless other new ones are proposed). This could be brought into the picture by repeating the entire analysis outlined above in separate chapters entitled Budget, Setting Objectives, and so forth. These might also be separate books in a multivolume set. Many cells representing illogical combinations would be left blank; thus, there is no apparent meaning to the budgeting and Delphi combination.

There are several research projects or topics where there are unanswered questions but where it should be possible to develop answers that would be of benefit to the strategic planning community.

The preceding summary has outlined one such major research area. Steps would be to review the literature from the standpoint of the matrix suggested, to conceptualize and generalize, and to suggest efforts or investigations needed to rationalize or perhaps fill in blank spots. Much literature exists which could be a starting point, and the first effort should be to codify this literature.

Another interesting research project would comprise a sequence of investigations that would illuminate our understanding of top management practice, bringing out similarities or differences in policy, strategic man-

FIGURE 2.2   Relations between Phase, Technique, and Organization

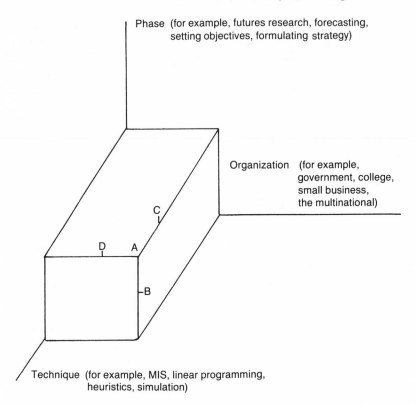

Phase (for example, futures research, forecasting, setting objectives, formulating strategy)

Organization (for example, government, college, small business, the multinational)

Technique (for example, MIS, linear programming, heuristics, simulation)

agement, and strategic planning. This could be done through in-depth interviews with a series of chief executive officers and their top staff.

Still another project would be in the area of evaluation, control, or monitoring. As already mentioned, it is difficult to say how closely the objective of a multiyear plan has been reached, because each year a new plan is introduced that modifies the previous objectives. In figure 2.3, point S is the starting condition at the beginning of a three-year plan, and point E is the planned ending condition. At the end of the first year, the plan is changed so that point B is the goal. At the end of the second year the plan is again changed, so that point C is the goal. The actual quantity reached at the end of the third year is point D. Even assuming that a single quantitative measure is available, how would we measure the degree of attainment to plan S? The differential D-E is not correct, because the plan was altered at points A and

FIGURE 2.3   Determining If Planning Objectives Have Been Reached

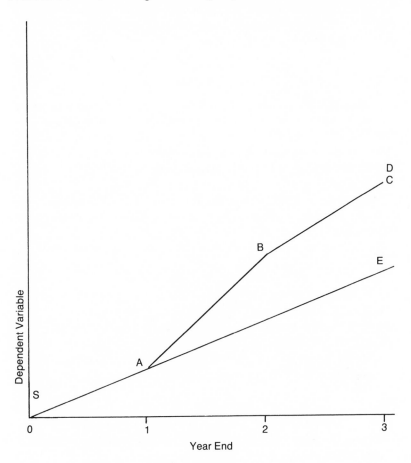

B. The differential C-D does not relate to plan S because the corporation readjusted its sights in accordance with reality at points A and B. Perhaps some sort of weighting function, including differentials at points A and B, could be used. In the real-life project, the weighting function would have to take into account multiple criteria, for example, maximizing return on investment while maintaining market share.

What are the specific causes of failures in planning as a whole or in a single component such as forecasting? We have already noted that the literature contains many references to the problem. Such a project could be approached through reference to figure 2.2 and to the work outlined for the first project above. Generalizations would be sought on the actual content of cells in the matrixes or combinations of cells compared to what should have been in those cells.

EXERCISE 2

Like all exercises in the book, this one is intended to form the basis for a part of the term project: preparing a strategic plan for an organization of your choice. For this exercise, present a typed, one-page report, outlining your answers to the following questions: What form and content should characterize strategy in your organization? What are the structural implications of strategy in your organization?

In addition to the material of this chapter, the following references are pertinent: King and Cleland (1978), chapter 8; Ackoff (1970), chapter 5; Steiner (1969), chapter 1.

REFERENCES

Ackoff, R. L. *A Concept of Corporate Planning.* New York: Wiley, 1970.

Ackoff, R. L. *Redesigning the Future.* New York: Wiley, 1975.

Ansoff, H. I. *Corporate Strategy.* New York: McGraw-Hill, 1965.

Ansoff, H. I. "The Changing Shape of the Strategic Problem." In Dan E. Schendel and Charles W. Hofer, eds., *Strategic Management: A New View of Business Policy and Planning.* Boston, Mass.: Little, Brown, 1979. P. 30.

Ansoff, H. I., and Leontiades, James C. "Strategic Portfolio Management." *Journal of General Management* 4, no. 1 (Autumn 1976).

Armstrong, R. H. R., and Hobson, M. "The Use of Games in Planning." *Long Range Planning* (Mar. 1972), p. 62.

Baer, William. "Counterfactual Analysis—An Analytical Tool for Planners." *Journal of American Institute of Planners* (July 1976).

Berg, Norman, and Pitts, Robert A. "Strategic Management: Multi-Mission Business." In Schendel and Hofer, eds., *Strategic Management.* P. 339.

Boulding, K. E. "Reflections on Planning: The Value of Uncertainty." *Planning Review* (Nov. 1975), p. 23.

Canning, Gordon. "A Strategic Framework for Analyzing Product Development." *Planning Review* (Nov. 1975), p. 349.

Channon, D. F. "Strategic Portfolio Planning Models: Practical Progress and Problems in Practice.'' In Schendel and Hofer, eds., *Strategic Management*, P. 122.

Cohen, K. J., and Cyert, R. M. ''Strategy: Formulation, Implementation, and Monitoring.'' *Journal of Business* (July 1973), p. 349.

Cooper, A. C. ''Strategic Management: New Ventures and Small Businesses.'' In Schendel and Hofer, eds., *Strategic Management*. P. 316.

Culhan, R. H.; Stern, L. W.; Drayer, W.; and Seabury, S. ''Linear Programming—What It Is—A Case Example.'' *Planning Review* (Sept. 1975), p. 21.

Dobbie, J. N. ''Formal Approaches to Setting Long Range Goals.'' *Long Range Planning* (June 1974), p. 75.

Dobbie, J. N. ''Strategic Planning in Big Firms—Some Guidelines.'' *Long Range Planning* (Feb. 1975), p. 81.

Dory, J. P., and Lord, R. J. ''Does Technological Forecasting Really Work?'' *Harvard Business Review* (Nov. 1970), p. 16.

Duncan, R. B. ''Qualitative Methods in Policy Research.'' In Schendel and Hofer, eds., *Strategic Management*. P. 424.

Duncombe, H. L. ''The Dangers of Centralized Economic Planning.'' *Long Range Planning* (June 1976), p. 16.

East, R. J. ''Comparison of Strategic Planning in Large Corporations and Government.'' *Long Range Planning* (June 1972), p. 2.

Forbes, A. M. ''Long Range Planning for the Small Firm.'' *Long Range Planning* (Apr. 1974), p. 43.

Friedman, Y., and Segev, E. ''Horizons for Strategic Planning.'' *Long Range Planning* (Oct. 1976), p. 84.

Galbraith and Nathanson. ''Strategy Implementation: The Role of Organization Structure and Process.'' In Schendel and Hofer, eds., *Strategic Management*. P. 249.

Gols, A. C. ''The Use of Input-Output in Industrial Planning.'' *Planning Review* (Mar. 1976), p. 17.

Goodman, D. A. ''A Goal Programming Approach to Aggregate Planning of a Production and Work Force.'' *Management Science* (Aug. 1974), p. 1569.

Grant, John H., and King, William R. ''Strategy Formulation: Analytical and Normative Models.'' In Schendel and Hofer, eds., *Strategic Management*. P. 104.

Grinyer, P. H., and Wooller, J. ''Computer Models for Corporate Planning.'' *Long Range Planning* (Feb. 1975), p. 14.

Gup, B. E. ''Portfolio Theory—A Planning Tool.'' *Long Range Planning* (July 1977), p. 10.

Hammond, J. S. "Do's and Don't's of Computer Models for Planning." *Harvard Business Review* (Mar. 1974), p. 110.

Harrison, F. L. "How Corporate Planning Responds to Uncertainty." *Long Range Planning* (Apr. 1976), p. 88.

Hatten, K. J. "Business Policy Research, the Quantitative Way, Circa 1977." In Hofer and Schendel, eds., *Strategic Management*. P. 448.

Hayes, R. H., and Radosevich, R. "Designing Information Systems for Strategic Decisions." *Long Range Planning* (Aug. 1974), p. 45.

Hobbs, I. M., and Heany, D. F. "Coupling Strategy to Operating Plans." *Harvard Business Review* (May 1977), p. 119.

Holloway, Clark. "Developing Planning Models." *Long Range Planning* (Feb. 1974), p. 52.

Holloway, Clark. "Using the Computer in Planning." *Planning Review* (July 1976), p. 9.

Holloway, Clark. "Does Future Research Have a Corporate Role?" *Long Range Planning* (Oct. 1978).

Holloway, Clark. "Strategic Management and Artificial Intelligence." *Long Range Planning* (Nov. 1983), p. 89.

Holloway, Clark, and King, William R. "Evaluating Alternative Approaches to Strategic Planning." *Long Range Planning* (Aug. 1979), p. 74.

Holmberg, S. R. "Monitoring Long Range Plans." *Long Range Planning* (June 1974), p. 63.

Humphries, G. E. "Technology Assessment and a New Imperative for Corporate Planning." *Planning Review* (Mar. 1976), p. 6.

Kahalas, Harvey. "Planning for R&D—The Impact on Society." *Long Range Planning* (Dec. 1975), p. 37.

Kahalas, H., and Bjorklund, R. L. "An Environmental Decision Model for Dynamic Planning." *Long Range Planning* (Feb. 1976), p. 81.

Kami, M. J. "Revamping Planning for This Era of Discontinuity." *Planning Review* (Mar. 1976), p. 1.

Kaye, Doris. "Astrology: A Tool for Planning." *Planning Review* (May 1975), p. 1.

Khalhaturov, T. S., ed. *Methods of Long Term Planning and Forecasting*. London: Macmillan, 1976.

King, William R., and Cleland, David I. "Environmental Information Systems for Strategic Marketing Planning." *Journal of Marketing* (Oct. 1974), p. 35.

King, William R., and Cleland, David I. *Strategic Planning and Policy*. New York: Van Nostrand Reinhold, 1978.

Koontz, Harold. "Making Strategic Planning Work." *Business Horizons* (Apr. 1976), p. 37.

LaLonde, B. J., and Zinszer, P. H. "Managing in Uncertain Times: The Case for Planning." *Long Range Planning* (Oct. 1975), p. 18.

Lanford, H. W., and Immundo, L. V. "Approaches to Technological Forecasting as a Planning Tool." *Long Range Planning* (Aug. 1974), p. 49.

Lee, D. R., and Orr, D. "Further Results on Planning Horizons in the Production Smoothing Problem." *Management Science* (Jan. 1977), p. 490.

Lesko, M. J. "How to Tap Big Brother for Information." *Planning Review* (Jan. 1977), p. 25.

Leyshon, A. M. "Marketing Planning and Corporate Planning." *Long Range Planning* (Feb. 1976), p. 29.

Linstone and Turoff, eds. *The Delphi Method—Techniques and Applications.* Reading, Mass.: Addison-Wesley, 1975.

Litschert, R. J., and Nicholson, E. A. "Corporate Long Range Planning Groups—Some Different Approaches." *Long Range Planning* (Aug. 1974), p. 62.

Locander, W. B. "A Planning Model for Multiple New-Product Introductions." *Journal of Business Administration* (Spring 1976).

Lorange, Peter. "A Framework for Strategic Planning in Multinational Corporations." *Long Range Planning* (June 1976), p. 30.

Martin, W. H., and Mason, S. "Leisure 1980 and Beyond." *Long Range Planning* (Apr. 1976), p. 58.

Massey, W. F. "A Dynamic Equilibrium Model for University Budget Planning." *Management Science* (Nov. 1976), p. 248.

McClain and Thomas. "Horizon Effects in Aggregate Production Planning with Seasonal Demand." *Management Science* (Mar. 1977).

McNamara, J. H. "A Linear Programming Model for Long-Range Capacity Planning in an Electric Utility." *Journal of Economics and Business* (Spring 1976), p. 227.

Michael, S. R., and Carlisle, A. E. "National Planning in the United States." *Long Range Planning* (June 1976), p. 21.

Naylor, T. H. "The Politics of Corporate Model Building." *Planning Review* (Jan. 1975), p. 1.

Naylor, T. H., and Schauland, "Experience with Corporate Simulation Models—A Survey." *Long Range Planning* (Apr. 1976), p. 94.

Naylor, T. H., and Schauland, "Survey of Users of Corporate Planning Models." *Management Science* (May 1976), p. 927.

Neubauer, F. F. "A Management Approach to Environmental Assessment." *Long Range Planning* (Apr. 1977), p. 13.

Noonan, F., and Giglio, R. J. "Planning Electric Power Generation: A Nonlinear Mixed Integer Model Employing Benders Decomposition." *Management Science* (May 1977), p. 946.

Nutt, A. B.; Lenz, R. C.; Lanford, H. W.; and Cleary, M. J. "Data Sources for Trend Extrapolation in Technological Forecasting." *Long Range Planning* (Feb. 1976), p. 72.

Orwell, George. *1984.* New York: Harcourt, Brace, 1949.

Pekar, P. P. "A Typology for Identifying Risk." *Managerial Planning* (Sept. 1976), p. 13.

Pennington, M. W. "Why Has Planning Failed? *Long Range Planning* (Mar. 1972), p. 2.

Pennington, M. W. "Why Has Planning Failed and What Can You Do about It?" *Planning Review* (Nov. 1975), p. 12.

Perry, P. T. "Organizational Implications for Long Range Planning." *Long Range Planning* (Feb. 1975), p. 26.

Power, P. D. "Computers and Financial Planning." *Long Range Planning* (Dec. 1975), p. 53.

Rasmusen, H. J. "Multilevel Planning with Conflicting Objectives." *Swedish Journal of Economics* (June 1974), p. 155.

Rhenman, E. *Organization Theory for Long Range Planning.* New York: Wiley, 1972.

Rosen, Stephen. "The Future from the Top: Presidential Perspective on Planning." *Long Range Planning* (Apr. 1974), p. 2; (June 1974), p. 34; (Aug. 1974), p. 73.

Rue, L. W. "Tools and Techniques of Long Range Planners." *Long Range Planning* (Oct. 1974), p. 61.

Sackman, H. *Delphi Critique—Expert Opinion, Forecasting and Group Process.* Farnborough: Lexington and Heath, 1975.

Schendel, Dan, et al. "Corporate Turnaround Strategies—a Study of Profit Decline and Recovery." *Journal of General Management* (Spring 1976), p. 3.

Scherer, C. R., and Joe, L. "Elective Power System Planning with Explicit Stochastic Reserves Constraints." *Management Science* (May 1977), p. 978.

Schoeffler, Sidney. "COPE Team Tells How PIMS Academic-Business Search for Basic Principles Can Get Line Managers into Strategic Planning." *Marketing News* (July 16, 1976), p. 6.

Shuman, J. C. "Corporate Planning in Small Companies—A Survey." *Long Range Planning* (Oct. 1975), p. 81.

Stander, A., and Rickards, T. "The Oracle That Failed." *Long Range Planning* (Oct. 1975), p. 13.

Steiner, G. A. *Top Management Planning.* New York: Macmillan, 1969.

Steiner, G. A. "Contingency Theories for Strategy." In Schendel and Hofer, eds., *Strategic Management.* P. 405.

Stevenson, H. H. "Defining Corporate Strengths and Weaknesses." *Sloan Management Review* (Spring 1976), p. 51.

Taylor, Bernard. "Strategies for Planning." *Long Range Planning* (Aug. 1975), p. 27.

Tersine, R. J. "Forecasting: Prelude to Managerial Planning." *Managerial Planning* (July 1975), p. 11.

Thomas, P. S. "Environmental Analysis for Corporate Planning." *Business Horizons* (Oct. 1974), p. 27.

Thurston, P. H. "Make Technological Forecasting Serve Corporate Planning." *Harvard Business Review* (Sept. 1971), p. 98.

Tipgos, M. A. "Structuring a Management Information System for Strategic Planning." *Managerial Planning* (Jan. 1975), p. 10.

Utterback, J. M. "Environmental Analysis and Forecasting." In Schendel and Hofer, eds., *Strategic Management.* p. 134.

Vancil and Lorange. "Strategic Planning in Diversified Companies." *Harvard Business Review* (Jan. 1975), p. 81.

Van Dam, Andre. "Taxonomy." *Planning Review* (Nov. 1975), p. 20.

Van Over, Raymond. "Altered States of Consciousness: Creative Alternatives in Decision Making." *Planning Review* (July 1975), p. 24.

Wacht, R. F. "A Long Range Financial Planning Technique for Non-Profit Organizations." *Atlantic Economic Review* (Sept. 1976), p. 22.

Waller, R. A. "Assessing the Impact of Technology on the Environment." *Long Range Planning* (Feb. 1975), p. 43.

Walters, Mangold, and Haran. "Comprehensive Planning Model for Long Range Academic Strategies." *Management Science* (Mar. 1976), p. 727.

Watt, K.E.F. *The Titanic Effect: Planning for the Unthinkable.* London: Freeman, 1974.

Weir, G. A. "Developing Strategies: A Practical Approach." *Long Range Planning* (Mar. 1974), p. 7.

Wilson, A. C. B. "Human and Organization Problems in Corporate Planning." *Long Range Planning* (Mar. 1972), p. 67.

Wortman, M. S. "Strategic Management: Not-for-Profit Organizations." In Schendel and Hofer, eds., *Strategic Management.* P. 353.

Chapter 3

Determining Objectives and Developing Strategy

An organization has a spectrum of objectives, and it also has a spectrum of *types* of objectives. These go under many names, which are not always used in the same way by all authors. We have selected the terms "mission," "objectives," and "goals," in decreasing order of generality, to cover this hierarchy. The terms are representative of the best of the literature and are logical, as we will demonstrate.

All organizations have objectives: all levels of government; religious, fraternal, charitable, educational, political, and terrorist groups; and businesses. In this chapter it will be convenient to talk in terms of corporate or business objectives, but the same principles apply over the complete range of organizations.

It should be apparent that objectives are necessary. Objectives are road markers. But, all objectives do not have equal weight, and some may be contradictory.

Until a relatively few years ago it was thought that business had only one objective: to maximize profits. This is the view expressed by Adam Smith in 1776. More recently the thought has arisen that each organization has a spectrum of objectives, including social responsibility, that to some extent may be incompatible with profit maximization. All objectives in the spectrum are not of equal weight. Some would say that the essential objective in business continues to be profit, since no company can improve the environment, provide social improvement, and give its employees security if it is bankrupt. Also, if a company were to maximize customer service (a typical and valuable objective), it would probably impair profit.

Balance is therefore necessary, and the ranking of objectives depends largely on the values of management. Since objectives may have differing weights, it is well to prioritize them, both by placing them into the different categories suggested above and by their order of importance within each category.

We will use the word *objective* in the generic sense to include the entire hierarchy and also specifically, as the name for the second level in the hierarchy. The meaning should always be apparent from the context of the discussion.

There is a clear difference between strategy and objectives. Strategy tells us *how* something is to be accomplished. In a sense it is synonymous with plan, although strategy refers to significant major elements and not to the details of dollars and volume. We also use it as an adjective, as in strategic planning.

An objective states *what* is to be accomplished: raise return on investment (ROI) to 15 percent; bring product X into the market; construct a plant in Wales. Each objective could perhaps be accomplished by any one of a variety of strategies.

THE HIERARCHY OF OBJECTIVES

The hierarchy of objectives (in the generic sense) is sometimes shown as a pyramid, with the corporate mission at the peak; a group of objectives (in the specific sense) is in the next, wider step below; this is followed by the corporate goals in the base of the pyramid.

An even clearer picture is given by depicting the hierarchy as a tree, in the way an organizational chart is often shown. In figure 3.1, the mission is found in the upper box. Directly related to the mission are a number of objectives. Each objective then suggests a number of goals. Notice that the common "dotted-line" relationship can be used to display secondary tie-ins. In the figure, the second goal is primarily concerned with advancing toward the first objective, but it also has something to do with the second objective. Similarily, goal 4 is mostly related to objective 3, but it is also concerned with objectives 1 and 2.

It is suggested that an organization could profitably use a similar graphic approach to visualize the interrelationships in its own framework of objectives.

Mission

The mission statement exists as the highest guiding principle within the organization. It is usually simply expressed in a paragraph or two. It may

FIGURE 3.1   The Hierarchy of Objectives

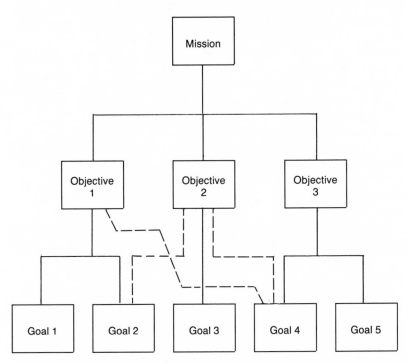

cover any or all of such topics as social aims; relations with customers, employees, the public, or stockholders; and type of business to be engaged in. Since the mission statement should guide all levels of management, it is best that it be explicit, that is, written down. Since it is a guide, all lower levels of objectives must be in agreement with it.

Because of its position as a broad guideline, the mission statement often exists unchanged for a decade or decades. It is important to realize, however, that it *may* be changed if necessary. The planning cycle is typically an annual one. Each year, the executive officers would review the mission statement not only for possible modification, but also to have clearly in mind the guidelines for the other (subsidiary) objectives and goals.

The mission statement for a multinational petroleum company might be: *To engage in all aspects of the worldwide energy business and to maintain dealings with customers, suppliers, competitors, and the general public on the highest ethical levels.* Notice that, although it is very broad and rather short, the statement offers specific guidance to the executive. Suppose the company were to consider a shipbuilding venture. Constructing petroleum tankers might allow the company to use its oil transportation expertise and would logically fall within the limits of the mission statement. It would be harder to justify building luxury liners. Producing agricultural chemicals could be easily justified if petroleum were the raw material, less so if coal tar were the starting point.

The recent entry of Exxon into office automation and word processing offers the reader an opportunity of constructing, in retrospect, a suitable mission statement.

To illustrate a change in mission, we might recall that the March of Dimes campaign was founded to be a force against polio and that President Franklin Roosevelt, who had experienced polio, was a major figure in the initial efforts. When the Salk vaccine was developed and polio virtually eradicated, contributions to the March of Dimes nearly ceased. The leaders of the organization had two alternatives: disband or change the mission. As we know, they chose the latter option, and today the March of Dimes is structured to operate against birth defects.

Objectives

Here the word *objectives* is used to denote the second level in the organizational hierarchy. In this sense, an objective is a desired result to be achieved in the long-range future.

Notice that an objective is more specific than the mission statement. Something specific is to be achieved, but the precise calendar time is not specified. The tendency as we move down the hierarchy is to begin to target particular goals, to start to think about timing, and to begin to expand the number of aims.

In the petroleum company, one of its objectives might be: *To enter the West Coast with an integrated refining-marketing capability.* Another objective could be: *To engage in concentrated research on the production of synthetic fuels from lignite and to acquire mining rights to adequate lignite coal deposits.*

It is important that objectives be well written so that guidance will in fact be given to the organization. We offer the following guidelines for this effort:

Road marker. The objective should be recognizable as a signpost. It should also be clearly in agreement with, and leading toward, the mission.

Guide to action. Remember that strategic planning is action oriented. The objective helps the manager make decisions by stating specifically what is to be accomplished.

Explicitness. Vague wording should be avoided: not "make profits," but "expand our profitable service station chain." Not "consider building a refinery in Toledo," but "Build a refinery in Toledo." The planner has, of course, considered numerous alternatives, but when objectives are written, conclusions must have been drawn.

Measurement and control. The objective should state more than a desire or a generality. Each year as the objective is reviewed it should be possible to see exactly whether or not it has been attained or whether progress has been made toward it.

Ambitious. The objective should cause the organization to reach, to stretch. In other words, it should be challenging. Setting objectives that are routinely achievable is of no inspirational value to the organization.

Recognizing strengths and weaknesses. It would be ridiculous to state an objective that is patently impossible because of a glaring weakness in the company. A worthwhile objective in a preliminary planning year might aim to correct that weakness, however. Conversely, it would be unwise to ignore or overlook company strengths in formulating objectives.

Recognizing threats and opportunities. Factors in the environment should also be recognized. One would not suggest an objective that meets an external threat head-on without first acting to remove or circumvent that threat.

Hierarchical relationships. As already discussed, objectives must be compatible and consistent not only with other objectives at the same level, but also with those at a higher level (the mission) and with those at a lower level (goals, yet to be discussed). Furthermore, there is the matter of the organizational hierarchy remaining to be discussed. Objectives at the corporate level, at the marketing-division level, and at the manufacturing level must all be compatible.

In summary, a set of objectives is a framework of organizational aims that can be used to guide all parts of an organization in its progression into the future. They are challenging, attainable, and mutually consistent.

Goals

Goals are at the lowest level in the mission-objectives-goals hierarchy. A goal is a specific accomplishment that the organization intends to achieve by a specified date. The goal is a stepping stone in the pursuit of the organization's broad objectives.

To continue the example of the petroleum company, goals might be: *to build a 50,000-barrel-per-day refinery near Los Angeles by 19xx; to acquire the Blank Marketing Company during the year 19xx.*

It might be proposed that goals relate to tactical planning while objectives relate to strategic planning. We do not find this a useful distinction.

The tactical-strategic interface is another elastic concept. What is tactical to one company may be strategic to another. In our frame of reference, which would apply to the vast majority of organizations, strategic planning extends five to ten years into the future. Each year of the plan for this period is expressed in considerable detail from the standpoint of dollars, volume, and new facilities. It is immediately obvious that setting goals is a prerequisite to this effort.

The checklist given above under objectives applies equally well to goals, since a goal is only a specifically stated, time-based objective. Setting goals is another important phase of the strategic planning effort.

THE ORGANIZATIONAL HIERARCHY

The authority relationships among various executives within an organization typically are shown by an inverted tree diagram similar to that of figure 3.2. One can easily see who reports to whom. So-called dotted line relationships are often included. These are perhaps most common in the finance or personnel areas. Each business unit often has its own controller, reporting to the vice president for that business unit. In addition, however, that controller has responsibilities to the corporate vice president for finance.

We have already seen in chapter 1 that there is a planning hierarchy referred to as the "cascade" system (see figure 1.5). Some of the same concepts would apply here, so that we might have a two-dimensional hierarchy, as illustrated in figure 3.3. If we follow the vertical dimension, a group vice-president could regard the corporate-level objectives as his group-level mission, and a still lower-level corporate objective could become a mission for a business unit. Figure 3.3. should be regarded as illustrative rather than as a hard-and-fast framework. The mission, objectives, and goals at the lower organizational levels will undoubtedly require modification and restatement from their higher level counterparts. What the figure does illustrate is the requirement of mutual interdependence of all objectives not only within a particular corporate level but also across all corporate levels. We cannot have, for example, a business unit pursuing goals incompatible with the corporate mission.

What we achieve is a way of communicating objectives to the lower-level managers. Each of these managers can then develop a specific spectrum of objectives. As will be discussed below, we suggest a recycle, or feedback, system. Some of the objectives developed at lower levels may suggest changes desirable in the higher-level objectives.

FIGURE 3.2   The Organizational Hierarchy

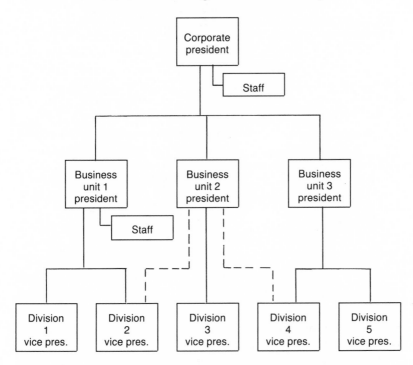

THE HIERARCHY OF STRATEGY

Remember that strategy is the *how* of accomplishing an objective. There are usually many different ways of doing this. For example, if the objective is to increase profits, strategies could include raising prices, cutting costs, increasing volume, introducing high-margin products, or combinations of these actions.

Objectives necessarily come before strategy. We cannot specify how something is to be accomplished until we know what the thing is. However, the feedback principle applies here very strongly. It is entirely possible that early in the planning process a worthwhile objective will be agreed on, and then it is found that there is no acceptable strategy for achieving that objective. The objective, of course, must be modified or abandoned.

Strategy is not the same thing as strategic planning. In a sense, strategy is the general or macro approach to be followed in achieving an objective; it is the big picture. Strategic planning follows the guidelines of the strategy statement but adds the details of dollars, volumes, and timing. Strategic

**FIGURE 3.3   A Two-Way Hierarchy of
Organization and Objectives**

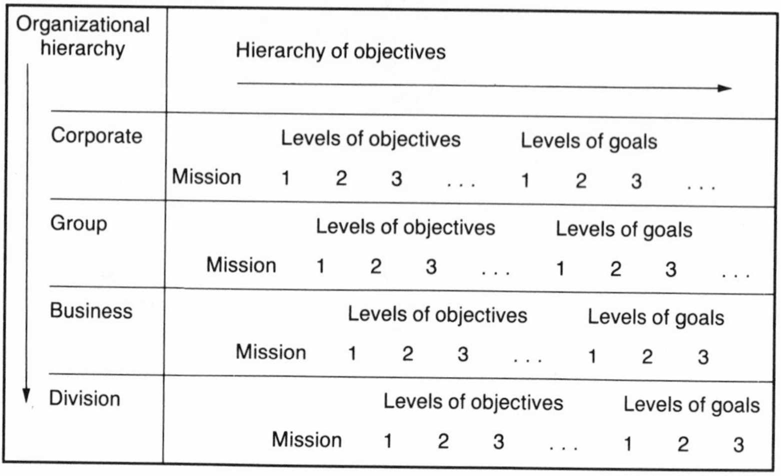

Organizational hierarchy	Hierarchy of objectives
Corporate	Levels of objectives Levels of goals Mission 1 2 3 . . . 1 2 3 . . .
Group	Levels of objectives Levels of goals Mission 1 2 3 . . . 1 2 3 . . .
Business	Levels of objectives Levels of goals Mission 1 2 3 . . . 1 2 3
Division	Levels of objectives Levels of goals Mission 1 2 3 . . . 1 2 3

planning retains the big picture aspect but adds specifics so that strategic plans, tactical plans, and operating plans for lower organizational levels can be produced in conformity with the strategic plan.

We do not have names for the hierarchical levels of strategy, and it does not seem profitable or necessary to create them. In fact, as depicted in figure 3.4., it is necessary to visualize a three-dimensional array. At the highest level, mission leads to thinking about corporate strategy, which in turn leads to a mission plan. Many organizations may not find it desirable or necessary to write explicit strategic statements or mission plans (that is, high-level strategic plans) at this highest point in the hierarchy.

At the next level, the recommended procedure becomes highly practical. Each objective must be amplified by a concept or strategy of how to achieve it. These concepts are then expanded into a strategic plan by adding the necessary dollars, volumes, and calendar dates.

At the lowest, or goals, level, the same steps are followed. Each goal requires a strategy, and each strategy must be fleshed out to become a part of the corporate strategic plan. Notice that, although seven different blocks in figure 3.4 are labeled ''Strategic Plan,'' these are not a series of independent strategic plans. Rather, each is a subset of the single corporate strategic plan. We refer to our earlier diagrams, figures 1.3, 1.7, and 3.3, which have already discussed aspects of the system of plans.

FIGURE 3.4 The Hierarchy of Strategy

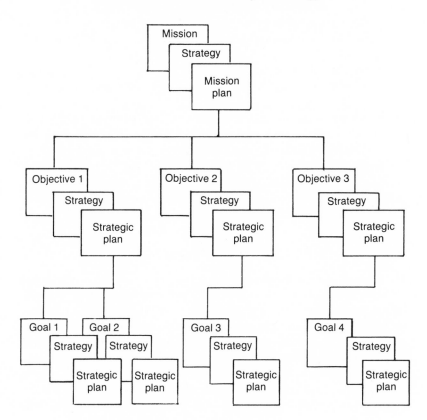

HIERARCHICAL ANALYSIS

By now you should be aware that strategic planning requires consideration of complex, interrelated, and ill-structured factors. Simon (1962, 1973) has proposed that problems of this type can be attacked by breaking them down into subproblems of less complexity, thereby multiplying structure. The hierarchical charts (figures 3.1, 3.2, 3.3, and 3.4) already discussed are starting points in this effort.

As we know, objectives and goals may be to some extent inconsistent; within the resources of an organization we may have to set priorities on what will be undertaken and what may have to be neglected. Some feel that prioritization must remain a subjective process. However, it is necessary in strategic planning to reconcile the inputs received from various organizational levels in some way.

- We receive data from both individuals and groups.
- The data include objectives-strategy matrixes as seen by each of the above.
- The data may include a statement of priorities.
- We ordinarily know little about the consistency of priority setting in the various data sets.
- While feedback has been proposed as a means of arriving at a consistent objectives-strategy matrix, the only present procedure for achieving this is by means of managerial intuition.

Research on this quantification problem is needed. One approach that appears to have promise is the scaling technique proposed by Saaty (1974, 1977, 1978). This is carried out in two steps: forming paired comparison matrixes followed by eigenvector analysis of the matrixes.

TYPES OF OBJECTIVES

Although this discussion is couched in terms of a business organization, the principles apply to all organizations, and the translation of concepts should be apparent.

Each business has many claimants, or stakeholders. Each stakeholder regards the business in his own way and would prefer that the business have specific objectives that serve the stakeholder's interest. Most of the recognized types of stakeholders are listed in figure 3.5. To a limited extent, the figure classifies stakeholders into adversary groups on the left and into benevolent groups (including stockholders) on the right. Also, long-term interests tend to characterize claimants at the top of the pyramid, phasing into shorter term interests as the pyramid is descended. Exceptions might be proposed, so that these relationships should only be considered fuzzy and tentative.

For the most part, of course, claimants do not have authority to impose objectives on the company. Objectives are written by all levels of the company's management, as indicated in figure 3.3 and as will be discussed in the next section. When objectives relating to particular stakeholders are included, it is because explicit statement of such objectives will be beneficial to the company in its strategic planning horizon.

Figure 3.6 again shows the list of stakeholders together with a partial list of the classes of objectives in which each might be interested. The figure is suggestive only of the major classifications. Executives, for example, would be interested in every objective the company proposes. Remember

**FIGURE 3.5 The Various Stakeholders and
Their Influence on Objectives**

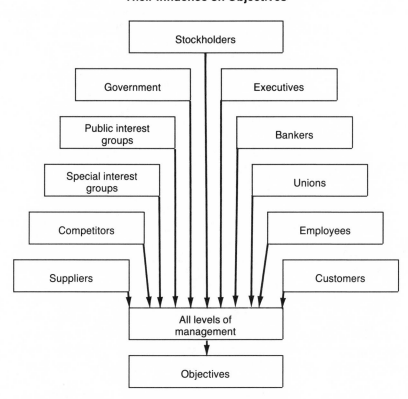

too that some objectives may be implicit rather than stated. For example, a
very real objective of executives might be to resist takeovers so as to retain
their position within the company.

As already noted, there may be inconsistencies inherent in a series of
objectives. It is still desirable to state them so that conflicting viewpoints are
on record. It is then the function of operating management to strike an appropriate balance. For example, a public-interest group might pressure the
company to respond to its concern with pollution; however, the stockholders and the executives may fear the consequences of pollution control on the
company's profits. Examples of even more complicated interactions could
be given. A fair-play objective might protect relations with a firm's customers at the expense of a profit and a dividends objective. This, in turn,

FIGURE 3.6   Topics for Objectives of Interest to Various Stakeholders

The Topic	The Stakeholder	Stockholders	Executives	Bankers	Unions	Employees	Customers	Government	Public interest groups	Special interest groups	Competitors	Suppliers
	Pollution							X	X			
	Profit	X	X			X						
	Product quality						X				X	X
	Equal employment				X	X		X				
	Fair play				X	X					X	X
	Debt policy			X								
	Dividends	X		X								
	Research and development									X		

could impinge on an objective regarding debt policy, to the alarm of the firm's bankers.

DEVELOPING OBJECTIVES AND STRATEGY

It is people who have objectives, not the organization. As shown in figure 3.5, the impetus for various objectives comes from the claimant groups, who work to influence definitions of objectives reached by various levels of management.

There are three important concepts related to the question of who develops objectives and strategy: feedback, organizational level, and planning time. These have already been outlined in chapter 1, but the thoughts will be consolidated here. Figure 1.2 illustrated the cyclic nature of planning and showed that, at any point in the cycle, events might trigger a reconsideration of objectives (the feedback principle). Figure 1.6 showed the cascade system based on organizational levels. Broad objectives are considered and set at top corporate levels, narrower objectives are developed at the group executive level, and so on. Objectives at any level are influenced and molded by considerations from the levels above and the levels below. Figure 1.7 combined the feedback and the organizational level thoughts into a single diagram.

Planning time was discussed in connection with figure 1.4. This diagram illustrated that strategy and objectives must form a continuum through time: an objective for a given year will be essentially the same as those for the preceding and following years.

All of these interrelationships can be combined, together with the three hierarchical diagrams figures 3.1, 3.2, and 3.3, as in figure 3.7. In brief, this figure shows that different organizational levels specialize in different levels of objectives and strategy but are not restricted to those levels. The diagram further shows that the process continues over time, so there is always opportunity for change from year to year.

The solid horizontal arrows (0) show that the process starts with the people in the organization. There are also some dotted arrows directed towards the organization, indicating that the strategy as developed has suggested that organizational changes are necessary. The dotted arrows (H) are representative of horizontal feedback. One must express objectives before strategy can be considered (some arrows are right-directed). By the feedback principle, after having considered strategy, we may find it necessary to modify our objectives (some of the H arrows are left-directed). In general, managers formulate both objectives and strategy at their own level; therefore, we find the approximately horizontal orientation in the H arrows.

The dotted arrows marked V symbolize vertical feedback. Some organizations tend to follow more of a top-down approach in formulating objectives and strategy; others follow more of a bottom-up approach. In either case, there must be both up and down feedback, so that objectives and strategy at all levels of the organization are in agreement.

The figure also illustrates the time dimension. Any or all of the three hierarchies may change as the organization is subjected to new threats, as it becomes aware of new opportunities, and as it develops internally.

Who Develops Objectives and Strategy?

Objectives and strategy do not spring into being fully formed, as our discussion up to this point has perhaps intimated. Someone must do the nitty-gritty; someone or rather, an entire echelon of someones must get their hands dirty.

**FIGURE 3.7   Relations among the Dimensions of Phase, Time, and
Organizational Levels**

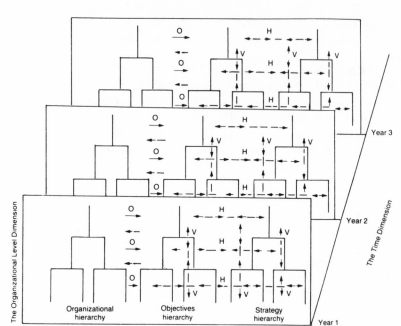

Ideally, the organization is planning oriented. Managers at each level
are expected to create their objectives and the interrelated strategies for accomplishing them, and are rewarded when they do the task. We have already given criteria and guidelines for stating good objectives. These may
be paraphrased in the following action list for each manager:

- Since the manager has the benefit of knowing the objectives of organizational superiors, the manager's own objectives can be made to fit
  into the corporate hierarchy. They will be acceptable to superiors.

- The objectives for each unit are created by its own manager, who
  thus will understand them and will ensure that they are specific. They
  will identify results to be expected.

- The manager will consider the strengths and weaknesses of the unit
  as well as environmental threats and opportunities, so that the objective as written is within the power of the unit to achieve.

- The manager must understand that while potentially conflicting objectives may each be desirable, a balance must be struck among
  them.

- The objectives will be measurable and quantitative so that both manager and superiors know when they have been achieved.

In a very real sense, the action list for writing strategy parallels the action list for managers, although it is simpler:

- Unit strategy must fit into the hierarchy of corporate strategy.
- Specific objectives lead to specific strategy.
- Considering strengths and weaknesses, threats and opportunities is as much a part of planning strategy as it is of identifying objectives.
- Strategy is the *how* of reconciling conflicting objectives.
- Measuring the fact of having achieved an objective does not have a counterpart in planning strategy.

The manager who works in an organization that is not planning oriented has several courses of action. Applying planning principles to his or her own career may among other things suggest a move into a different organization. To the extent permitted, the manager's own unit may be run with planning techniques. Finally, the manager may endeavor to convince superiors of the advantages to be gained by bringing formalized planning into the organization.

STRATEGIC CHOICE: WHAT IS IMPORTANT?

Henry David Thoreau wrote, "It is not enough to be busy; so are the ants. The question is: What are we busy about?"

The Swiss professor of economics Vilfredo Pareto used a chart called the "Pareto chart" to study the distribution of wealth and income. From such a chart, as shown in figure 3.8, we might observe that 80 percent of the people of Great Britain hold about 10 percent of the wealth. If different coordinates were attached to the chart, we might find that 60 percent of United States citizens receive less than 30 percent of the total U.S. income.

The Pareto effect has applications far beyond its original use in economics. Let us rename the coordinates, as is done in figure 3.9. Based on part a of the figure, we could make statements like: *Eighty percent of our products bring in only 20 percent of our profits. Seventy percent of our quality complaints arise from only 30 percent of our products.*

With regard to planning, the lesson is clear. Plan to take advantage of your strengths and stay away from your weaknesses. Discontinue the weak 80 percent of your products. Perhaps this cannot be done arbitrarily or unilaterally: if a full range of products is not available, the customer may not buy any. When such a problem actually occurred in a company, sales commissions were withdrawn on the weak products. Salespersons were thus in-

FIGURE 3.8   The Distribution of Wealth

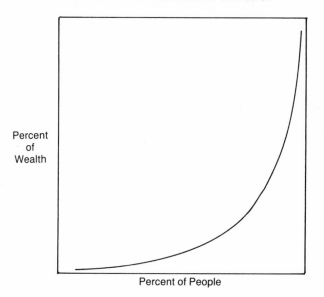

Percent
of
Wealth

Percent of People

spired to work with the customers in finding alternates for the no-commission items.

The reactive planner accepts his environment; he reacts to it; he tries to work within the confines of figure 3.9a. The proactive planner, on the other hand, tries to change the environment for the better and, by one means or another, to remove the undesirable lower tail of the figure in order to arrive at the more linear representation of figure 3.9b.

The principle extends beyond the Pareto effect. The successful planner is one who keeps the big picture in mind and is not diverted by details. One international petroleum company would periodically hold meetings in each of its subsidiary marketing companies. Invariably, one of the headquarters executives would suggest going out to visit a service station. Is this the big picture? Some of the pro and con arguments might be:

- The visit helps the executives relate accounting numbers to real life in that country.
- The visit is good from a political standpoint, since the host country thereby feels the executives have an interest in it.
- The executives increase their knowledge of marketing techniques and service station operations by the visit, even though each of them has visited service stations in the role of executive or customer thousands of times.

FIGURE 3.9 The Pareto Effect

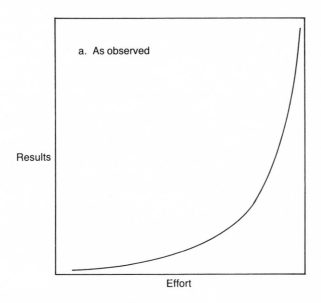

a. As observed

Results

Effort

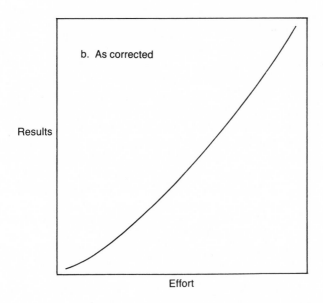

b. As corrected

Results

Effort

- Only service stations are visited, never bulk plants, unloading docks, or other marketing facilities, even though they too have problems.
- The executives enjoy recalling their earlier days as a service station manager or a branch manager.
- The executives have seized on an excuse to avoid getting down to work.

As another example we might cite the dynamic, intellectual, hard-working, and numbers-capable executive who regularly read and absorbed reports from each of his many retail-chain outlets. Each of these reports was blue-penciled with commands on what to do about product line, inventory levels, discount policies, merchandise returns, and similar matters. He gave no thought, however, to major demographic shifts in customer location, customer age, or customer buying habits, so that over the period of his tenure many of the branches experienced major setbacks.

In both of these examples, the big picture was not being kept in mind. It is not always easy to determine what factors will be important, but remember that strategic planning is concerned with the future. We must estimate what will be important over the entire strategic planning horizon—the big picture may be modified over that time span.

The same principles apply to a person's career. Individuals should evaluate their own strengths and weaknesses, objectives, threats, and opportunities. They should regularly ask themselves questions like:

- On each of my assignments, should I maintain a high profile or a low profile? (This may vary by assignment.)
- Should I work hard in my present job, or should I look for a transfer to greener pastures?
- Should I join professional societies?
- For what type of special assignments should I volunteer?
- How should I spend my free time? Study? College courses? Making contacts?
- Should I seek out a mentor in the higher levels of my organization?

A separate section will be devoted to job opportunities and requirements in the strategic planning field.

EXAMPLES

This chapter has given suggestions on how to develop a coordinated, consistent, and interrelated system of objectives and strategy. This is an ideal toward which each organization would be well advised to progress.

In the real world, organizations often fall short of these recommendations. It may be instructive to include an example of a hierarchy of objectives as prepared by an actual company. No doubt the reader will immediately notice deficient areas in the example.

This example displays documents prepared by various executive levels of a multinational petroleum company for a recent planning year. Only representative segments are shown. Figure 3.10 gives the corporate-level mission statement. Figure 3.11 shows objectives and goals as expressed by the European division of this same company.

Obviously, the precise objectives and strategy expressed in these figures are not of interest; rather, the level of detail they demonstrate is illustrative. Notice that as we proceed from the corporate mission to the objectives and to the goals, we become more and more specific and more conscious of calendar time. In the petroleum industry, "upstream" refers to exploration, production, and crude-oil transportation, and "downstream" refers to refining and marketing.

Figures 3.12 through 3.16 provide, respectively, objectives statements for North Europe, South Europe, the United Kingdom and Ireland, Scandinavia, and Exploration and Production. Each of these areas is a part of the European division of the corporation. Notice several things:

- Some divisions have done better work than others.
- There is general agreement throughout the hierarchy.
- So as not to impair creativity, stylized formats have not been insisted upon.
- Different areas emphasize different points, as would be expected.
- In most areas, there is not as clear-cut differentiation between objectives and goals as is desirable.
- Some areas include comments on strategy. For the most part, this is not done, and should not be done, and strategy is and should be discussed as a part of the resulting plans.

FIGURE 3.10 The Corporate Mission Statement*

Disturbing crosscurrents in the world economic and energy environment affect X Corporation and will shape its course in the years ahead. Although this environment is beyond our control, we believe we have the ability, as well as the duty, to respond in a way that is beneficial to our shareholders while remaining a responsible world citizen.

X's primary objective is to continue to be a growing and profitable supplier of energy to world markets. While petroleum will still be the largest part of our business for many years, we intend to grow as a supplier of other energy forms as the demand for them develops, particularly in coal, uranium, tar sands, and synthetics. We may also continue to extend this diversification into other related fields, as opportunities arise and investment funds are available.

The overwhelming majority of our investments will continue to be energy related. The amounts spent in developing energy resources already in place will be accompanied by growing investments in new energy resources in the United States and abroad. We see no lack of opportunities to capitalize on the corporation's financial, technological, and managerial strengths.

If, as some believe, scientific knowledge grows exponentially, the next 100 years could make the last 100 look elementary by comparison. Beyond a doubt X's future will depend on technological innovation and the management of technological change.

While the energy industry now has a freer market environment in which to operate, it must be recognized that government everywhere, including the United States, will remain a major factor in energy matters. X will continue its efforts to encourage government energy policies that provide the incentives needed for future energy development.

FIGURE 3.11 Objectives and Goals for European/Mideast Operations

A. *General corporate objectives*
1. To protect and enhance the investment of its shareholders through a consistent pattern of growth by:
   - Expanding present areas of business that are profitable and are expected to continue to be profitable in the future.
   - Making full and best use of all manpower skills, research and planning capabilities, raw materials, plant and equipment, and capital resources.
   - Diversifying into potentially profitable new areas consistent with availability of the necessary management skills, operating capability, and raw material and financial capabilities.
   - Selecting a balance of investments providing both near-term and long-term profitability.
   - Increasing the capabilities, motivation, innovation, initiative, and expertise of present and future personnel.
2. To continue to be one of the major energy companies in all activities where profitability is attractive when balanced against risks.
3. To reverse the trend of recent years and increase net income and return on investment to more favorable levels as quantified by specific profitability goals.
4. To anticipate change and develop opportunities to take advantage of expected change.
5. To maintain flexibility to act quickly and effectively in response to changing circumstances and new opportunities.
6. To achieve recognition by each employee of his or her personal responsibility for the Corporation's image, profitability, and well-being.

---

*Synthesized from several company statements.

FIGURE 3.11 (*Continued*)

7. To have the Corporation fulfill its social and environmental responsibilities.

B. *Specific corporate goals for the period 19xx–19xx*
1. Increase return on employed capital from the current level of 7% to a minimum of 9.5–10.5% by 19xx.
2. Increase net income by a minimum of $50–$60 million per year and an average rate of 10% per year for years 19xx through 19xx.
3. Reduce long-term debt by $150 million per year over the next three years from the current level of 28% of capitalization to less than 20% by 19xx.
4. Increase gross operating revenue as a percent of gross fixed assets from the current level of 54%.
5. Existing investments which are not expected by good planning and economics to yield the minimum of 8% return on employed capital after taxes by 19xx should be identified and made the subject of special study and executive review.
6. Consistent with corporate profit goals, the share of capital allocated to new projects expected to contribute profits within three to five years should not be less than 60%.
7. New projects should be expected to yield a minimum ROI of 12% after applicable foreign and U.S. tax.
8. To reduce physical, political, and economic risks, the Corporation's exposure through any single future investment program should be limited to 5% of employed capital, or loss exposure equivalent to 5% of current earnings.

FIGURE 3.12 Objectives and Goals for North Europe

A. *Achievement Sought*
   Within the following constraints:
New investment is to be self-generated; is not to exceed 85% of the cash flow; is to yield 20% DCF after local tax; payout period is to be less than six years; is to yield 20% ROI on average net investment.
1. To continue to generate an adequate return on invested capital in this area and raise it to 20% by 19xx.
2. To expand and solidify the base load business of gasoline and lubricants in the area to provide for continuous growth of the business apart from the traditional price volatility in the distillates and fuel markets.
3. To add further strength to the lubricants/specialties business by forward integration into consumer good manufacturing, which consists essentially of upgrading our feedstocks.
4. To capitalize on the quality image of the X brand, which in the Benelux nations has special drawing power.
5. To minimize risk by working with third parties interested in assuming risks so far carried by X.
B. *Quantification*

Note: This section on goals consisted of a table, showing for the last historical year, for the current year, and for six planning years, the quantities:

Volume sales	Revenues
Costs	Margin
Marketing expenses	Net income
Employed capital	ROI

FIGURE 3.12 (*Continued*)

Three profit-improver projects yielding more than 30% ROI could have been added to this base plan. These investments, which would materially improve the North European Operation, would have cost about $9 million in total.

FIGURE 3.13   Objectives and Goals for South Europe

1. To increase to a satisfactory level the area's:
   a. Rate of return on employed capital.
   b. Operating revenue per dollar invested in fixed assets.
   c. Total net income.
   d. Net income per dollar of operating revenue.
2. To improve the area's profitability by maintaining or eventually reducing the amount of investment in the area's subsidiaries.
3. To increase manpower productivity expressed as the number of barrels sold and of dollar revenue per person employed.

FIGURE 3.14   Objectives and Goals for the United Kingdom and Ireland

The objective of the United Kingdom and Ireland area for the next five years will be to raise earnings to an average of 9% (income defined in the manner of the 19xx budget) on employed capital over the period 19xx through 19xx and 10% in 19xx–19xx. A three-rolling-year average will be taken as the criterion in view of the manner in which U.K. market prices react to changes in international product values and industry costs and the dependence of the U.K. area net income on international market prices.

Within the following constraints:

1. Investment should not exceed 85% of funds generated (about $14 million p.a. based on 19xx).
2. New projects will not require corporate funds.
3. New investments will yield 15% DCF after local income tax with a maximum payout period of six years and 15% ROI on average investment.
4. If funds are not available from cash flow, new retail outlets will be financed by local risk finance.
5. Long-term leasing *will* be employed when advantage can be taken of favorable tax conditions associated with refinery investments and automotive equipment.
6. No subordinate positions will be taken in joint ventures involving X's currently owned facilities except to obtain political positions for concessions locally or in producing countries.

Goals will be:

To create by 19xx a commercially viable company having

1. The financial strength,
2. The security of income, and
3. The organizational strength required to enable it to consider operating as a publicly quoted company in the United Kingdom with minority interest by X.

For Which it will be Necessary:

To develop three levels of management with a strong commercial understanding and a high degree of entrepreneurial aggressiveness within an environment (including compensation, benefits, and job satisfaction) that will attract high-caliber personnel.

The management should have continuity and be composed of United Kingdom subjects except in positions that have unique technical requirements.

FIGURE 3.15   Objectives and Goals for Scandinavia

A. *Objective* We believe that profits will be made in the future in downstream operations in Scandinavia, and we are confident that company X is in position to compete effectively for a fair share of these profits.

Our objective is to participate in the downstream activities in Scandinavia in a manner that will ensure an equitable rate of return on capital employed to the best interest of shareholders and employees.

B. *Strategy* Our strategy is to safeguard our future competitive position relative to our main competitors to ensure that our profit performance at all times is equal to or better than theirs. Strategy can be summarized under the following headlines, which are largely self-explanatory:
- Create a profit-oriented organization.
- Fully integrate and optimize manufacturing, outside supply, and marketing.
- Improve productivity and profitability of existing assets.
- Divest unprofitable assets or assets with unsatisfactory potential.
- Channel new investment into areas where X has unique opportunities.
- Control operating costs.

FIGURE 3.16   Objectives and Goals for Exploration and Production

The problem facing Exploration and Production is to devise a realistic approach to reach three main objectives:
- Maintain security of invested capital and future earnings.
- Increase net income after foreign tax by an overall average of about 10% per year.
- Aggressively develop business opportunities in competition with other oil companies.

There is no easy approach to any of these objectives, particularly since a solution today in any one country is not likely to be the correct one tomorrow in that country or in any other. The following guidelines will be the basis for our operating strategy:

A. To maintain security of invested capital and future earnings and increase net income after foreign tax by an average of 10% per year, X will:
1. Aggressively pursue exploration in potentially stable areas that present scope and the promise of finding major reserves. Emphasis will be given to:
   a. improving X's position in the offshore portion of Northwestern Europe.
   b. vigorously developing X's excellent properties in West Africa.
   c. reconsidering X's stance in the Middle East and North Africa, bearing in mind the remaining high productivity potential, the competition, and the need to promote ingenious business schemes.
   d. generating new exploration ventures in virgin areas showing good geological prospects and political stability.
2. Properly assess the political and technical factors in the initial stages of a venture.
3. For certain high-risk programs, attempt to soften the impact of the possible loss of capital by limiting the size of the investment directly, or indirectly by sharing the program and spreading the risk with another investor.
4. In the case of high-risk development projects, political and/or technical, only consider projects with four years payout and 20% DCF rate of return. This will not give absolute protection but statistically should be satisfactory.
5. In new high-risk exploration ventures, arrange for a low commitment during the initial stage and an early back-out point in case the property is evaluated as uncommercial.
6. In capital-intensive projects, such as a development program for the North Sea

FIGURE 3.16 (*Continued*)

    or the liquified natural gas facilities in Nigeria, obtain as much capital as possible through unconventional loans covered by risk insurance.

    7. Optimize production of the better existing projects by vigorous development.

B. To actively develop business opportunities in competition with other oil companies.

    To satisfy the aspirations of the producing countries to become directly involved in the oil business, X must take the lead in devising unique arrangements or joint operations as follows:

    1. Set up a joint operating company with state-owned oil companies, which would participate in decision making and responsibility from the beginning of operations. In this concept, which has been proposed to the Norwegian government for operations in the North Sea, each partner will own equal interests and have equal rights and management responsibilities. This joint company will have the potential for providing a vehicle for marketing the partnership's production—X will contribute the initial capital to this venture and will carry the state oil company through the exploration phase and a portion of the appraisal phase of developing the first discovery. In its operation the joint company will utilize to the maximum local personnel and the potential of local industry.

    2. Offer a similar arrangement to other countries where exploration prospects are promising but where our competitors are still proposing a company-controlled operation until commercial production is found.

    3. Of even more importance, devise for countries that have achieved 100% participation profitable arrangements whereby X would furnish capital and technical expertise in exchange for a long term supply of crude oil at a favorable price.

To achieve these objectives, the critical requirement is outstanding professional skill in dealing with technical problems and negotiating with governments. Accordingly, our plan envisions positive steps to upgrade manpower in order to strengthen resources in executive and supervisory abilities, advisory efficiency, exploration and engineering expertise, and business ingenuity.

Exercise 3

    This and every exercise is intended to facilitate and be the basis for a part of the term project: Prepare a Strategic Plan for an organization of your choice. For each exercise, present a typed, one-page report showing the directions your analysis will take.

    For this exercise, develop charts showing the networks of hierarchy for the organization and objectives and strategy for your selected company.

    In addition to the material of this chapter, the following references are pertinent: King and Cleland, (1978), Chapters 7, 8, 9; Steiner (1969) Chapters 1, 6, 7; Ackoff (1970), Chapter 5.

REFERENCES

Ackoff, R. L. *A Concept of Corporate Planning*. New York: Wiley, 1970.

Allen, L. A. *Making Managerial Planning More Effective*. New York: McGraw-Hill, 1982.

Argenti, John. *Systematic Corporate Planning*. New York: Wiley, 1974.

Hussey, David. *Corporate Planning Theory and Practice*. Oxford, England: Pergamon Press, 1974.

King, W. R., and Cleland, D. I. *Strategic Planning and Policy*. New York: Van Nostrand Reinhold, 1978.

McNichols, T. J. *Executive Policy and Strategic Planning*. New York: McGraw-Hill, 1977.

Rogers, R. E. *Corporate Strategy and Planning*. Columbus, Ohio: Grid Pub. Co., 1981.

Saaty, T. L. "Measuring the Fuzziness of Sets." *Journal of Cybernetics*, 4 (1974), pp. 53–61.

Saaty, T. L. "A Scaling Method for Priorities in Hierarchical Structures." *Journal of Mathematical Psychology* 15 (1977), pp. 234–81.

Saaty, T. L. "Exploring the Interface between Hierarchies, Multiple Objects and Fuzzy Sets." *Fuzzy Sets and Systems* 1 (1978), 57–68.

Simon, H. A. "The Architecture of Complexity." *Proceedings of the American Philosophical Society* 106 (December 1962), pp. 476–82.

Simon, H. A. "The Structure of Ill-Structured Problems." *Artificial Intelligence* 4 (1973), pp. 181–201.

Steiner, G. A. *Top Management Planning*. New York: Macmillan, 1969.

Chapter 4

Feedback and Alternatives Analysis

Having developed a set of strategic objectives, we now raise the obvious question: How do we get to where we want to go as efficiently as possible? Once objectives have been set, we must propose various means of attaining in each time period an acceptable amount of progress toward their realization. This phase of the planning process will be referred to as "alternatives analysis," a term that implies that there can be more than one approach to take to meet an objective.

Before we choose from among a number of alternatives, we should try to make sure that the set of alternatives includes all potentially successful means of attaining the goal we have in mind. Thus, the process of generating alternatives is important.

It should be stated at this point that there is no guarantee that an organization will succeed in choosing the single best alternative, even if in theory it does exist. This is not to say that the alternative selection process is not successful. Careful consideration of alternative approaches, as a minimum, will serve to protect against adoption of an approach grossly inappropriate and therefore predestined to failure.

THE PRACTICAL APPLICATION OF ALTERNATIVES ANALYSIS

Corporate objectives and the means of attaining them are constrained in advance by the existence of a well-defined company mission and statement of ethos. Company mission often includes a reference to generation of an adequate return on shareholders' capital. It should be noted that this profit objective is not universally accepted and has been challenged by the stakeholders' theory and consensus theory.

Ethos may be defined officially as the disposition, character, or attitude peculiar to a specific people, culture, or group that distinguishes it from other peoples or groups. In this context, ethos refers to the manner in which an organization behaves towards its employees and those external to the organization.

Ethos is similar to what Rogers (1981) refers to as constraints. These constraints determine what the firm will not do, on moral grounds. Constraints include such considerations as the law, deceptive dealings, discrimination, product quality, unfair labor practices, and employee safety.

According to both Rogers (1981) and Argenti (1974), the logical progression leading to the alternatives-generation phase of the planning process involves:

1. Definition of company mission
2. Determination of ethos or constraints
3. Generation of alternatives

It may be useful to point out that each of these processes contributes to the formulation of strategic objectives, but the final step involves the actual selection of alternatives. The mission and constraints may provide broad objectives, but not until the alternatives or means for accomplishing these objectives are selected can we begin to quantify and set targets or goals that become an integral part of a company's strategic objectives.

ALTERNATIVES GENERATION

Alternatives generation involves the preparation of a list of possible actions the company might pursue in order to achieve its objectives. Great care must be taken to avoid a myopic or biased list of alternatives. It is also important that a complete list of alternatives be generated.

A technique that has potential advantages at this stage is a group decision-making process known as the Delphi technique, discussed in detail in chapter 8. This technique was originally developed by the RAND Corporation in an effort to forecast military events. The Delphi technique as normally applied is useful in enabling a panel of experts to arrive at a consensus. When this technique is adapted to alternatives generation, members of the planning committee should be familiarized with company objectives and asked to make a list of alternatives for accomplishing them. It should be noted that this process is conducted confidentially, so that the names of sponsors are not attached to their suggestions. A complete listing of all proposed alternatives is supplied to all participants, who are asked to reconsider their original proposals. A new list of alternatives is then compiled.

This technique allows the generation of a list of alternatives unimpeded by "groupthink," status, or interpersonal conflict. The result should be a higher quality, more varied, and less biased list.

Argenti's (1974) model of alternatives generation suggests that one way to avoid omitting important options is to review seven possible means to accomplish objectives:

1. Invest capital
2. Overcome obstacles
3. Exploit opportunities
4. Use strengths
5. Overcome weaknesses
6. Institute a profit-management plan
7. Use management techniques

Specific alternatives could be classified under one or more of these categories.

A second type of review suggested by Argenti involves:

1. Examining existing business areas to see what should be
   a. reduced
   b. maintained
   c. increased
   d. forced
2. Taking a look at potential new business areas that may arise out of a need to
   a. integrate forward
   b. integrate backward
   c. diversify
3. At least a consideration of that often overlooked but sometimes prudent alternative: liquidation.

The second item in the above list is quite similar to the Boston Consulting Group matrix of Stars, Dogs, Cash Cows, and Question Marks, discussed in chapter 12. It may be noted that Argenti's model of alternatives analysis has been extended by other authors in terms of network analysis.

THE MECHANICS OF ALTERNATIVES GENERATION

All levels of management will have ideas and wishes on how the objectives of the company are to be pursued. These various alternatives, many of which are conflicting, must be examined, and one chosen. A logical means of doing this is presented in figure 4.1.

FIGURE 4.1   Sequence of Operations in Alternatives Generation

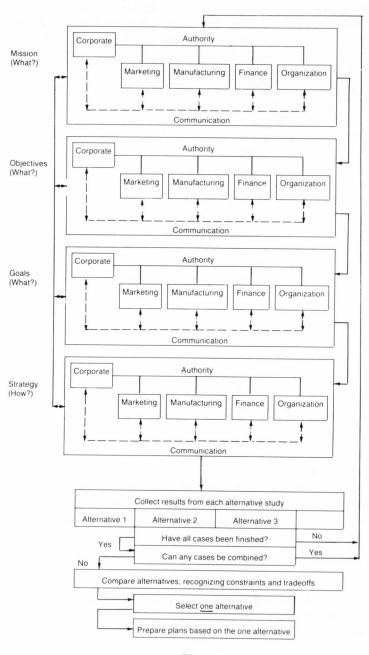

The figure depicts a company with four functional areas: marketing, manufacturing, finance, and organization. Of course, a real company would add or substitute its actual functions. The process must always begin with the top block of the figure: consideration of the company mission. This must be done during the consideration of each alternative. As brought out in previous chapters, it is rare that a mission is changed, but it is not impossible to do so. Within the block we see the usual lines of authority flowing from the corporate level to each of the functional areas. In addition, dotted lines indicate that there is complete communication not only between the corporation and each of the functions but also between each pair of functions. Through this feedback process, the parties agree that the mission is acceptable for the alternative in question. More rarely, it may be noted that changes in the mission statement would be required for that alternative. Also, at this point, each function derives its own mission statement, which is in some sense a sub-mission of the corporation. Sometimes a sub-mission is more closely related to the corporate objectives, now to be discussed. See chapter 1 for a definition of "mission" and the other terms.

In the second block, the same feedback process obtains, so that a mutually agreeable set of corporate and functional objectives results. Flow now passes to the third block, as shown by the arrows at the right of the diagram, where goals (sometimes called short-range objectives) are derived and mutually reconciled. Finally, the fourth block is reached, where, again by the same feedback process, the strategy of how to achieve all of the above is determined.

Remember that this process is carried through for each alternative. As each alternative is finished, its details are recorded, as indicated at the bottom of figure 4.1. If more cases need to be considered, the process repeats, beginning again at the top of the figure. At some point it may result that several alternatives, sometimes called cases, can be combined to form a new case, either in addition to or in place of, the original cases.

When a final set of alternatives is achieved, they must be compared, taking into account all the various constraints and tradeoffs, and one (and only one) chosen for implementation. We now discuss how the selection of one alternative may be achieved. Contingency planning, where alternate plans are kept in mind for emergencies, is discussed in another chapter.

EVALUATION OF ALTERNATIVES

Evaluation of alternatives can be thought of in terms of "gap analysis" (Ansoff 1965). Such analysis can be made at the corporate level, or a preliminary gap analysis can be made at the group, divisional, or functional level prior to the corporate-wide analysis.

Regardless of the level, the procedure is much the same. The projected performance of the selected level (corporate or lower) is compared to the targets that have been established for the level in question. In the case of multiple goals, it may be desirable to do the analysis for each goal. The gap—the difference between goal and projected achievement—would be calculated year by year for each year of the planning horizon. This procedure is often a valuable stimulus in the search for new strategies to achieve company goals.

It is during the stage of alternatives evaluation that specific courses of action are analyzed in accordance with company objectives. This leads to the dismissal of a number of alternatives and eventually to a ranking of the remaining alternatives in terms of their degree of consistency with company objectives.

At the initial stage of alternatives evaluation, there is a need for some type of screening operation to reduce the list of alternatives to a manageable number. Clearly, those alternatives that are not consistent with company mission (profit) and environmental constraints (ethos) should be eliminated without further consideration.

The following checklist gives further guidance on the elimination of alternatives.

1. Does the alternative give the company a performance risk curve compatible with that of its shareholders?
2. Does the company have the competence to carry it out?
3. Does it capitalize on company strengths?
4. Does it eliminate or reduce company weaknesses?
5. Does it allow the exploitation of opportunities?
6. Does it reduce potentially severe threats?
7. Does it call for morally objectionable actions?
8. Are any ethological constraints infringed?
9. Can the proposed strategies realistically be executed?

Any alternative not consistent with these guidelines may be eliminated.

Once a number of alternative strategies have been ruled out, the remaining list may be more closely scrutinized. Every alternative may be looked at from two perspectives: operational objectives and project objectives. The operational objectives consist of proposals for modifying the existing business, whereas the project objectives involve proposals for entirely new activities. At this point, company models become extremely valuable.

QUANTITATIVE TECHNIQUES

Sensitivity testing is often useful in evaluating alternatives and involves estimating the effect on the return on investment (ROI) caused by errors in each of the underlying assumptions of a particular alternative. Among the advantages of sensitivity testing are the following:

1. It shows which assumptions are most critical.
2. It shows the ranges of possible outcomes.
3. It does not rely on probability; rather, it asks, What would happen if X occurs?

An outcome matrix examines the probabilities associated with various potential outcomes for a particular strategy so as to determine an "expected value" or most likely result.

General-purpose modeling in a corporate planning context is discussed in chapter 12. Any such models may be used for alternatives analysis. For example, cash-flow models, income models, production models, and purchasing models can be constructed. They may be separate models to be used for planning of subsystems, or they may be parts of one integrated corporate model to support the quantitative aspects of corporate planning generally.

IMPLEMENTATION

The implementation of the strategic plan involves the development of operating strategy. Functional area plans are coordinated with overall firm objectives through the formulation of coordinating subobjectives. Each functional area involves different factors peculiar to that area. This can be illustrated by listing details for a number of typical functions:

1. Marketing considerations
    a. Product line, extent, purpose
    b. Pricing, packaging, design
    c. Channels of distribution
2. Production considerations
    a. Capital-equipment expenditures
    b. Plant size, location, etc.
    c. Production methods
3. Financial considerations and policies
    a. Dividends
    b. Retained earnings
    c. Debt

d. Cash flow
e. Budgeting
f. Long-range planning

ORGANIZATIONAL STRATEGY

The adopted corporate strategy should be the major factor that shapes the structure of the firm. Strategic considerations in this area involve:
1. Communications-net requirements
2. Skill requirements based on basic overall objectives and subobjectives
3. Staff requirements and relationships
4. Centralization versus decentralization
5. Product management versus functional management versus geographical management, etc.

DEVELOPMENT OF THE CONTROL SYSTEM

Interpretation and evaluation of results must flow through the organization and must be based on responsibility and performance of individuals strategically placed in the organizational structure. The feedback mechanism is a function of the organizational structure and the intangible factors of organizational behavior. The control strategy must flow from the organizational design and must measure progress toward the corporate objectives and subgoals as developed from corporate purpose and constraints.

Factors that should be considered in the development of control strategies include:
1. Selection of key control variables
2. Coordination of control measures
3. Balance between qualitative and quantitative control measures
4. Use of systems analysis in structuring a control system
5. External monitoring systems
This evaluation of the strategic planning process and results is referred to as "reformulation."

The control system may indicate weaknesses in the corporate strategy as a whole. Such an indication signals the need for the development of a recovery strategy, which involves the complete recycling of the policy-making process and a redesign of the overall strategic plan. Complete recycling involves a change in operating, organizational, and control strategies.

Reformulation is more likely to focus on one or more of the successive phases of the policy-making process. Many successful reformulation strategies have been executed through changes in operating, organizational, or control strategies singularly. Reformulation of separate business units in decentralized organizations represents special problems. Organization strategies and structure of most organizations lag behind their operating strategies.

While planning has evolved from short to long term and from operating to strategic control, control systems at top-management level still tend to focus on monitoring short-term operational performance. The remedy lies in new tools, known collectively as strategic controls, which focus on setting standards and on measuring and evaluating performance in the following areas:

1. Key assumptions concerning the evolution of the environment and the resources of the firm
2. The constancy of crucial factors of success
3. The development of distinctive competences and key results

These factors are not adequately covered by current accounting practices. The expectations approach appears to offer a tool for planning and control. Whereas management by objectives was based on the concept of an "objective," the new approach is based on the concept of an "expectation," specifically a requirement that one person (or group) holds of another person (or group) in connection with a job. One board of directors chose to classify the relative importance of expectations in the following way:

H: High priority
M: Medium priority
L: Low priority

Accurate, relevant performance reporting is essential for effective planning and control. One group of managers chose a simple reporting format on expectation of achievement:

A: Above expected level
E: Expected level
B: Below expected level

Performance review is a disciplined communications process, relying heavily on the interview process, in which people in the organization cooperatively express their hopes and aspirations for a stated period and rationalize them within the context of the overall goals of the corporation.

THE SELECTION OF A SINGLE ALTERNATIVE

Previous sections have discussed aids to help in the elimination of less-desirable alternatives (cases). Quantitative methods and computer models are certainly one such aid. Considerations regarding the implementation of an alternative case are highly relevant; if the case cannot be implemented it is worthless. Organizational factors are relevant: Is the needed organization attainable, and will it generate enthusiasm? Control techniques are pertinent: Are there factors that could serve to measure progress toward goals? The time factor has not been specifically mentioned above: What are the visualized results in each year of a proposed case? How does the summation appear? Is there a trend with time? What are the factors regarding momentum of the results?

The analysis already given may have resulted in the selection of one alternative, which can then be fleshed out into the formal corporate strategic plan. At this point, no more than four alternatives should remain. If there are more, some should be eliminated by reviewing the guidelines already given.

In order to select the winning alternative, the use of a questionnaire such as that outlined in figure 4.2 is suggested. Our present state of knowledge does not provide a simple technique for the selection of one best case out of a series of cases. Rather, the process must be one of negotiation, discussion, and consideration by various corporate and functional executives. We do not claim that the questions of figure 4.2 are applicable for every company. They will certainly serve as a starting point; some may have to be deleted and others added.

The first step, therefore, is for the company to develop its own version of the figure. Judgment is required to interpret answers to the various questions; sometimes a yes answer may denote an inferior position (rank = 1); other times it may have a superior connotation (rank = 5).

One approach would be for each of a number of executives to complete the form independently, resulting in a numeric "grade" for each case. Adding these grades from all executives would indicate the winner. Alternatively, the grade summation could be used to eliminate the lowest case, followed by additional discussion and negotiation on the remaining cases. The exact procedure to be followed is a matter of judgment for each particular company.

FIGURE 4.2 Alternatives Spread Sheet
Insert rank number ranging
from 1 = very inferior
to 5 = very superior.

	Alternative Number			
	1	2	3	4
1. Does alternative fit mission?	___	___	___	___
2. Is the strategy identifiable and understood by all?	___	___	___	___
3. Does the strategy agree with objectives?	___	___	___	___
4. Will the strategy promote profitability, growth, survival?	___	___	___	___
5. Does the strategy conflict with other strategies?	___	___	___	___
6. Is the strategy properly interrelated with the functional substrategies?	___	___	___	___
7. Considering organization and personnel, can the stated objectives be achieved?	___	___	___	___
8. Does the alternative build on strengths?	___	___	___	___
9. Is the alternative consonant with resources?	___	___	___	___
10. Is it consonant with size of firm?	___	___	___	___
11. Is it consonant with share of market sought?	___	___	___	___
12. Is it consonant with skills and resources?	___	___	___	___
13. Can skills and resources be acquired?	___	___	___	___
14. Does the alternative avoid or minimize weaknesses?	___	___	___	___
15. Is it consistent with personal values of managers and employees?	___	___	___	___
16. Does it suggest agreement with stated policies of horizontal or vertical integration?	___	___	___	___
17. Is the alternative within acceptable environmental restrictions?	___	___	___	___
18. Is it consistent with company environment?	___	___	___	___
19. Has it been checked for consistency with past, present, and prospective trends?	___	___	___	___
20. Has it been checked by developing acceptable and realistic subplans for an extended period into the future?	___	___	___	___
21. How will it relate the firm to the desired social order?	___	___	___	___
22. What need or service will it supply?	___	___	___	___
23. Is it based on a known technology?	___	___	___	___
24. Is the alternative's timing good?	___	___	___	___
25. Is this a new or an ongoing industry?	___	___	___	___
26. What is the nature of the industry structure and its competitive patterns?	___	___	___	___
27. Will this alternative force a technological breakthrough?	___	___	___	___
28. Are we familiar with marketing these products or services?	___	___	___	___
29. Do we understand these customers?	___	___	___	___
30. Do we understand this specific market?	___	___	___	___
31. Do we understand the regulatory environment?	___	___	___	___

FIGURE 4.2 (*Continued*)

32. Do the ethics and business practices fit in with our beliefs? _____ _____ _____ _____
33. What is the projected return on investment? _____ _____ _____ _____
34. Are financial resources adequate? _____ _____ _____ _____
35. What are estimated annual sales? _____ _____ _____ _____
36. What is estimated new dollar payout? _____ _____ _____ _____
37. Does the alternative balance risk and profit potential consistent with resources and prospects? _____ _____ _____ _____
38. Does the option effectively employ existing investment? _____ _____ _____ _____
39. Is there flexibility (or reversibility) in using present investment? _____ _____ _____ _____
40. What are inflation or pricing considerations? _____ _____ _____ _____
41. How many years would be required to reach acceptable sales? _____ _____ _____ _____
42. What specific products or services are involved? _____ _____ _____ _____
43. Is this a single-product or a many-product venture? _____ _____ _____ _____
44. Are products new to the market and innovative? _____ _____ _____ _____
45. Do we have needed production and marketing skills and resources? _____ _____ _____ _____
46. Could competitors enter the market easily? _____ _____ _____ _____
47. Are raw materials readily available? _____ _____ _____ _____
48. Are we familiar with processes required? _____ _____ _____ _____
49. Are R & D staff and resources available? _____ _____ _____ _____
50. Is production know-how available? _____ _____ _____ _____
51. How probable is successful implementation? _____ _____ _____ _____
52. What is the status of patents in the field? _____ _____ _____ _____
53. How energy-dependent is the project? _____ _____ _____ _____
54. Is the present sales force adequate? _____ _____ _____ _____
55. How large are estimated markets? _____ _____ _____ _____
56. What are market-growth prospects? _____ _____ _____ _____
57. How stable is the market? _____ _____ _____ _____
58. What are market trends (up, down, static)? _____ _____ _____ _____
59. Is a regional, national, or international market involved? _____ _____ _____ _____
60. What are the requirements for market development? _____ _____ _____ _____
61. What are the requirements for promotion? _____ _____ _____ _____
62. What are the requirements for technical services? _____ _____ _____ _____
63. Does the alternative involve cyclic or seasonal demand? _____ _____ _____ _____
64. What is the potential market position for this alternative? _____ _____ _____ _____
65. Are present products similar? _____ _____ _____ _____
66. Does this alternative involve the production of a new product for a new market? (Be careful!) _____ _____ _____ _____
67. Will this alternative pioneer a new industry? _____ _____ _____ _____

FIGURE 4.2   *(Continued)*

68. How will this alternative affect present products?	___	___	___	___
69. How might present customers react?	___	___	___	___
70. How many potential customers are there?	___	___	___	___
71. Does this alternative fit a niche in the market that is now open?	___	___	___	___
72. Will this niche remain open long enough to recover capital investment and earn a profit?	___	___	___	___
73. Is this niche or industry position desirable?	___	___	___	___
74. Does this alternative imply vulnerability to the power of one major customer?	___	___	___	___
75. How stiff is competition with other products?	___	___	___	___
76. What are the advantages of this product?	___	___	___	___
77. How long is product life?	___	___	___	___
78. What is product life cycle?	___	___	___	___
79. Is there exposure to legal liability?	___	___	___	___
80. How steady is customer business stability?	___	___	___	___
81. What is the potential for competitive action?	___	___	___	___
82. Is there a single powerful competitor?	___	___	___	___
83. Is this alternative patterned after that of a competitor? (Be careful!)	___	___	___	___

Exercise 4

This exercise, like the others, is intended to facilitate and to be the basis for a part of the term project: Prepare a strategic plan for an organization of your choice. For each exercise, present a typed, one-page report showing the directions your analysis will take.

For this exercise, indicate what factors your company should consider in preparing alternatives and how it should go about the work.

In addition to the material of this chapter, the following references are pertinent: Ansoff (1965), chapter 8; Argenti (1974), chapters 5, 7; Sawyer (1983), chapters 9, 15.

References

Ansoff, H. Igor. *Corporate Strategy.* New York: McGraw-Hill, 1965.

Argenti, John. *Systematic Corporate Planning.* New York: Wiley, 1974.

McNichols, Thomas J. *Policymaking and Executive Action.* New York: McGraw-Hill, 1983.

Rogers, Rolf E. *Corporate Strategy and Planning.* Columbus, Ohio: Grid Pub. Co., 1981.

Sawyer, George C. *Corporate Planning as a Creative Process.* Oxford, Ohio: Planning Executives Institute, 1983.

Chapter 5

Strategic Planning
and Top Management

Earlier chapters have outlined the areas of strategic planning and have indicated that this responsibility logically belongs to corporate headquarters. Divisions or functional subunits cannot see or take full advantage of available opportunities, and they cannot see or counter the threats to the enterprise. This does not imply any reduction in divisional strategic responsibilities; indeed, much strategic work needs to be exploited at divisional levels.

Planning is regarded by all authorities as the prime responsibility of the chief executive. This does not imply that all executives rise to their posts through the staff planning function. Indeed, few do. Further, there is no implication that all CEOs fit a particular stereotype, certainly not that of a staff planner. McNichols (1983) illustrates this point well in his description of three men being considered for the top executive position of an international corporation. The comparisons are summarized in table 5.1. All three candidates are successful, but there is no single characteristic and no grouping of characteristics that can be pointed to as the reason for success. It has been said, only partly in jest, that the way to become a top executive is to have no discernable faults. If one of the persons described in table 5.1 tended to fly off the handle at awkward moments and another was prone to make poor assumptions and jump to conclusions, the third might be chosen, even though he had no outstanding qualities. Perhaps one universal requirement for a CEO is political sense, and this is discussed later in the chapter. As will be seen in another section, such an ability is also important for the corporate planner.

TABLE 5.1   Characteristics of Candidates for a Particular Chief Executive Position

Name	Scheer	Diederich	Boyd
Age	Forty-eight	Fifty-four	Fifty-one
Citizenship	Switzerland	Germany	United States
Position	Director of finance	Director of manufacturing	Director of marketing
Religion	Roman Catholic	Lutheran	Protestant
Health	Hearing poor	Good	Good
Education	Ph.D., Economics	B.S., Electrical Engineer	60 hour busines diploma
Experience	Business	Technical	Sales
Married	Yes	Yes	Yes
Children	Four	Eight	None
Languages	German, French, English, Swedish, Danish	German, English, Swedish	English Swedish
Professional associations	Many	Many	One
Outside interests	Music, sailing, author of professional articles	Radio, music, gardening, chess	Spectator sports, reading, travel

THE TOP EXECUTIVE AND THE REAL WORLD

It is a truism to state that the executive accomplishes the purposes of the organization by delegating work to others. When a task needs to be done, the executive directs another person to do it. Others provide descriptions of the real world—past, present, and future. As shown in figure 5.1, inquiries about past results are answered by an accounting department, feedback on current actions is provided by an operating manager, and the outlook for strategic plans comes from a corporate planning department.

Since our interest is in strategic planning, we will discuss this last sector. Ansoff and Leontiades (1976) have listed eleven facets of the planning work of the top manager:

1. Monitor the environment for trends and events likely to have a major impact on the firm
2. Formulate the portfolio objectives (that is, the mix of businesses) of the firm

FIGURE 5.1 The Central Role of Top Management

3. Select the desired portfolio (that is, mix of businesses) by specifying it over time, including entry timing, penetration rate, and divestiture
4. Analyze the vulnerabilities of the firm
5. Define acceptable trade-offs between objectives and vulnerabilities
6. Determine the responsibilities and contributions of the various divisions
7. Determine resource allocations and transfers among the divisions
8. Select the broad strategy: horizontal, vertical, concentric, or geographical diversification; wholly owned; joint ventures; franchises
9. Determine the common thread for the firm to pursue

10. Set up a strong and unsentimental divestiture policy

11. Identify new businesses that meet the requirements of the portfolio strategy

The planning function of the CEO calls for heavy reliance on information concerning the environment of the company in addition to information about the company itself. Much of this information will be developed by the corporate planner, but it may be well for the CEO to have independent sources, both as a check and to enhance personal stature and ability.

Chapter 9 reviews some of the places that information pertinent to planning may be found. Membership in planning societies can increase awareness about both planning methodology and specialist sources of information. Membership typically is made up largely of nonplanning executives. The appendix provides a list of such societies as well as a list of consultants who specialize in forecasting, planning, and corporate modeling. Finally, it is wise to sound out the opinion of people outside the company. Helpful sources might be:

1. Bankers
2. Major institutional stockholders
3. Stockholders' committees
4. Survey of stockholder opinions
5. Stockbrokers
6. Financial consultants
7. Interfirm comparison studies (for example, Dun and Bradstreet)
8. Industry studies (for example, Dun and Bradstreet)

In some cases, the prestige of the CEO may provide access to information that a corporate planner could not obtain.

ROLE OF THE CORPORATE PLANNER

The borderline between what the CEO does and what the corporate planner (CP) does is fuzzy and varies from company to company. There are three major functions for the CP: innovator, recorder, and communicator. The subheadings proposed by Sawyer (1983) are classified in figure 5.2 into these three main headings. The borders between topics are also fuzzy. Recording, for example, may be classed as a form of communication.

Innovator

The planner seeks the best possible combination of available resources and then recommends the acquisition of new resources. As alternate plans

FIGURE 5.2 Functions of the Corporate Planner

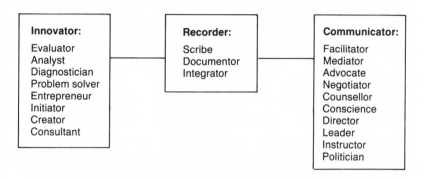

Innovator:	Recorder:	Communicator:
Evaluator	Scribe	Facilitator
Analyst	Documentor	Mediator
Diagnostician	Integrator	Advocate
Problem solver		Negotiator
Entrepreneur		Counsellor
Initiator		Conscience
Creator		Director
Consultant		Leader
		Instructor
		Politician

are put together, they must be evaluated. In the course of this activity, the CP needs analytic skills and the ability to use models and other tools of analysis. Being a diagnostician is perhaps different from being an analyst; one must understand what is driving events and what is controlling variables. Problem solving adds another dimension; having produced an analysis and a diagnosis, the CP now must decide what should be done in order to solve the problem. The mere fact of recognizing when there is a problem is a valuable ability. A CP who is put in charge of a business project that does not fit elsewhere or that for any other reason is an ''orphan'' ceases to be a CP. It is possible to use managerial and entrepreneurial skills, however, without acting as an advocate for entrepreneurial actions by the corporation. To be an initiator is to put forth suggestions and new ideas on which the CEO may take action. The CP must always seek to ''create the future'' for the firm. He attempts to be proactive rather than sit back and let the future come as it will. Finally, the role of consultant in which the CP often finds himself has innovative aspects. This is a sensitive position, requiring confidential treatment of information received, balanced with the requirement of keeping the CP's superior informed.

Recorder

Being a scribe or secretary is sometimes the stereotype of a CP. It is hard work to put the results of group discussions on paper as a record of planning progress and as a stimulus for further ideas. The function is extremely important; it may help the CEO to grasp concepts behind objectives and strategies as stated, and it may help the chief executive to tackle issues and to shape and polish concepts. The function of documentor perhaps carries an additional function of preparing a summary of significant conclusions. The integrator aspect of recording is one of reconciling the existing needs of various divisions and departments and helping each department understand the necessary process of give and take.

Communicator

The documentation described above is certainly a part of communication. But even though a written report states the facts, personal discussion amplifies and fills in details and thus permits fuller understanding. For this reason, many corporations have the planning department put on a "road show" of both preliminary and final versions of the strategic plan, covering all significant geographic areas. Alternatively, or in addition, selected key managers may be brought to corporate headquarters for similar discussions. As a result of the interpersonal relationships that grow in the course of such a program, the CP becomes a facilitator, capable of recognizing and cutting red tape and having the proper contacts in the organization to get things done quickly. Very often, when a group is struggling with the planning process, issues and controversies arise between units. The CP has the opportunity to act as a mediator, pointing out the benefits of the final plan and the undesirability to all of allowing such disagreements to surface. The position of advocate has already been alluded to. Sometimes one of the divisions will formally request the CP to act as advocate, to help it tell its story. The above roles often merge into negotiating among several parties. The CP is an obvious choice for negotiator, by virtue of being neutral and well-informed. Often a counselling relationship arises between the CP and a line executive. The executive also needs a neutral and well-informed person from whom to seek advice or to serve as a sounding board. The executive might be reluctant to relate to subordinates, superiors, or peers in this manner.

In any of the above roles, but particularly, perhaps, in mediating or counseling, the CP may find it necessary to act as a conscience, pointing out possible illegal, unethical, or otherwise undesirable aspects of a suggested course of action. The CP is the leader and director of the corporate planning group and may also assume these functions for a task force established to carry out a planning function. The CP is always an instructor; teaching duties may range from guidance of a group of managers who have never put together a plan to the presentation of sophisticated information on new techniques.

THE TOP MANAGEMENT-CORPORATE PLANNER INTERFACE

There is no iron-clad regulation that separates the domain of the executive from that of the planner. The borderline between the two varies among companies and with time in the same company. For example, a new CEO may relinquish functions or usurp functions.

The situation is presented in figure 5.3. The functions of the CEO have been discussed, as have those of the corporate planner. Depending on the company and the personalities, the statement of these functions is flexible. Similarly, there is interaction between the chief executive and the operating departments and between the CP and the operating departments. As a result of these various communication channels, a corporate strategic plan emerges. At this point the "fuzziness" must disappear. It is up to the CEO to affix a stamp of approval and to say, "This is the plan." The CEO must present the plan to the operating divisions and state, "This is what you will do." At this point the plan passes from the realm of a staff planning matter and becomes an operating directive.

THE RATIONAL VERSUS THE POLITICAL

Politics is not a dirty word; rather, it is the process of discovering what others want in order to endeavor to give it to them—as well as to find out how to get others to act in ways that you believe to be in the best interests of your firm and the community. Line and staff executives at all levels must manage relationships. If you will, this is "playing politics."

Both the corporate planner and the CEO must be aware of the need for politics. The needs and ambitions of all executives are a major influence on the CP; the power and beliefs of the comptroller, the chief of the firm's most profitable division, the executive who did not get the CEO post, the people who are now vying for that spot—are legitimate concerns. Further, the CP's position is almost never one of power. In any direct confrontation with a line officer, the CP will usually lose. Therefore, this position demands political awareness. It has been said that the success of a CP depends more on the ability to manage and balance relationships than it does on technical competence.

Before discussing politics at the CEO level, let us consider a completely rational planning system. This might take the form of a massive linear programming (LP) system. The requirements and details of such systems are described in chapters 12 and 18. In theory it is possible to represent product movements, sales, relations with customers, competitors, local, state, and

FIGURE 5.3   Interfaces in Planning Relationships

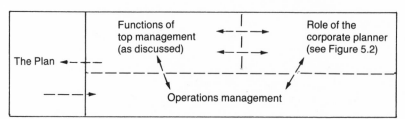

national governments, and the general public—in short, all aspects of an on-going business. It is also possible to replicate this matrix for each year of the planning period.

At our present state of knowledge, no CEO would be willing to base a plan strictly on the outcome of such a model. Because of the unlimited number of possible alternatives, the complexity of the managerial function, and the unpredictability of people, the CEO is constrained to "satisfice"—obtain the best conditions perceived possible rather than to use an optimizing model. Often the CEO is forced to negotiate with various factions or coalitions representing disparate views. Many decisions are primarily designed to reduce conflict and set up strategic plans acceptable to a number of conflicting factions.

Many examples could be given where failure to play politics has been harmful to a firm. Recently, a major bank foreclosed on a bankrupt firm, thus freezing funds set aside for making unemployment payments to the employees. Since this occurred in a major depressed area, there was a large outcry from all segments of the population, including the clergy. Although the action of the bank was technically correct and proper, it will take much time and effort before the bank can seriously use its former slogan: This bank is a good neighbor.

THE HIERARCHY OF MANAGERS

At every level in every organization, managers go through similar processes of management and planning, although the style, the manner, and the content differ for each manager and each task. In most organizations the relationship between managers is hierarchical, that is, each manager reports to a superior and has several subordinates.

Some managers manage without any assistance from advisors. They make decisions, give instructions, and check results themselves. A planner is, strictly speaking, someone who helps a manager to perceive how best to perform the "decide how" function. In practice, the planning of a task is intimately linked with checking results. We often speak of planning and control as if they were one activity.

ACCOUNTABILITY AND PLANNING

In managerial planning the idea that individuals, not groups, are accountable is vital. Business, corporate, financial, marketing, and production plans become useful tools and not display pieces only to the extent that we can hold individuals accountable, both for making plans and for carrying them out. The prevailing attitude is that the manager is solely and personally responsible for a unit's success or failure. We must be able to hold individuals to account if work is not done as planned. Theories of group or team accountability do not hold up in practice. Too much time is required, and there is strong likelihood of evasion if we try to hold several people to an obligation for reaching sales objectives or meeting a quality standard. Control aspects are further developed in chapter 11.

"Accountability" is defined as the obligation to carry out the duties or responsibilities and to exercise the authority of a position in conformance with understood and accepted standards. Three terms must be further defined: "Responsibility" is the work assigned to a position. "Authority" is the sum of the powers and rights assigned to a position. If you have responsibility you are assigned the work; if you have authority you have both the right and the ability to make the decisions, spend the money, or mobilize anything required by the work. "Performance standards" are the criteria by which the work and results are measured.

A manager can delegate to others the work of developing plans and can permit others to make decisions with respect to what goes into plans. A manager, however, cannot hold others accountable for his or her plans or for carrying them out, no matter how much others have contributed. Planning can be effective only to the degree we can hold people accountable for doing work and achieving results in an agreed-upon manner. While there is substantial agreement on the need for accountability, the way to establish it is another matter. Most plans are developed by staff. A key is to develop teamwork by identifying the part each plays and ensuring that there is generous credit for all. Managers are accountable for the plans that are developed for them by staff. But people in a staff relationship have, in turn, their own accountability for the content and quality of the work they do.

Accountability is the overriding reason that planning is called a top-management function. Planning and implementation must be carried out together. If a plan is not to be implemented, designing it is a waste of time.

EXERCISE 5

This exercise, like the others, is intended to facilitate and to be the basis for a part of the term project: Prepare a strategic plan for an organization of your choice. For each exercise, present a typed, one-page report, showing the directions your analysis will take.

For this exercise, discuss the role of top management in your company and its interactions with the corporate planner.

In addition to the material of this chapter, the following references are pertinent: Allen (1982), chapters 3, 4; McNichols (1983), chapter 1; Uyterhoeven et al. (1977), chapters 1, 2.

REFERENCES

Allen, L. A. *Making Managerial Planning More Effective.* New York: McGraw-Hill, 1982.

Ansoff, H. Igor, and Leontiades, James C. "Strategic Portfolio Management." *Journal of General Management* 4, 1 (Autumn 1976).

Argenti, John. *Systematic Corporate Planning.* New York: Wiley, 1974.

McNichols, Thomas J. *Policymaking and Executive Action.* New York: McGraw-Hill, 1983.

Sawyer, George C. *Corporate Planning as a Creative Process.* Oxford, Ohio: Planning Executives Institute, 1983.

Uyterhoeven, H. E. R.; Ackerman, R. W.; and Rosenblum, J. W. *Strategy and Organization.* Homewood, Ill.: Irwin, 1977.

Chapter 6

Environmental Factors Affecting Strategic Planning

Each organization exists in a complex mix of factors, forces, and entities that we call its environment. In a broader sense, the organization is itself part of the overall environment in which all organizations exist.

We have already introduced the terms reactive and proactive. A reactive firm, or organization, is one that reacts to its environment; in the vernacular, it takes what it is given. On the other hand, the proactive firm attempts to shape its environment, to make it more favorable to the organization. The situation is somewhat as depicted in figure 6.1. Some of the many environmental forces are listed in the center of the figure. The proactive firm, as shown by the arrows directed outward, actively attempts to shape these environmental forces more to its liking. In contrast, the reactive firm, at the right of the figure, is passively being shaped by the environment.

Naturally, the figure shows the most extreme situation. In practice, a firm cannot restructure all the environmental components that are significant to it. The restructuring that can occur happens in differing degrees. A firm may be proactive toward certain factors and reactive toward others. The firm must also keep the cost-benefit relationship in mind; some factors could cost more to reshape than the results would warrant.

As the list of factors in figure 6.1 suggests, there are both internal and external environments. Rogers (1981) points out that the factors in each of these environments can be grouped into five major categories: economic, social, legal, technological, and ecological.

1. Economic factors. External economic factors include gross national product (GNP), taxation, money supply, unemployment rate, and many

FIGURE 6.1   The Environment and the Organization

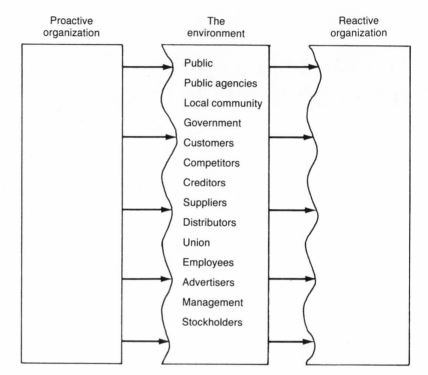

others. The borderline between external and internal economic factors is not clear-cut, but internal factors are those of direct concern to the firm: for example, market share, competition, and product price.

2. Social factors. Cultural values are quite different in the United States than, for example, in the Middle East. Societal attitudes towards the profit motive, social responsibility, taxation, and advertising must be taken into account. Internal social factors include such matters as management style and personnel policies.

3. Legal factors. It would seem that this is a purely external category. There are laws concerning how the firm may be formed, modified, or dissolved and how it can conduct its business. Legal factors are closely related to planning, because management must be aware of the legal implications of any planned strategy. Of course, there is the hierarchy of government to be considered: federal, state, county, and municipal. This matter is further complicated in the case of multinational companies.

4. Technological factors. This factor is both a threat (a competitor may make a breakthrough) and an opportunity (the firm may develop new products or processes). Even if the firm does not itself conduct research, it at the least must be aware of potential developments in its areas of interest. The internal-external dichotomy here seems obvious.

5. Ecological factors. This factor is closely related to social, legal, and technological factors. Many natural resources are nonrenewable, while industrial pollution, in the extreme, may threaten a civilization. An internal component could be visualized, as in the management and replanting of forest reserves by a paper company.

FORECASTING THE ENVIRONMENT

The framework for strategic planning is based on the idea that an organization must balance its internal capabilities with its external environment. Since this balance is achieved by apportioning the organization's resources to achieve goals consonant with external characteristics and demands, analysis of the environment is an extremely important issue.

A distinction must be made between economic forecasting and environmental forecasting. The environment is made up of a number of factors, some quantitative and some qualitative. Examples of quantitative factors would be gross national product, the fraction of women in the labor force, and sales of the firm's product. Qualitative factors could include such things as a coming national election and the expected bankruptcy of a major competitor. Techniques for economic forecasting are discussed in chapter 8.

Environmental forecasting is difficult because of the many factors involved and also because many of the single factors within the business environment are undergoing rapid change. There is increased instability in political systems and associated regulations and in interdependencies with other firms, labor unions, and various institutions. In addition, there is uncertainty about which of the factors will become important in the future.

Before environmental forecasting can begin, we must decide which of the host of all possible factors are relevant to the firm's costs, operations, and profitability. Sometimes, only one, two, or three factors in the environment turn out to be significant. Moreover, the relevant environment can often be narrowed down for individual divisions within the organization—a valuable finding that allows decentralization of planning in the organization.

The situation is shown in figure 6.2. At time = 0 (the present), it is necessary to predict the environment for a series of planning years (1,2,3 . . .). At the end of the process, we know exactly what our predic-

FIGURE 6.2 Forecasting the Environment

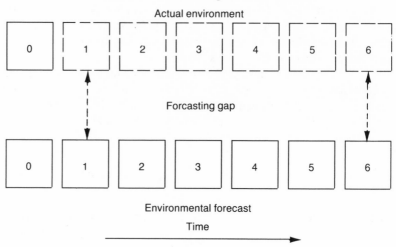

tions are, therefore the blocks are shown with solid lines. At time $= 0$, we do not have exact knowledge of the future, so that the blocks for the actual environment are outlined with dotted lines. The forecasting gap indicated on the figure thus becomes known only in the future as each planning year is reached.

Distinction must be made between the forecasting gap and the planning gap. The organization's objectives represent a desired future state that management wishes to attain. A strategic plan expresses what the organization expects to be able to attain. Any difference between this and the objectives is the planning gap. Chapter 4 discussed the preparation of alternative plans as part of an effort to reduce the planning gap. The planning gap, therefore, is something that can be noted, worked with, and probably reduced at time $= 0$ when plans are being developed.

The only way to reduce the forecasting gap is by gaining experience in using good forecasting methods and using them well. Only after a number of planning years have elapsed can we observe the forecast gap and thereby determine how to improve our methods. No "cookbook" approach is available beyond restating the precepts emphasized throughout this book: break a problem into simple components, use extensive feedback in all conceivable directions, and employ the best analytic techniques available.

Relating Opportunities, Threats, and Resources

Many of the world's changing environmental factors affect the markets for a firm's products now and in the future. Each firm is a system and, in turn, is subject to a variety of interrelationships in other larger systems. These comprise a host of economic, technological, social, and political factors. Change challenges all established strategies and opportunities, poses new threats, offers new opportunities, and raises questions about the continuing availability of a firm's resources, both physical and human.

If the precepts of this and other chapters are heeded, perhaps nothing more need be said. This section will summarize some of the precepts from an environmental viewpoint. First, means must be found for gathering intelligence concerning the many environmental factors and for organizing that intelligence into systematic data banks. This is discussed in chapter 9. Second, it is necessary to be able to explore the effects of these environmental factors on the mission and objectives of the organization. Some of the available approaches are brought out in chapters 4 and 12. It should be clearly stated again that there are no infallible approaches to this process. Each organization must select its own techniques and must ensure their validity over time.

Corporate versus Business Level Planning

Previous chapters have pointed out that strategic planning is done at various levels in the firm, and the guidelines with respect to the environmental forecasting part of the planning process are perhaps self-evident. In the case of competitor analysis, corporate planners will concentrate on those firms that compete with many of their firm's divisions, leaving divisional planners to handle the one-on-one examples. In both situations, it is often useful for the firm to put itself in the place of the competitor and to prepare a hypothetical, but fairly complete, strategic plan for that competitor.

Similarly, assessing the availability of input resources would be done at the corporate level if the resources are used across a large segment of the firm and at the divisional level when resources concern primarily that division. Thus, an energy firm would be concerned with petroleum reserves at the corporate level, but only the nuclear division would study the problem of uranium deposits.

The same principles apply to all the various economic, demographic, social, political-legal, and technological factors already mentioned. At the corporate level, a broad overall study of the environment is often made, followed by a study of the possible or probable impact of the forecast changes on segments of the firm. At the divisional level, a more specific approach is possible. Identify the factors that have in the past had an impact, or that are forecast to have an impact, on that division alone; then study those factors.

COMPUTER MODELS IN ENVIRONMENTAL FORECASTING

Management is always confronted by a spectrum of environmental problems:

- Economic uncertainty
- Local and international competition
- International liquidity problems
- Various types of shortages
- Energy crises
- Political events

No one will ever be able to make precise, calendar-date forecasts of events in the above list. What is needed is a systematic approach for evaluating the consequences of alternate policies, economic events, and political events on the future of the firm. Computer models are essential in order to be able to obtain answers to the difficult ''What if?'' questions that arise in the course of exploring these complex and interacting environmental factors. Chapter 4 has discussed the question of generating planning alternatives. Chapter 12 will outline the possible formats of management science techniques. Without the ability to look at large numbers of alternate scenarios and to do this in a reasonable space of time, strategic planning would be impossible. In a complex business, where there are multiple interacting environmental factors, computer models give the manager such a capability.

THE CHALLENGE OF THE FUTURE

The title of this section may seem redundant in a work on planning, but there is a particular challenge where environmental variables are concerned. Some variables might be called controlled; a firm could decide to build a plant in a certain planning year, or it could decide to fund and staff a new organization in another planning year.

By contrast, environmental variables are partly or even largely uncontrollable, in spite of the discussion about the proactive organization shown in figure 6.1. Although the planner or the executive cannot predict the future value of a factor with guaranteed accuracy, it is possible to determine a logical outcome of events if a prediction proves correct. The procedure is thus to make an assumption about the future of each of the pertinent environmental variables. A plan based on such a set of assumptions becomes one of the alternative plans already discussed in chapter 4.

The set of assumptions underlying each alternative must be clearly understood by everyone involved in the planning process. This has already been indicated as one of the functions of the planning staff in figure 1.5: to communicate planning assumptions and guidelines. Each assumption is treated as a fact during the planning work. At the same time, however, the assumptions must be labeled as such in the final publication of the alternative, so that proper assessment of probabilities and risks can be made when choosing between alternatives.

The above thought is so important that it will be repeated. It is imperative that, during the preparation of a given alternative, the same set of assumptions be used by all levels of managers and in all segments of the firm. It would be fatal for one manager to use a different assumption, even though the manager distrusted the validity of the official assumption.

In line with previous remarks, the divisional plan will contain assumptions that do not directly affect other divisions or the corporation. Nevertheless, these assumptions must be stated and labeled as such so that the final corporate alternative (which includes the divisional plan) can be properly evaluated.

One caveat about the statement of assumptions is that they must not be used as a device for any manager to evade responsibility. An action that is or should be under the control of a manager must not be stated as an assumption. It would be incorrect for a manager to say that he assumes his division will have erected a plant by the target date.

Oftentimes, assumptions must be made even though the firm has little or no information on which to base them. Even in this uncomfortable situation, it is better to go through the explicit planning process as outlined rather than to include implicit and unstated assumptions in a plan. The firm must also decide whether to make the effort to get hard data. There are two approaches to this decision. The first is to study the cost-benefit balance. Would the cost of gaining the needed information pay out in possible benefits? A later chapter will discuss the matter of information for strategic planning, including environmental information. Second, the firm might engage in risk analysis if a probability statement can be attached to the quality of the assumption. Standard works on decision analysis should be consulted if this approach is seriously considered (Schlaifer 1969).

Our old standby, the feedback approach, applies also in the creation of assumptions. First, initial assumptions are proposed by a particular manager or by a group of managers. Next, these are used as working assumptions in preparing alternate cases. Revision and modification may take place in this step as the result of discussion and negotiation. Lastly, when the accepted written alternative case appears, it contains the final assumptions as they have been distilled out of the feedback process. One-point plans are still made by some firms but should be avoided. If a firm makes one set of assumptions and creates one alternative as its plan, its approach is inflexible. Should the fundamental assumption fail, the entire plan will fail.

CONTINGENCY PLANNING

A contingency is something that may happen but is not certain to happen. All environmental factors have a strong contingency aspect. To a large extent, we have already provided for contingency planning. Figure 1.4, for example, points out that plans are modified each year for the entire planning horizon. In the figure, Plan 35 is essentially the same as Plan 05, but the planner has had the opportunity to modify the plan in intermediate years as contingencies have arisen.

A second way of providing for contingencies is contained in the chapter 4 discussion of alternatives analysis. A particular contingency would be contained in one of the cases studied. Should that contingency arise, then the corresponding alternative plan would be put into effect. The planner needs an additional indicator, that of a trigger point. This is something that clearly specifies when the particular contingency has occurred. If this is not provided for, a series of small changes in the environment (a competitor's behavior, for example) might take place without the firm's becoming aware that the contingency has in fact happened. After each action, the manager, being busy with day-to-day emergencies, would like to believe that the action is not great enough to get excited about.

Finally, sensitivity analysis, usually carried out via studies on a computer model, is a great help in contingency planning. It is sometimes possible to find a strategy that is resistant to a number of environmental contingencies, and where this is possible, the need for particular contingency plans is eliminated. In sensitivity analysis, a model of the corporation is run with the value of a particular environmental variable first at a low level and then at a high level. The effect on the corporation of the change in the variable is immediately evident.

ETHICS, MORALITY, AND STRATEGIC PLANNING

Some would say that men like Mellon, Carnegie, and Rockefeller played a large part in making America great. In contrast, during the 1960s the media, unions, minority groups, university faculty, and students often complained that business uses its power illegitimately and in fact makes obscene profits. Perhaps, the pendulum is swinging back from this extreme position, and many will admit that business is not all bad.

Ethics is the fuzziest topic in the subject of business policy, which itself is full of fuzzy concepts. What is acceptable in one sector of the environment may be considered reprehensible in another. For example, in some countries it is considered entirely acceptable for an employee to receive part of a salary ''under the table'' to avoid paying income taxes.

Changing beliefs on the part either of the public or of regulatory bodies can have a profound impact on the profits of a firm. The Ethyl Corporation was formed to produce and market tetraethyl lead, a component of high-octane gasoline. Recent public and political campaigns against air pollution have strongly restricted the sale of leaded gasoline, to the great detriment of Ethyl's profits. For many years, cigarette manufacturers have been forced to label their product as a potential cause of lung cancer, and it now appears that even stronger warnings will be required. These and other threats to cigarette sales have caused most major tobacco companies to diversify into new industries.

Such examples are usually classed under the heading of social responsibility (SR), but again the boundary between SR and ethics-morality is fuzzy. Nobel Prize winner economist Milton Friedman (1962) once said that the only responsibility of business is to make a profit, and that by so doing, it will contribute to the efficient use of resources and to the improvement of the environment. When a firm exercises SR, it is sometimes difficult to determine whether it has a corporate conscience, whether it hopes thereby to maximize its long-run profit and growth potential through preservation of its local ecology, or whether it hopes to capitalize on the public-relations aspects of the SR position.

Regardless of corporate motives, it is invaluable for the corporation to have a written creed or statement of ethical principles. Many major corporations do have such written statements. These act as a guide to managers at all levels, but they can also act as a protective device if a manager should be asked by a customer or government official to behave improperly. An excellent example of such a creed is that of Eaton Corporation, shown in figure 6.3.

FIGURE 6.3   The Eaton Corporation Code of Ethics
Corporate Statement on Ethical Business Conduct

Eaton Corporation's commitment to the highest degree of integrity and honesty in the management of its business affairs is stated in the following letter dated April 30, 1982.

E. Mandell de Windt
Chairman of the Board

Eaton Corporation
World Headquarters
100 Erieview Plaza
Cleveland, Ohio 44114

April 30, 1982

Dear Fellow Employee:

My purpose in writing to you is to reaffirm that Eaton is dedicated to the concept of personal integrity in the conduct of our business affairs and that all of our policies and practices flow from that principle.

Eaton has operated as a responsible and responsive corporate citizen since it was founded. A policy of the Board of Directors states that "Eaton's affairs should be conducted in conformity with high moral and ethical standards."

The laws of the cities, states and nations in which we operate are inviolable contracts with the people in those communities. We must continue to respect and obey these laws. Any effort by Eaton to change existing laws or to affect proposed legislation must be conducted within the legal and morally acceptable means available for such activity. In this connection, our policy prohibits contributions of company funds to political candidates or parties even where such contributions are lawful.

Throughout the world, Eaton products are marketed through vigorous competition, and the only advantages we seek are those that can be gained through the superior quality of our research, engineering, manufacturing and marketing.

In every business transaction and negotiation, Eaton managers are expected to respect the rights of competitors, customers, suppliers and employees. All laws governing price fixing, division of customers and territories and other trade practices must be strictly complied with.

Bribes and illegal payments subvert the very essence of competition and erode the moral fiber of those involved. Such activities are not condoned and will not be tolerated.

Conflicts of interest with the business of the Company are to be avoided. Neither an employee nor any member of his or her family (spouse, parent or child) shall have an interest of more than 1% in any firm which deals with the Company if he or she is in a position to influence transactions. Also, no gifts of substantial value shall be accepted from suppliers or customers of the Company.

I am confident that each of you shares my conviction that integrity is a personal and absolute quality. To compromise it for commercial advantage is literally and figuratively, bad business. Be assured that any violation of our policies will result in disciplinary action.

FIGURE 6.3 *(Continued)*

It is important that the policies set forth in this letter be thoroughly discussed with those people who report to you and for you to advise them of your full endorsement of the company's commitment. I'm sure you will stress the necessity that we operate worldwide within the company's policies and with the highest degree of integrity and honesty.

Sincerely,

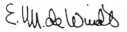

I have read and fully understand the above Corporate Statement on Ethical Business Conduct. I understand, too, that I am responsible for full compliance with it in my activities on behalf of Eaton Corporation, bringing to the attention of management any activity which appears to be in violation of or inconsistent with these principles.

Date _____

Signature _____

Name _____

Title _____

Location _____ Div. No. _____

Reprinted with permission of the Eaton Corporation, Cleveland, Ohio.

We thus have three approaches or courses that a firm could take:
- Anything goes, as long as it is legal and makes a profit.
- A middle ground may be seen as a pragmatic choice.
- The firm may opt to be a crusader, actively promoting SR and good citizenship.

Perhaps the first course is a bit like skating on thin ice. Under certain circumstances the firm could be open to criticism, especially if the judgment of the management and the public diverge slightly, as must happen from time to time. The third course may also be extreme. If the firm is expending money for SR activities not actually required and its competitors are not, the first firm's stockholders are losing returns. As is so often the case, the middle ground seems best.

EXERCISE 6

Each exercise is intended to facilitate and be the basis for a part of the term project: Prepare a strategic plan for an organization of your choice.

For each exercise, present a typed, one-page report, showing directions your analysis will take.

For this exercise, outline the nature of the major environmental factors affecting your company. Trace any interactions and suggest opportunities for proactive behavior.

In addition to the material of this chapter, the following references are pertinent: Grant and King (1982), chapter 9; Hussey (1974), chapter 5; Rogers (1981), chapter 1.

REFERENCES

Andrews, Kenneth R. *The Concept of Corporate Strategy*. Homewood, Ill.: Dow Jones-Irwin, 1971.

Friedman, Milton F. *Capitalism and Freedom*. Chicago, Ill.: University of Chicago Press, 1962.

Grant, John H., and King, William R. *The Logic of Strategic Planning*. Boston: Little, Brown, 1982.

Hofer, Charles W., and Schendel, Dan. *Strategy Formulation: Analytical Concepts*. St. Paul, Minn.: West Pub. Co., 1978.

Hussey, D. E. *Corporate Planning: Theory and Practice*. New York: Pergamon Press, 1974.

McNichols, Thomas J. *Executive Policy and Strategic Planning*. New York: McGraw-Hill, 1977.

Naylor, Thomas H. *Corporate Planning Models*. Reading, Mass.: Addison-Wesley, 1979.

Paine, Frank T., and Anderson, Carl R. *Strategic Management*. Hinsdale, Ill.: Dryden Press, 1983.

Rogers, Rolf E. *Corporate Strategy and Planning*. Columbus, Ohio: Grid Pub. Co., 1981.

Schlaifer, Robert. *Analysis of Decisions under Uncertainty*. New York: McGraw-Hill, 1969.

Steiner, George. *Top Management Planning*. New York: Macmillan, 1969.

Chapter 7

Organizing the Planning Effort

There are many viewpoints from which one could consider the organization of a planning effort. We will list some of them here and then go on to consider factors that impinge on each of the viewpoints and suggest how the planning effort might differ from one to another.

- A new organization is to be created.
- Planning is to be introduced into an ongoing organization.
- A new planning year is to begin in an organization that has previously planned.
- The planning basis is to be changed—for example, from annual to continuous.
- A plan description is to be made from which planning duties can be inferred.
- Job descriptions are wanted from which a planning organization can be inferred.

Again we call attention to the contingency aspect of planning. While the remarks to be made will cover most situations, for example, profit versus nonprofit and large versus small organizations—each CEO should carefully evaluate his own organization for exceptions, perhaps creating a checklist of factors that need to be considered differently.

A TYPICAL STRATEGIC PLAN

A basic outline for a strategic plan is given in figure 7.1. This could serve as the corporate plan or as a plan for one of the corporate divisions. It

FIGURE 7.1 Outline for a Strategic Plan

I. Executive Summary
II. Description of the Organization
III. Objectives and Goals
IV. Environmental Considerations
    A. Economy
    B. Consumers
    C. Competitors
    D. Government and Politics
    E. Societal Values and Styles
    F. Technology
    G. Market Research
V. Internal Assessment
    A. Strengths and Weaknesses
    B. Requirements for Success
VI. Strategy
VII. Evaluation of Alternatives
VIII. Tactics
    A. Marketing and Supply and Demand Balances
    B. Manpower and Skills
    C. Raw Materials
    D. Capital
    E. Operations
    F. Research and Development
IX. Economic Projections and Results
    A. Basic Assumptions Underlying the Plan and Its Economics
    B. Economics: Revenues, Costs, Profits, Returns
    C. Sensitivity and Risk Analysis
X. Monitoring
    A. Measurement
    B. Control
XI. Contingency Plans
XII. Summary and Conclusions

is only by considering what has to be accomplished that we can decide how to organize to do it.

Executive Summary

It is always a mark of good writing to begin with a short summary of the salient points of what is to be presented. The writer has an opportunity to sell a particular outlook, while the busy reader can decide what to study in detail and perhaps what to skip over.

Description of the Organization

The general nature of the plan should be described in terms of size, scope, and broad characteristics. This section should outline the particular type or types of business being done and give a broad view of present and forecasted future operations on an overall basis and also on a year-by-year basis. Some would say that management should already be aware of these facts. Remember, however, that a plan is partly a communication device to insure that *all* levels of management see the facts in the same light and are in agreement on these facts.

Objectives and Goals

The plan should outline and describe the objectives that are sought for the activity. This section might include a restatement of the organization's mission. Desired achievements may be enumerated by categories, such as financial, operating, manpower, social, political, environmental, and technological.

The goals or targets associated with the objectives should be quantified both in size and in timing. For example, financial goals would include specific numbers for such results as return on invested capital, net income, long-term debt, gross operating revenue, gross fixed assets, ROI, DCF rate of return, and payout period for forecasted new investments.

Environmental Considerations

This section should contain a description of the basic state of the industry and of all factors within the environment that could have a significant effect on the firm's business. For the sake of simplicity, in much of the following we speak in terms of a profit-oriented organization. One should remember that the ideas can easily be transferred to the nonprofit case. Specific pertinent categories, such as the following, should be included.

The Economy. Because of the interrelationship between the degree of profitability of a business activity and general economic conditions, the latter should be explained and forecasted for the planning period. Often, the general state of the economy of a region or its point on the business cycle will determine whether the timing of a given activity is attractive or not. Traditional growth patterns, business cycles, or successive phases of GNP upturns and downturns can be demonstrated in most industrialized countries. For international or interregional firms, the interactions of factors across geographic borders may be important.

Consumers. In business activities where consumer opinions are important in determining demand, adequate customer research should be performed. This can substantiate sales forecasts, reduce the possibility of unpredicted customer reactions, and provide a basis for innovative and creative planning input. A breakdown of customer types and purchasing characteristics is necessary to understand the business environment, plan strategy, and design tactics for acceptance of the firm's products.

Competitors. An understanding of the size, strength, and marketing philosophy of each major competitor is necessary to provide a logical basis for strategy formulation. It will aid in determining the required resources, degree of competitive aggressiveness, financial structure, product mix, promotional methods, and market penetration necessary for a successful business.

Government and politics. The set of laws, regulations, and other constraining factors, including incentives for growth imposed or likely to be imposed by governmental agencies or by political decrees, should be detailed in the plan. These factors can often mean the difference between a profitable and a losing activity. This area is one that is most susceptible to change, and therefore it is a major source of risk.

Societal values and styles. The social environment is important to a business activity because it gives rise to changes in consumer habits and reactions. It also influences governmental legislation and other political factors.

Technology. Knowledge of the state of the art of technology and planned or anticipated improvements is important in order to be able to predict future competitiveness and to estimate required research and development activities.

Market research. The plan ideally should include a long-range forecast of industry growth in various market segments with the firm's projected market share added. It should also contain a listing of the major competitors' present market shares. This section should describe the ground rules established for conducting market surveys, the responses obtained, and the firm's interpretation of those responses. If the projections show that the firm is expected to increase its market share over the life of the business activity, then the reasons for this should be given. In other words, unsupported optimism can be regarded only as wishful thinking.

Internal Assessment

The firm's strengths and weaknesses with respect to the environment and to the basic state of the industry should be enumerated and analyzed. This information will enhance the manager's ability to assess competitive viability.

An analysis should be made to identify the requirements for success in this particular business activity. The principal areas to be considered include characteristics of a successful company and reasons why the firm or competitor companies are presently successful. This and the foregoing analysis of the firm's strengths and weaknesses show if and how the firm needs to improve.

Strategy

It is necessary to outline the strategy to be used to accomplish the objectives set forth for the firm. This should explain in broad terms how the activity is expected to deal successfully with competition within the industry and to what trends and forecasts the strategic plan will be adapted. It should explain how the firm can use to best advantage opportunities for earning profits. The strategy should describe how the strengths and resources of the firm may be applied to make the business successful and how use of these strengths will overcome competitive resistance in various areas without initiating destructive counterattacks.

Evaluation of Alternatives

Alternative courses of action for the pursuit of each business activity should be enumerated and evaluated as discussed in chapter 4. A summary of the strengths and weaknesses of the alternatives should be attached, and options should be ranked in order of relative attractiveness to the firm. As already explained, the ranking procedure may require the development of preliminary sets of economics for many of the cases. If political or other factors are important enough to rule out, even temporarily, the pursuit of the economically most attractive alternative, the reasons must be clearly stated. Lack of manpower, lack of technological capability, or lack of administrative time can kill an alternative if the lack would be detrimental to ongoing profitable activities. It is particularly important to explain each factor that makes any proposed activity compelling as, for example, if the proposed activity is required for ecological or public relations reasons, or if, for any reason, there is no detailed economic statement.

This section should include explanations of why the course of action proposed in the strategic plan has been recommended under the existing constraints. If the constraints are proposed by corporate guidelines, it may be desirable to show how much profitability would increase should constraints be lifted. A revision of the guidelines might be justified.

Tactics

This section details methods for implementing the strategy. It is therefore slanted toward practical and innovative ways of conducting operations in order to achieve an advantage over competitor operations. The delineation of tactics enables the manager to determine how each competitive business activity should be conducted. Tactics differ from strategy in the same way that conduct of a specific battle differs from conduct of a war. The following paragraphs illustrate how to set up such tactical plans properly.

Marketing and supply and demand balances. The manager should formulate expected pricing policy, advertising and promotion methods, target markets, product mix, class of trade, distribution channels, and other such short-term and long-term marketing tactics. In addition, supply and demand analyses and balances are required to validate the extent of customer needs and industry ability to satisfy those needs. An understanding of those supply-demand relationships will enable the manager to predict price and demand fluctuations more accurately.

Manpower and skills. The extent of functional and administrative skills required to develop a strong competitive stance should be ascertained. The timing for development of skills in different areas should correspond to the overall strategic plan for implementation of tasks as each opportunity develops.

Raw materials. Tactics are also to be developed regarding the sources, availability, and cost of raw materials. This facilitates the development of logistics to assure the availability of the raw material supply at minimum cost. In the case of a petroleum company, details might involve tanker movements, tanker capacities, fleet size, distributions systems, and terminal locations.

Raw-material sources should be enumerated, and non-firm sources should be specifically identified along with alternative sources whenever possible. If a within-firm source of raw materials has no alternative outlet for disposition of their materials other than the proposed within-firm business activity, then that raw material activity is dependent on the proposed activity for its success. Structuring of transfer prices between divisions may be required. The setting of transfer prices is done in order to give or apportion incentives between divisions so that corporate objectives are met. Transfer prices do not, of course, directly affect corporate profits in the short term. These incentives do control the tendency for expansion of some areas relative to others, and this may indeed give rise to increased profits over the long term.

Capital. The amount and timing of forecasted capital and expense disbursements should be detailed in this section. This will not only provide the basic figures but also explain what these figures represent and why the timing is correct for strategic and tactical reasons. If any portion of the capital requirements for new facilities and investments is expected to be obtained through direct external financial arrangements, these should be described.

Operations. Operational considerations determine the degree of flexibility the activity must have in order to enable it to respond to environmental influences. This section must therefore include a discussion of such factors as plant location, size and makeup of facilities, production layout, output capacity and quality, and degree of vertical integration or self-sufficiency with respect to procurement of component parts or inventory.

Research and development. Planned posture with respect to basic and applied R&D is necessary in order to acquire the skills and resources necessary for product improvement, increased reliability, more efficient production, and cost minimization.

Economic Projections and Results

Assumptions. The strategic plan should contain a comprehensive list of basic assumptions as a preface to the development of the plan and the economics. The list should encompass key assumptions regarding the firm's competitive position in the market and all other factors that might significantly affect the business. Some of the key assumptions to be included are rationales for the establishment of prices, volumes, market share, manufacturing cost, investment cost, other operating costs, manpower, the research and technological capability required, taxes (including any special concessions), working capital, and the growth of industry demand over the forecast period.

Before a strategic plan is built on these basic assumptions, the managers and planners should review the assumptions and assess their validity. This procedure involves standard tests such as checking for consistency with historical rates or forecasted trends, looking for logical cause-and-effect relationships, deciding whether expectations are realistic under the circumstances, substantiating the findings of market-research, and considering written contracts and agreements.

Economics. This section should contain detailed elements of income for each year: sources and uses of funds and a balance sheet both for the beginning and ending projected year, the projected economics, and the cash flow for each year. The cash flow sheet should include the conventional measures of profitability—DCF return, average ROI, and payout period. In addition, a chart showing net present value versus discount rate would be helpful in determining the attractiveness of the business. Detailed elements would include revenues, costs, profits, and returns, using different bases. The numbers should be summarized for the period and also given on a yearly basis. If the items are numerous and the explanation of items becomes complex, significant milestones should be highlighted.

Sensitivity and risk analysis. A complete strategic plan should contain a risk analysis and some evaluation of the chance variables that might influence the outcome or profitability of the different business activities. This is not an easy task. It may be difficult to quantify the risk inherent in a particular decision of a governmental or legislative agency, for example, but it can be done. The quantification will result in a better prediction of economics. Of course, identification of hidden influences or factors that might materially affect a business are dependent on the insight of the planner and of the manager. However, the sensitivity of economics to such conventional variables as price, volume, costs, and investments can be easily ascertained after the most likely set of economics is developed. The very minimum that should be contained in this section is a listing of the most sensitive chance factors, their probable variance, and their consequent influence on the ROI, DCF return, and payout period. A full-scale risk analysis would result in plotting cumulative probability charts showing the likelihood of achieving no less than prespecified ROI or DCF returns in no greater than a prespecified payout period. To minimize the cost and effort and to maximize the credibility of risk analysis, data acquisition should be undertaken by an expert in this field of the business activity and with consultation as required with an expert risk analyst.

Monitoring

Measurement. A description of the measurement tools for monitoring and control of the business activity is required. Variance reporting is an accounting management tool often used to monitor the progress of a given activity. This tool can be applied to operational areas as well as to profit performance and other financial budget items. The procedure requires setting specific intermediate and short-term goals and measurement of performance against these goals at regular intervals.

Control. Methods for control of the business activity should be explained for the benefit of planning, executive, and operating personnel. Depending on the type, complexity, and sophistication of the business activity, they may use such methods as scheduling techniques, optimization techniques, model building, other computer applications, break-even analysis, variance reporting, or project-activity report reviews.

Contingency Plans

It would be appropriate to construct a contingency plan in the event that variation of certain sensitive factors causes forecasted operating results to fall short of expectations. Upon the occurrence of an event known to affect significantly a sensitive variable, part or all of the contingency plan may be called into play. For example, if price is a sensitive variable in a business activity and if the price leader suddenly changes its price structure drastically, this could be cause for immediate retaliatory action. A planned response will have much greater probability of success than an instinctive reaction. If the factors influencing the economics are slow to change, an adverse outcome may not be as obvious as in the price-cutting example. In this case, they may have to be identified by a control mechanism such as variance reporting. The contingency plan, in anticipating such an event, would propose a solution and determine the consequent impact on profits, cash flow, ROI, DCF return, and payout period.

Summary and Conclusions

The final section of the strategic plan winds up the set of proposals, goes into more detail than was done in the executive summary, and summarizes the benefits to be gained from the plan. It may indicate the planning effort for the next planning period and offer a final ''selling'' opportunity.

CREATING A NEW ORGANIZATION

When it is desired to form a new organization, there must be a process something like the effort needed to create the strategic plan of the previous section. When outside financing is being sought, the preparation of such pro forma statements is mandatory. Unfortunately, the process is perhaps not always as complete and thorough as has been described. The entrepreneur is anxious to get something started. Resources may be conserved until something is ''coming in,'' and for one reason or another, the outlook may tend to be more optimistic than realistic.

You cannot raise money without a detailed and thorough written strategic plan, but perhaps even more important, it is one of the greatest failure preventing tools. Success may start with a brilliant concept, but implementation requires consideration of a vast number of small details. Starting a business without a plan is like starting a journey without a map: "If you don't know where you are going, any road will get you there."

Everything important to the business should be contained in the plan. Furthermore, if you are raising capital and if your plan will be studied by a great many people, it should be reviewed by an attorney, since there are SEC and other governmental restrictions to keep in mind.

Two other thoughts are relevant for the new business particularly. First, it would be well to devote a section in the plan to the management team—who are they, what is their relevant experience, what is the ownership, and what is the proposed compensation. Second, something like a PERT chart showing a timetable of what needs to be done, is useful and impressive.

One thing not usually done at this stage which certainly should be done is to provide for an ongoing planning facility in the new business. Organizing the new firm is a planning task. It would be well for the entrepreneur to specify who is to continue the planning effort on a continuing basis. If the firm is small, it may be the founder, who would then be well advised to acquire a certain amount of planning knowledge.

If the firm is larger, the entrepreneur undoubtedly has staff to assist in the organizing efforts. One of these persons should have been recruited with the idea of continuing with the firm as the staff planner. If the guidelines of figure 7.1 have been followed in creating the firm, it will be natural and convenient to continue to use these guidelines for the annual planning effort.

The entrepreneur is apt to feel that it is a waste of resources to think about the future, since the present must be managed or there will be no future. This is not true, as already pointed out, because the work required to gain financial and other approvals for starting the business will constitute a strategic plan. All that is needed is to add a proper planning perspective.

PLANNING JOB DESCRIPTIONS

The planning department itself needs to create a version of figure 7.1 for use in its own operations. It should be clear what the mission and objectives of the planning department are. Preparing job descriptions for members of the department is a good starting point.

The chief executive officer can gain help in determining how best to organize planning by studying the setups used successfully by similar firms. O'Connor (1981) has given job descriptions for numerous planning posts and organization charts for a variety of firms. It must be emphasized again, however, that what worked for a company similar to yours may be useful only as a starting point for much head scratching and soul searching.

Figure 7.2 is an organization chart based on the belief that there are four imperatives in successful planning:

- Communication with all levels of management
- Environmental study
- Systematization of the planning
- Preparation of the strategic plan

Each of these functions is represented in figure 7.2. The planning vice president could also be called the corporate planner. In any case, this person certainly must be adept at communicating upwards, downwards, and sideways.

The importance of knowing about the environment has been brought out in chapter 6. Data are often gathered and studied by economists, and as the figure shows, there may be a number of subdivisions in this department.

We have also brought out the importance of analysis and the study of alternatives, probably aided by computer models and computer techniques. Computer models of a firm often are controlled, and modified and sometimes created by the planning department. This department could well have a number of subdivisions dealing with these techniques.

Finally, we come to the making of the strategic plan. Communication is essential. The planning department must receive directives, request infor-

FIGURE 7.2 A Possible Organization Chart for Planning

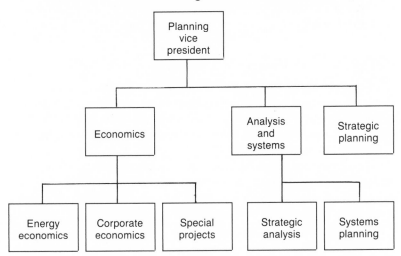

mation, request analyses, study alternatives, prepare and circulate preliminary plans, and finally issue the plan agreed upon. It is not intended to imply that this department will usurp the functions of the vice president. Rather, close working relationships at all levels within the planning department are essential.

To give further clarification to the various duties, figures 7.3 to 7.6 give job descriptions for four positions. The contingency principle must again be emphasized. Each CEO must analyze his or her own firm. One or more of the positions may not be needed, work may be subdivided differently, or the planning function may be integrated with another position. In spite of these factors, careful study of the principles given here will give the CEO and the corporate planner invaluable guidance with regard to their own firm.

There is some overlap in figures 7.3 through 7.6, and in some firms the CEO may wish to assign duties differently. For example, the planning vice president may not directly perform some of the duties outlined in figure 7.3, but merely oversee them, delegating the detailed work to staff.

CONTINUOUS PLANNING

The discussion so far in this chapter has assumed a traditional planning cycle, that is, planning begins at a particular calendar date, moves through various stages according to a preset schedule, and has a final termination date.

Much is to be gained by encouraging the planning process to continue year round. There are a number of benefits to be derived from the use of such an approach.

Desirable Elements in Continuous Planning

Level workload.   Specifications for annual planning usually call for an intense level of effort during a two- or three-month period, with few specific instructions for planning tasks to be conducted for the remainder of the year. This is not to say there is no useful planning work done during the rest of the year. There is, of course.

The environment is not on a calendar. One of the major purposes of the planning process is to identify new opportunities and changes in the environment so that proper analysis and consideration can be given to them. Since new threats and opportunities do not follow any calendar schedule, the once-a-year planning approach does not assure their timely transmittal.

Early warning.   A continuous planning approach provides an early warning system for new directions in the business environment so that plans

FIGURE 7.3 Job Description: Vice President for Planning

1. Assist the CEO and other executives in developing corporate mission and objectives.
2. Initiate and implement the planning process. Educate and orient divisions to the planning process. Modify the process as needed each year, and establish the planning calendar for the year.
3. Assist the CEO and divisions in identifying data needs, in locating sources of information, and in acquiring data. Monitor the external environment and distribute key planning assumptions.
4. Supply direction, guidelines, and coordination to help each division prepare its own strategic plan. Manage a feedback process so that the divisions' planning process, planning methods, and final strategic plans meet corporate requirements in scope, intensity, and timeliness. Schedule plan and program review meetings.
5. Receive divisional plans and programs, consolidate them, write executive summaries, secure CEO approval, and distribute the approved plans to those recipients with need to know.
6. Monitor the implementation of divisional strategic plans and the timely adjustment or updating of the plans or the timely introduction of contingency plans. Review progress against plans and evaluate planning effectiveness.
7. Develop corporate computer models and various computer techniques to support the programming effort. Ensure compatibility and agreement of such models with corporate accounting files.
8. Keep informed on strategic planning methods and techniques. Disseminate this information to all appropriate personnel for the continued development of planning skills and disciplines throughout the corporation.
9. Perform special assignments and handle special support projects as required.
10. Establish department budget. Train new MBA employees. Maintain integrity of planning files.

FIGURE 7.4 Job Description: Economist

It is expected that the incumbent will have a college degree in economics and probably an MBA.

1. Assist in all environmental studies as assigned. Provide support to other segments of the planning department.
2. Develop semiannual economic forecasts to be used in the strategic plan and in the budget. Do updates as required by changing conditions.
3. Develop information pertinent to the planning function as requested. Use available economic data bases and services as appropriate.
4. Evaluate and disseminate market intelligence concerning competitor posture, plans, and programs as required to support the firm's strategy. Assess impact on the firm's corporate objectives and opportunities.
5. Function as the in-house consultant at all levels on any and all economic considerations.
6. Develop and maintain capability to construct economic scenarios, projections, and analyses as requested.
7. Provide skill and expertise in looking at the external environment and identify conditions that have potential impact on the firm or the industry. Participate in and provide company liaison with future-oriented societies, research groups, and contacts in the community. Develop or provide input to special studies on the assessment of future technical problems.

FIGURE 7.5 Job Description: Analyst

It is expected that the job holder will possess a degree in management science or in business administration and will have an MBA.

1. Assist in all analysis activities as directed and provide consulting service to department members as requested.
2. Identify gaps or shortfalls that would prevent achievement of corporate objectives and recommend areas of emphasis for expansion, diversification, acquisition, or divestment.
3. Conduct continuing assessment of corporate performance compared to corporate plans to identify strengths and weaknesses in coping with the present and with the future environment.
4. Analyze historical and projected future characteristics of the firm under various economic, competitive, and resource scenarios so as to give planning staff and corporate management a strategic view of the firm.
5. Manage special planning projects aimed at understanding in depth aspects of the firm's internal or external environment.
6. Develop and maintain, in conjunction with internal or external experts, a strategic corporate structural model and computerized x-year strategic plan that corresponds with corporate objectives and assumptions. Develop procedures, models, and analyses necessary to produce long-term financial and other forecasts in a time-efficient manner. This system will incorporate the latest MIS technology and will facilitate the rapid evaluation of strategic alternatives.
7. Assess and develop new planning techniques and recommend them to appropriate places in the firm.
8. Coordinate corporate efforts in developing planning assumptions, consulting with internal experts as necessary.

FIGURE 7.6 Job Description: Strategic Planner

The strategic planner will probably have a degree in business administration as well as an MBA.

1. The strategic planner will act as the executive for the vice president for planning and assist in all functions as directed.
2. Integrate the divisions' strategic plans into a consolidated plan. Assist corporate management in extending this into a corporate strategic plan.
3. Assist corporate management in the development of acquisition guidelines and in the evaluation of acquisition candidates.
4. Administer and implement the corporate planning process. Assist divisions in identifying critical issues and in developing their strategic plans.
5. Coordinate and participate in the review, feedback, revision, and consolidation of strategic plans at all corporate levels.
6. Prepare the conceptual design of the strategic planning process and its methodology, forms, and review procedures.
7. Develop a perspective of standard industry performance, fix the firm's position within a broad market and competitive context, and identify growth opportunities. This will be the basis for properly analyzing and evaluating strategic plans at all corporate levels and for evaluating corporate alternatives.
8. Establish key planning dates and outline the flow of activities in a planning calendar, possibly in PERT format.
9. Maintain a planning handbook that includes instructions, forms, and basic information for the entire planning cycle.

for these new directions can be tested for their fit with corporate and regional objectives before a great deal of effort in analysis has been expended. Not waiting for the annual planning period may allow a new opportunity to be expedited when appropriate.

Evaluation in a broader context. The evaluation of new opportunities or changes in business climate creates difficulties at both corporate and regional levels when they occur at the same time the respective strategic plans are being finalized.

Time for review and experimentation. The review, modification, and refinement of any strategic plan is a predictable, necessary, and useful phase in the planning process. By viewing the planning process as continuous, planners can devote more time and attention to this aspect of the process to make the strategic plan product entirely consistent with the CEO's position.

Updating. Updating may not be desirable. Many new opportunities or substantive changes in the business climate warrant careful analysis, but these may affect only a small portion of the total strategic plan. Hence, they do not necessitate major revisions in the entire strategic plan.

Undesirable Elements in Continuous Planning

Attractive as the continuous planning system is, there are a number of undesirable conditions to be guarded against.

Missed deadlines. Deadlines serve a purpose. The rigor of a schedule with appropriate deadlines for phases of the planning process, including completion of the strategic plan, is valuable. It encourages not only the planner but also all the staff and line personnel involved to develop the plan as a tool to be used by management in the conduct of the firm's business. The assembly of a comprehensive strategic plan is a complex and time-consuming process. There must be incentives to bring it to an orderly conclusion even if some level of detail or some subject of further study must be slighted.

Cumulative small changes. Some new opportunities or changes in the environment are quite apparent when they happen, and we can focus our attention on them. However, many small changes in internal operations, in the external environment, or in legislation and regulation are not in themselves significant enough, or identified as being significant enough, to warrant major review, although their combined impact may be rather substantial. Periodically, perhaps annually, there is need for a comprehensive reassessment of the entire strategic picture.

Annual cycle fits available data. A calendar-year cycle is consistent with major units of time and resource forecasting. A large percentage of the data and information used and interpreted in a strategic plan is available on a calendar-year basis. These need not be revised or reevaluated more frequently.

No consistent corporate image. If a continuous planning system allows different elements of a corporation to be in different stages of completion of their planning at any one time, it may be difficult to provide a consolidated picture of the corporation's plans. Similarly, it would be difficult to provide a consistent comparative picture of several divisions at any specified date.

Basis for comparison. The annual period of forecasting has been used for many years in financial budgeting. The annual increment provides a convenient grid for comparison purposes in understanding change and the impact of new opportunities.

The Continuous Planning Process

In a continuous planning process, the preparation of, say, a five-year plan may take six months or it may take fourteen months. When the plan is finished, it is implemented. A little thought will reveal that this is not necessarily a disruptive process. If a short time has been required, probably few changes will have been necessary, and the previous plan will not have been greatly changed. The new plan does have the benefit of all recent environmental factors, however, and the firm is thus always kept on an optimum course.

The emphasis in a continuous strategic planning system should be on the planning process with the objective of encouraging the best product, including alternatives to help regional CEOs plan for and conduct business. This should be done with particular regard for future conditions under which that organization can meet its objectives. The planner should view his or her role in the process as "causing good planning to happen."

Modification of draft plans. A vital step in the planning process is the recycling of the draft plan. This occurs after the initial draft is developed for CEO review, whether at the regional or the corporate level. The initial plan is usually prepared by lower levels of management with the assistance of the planning staff. It is almost predictable that the draft plan will not reflect precisely the view of the appropriate CEO in terms of the balance of external and internal influences and available resources, opportunity, and achievement. Modification and redirection are called for. Because the first draft has begun to identify directions and alternatives, the CEO is able to direct this modification efficiently. In other words, the draft plan provides a medium for efficient communication regarding operational, logistical, financial, and manpower aspects of the firm. This is a healthy and necessary step in the planning process. It must be recognized so that time and effort are allocated to allow it to occur. It has a two-way communication value not only in identifying alternatives and implications to the CEO but also in communicating the CEO's view to other management levels and to the planning staff on directions and achievements that will be expected.

Special studies throughout the year.   It is important that the CEO and corporate planning be aware of major new opportunities being considered at the divisional levels in the early stages of their development. A variation on the continuous planning system proposal may be to continue the annual development of the major base strategic plan but with the addition of periodic special studies. These can address such areas as new opportunities, business problems, and changing business environment. Such studies would recognize the impact of these changes on the established base plan. It is a substantial task to develop a comprehensive strategic plan including the refinement of plans for several interrelated businesses to the point of CEO approval. Special studies of new opportunities or new directions including plans for contingency actions are significant tasks and can have a load-leveling effect on the activities of a professional planning staff.

Strategy review.   It may be necessary in large part to separate the effort concerned with strategies to meet long-range objectives and the effort of conducting operational planning dealing with realities of the current and near-term business situation. A strategies group could deal effectively with the fundamental long-term issues of resource allocation, economic and social climate, competitive environment, legislation, and regulation. It could provide the CEO a basis for an increasing awareness and calibration of the directions and alternatives of the business.

Conclusions.   A continuous planning system that imposes a reasonable schedule, recognizing the time and effort requirements for the various planning phases at the divisional and at corporate levels, is an attractive alternate to the traditional approach. Recognition of the role of strategic thinking, the need for planner talent, and the value of CEO review and modification of plans will help assure the value of the product of planning efforts. It will enable corporate, divisional, and subsidiary operations to achieve their respective objectives in a better, more organized way.

CREATING A PLANNING DEPARTMENT

It is possible to visualize an organization run on a hit or miss basis. Decisions are made day to day as crises arise. The firm is reactive with respect to its environment; the proactive concept is unheard of. The preparation of an annual budget for the coming year is the closest approach to planning.

One day, the CEO says, "Let there be planning!" He may be impelled to say this for any of a multitude of reasons—conversation with a peer, outside reading, study of a competitor, or the suggestion of a subordinate. It is the purpose of this section to indicate how the planning process can begin and how it should be structured. In any case, the introduction should be gradual, using, perhaps, the SEE principle:

- *S*tart simple. Set up one of the functions of planning that can be implemented reliably. Get it running and producing useful results.
- *E*xpand stepwise. As each function is operating, add another and then another, until a full planning system is achieved.
- *E*nd development. When this usable system is gained, stop development and use it for at least a few years. Avoid trying to gild the lily.

The experienced CEO is certainly aware of the need for a political approach to instituting a major new effort. A planning system may start on just his say-so, but it will not necessarily be successful using this basis. A particularly powerful divisional head may need some private talks or "softening up." Sometimes planning is felt by the operating people to be a device to assess how effectively each division is working. The operating people might get a false message that the CEO is trying to drop unsuccessful parts of the firm. Making individual departments justify their existence, when they have never before had to, can be quite distasteful. The operating executives may be resentful because the incoming corporate planner has never run a business. Politics is not a dirty word, and politics are important.

The CEO must be sure that the organization has the proper planning climate, sometimes called "planning culture." In order to create this and to ensure that managers at all levels are aware of and are enthusiastic about the advantages of strategic planning, it is sometimes useful to conduct workshops or off-site retreats. Here, the CEO, with the help of outside consultants, can bring out the many advantages of strategic planning not only to the corporation but also to the divisions and to divisional management.

Several steps should be followed to bring in strategic planning. These are outlined in figure 7.7. The first, "Plan to plan," is started by the CEO as described in the preceding paragraph. Next, the CEO will need staff help, which may be obtained either by hiring a new person or by reassigning an employee. There are several approaches. The CEO might hire the strategic planner shown on figure 7.2 and might personally fill the position of vice president of corporate planning on a temporary basis. Alternatively, a vice president for corporate planning might be hired as a staff assistant to get planning started. Perhaps it would be well to reaffirm one of our basic prop-

FIGURE 7.7   Organizing for Planning

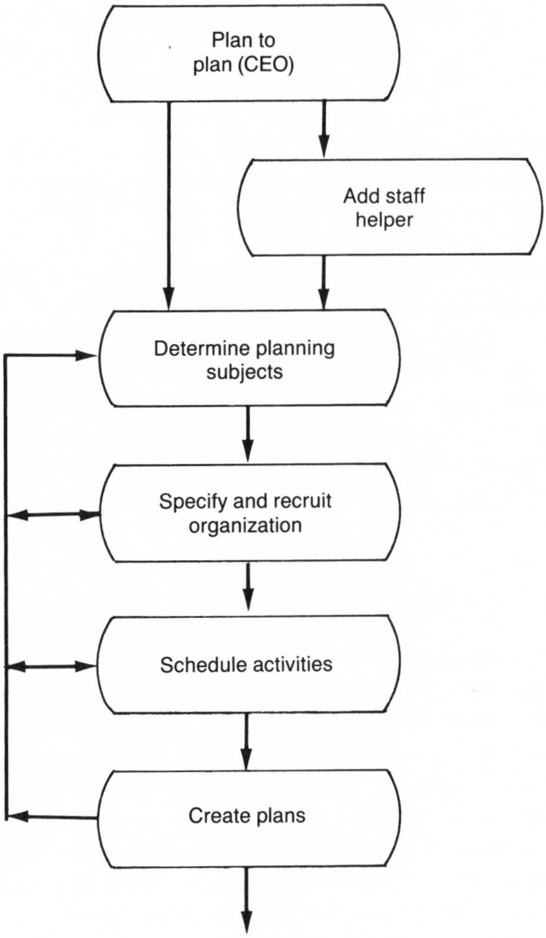

ositions at this point: the CEO will do the planning, and the newly hired assistant will expedite the process.

The third block in figure 7.7 indicates that the functions of planning must be decided. A checklist of such functions can be prepared by reviewing the suggestions of this chapter, particularly the strategic planning outline given in figure 7.1. We emphasize again the contingency principle. Each firm must determine its own priorities and desiderata, depending on its strengths, weaknesses, and wishes.

Having settled on the strategy to be followed, the firm must set up the organization for planning, shown in the fourth block. We agree with Chandler (1962) that strategy must precede structure. There are many possible formats for a planning organization beyond the typical line structure shown in figure 7.2, for example, task force, venture team, or matrix. In addition to choosing the planning structure, this block includes recruiting the necessary personnel.

In the fifth block, planning actually begins. Data files are developed and maintained. All activities are scheduled, perhaps using a PERT chart approach. Analyses are made, and models are developed.

In the last block, the firm and its new planning organization begin to create and publish plans for discussion, debate, and recycling. Throughout the diagram it is something of a matter of taste as to whether to outline the process all at once or to outline the details of each step when that step is reached. After one year's planning has been completed, of course, that question largely loses its significance.

Organizing for a New Planning Year

Once the first planning year has been completed, the organizational effort for the next year is minimal. Essentially the process of figure 7.7 can be repeated, with the top block omitted. In forming a checklist for the new year, questions would be modified to address such matters as:
- What went wrong?
- What was successful?
- What environmental changes do we foresee, and how should our organization change to meet them?
- What planning functions do we need to add? Delete?
- How could our schedules be improved?
- Are there weak points in staffing?
- Is the timing of our planning correct?

Further insight is given by figure 7.8. The upper level shows corporate activities. Early in the year, environmental studies are begun, and results are passed to the divisions. Later in the year, divisional plans are received and studied, and resources are allocated to the divisions. Finally, after considerable discussion and feedback to and from the divisions (shown by the arrows on the diagram) a corporate strategic plan results. The lower level shows the similar activities of the divisions, with the arrows clearly indicat-

FIGURE 7.8 Organizing the Annual Planning Cycle

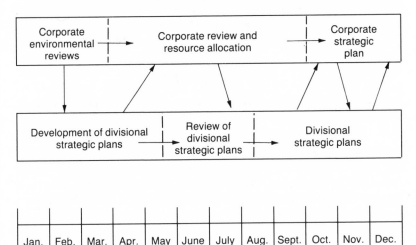

ing that consultation with other divisions and with the corporate level is required.

SUMMARY

We reject the thought that there can be a "cookbook" approach to organizing for strategic planning. We affirm instead the merit of the contingency approach. No firm should select a particular organization or process because another successful firm uses it. It is up to the CEO to believe in strategic planning and to inspire the organization by implanting the required strategic planning culture. By following the precepts of this chapter, each firm can develop a successful strategic planning organization and process, which will lead to successful strategic plans.

EXERCISE 7

This and every exercise is intended to form the basis for part of the term project: Prepare a strategic plan for an organization of your choice. For each exercise, present a typed, one-page report, showing directions your analysis will take.

For this exercise, select the situation that fits your organization—new firm, new planning department, new planning year, new planning style—and describe what needs to be done (who, what, how).

In addition to the material of this chapter, the following reference is pertinent: King and Cleland (1978), chapters 13 and 14.

REFERENCES

Chandler, Alfred D., Jr. *Strategy and Structure.* Cambridge, Mass.: M.I.T. Press, 1962.

King, William R., and Cleland, David I. *Strategic Planning and Policy.* New York: Van Nostrand Reinhold, 1978.

O'Connor, Rochelle. *The Corporate Planning Department: Responsibilities and Staffing,* Report 806. New York: Conference Board, 1981.

Steiner, George A. *Top Management Planning.* New York: Macmillan, 1969.

Chapter 8

Economic Forecasting and Strategic Planning

Strategic planning is a forward looking activity. The culmination of the planning process is the preparation of written plans, including both volumetric and financial numbers, for a period five to ten years in the future. The plans have considered and have struck a desirable balance among many individual factors and classes of factors including the following:

- Demographic factors
- Competitive factors
- Company strengths and weaknesses
- Environmental threats and opportunities
- Political factors
- Business and industry climate
- Management desires and values

It seems self-evident that information on each of these factors (and perhaps others) is needed before realistic plans can be prepared. This is equivalent to saying that a data base is required for each of the factors. The data base must also pertain to the planning period, that is to say, we need an estimate of what our competitors will be like for each year of the planning period, not merely what they are like today.

It is the purpose of this chapter to present some of the methods for deducing these future values. Notice that there is a strong contingency aspect. No two organizations will find it best to go through the identical sequence of Delphi, scenarios, and the other techniques. The procedure will even vary in different parts of the same organization. Knowledge of the inputs and out-

Adapted from Clark Holloway, "Does Futures Research Have a Corporate Role?" *Long Range Planning* 2 (Oct. 1978). Reprinted with permission of Pergamon Press, Ltd.

puts of the available techniques, however, will permit each executive and planner to chart a realistic and profitable course.

COMMERCIAL DATA BASES

In addition to data bases maintained by the individual organization, many data bases can be accessed on a rental basis (Holloway and Meadows 1981). Determination of an appropriate data base for searching requires knowledge of the coverage provided by the various bases available. The addition of three or four new data bases each year has broadened the number of sources from which information can be obtained but has increased the task of staying abreast of the location of this information. Frequently, two or more data bases must be searched to locate needed information.

Figure 8.1 lists some of the principal on-line business and economic data bases, as well as some from related areas containing information relevant to business research. Journals such as *Interfaces, Management Science, Operations Research,* and, of course, *Harvard Business Review* typically are included.

The producer of a data base is the organization that creates the data base and maintains it by continually adding new information as it appears in the literature. The producer may be a private company or a trade or professional association. The vendor is an organization (e.g., Lockheed, SDC) that makes files from various producers available to the public.

Once the search question has been analyzed and a strategy developed, the procedure to obtain printed results is straightforward.

1. Connect with the vendor's computer by telephoning the vendor, either by direct dial or through a communications system (Telenet or Tymshare).
2. Enter password to identify user.
3. Specify data base desired (Management contents, ABI/INFORM, and so on).
4. Enter commands for the search logic. Specific commands will vary with vendor.
5. Order the information desired and instruct the computer to print search results either on-line or off-line.
6. Sign off.

The total cost of a search depends on telephone connect costs, hourly computer connect rate, vendor method of charging for search results, and technical services.

FIGURE 8.1   **Data Base Survey**

Data Base	Coverage	Number of Citations and Dates
ABI/INFORM	Management and administrative methods and concepts	235,000 1971 to present
Economics Abstracts International	All areas of economics including international economics	148,000 1974 to present
EIS Industrial Plants	Current information on 135,000 businesses with annual sales of more than $500,000	161,000 current data
EIS Nonmanufacturing Establishment	Current information for over 300,000 nonmanufacturing establishments that employ 20 or more people	306,200 current data
Management Contents	Articles from over 700 United States and foreign journals and proceedings on a variety of business and management-related topics	177,000 1974 to present
Pharmaceutical News Index	Articles from major industry newsletters and reports covering news about pharmaceuticals, cosmetics, medical devices, and related health fields	114,000 1975 to present
PTS International Time Series	Time series of historical and projected data on production, wages, prices, and demographics	114,000 1957 to present
PTS U.S. Time Series	Time series of historical and projected data on population, income, employment, and earnings by industry in the United States	47,400 1957 to present
Psyc INFO	Coverage of the world's literature in psychology and the behavioral sciences from over 900 periodicals and 1,500 books, technical reports, and monographs	456,500 1967 to present

Data courtesy of the DIALOG™ Information Retrieval Service of DIALOG Information Services, Inc. Reproduced with permission.

Defining and Outlining the Forecasting Field

Strategic planning deals with the future, typically five to ten years beyond the present. Obviously, there is a need for forecasting techniques.

As always, the possibility of semantic difficulties exists. The word *forecasting* perhaps has a one-dimensional image: we forecast the GNP or the Dow-Jones Index. In strategic planning we are interested in multidimensional forecasts and in the creation of scenarios (to be defined and discussed below).

The term "futures research" has arisen to be descriptive of the type of forecasting particularly interesting to strategic planning. We are all familiar with the term "think tanks"—organizations with the purpose of speculating about the future and arriving at defensible projections. These may be captive groups existing within an organization such as the U.S. Army. They may be public firms available for hire, such as the well-known Hudson Institute, the RAND Corporation, or the Futures Group. Roy Amara, president of the Institute for the Future, has selected two useful definitions of futurism: Any systematic attempt to improve our understanding of the future consequences of present developments and choices, and any effort to systematize our assumptions and perceptions about the future: possible futures, probable futures, or preferable futures. However, futures research (FR) is not the same thing as strategic planning (SP). The characteristics of SP can be stated as being:
- decision-oriented
- about important matters
- with long-range implications
- about things that do not now exist
- about organizational rather than personal matters

Characteristics of futurism are:
- systematic strategies for getting from here to there
- a mode of thought
- combinations of planning and prognostication
- comprehensive and multidisciplinarian
- "alternative future" concept is fundamental

Thus far, we do not have a clear-cut dichotomy. One might expect that the time dimension would offer a means of distinction, but it does not. Just as the time-span of tactical planning for one company suggests strategic planning to another, so the time-span of FR varies with the institution. Kahn's book *The Year 2000* (Kahn and Wiener) was published in 1967. While futurists concern themselves with change fifteen, twenty-five, or even fifty years into the future, these times can be equalled or exceeded by SP. Long-range planning for capital improvements in the rail industry can occupy twenty-five years. U.S. Steel has surveyed its iron ore requirements out to the year 2020. Weyerhauser is planning tree growth from fifty to seventy-five years in the future. The definition of what future time is has not been answered.

Based on all of the foregoing, we propose the comparison of SP and FR shown in figure 8.2. In the first four categories, there is no difference between SP and FR. Both are concerned with the whole organization rather than one or two of its parts. Both restrict themselves to considering the big picture; both look into the future; both are concerned with new products or ideas; and both relate to the organization rather than to the individual. SP is aimed at decision making, while FR is not, as Amara's definitions indicate.

SP may consider alternate plans, but in the end only one is recommended; this is the decision orientation. FR may in some cases select a specific probable outcome, but one of its key phrases is "alternate futures," all more or less equally likely. If SP considers a number of alternate possibilities that a competitor, for example, might pursue, a specific response is planned for each responsibility. SP implies that an organization can put itself into a desired position by its planning; the future can thus be controlled. FR merely presents possible alternate futures without controls.

Pure research is undertaken without any anticipation of a specific benefit from the research. Applied research builds an outcome of pure research into a useful product or service. This distinction may summarize the difference between SP and FR. Investigation of the future and presentation of a list of possible alternatives (FR) corresponds to pure research. Preparation of a specific action plan (SP) corresponds to applied research.

Corporate executives do not distinguish between the terms SP and FR. In a recent questionnaire (Narayanan 1977), over 85 percent of the corporate response felt both the ideal and the actual planning time was in practice below ten years. While time itself is not a discriminating factor for separating SP and FR, this answer of ten years suggests the respondents did not have futurism in mind. Similarly, a poll taken at a meeting of the World Future Society found (*The Futurist,* Apr. 1972, p. 76) that 56 percent of the respondents used a time frame of under ten years for FR. While only 18 percent of the attendees were corporate representatives, this is felt to verify the premise that FR and SP are regarded as roughly equivalent.

Incentives for Futures Research

It seems evident that a corporation must have strategic planning before it would consider futures research. It would make little sense for profit-making organizations to speculate about alternative futures unless they were interested in making some decisions about their future. This suggests that

FIGURE 8.2   Comparison of Strategic Planning and Futures Research

	Strategic Planning	Futures Research
Global	yes	yes
Important topics	yes	yes
Long time-span	yes	yes
Concerns new things	yes	yes
Decision-oriented	yes	no
Specifies alternatives	yes	maybe
Alternatives	no	yes
Control	yes	no

FR and SP might occur as a two-stage process, implemented by either the same group or by separate groups. Whenever good SP has been found in a company, that company must have done FR, even though it did not realize it.

The chief executive is not likely to be directed by his board to espouse futures research (or strategic planning, for that matter). FR can prosper only if the CEO comes to the conclusion it is good for the company. He may reach this decision by a desire to mold his company's future, by his observation of successful FR in other companies, by enthusiasm on the part of a subordinate, or upon the advice of a management consultant. On the other hand, the CEO may not be attracted to FR, or the CEO may not want to spend money (so as to make a good showing in the current year). In these instances, the company is not then apt to have FR.

There is a strategic planning culture, or atmosphere, within a company conducive to the beneficial application of SP. The same thing would apply to FR. It is almost entirely the personality of the CEO which creates such a culture and inspires all departments to think in these terms.

The concept of futures research as a separately identifiable activity is useful but by no means indispensable. Strategic planning is critical to companies, and futures research comes along naturally with good SP. Molière tells of the man who was surprised to find he had been using prose all his life. Companies with competent SP departments might be surprised to realize they have been using FR for a long time. Having FR done by a group in a corporation separate from the SP group, however, would maintain objectivity, permit specialization, and alleviate the time pressures associated with getting out an annual strategic plan. Since the FR activity is an integral part of SP, any gain in setting it up as a separate discipline would consist only of these advantages, and principally that of specialization.

The Methods of Futurism

Many authors give lists of the multitude of methods which have been used in SP. Four of these lists are summarized in table 8.1. Gordon (1972) and Lanford and Imundo (1974) give descriptions of the methods they cite. In addition, the latter gives a reference list for a fuller outline of the workings of the methods.

The final column suggests those methods of particular interest in a corporate environment.

Scenarios. A recent survey (Lanford and Imundo 1974) suggests that the predominant technique in futures research is the writing of scenarios. Zentner (1975), head of the Shell Oil Company futurist team, gives us an excellent outline of the topics that must be considered, shown here in modified form:

What are scenarios?
Consulting the oracle
Development of corporate planning scenarios
Organizational placement of scenario group
Scenario selection and design
The extrapolative scenario 1985 to 2000
How many scenarios?
Scenario themes
Format of the scenarios
Where do the data come from?
The group
The energy crusade scenario 1985 to 2000
Techniques
Use of scenarios in corporate planning
The energy-limited scenario 1985 to 2000

Since futurism is a part of strategic planning, it would be sensible to use scenarios about twenty years ahead to support a five-year strategic plan. They can be constructed and ranked, using a mathematical approach with the computer. A good tactic to consider would be to let a computer run for a few hours (or days) putting together scenarios and flagging for further study those that look particularly disastrous or opportune.

A scenario is an internally consistent story about the future. To create the plot, the researcher must make assumptions concerning family life and modes of living, as well as demographic, economic, political, and technical factors. Scenarios are important in integrating broad bases of knowledge so that factor relationships can be understood. The scenario becomes the background within which the proposed strategic plans must operate.

TABLE 8.1   Methodologies in Futures Research

	Gordon	Lanford and Imundo	Narayanan	McHale	Corporate Usefulness
Scenarios	•	•	•	•	•
Relevance trees		•		•	
Consensus methods					
Delphi	•	•		•	•
Expert panels				•	
Brainstorming				•	
Genius forecasting	•				
Individual expert				•	
Simulation	•		•	•	•
Gaming			•	•	
Cross impact analysis	•	•	•	•	•
Input/output analysis	•		•		•
Models					
Operational				•	
Statistical				•	
Causal				•	
Forecasting techniques			•		
Trend extrapolation	•	•		•	•
Envelope curves		•			•
Precursive indicators		•		•	•
Probablistic forecasting				•	
Historical analogy				•	•
Analogy curves		•			•
Substitution effect		•			•
Contextual mapping		•		•	•
Network analysis				•	
Decision trees	•				
Morphological analysis			•		
Multi-echelon coordination			•		
Field anomaly relation			•		

In one sense, the reliability of scenarios is not a relevant question. It has been said, for example, that scenarios are an aid to thinking rather than a prediction of the future. Usually several are prepared for a particular study. They serve to call attention to the large range of possibilities that must be considered in the analysis of the future. Since no single one of the scenarios is intended to be a prediction, it is meaningless to speak of their accuracy. The set of scenarios is to be taken as a whole, and the objective of the corporation is to develop a strategic plan which will enable the company to survive and prosper under most of the scenarios, if not all of them. For this purpose, the set of scenarios would be considered reliable.

Scenarios are valuable because they give a consistent picture under particular assumptions. It is up to the strategic planner to choose one scenario out of all those available by justifying his assumptions. Given practical hydrogen fusion and solar energy collectors in space, for example, the average man could anticipate Utopian living conditions in the year 2000. Without these assumptions the scenario for mankind would present Victorian conditions of coal-based smog.

Precursive indicators. The progress of a later technology may follow the progress of an earlier technology but be separated by a time lag. If the progress of the later technology parallels the curve of the earlier technology the leader-follower relationship may be useful.

Economic, political, and social factors may serve as precursors as well as technological factors. The speed attained by military aircraft and the subsequent speed attained by commercial transport aircraft is an example of a precursive indicator. The speed of military aircraft plotted against time gives a positively sloped curve. The speed of commercial aircraft gives a similar curve, but displaced in time by nine to fourteen years.

The concept of a precursive indicator can also be based on an analytic rather than a graphic approach. I used a leading indicator in developing a forecasting system for petroleum product prices for the European office of a major petroleum company (Holloway 1981). An explication of this example follows.

In the petroleum industry, ocean transportation has tremendous leverage on profits. In periods of tight vessel supply and high market rates, transportation is one of the most critical factors to be considered in developing a maximum profit strategy. The cost for transportation taken for short periods (single voyage to one-year consecutive) may show deviations of 300 percent on Worldscale (a transportation cost index) in a single year. One might expect European product prices to lag behind Worldscale (WS). One reason this would occur is because prices are fixed at the beginning of a voyage when the vessel is loading in the Persian Gulf. This same crude oil does not appear in Europe as finished products until four or five weeks later. There are several independent variables that could influence petroleum product prices in addition to WS. Date and date squared were included as independent variables to permit accounting for the large changes in product prices over the time of the study. Otherwise, the WS variable might incorrectly appear as a surrogate for time. There are also seasonal trends in bulk petroleum product prices. Gasoline price will be higher in the summer, while heating oils will be more costly in the winter. To account for these effects, seasonal variables of the form

$$L(W) = Sin ((D-W/52) * 2\Pi)$$

were included in the regression studies, where D is date and W is week number in the year. Selection of a value of W between 1 and 52 permits accounting for seasonal effects.

Separate regression equations were developed for each of three products: gasoline, gas oil, and fuel oil. In each case, of course, the product cost was the dependent variable. Each regression equation is of the form:

$$P = Constant + a*WS + b*D + c*D*D + d*L(W1) + e* L(W2)$$

where   P is predicted price, five weeks hence.

WS is Worldscale index now.

D is date, five weeks hence.

L is the seasonal factor discussed above, and W1 and W2 indicate two different week numbers.

a, b, c, d, e are regression coefficients.

The regression coefficients from this study were found to be significant at the 0.05 level or better. The Worldscale rate was thus found to be an important precursive variable for the price predicted five weeks in advance.

Computer-assisted forecasting. Repeating the same intensive manual calculations for every year of a ten-year forecast year after year is highly wasteful of manpower. The purpose in computerizing long-range environmental forecasts is to reduce to a minimum the amount of time spent by professional staff in coordinating, summarizing and supervising production of the final multipage report, thus freeing up many man months per year for more important work.

This section describes a technique I developed for the European division of a multinational oil company. It provides a user who is without computer expertise the facility for maintaining, evaluating and adjusting a computer data base. It will find use in preparing stand-alone reports, in preparing input for sensitivity models and linear programming models, and other planning applications. It is recognized that each organization may have different requirements and may need different built-in calculations.

This technique is described using the forecasting of oil and energy for Western Europe as an example. The data for oil supply and demand in thousands of metric tons per annum for all countries forms a data file in the computer.

It would be interesting to determine the variation in the prediction in successive forecasts of a particular number for, say, two years in advance. If the number remains fairly constant or if it varies in a regular manner, then the proposed computer technique would be highly suitable as a starting point for each year's ten-year forecast. On the other hand, should the number vary randomly, then the manual approach would appear worthless, and the computer technique would introduce useful consistency. The procedure would allow incremental up-dating of individual forecasts within a county as new information becomes available, and it would offer an elementary analysis of the data to pick out quickly forecasts that may be suspect.

The subject of computer generated forecasts through use of growth rates and smoothing techniques, as visualized in this application, is intriguing. As much as 30 to 40 percent of the forecasts, particularly the unimportant ones, can be adequately generated through use of what economists call naive mathematical models. Perhaps another 30 or 40 percent of the forecasts could be created through use of more advanced mathematical models.

Data for about twenty years (several historical and the remainder future) remain on permanent file in the computer even though all of these years are not printed out during a computer run. Usually, twelve years of data would be printed out with the starting year at the user's option. In order to keep the file current, each year the oldest year's data would be deleted and data for a new future year added.

In the example, data for twenty countries were carried in the system. In addition, the computer automatically created seven area totals and subtotals. The list of the twenty areas is given in figure 8.3.

Each computer run also calculates the average yearly growth rate for three time-spans, as specified by the user. These growth rates are calculated for each line of the output. The report described would be printed in final form so it can be photoreduced and copied to eliminate a large amount of secretarial typing and proofreading.

The first report would be used by an economist in developing, verifying, and adjusting his data. The yearly growth rate is calculated for each year and each line. Scanning through these growth rates permits the analyst quickly to pick out data that may be suspect. More products are presented than in the reports that would be used for publication. The list of products is given in figure 8.4. Also given, but not shown in the tables, are the conversion factors presently in use to convert from metric tons to barrels. It is pos-

FIGURE 8.3   Example of Areas Used

Austria	Germany (West)	Luxembourg	Sweden
Belgium	Greece	Netherlands	Switzerland
Denmark	Iceland	Norway	Turkey
Finland	Ireland (Republic)	Portugal	United Kingdom
France	Italy	Spain	Yugoslavia

FIGURE 8.4   Products Reported

Aviation gasoline	Paraffin wax	Inland product demand
Motor gasoline	Asphalt	International bunkers
Solvents and other	LPG	Heavy fuel
Subtotal	Other refinery gas	Lubes
Jet fuel	Petroleum coke	Refinery fuel and loss
Kerosene	Chemical feedstocks	Total demand
Subtotal	Petroleum pitch	Crude runs to stills
Diesel (auto)	Naphtha for gas	Domestic production
Other distillate	manufacturing	Crude imports (net)
Subtotal	Road oil	Product imports (net)
Heavy fuels	Others	From other sources
Lubes and greases		

sible for the user to change any of the items appearing in this first report at will.

Following the report used for detailed checking, six reports are prepared. Individual reports may be selected from these for publication as desired. Certain products can be accumulated into subtotals as the user wishes. In this specific example, the following reports were presented:

Report 2: shows the data presented as thousands of metric tons.

Report 3: gives the same data in millions of metric tons.

Report 4: shows the metric tons data as a percentage of total demand.

Report 5: shows conversion to thousands of barrels, using the conversion factors listed in the first (checking) report.

Report 6: gives the data as millions of barrels.

Report 7: shows the barrel data as a percentage of total demand.

All of these reports are produced for each of the twenty areas listed in figure 8.3. Totals and subtotals shown on the reports are calculated from existing data, not from input.

If the analyst wishes to project data backward or forward in time at a particular growth rate, this can be done by entering the desired percentage for backward projection, for forward projection, or for both. If a new number has been entered under annual data, this is the figure that will be used as the starting point. If new annual data is not entered, then the figure in the computer file for the year in question will be the starting point.

It is also possible for the economist to select two years and have the computer calculate the average growth rate between these two years. The program will automatically enter data for the intermediate years to agree with the calculated growth rate.

It is perhaps best to use the growth rate and smoothing techniques in separate computer runs after it is certain that the necessary annual data have been provided. The reason for this is to ensure that both of the years required in the smoothing technique are in fact available when required or that desired values for annual data are not written over by the automatic growth rate procedure.

Although the features of this example system have been given in some detail, it should be evident that the ideas are intended solely for extrapolation to other organizations. Some of the specific points mentioned above may not be needed in different applications, while other additional features may be suggested by the above discussion.

Delphi. Of consensus methods, the Delphi technique is the unquestioned leader. The method uses a questionnaire to ask selected experts in many fields the approximate date they expect specified events to occur. Following the first survey, individuals who responded outside the middle 50 percent are provided with the survey results and are asked to consider changing their response, otherwise to give reasons for it. In subsequent rounds, all participants are given the intermediate results together with the justifications for extreme values. The survey usually terminates after five rounds.

The range of responses may be as important to the researcher as the consensus. Consensus may not be achieved for every question. If consensus is necessary when a bimodal response has been obtained, the researcher can either rephrase the questions or develop a rationale for bipolarity of the responses. A Delphi questionnaire used for researching progress on the artificial heart has been given by Lanford and Imundo (1974). For the most part, Delphi forecasts appear to be consistent with reality.

Genius forecasting. When the Delphi group decreases to size one, we have "genius forecasting," or the individual expert, generally not regarded as a valuable procedure. Since people are inclined to remember only the hits, this method is thought to be better than it is. Steinmetz, a towering genius in the electrical engineering field, had mixed success with a forecast of the future that appeared in the *Ladies Home Journal* in 1915. Steinmetz scored best in the technological parts of his predictions.

Contextual mapping. A contextual map portrays graphically the development of a technical area through time. It resembles critical path scheduling in showing interrelationships among technologies and devices. The need for future developments can be located on the same time scale. Figure 8.5 shows the typical components of a contextual map. The lowest line shows a calendar time scale. Above that a line indicates developmental plateaus to be achieved. The center line of boxes contains the names of specific devices or projects, located appropriately above the plateau line. Other lines of boxes may be added to show associated or contributing technologies to such specific devices.

In a contextual map for the development of artificial intelligence, the various plateaus could be things like: thinking robots, automatic planning, or executive alter ego. Specific projects could be: unsupervised factory or world class chess-playing machine. Supporting technology would include items like the LISP language or three-dimensional computer chips.

Other Techniques.   Many other methods may be useful, and their selection is limited only by the ingenuity of the economist. Some possibilities are:

Envelope curves	Relevance trees
Substitution effect	Critical path scheduling
Analogy curves	Game theory
Cross impact analysis	Corporate models

A few of these will be discussed in chapter 12.

Reliability

While for the most part Delphi forecasts appear to be consistent with reality and while many early forecasts using other techniques are found to be borne out, there can be no question of the hazards and errors in FR. Forecasting acts of God is easier than anticipating acts of man, because in the latter case one must understand the five social sciences, particularly economics, sociology, and political science. Because of sociological and other discontinuities, predictions beyond the year 2020 may be inherently impossible.

Unfortunately for FR, the future remains the future. In analyzing the workings of the world we must rely on the way the world has worked in the past. Lacking predestination, the world does not continue to work precisely as it did in the past.

Reliability also bears on the subject of self-fulfilling forecasts. Suppose that if no recognition were given to the possibility of event A, that event would not take place. Let a corporate futures group consider the matter and predict the event A will take place. Simply because of the prediction (possi-

FIGURE 8.5 Contextual Mapping Components

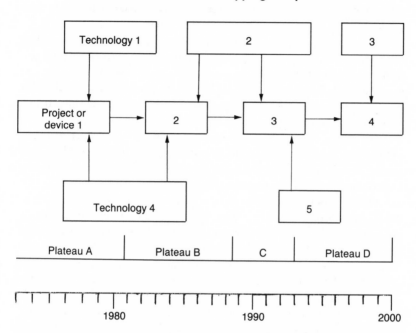

bly people begin to think about it and realize they would like it), event A does in fact take place; we have a self-fulfilling prophecy. The opposite can happen where event A is predicted, and because of the prediction it does not happen.

INPUT-OUTPUT ANALYSIS

Input-output (IO) analysis looks at the interindustry flows of raw materials, intermediate products, and technical and financial services, as well as the delivery of finished products to final markets. An input-output table displays the sales by each industry to other industries in its horizontal rows and the purchases by each industry from other industries in its vertical columns. It stresses the interrelationships between one industry, all other industries, producers, consumers, and the public and the private sectors.

IO models have validity as a management tool to forecast over the medium and long term and also to measure sensitivity. Sensitivity refers to the effect certain changes in inputs (such as tax changes or the introduction of a new trade policy) have on different elements of the industry.

IO is practical for strategic planning based on a wide variety of multi-industry data, on information concerning national and international economies, and on complex matrix analyses that are dependent upon the computer. All of these data and techniques are available.

Any industry will be affected to different degrees by changes such as innovation, public attitudes, government action, and international trade pattern changes. It is possible to measure the effects of these changes upon several hundred industry sectors and to estimate industrial markets, availability of producers' supplies, wage and price trends, opportunities for investment, repercussions of federal expenditures, and technological change.

For strategic planners, an input-output table provides a working model of the technological apparatus that helps to make and test economic projections. The originator of the technique was Wassily W. Leontief (1951), who received the Nobel prize in economics for its development.

Figure 8.6 shows a simple example (due to Carter 1966) of a hypothetical economy broken down into two sectors: agriculture and industry. Reading across the row of one of these sectors, the large figures in each cell show the distribution of its output of intermediate products to itself and to the other sector inside the interindustry matrix and its delivery of finished products to final demand. The figures down a column show the input of intermediate products required by the sector plus its value added, that is, inputs of labor, depreciation, and profit. The final demand and value added for the system as a whole are equivalent to the same gross national product (eighty-five arbitrary units such as billions of dollars). The total output for each sector redundantly adds its interindustry deliveries to its contribution to the gross national product. The input-output coefficients in small figures at bottom left of each cell express the ratio of the input shown to the total output of the sector in whose column it appears. Figures at bottom right are inverse coefficients, showing the direct and indirect requirement for the input per dollar of delivery to final demand.

Input-output is both an information base and a methodology. There are various topics to be considered. The development of dynamic input-output systems is discussed by Leontief (1970), Almon (1966), Waddell et al. (1966), and Bureau of Labor Statistics (1968). There are input-output studies for particular cities, counties, and states and other regions of comparable size, as pointed out by Isard and Langford (1968), Miernyk (1970), Bourque and Cox (1970), and Polenske (1970). Since it includes information from all sectors simultaneously, input-output provides a framework for consistent analysis of natural resource constraints and pollution. Work is reported by Ayres and Kneese (1969), Isard (1968), and Carter and Ireri (1970). Strategic planning requires information on the future. Studies of past changes in input-output matrixes give some basis for judging how vola-

FIGURE 8.6   Simplified Input-Output Table

	Agriculture		Industry		Final Demand	Total Output
Agriculture	25		20		55	100
	.25	1.46	.40	.66		
Industry	14		6		30	50
	.14	.23	.12	1.24		
Value Added	61		24		85	
	.61		.48			

From Anne P. Carter, "The Economics of Technological Change," *Scientific American* 214, 4 (April 1966), p. 25.

tile they are apt to be. A number of individual firms construct their own internal input-output tables, but these are not generally made available to the public. Work has been reported by Quantum Science Corporation (1968), Carter and Brody (1970), and Carter (1970).

It will be apparent that the matrix structure of input-output is strongly related to the matrix structure of linear programming. If a firm has available a linear programming representation of its operations, it is not likely that an internal input-output table would be of value, but bringing in external factors could be useful.

EXERCISE 8

This and every exercise is intended to form the basis for part of the term project: Prepare a strategic plan for an organization of your choice. For each exercise, present a typed, one-page report, showing the directions your analysis will take.

For this exercise, briefly describe the major technology of your organization and the forms of technological forecasting appropriate to the situation of the organization with respect to planning.

In addition to the material of this chapter, the following references are pertinent: King and Cleland (1978) chapter 11; Steiner (1979) chapter 7 and 14.

REFERENCES

Almon, C. *The American Economy to 1975: An Interindustry Forecast.* New York: Harper and Row, 1966.

Ayres, R., and Kneese, A. "Production, Consumption, and Externalities." *American Economic Review* 59, 3 (1969), pp. 282-95.

Barna, Tibor, ed. *Structural Interdependence and Economic Development: Proceedings of an International Conference on Input-Output Techniques.* New York: St. Martin's Press, 1963.

Bourque, P., and Cox, M. "An Inventory of Regional Input/Output Studies in the United States." Occasional Paper No. 22, University of Washington Graduate School of Business Administration, 1970.

Carter, Anne P. "The Economics of Technological Change." *Scientific American* (Apr. 1966), pp. 25-31.

Carter, A. *Structural Change in the American Economy.* Cambridge, Mass.: Harvard University Press, 1970.

Carter, A. P., and Brody, A., eds. *Applications of Input/Output Analysis. III: Stability of Coefficients and IV: Forecasting Coefficients.* Amsterdam: North-Holland Pub., 1970.

Carter, H., and Ireri, D. "Linkage of California-Arizona Input/Output Models to Analyze Water Transfer Patterns." In Carter and Brody, eds., *Applications of Input/Output Analysis.*

Chenery, Hollis B., and Clark, Paul G. *Interindustry Economics.* New York: Wiley, 1959.

The Futurist (Apr. 1972), p. 76.

Goldman, Morris, R.; Marimont, Martin L.; and Vaccara, Beatrice N. "The Interindustry Structure of the United States: A Report on the 1958 Input-Output Study." *Survey of Current Business* 44, 11 (Nov. 1964), pp. 10-17.

Gordon, T. J. "The Current Methods of Futures Research." In A. Toffler, *The Futurist.* New York: Random House, 1972. Pp. 164-89.

Holloway, Clark. "A Leading Indicator for Forecasting Petroleum Product Prices." Paper presented at ORSA-TIMS, Houston, Texas, 1981.

Holloway, Clark, and Meadows, Nolan R. "Searching the Business Literature by Computer." *Business and Economic Review* 8, 3 (Dec. 1981), pp. 31-38.

Isard, W. "On the Linkage of Socio-Economic and Ecologic Systems." *Papers of the Regional Science Association,* 1968, pp. 79-99.

Isard, W., and Langford, T. "Impact of Vietnam War Expenditures on the Philadelphia Economy: Some Initial Experiments with the Inverse of the Philadelphia Input/Output Table." *Regional Science Association Papers,* 1969, pp. 217-65.

Kahn, H., and Weiner, A. J. *The Year 2000.* New York: Macmillan, 1967.

King, W. R., and Cleland, D. I. *Strategic Planning and Policy.* New York: Van Nostrand Reinhold, 1978.

Lanford, H. W., and Imundo, L. V. "Technological Forecasting." *Long Range Planning* (Aug. 1974), p. 49.

Leontief, Wassily. *Input/Output Economics*. New York: Oxford University Press, 1966.

Leontief, Wassily W. "Input-output Economics." *Scientific American* (Oct. 1951), pp. 15–21.

Leontief, Wassily W. "The Structure of Development." *Scientific American* (Sept. 1963).

Leontief, Wassily W. "The Structure of the U.S. Economy." *Scientific American* (Apr. 1969), pp. 25–35.

Leontief, Wassily W. "The Dynamic Inverse." In Carter and Brody, eds., *Contributions to Input/Output Analysis*.

Leontief, Wassily W., and Hoffenberg, Marvin. "The Economic Effects of Disarmament." *Scientific American* (Apr. 1961), pp. 47–55.

MAPTREK Economic Services. New York: Quantum Science Corp., 1968.

Makridakis, Spyros, and Wheelwright, S. C. *The Handbook of Forecasting*. Somerset, N.J.: Wiley, 1982.

McHale, John. "The Changing Pattern of Futures Research in the USA." *Futures* (June 1973), p. 257.

Miernyk, W. "An Interindustry Forecasting Model with Water Quantity and Quality Constraints." *Proceedings of the Fourth Annual Symposium on Water Resources Research,* Ohio State University, 1970.

Narayanan, V. K. "Role and Status of Futurism: An Empirical Study." Unpublished paper, 1977.

Polenske, K. "Empirical Implementations of a Multiregional Input/Output Gravity Trade Model." In Carter and Brody, eds., *Contributions to Input/Output Analysis*.

Steiner, G. A. *Strategic Planning*. New York: Free Press, 1979.

Toffler, A. *The Futurists*. New York: Random House, 1972. Pp. 164–89.

U.S., Department of Labor, Bureau of Labor Statistics. *Capital Flow Matrix*. Bulletin No. 1601. Washington, D.C.: U.S. Government Printing Office, 1968.

Waddel, R., et al. *Capacity Expansion Planning Factors*. Washington, D.C.: National Planning Association, 1966.

Zentner, R. D. "Scenarios in Forecasting." *Chemical & Engineering News* (Oct. 1975), p. 22.

Chapter 9

Information for Strategic Planning

As is often the case, a word may be used by different people to mean different things. We define the word *data* as a collection of unstructured opinions, facts, and figures. To emphasize this notion, the term "raw data" is sometimes used. Strictly speaking, data requires a plural verb, but it is also used as a collective noun with a singular verb. When data are organized, classified, and otherwise interrelated, we have transformed the data into information. We regard "data base" as synonymous with information. The term "management information system" (MIS) is also well known. It refers to a further systematization of data beyond the information stage.

The MIS concept has usually been considered useful in operations or management control rather than in strategic planning. Cost accounting or financial studies have used evolving forms of MIS for many years. Earlier chapters should have made it evident that an MIS system is indispensable as an integral part of a successful strategic planning department. The very best situation is to have a corporate MIS facility that is used and relied on by all planning staff as well as by functional departments of the corporation.

Figure 9.1 shows that there are three steps in the development of strategic planning data bases. First, there must be a source for the needed data, and some of the many types of data which might be considered are indicated in the left-hand column. Such data may be free, it may be for sale, or it may be protected. A discussion of these terms is given in the next section. It should be pointed out that we are ignoring here the highly significant problem of analyzing the reliability of the data received. Some evaluation system must be a part of the data collection process in order to appraise both the

FIGURE 9.1   The Development of Information

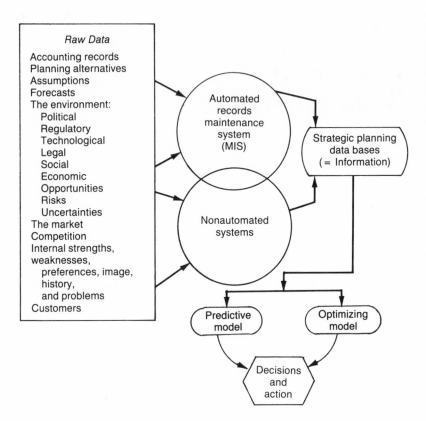

source and the content of the data. Perhaps this may be put into a statement of probabilities.

Second, there must be a process for turning the data into information, as suggested by the overlapping circles. Nothing more will be said about manual, or nonautomated, systems beyond pointing out that a manual system might be no more complicated than a set of notebooks to receive clippings or notations by various levels of management. Even a simple manual system can illustrate the difference between data and information. We might visualize two pieces of data, each of little or no interest. When considered jointly, however, they might become information of the highest significance. In any event, an MIS system will be computer based, and considerations for its establishment and operation are given in a later section. We do visualize possible overlap in manual and computer-based systems. A firm might have a complicated manual system with or without a computer-based system, and the computer system might be simple or complex.

Finally, the firm has created a set of strategic planning data bases, so that it has in fact succeeded in converting data into information. Information is useless unless it is a basis for action. With data bases available, models of the real world, whether intuitive or mathematical, can be created, and these in turn will lead to decisions and action.

SOURCES OF INFORMATION

This section gives a number of specific sources where data and in some cases information can be obtained. Note that the following remarks are meant to be illustrative. There are undoubtedly many other equally valuable sources that have not been listed. While every effort has been made to assure accuracy, it must be remembered that material of this type is apt to change rather quickly.

Another information source highly valuable for strategic planners, particularly when starting their careers, are the seminars and training sessions sponsored by many organizations. Discussion of such seminars is left to the chapter on training strategic planners.

Free Information

Actually, no information is free. The planner may find data in the *Wall Street Journal*, but there is a subscription cost. When the CEO gets a tip at lunch, he had to pay for the lunch. We suggest an arbitrary boundary line of about $200. If a book or a journal subscription costs less than that amount, we call the resulting information free. For example, Brownstone and Carruth (1982) have provided an in-depth directory of some five thousand English-language sources to the information a planner might need, ranging from newsletters to journals to books to computerized data bases and covering all industries and all countries.

Some of the sources of free data are listed in figure 9.2. Much can be gained by alerting members of the firm to the need for data, perhaps data of particular kinds. Salesmen have wide contacts. The purchasing department can talk to supplier salesmen. Accounting will be aware of payment habits and the financial condition of other firms. Executives are often in contact socially or professionally with executives in other firms.

Business periodicals are an obvious source of data. Most executives regularly read the *Wall Street Journal* as well as several other periodicals.

FIGURE 9.2   Sources of Free Information

Internal:
    Sales force
    Purchasing department
    Research and development
    Accounting
    Executives
Business periodicals
Books
Business reference services
Business literature indexes
Government
Professional associations
Trade associations
Customers
Suppliers
Distributors
Competitors:
    License agreements
    Local chamber of commerce
    Local press
    Local bank
    Trade press
    Stockbrokers
    Annual reports
    Stockholder meetings
    Investment bankers

Books, either on particular companies or on particular industries, are often helpful. Business reference services, such as *Moody's Industrial Manual* or the various Dun & Bradstreet reports give background information on industries and companies, although these are usually aimed particularly at financial information. One should also refer to the *Business Periodical Index*.

The federal government has been called the world's largest source of free information. It supports over 500,000 experts and spends billions of dollars annually on specialized subjects. For any problem you may face, there is likely to be an expert on the federal payroll who has spent years studying that subject. Figure 9.3 lists a few contact points. It may take a bit of persistence to find the specialist on your problem within the listed bureau, but once you find him, you will be deluged with free information. Lesko (1982) has prepared a 1,024 page guide to U.S. government sources. He is also the founder of Washington Researchers, an organization that publishes monographs and conducts seminars on government information topics. There are also newsletters that interview government and business leaders, analyze business forecasts, economic reports, and statistical abstracts, and present digested information (*Kiplinger*, 1983; and *U.S. News*, 1983).

FIGURE 9.3   Information Contact Points in the Federal Government

American Society of Association Executives
Information Central
1575 Eye St., N.W.
Washington, D.C. 20005
Identify association with information on your subject.

Conservation and Renewable Energy Inquiry and Referral
P.O. Box 8900
Silver Spring, MD 20907
(301) 427-7109
Research, publications, and other services on solar energy.

Environmental Science Information Center
NOAA
11400 Rockville Pike
Rockville, MD 20852
(301) 443-8137
Information relating to the environment.

Health Information Clearinghouse
P.O. Box 1133
Washington, D.C. 20013
(800) 336-4797
Reference services on health-related topics.

Library of Congress
National Referral Center
Washington, D.C. 20540
(202) 287-5470
Locate organizations that provide free information.

Library of Congress
Science and Technology Division
Reference Section
Washington, D.C. 20540
(202) 287-5639
Free and fee-based services.

Performing Arts Library
John F. Kennedy Center
Washington, D.C. 20566
(202) 287-6245
Reference services on the performing arts.

U.S. Department of Agriculture
Information Office
Office of Public Affairs
Room 1–13A Admin. Bldg. S.W.
Washington, D.C. 20250
(202) 447-2791
Research specialists provide help on agriculture-related subjects.

U.S. Department of Agriculture
National Agricultural Library
12301 Baltimore Blvd.
Beltsville, MD 20705
(301) 344-3755
Published material and research on general agriculture.

FIGURE 9.3 (*Continued*)

U.S. Department of Agriculture
Statistical Reporting Service
14th and Independence Ave., S.W.
Washington, D.C. 20250
(202) 447-2122
Agriculture and food statistics.

U.S. Department of Commerce
Bureau of the Census
Data User Services Division
Customer Services
Washington, D.C. 20233
(301) 763-4100
Economic and demographic statistics.

U.S. Department of Commerce
Bureau of Economic Analysis
Tower Building
Washington, D.C. 20230
(202) 523-0777
National, regional, and international economics.

U.S. Department of Commerce
Bureau of Industrial Economics
Room 4878
Washington, D.C. 20230
(202) 377-1409
Information about companies and industries.

U.S. Department of Commerce
Foreign Trade Reference Room
Washington, D.C. 20230
(202) 377-2185
U.S. import and export statistics.

U.S. Department of Commerce
Library
14th and Constitution Ave., N.W.
Washington, D.C. 20230
Reference services on commerce and business.

U.S. Department of Commerce
National Technical Information Service
5285 Port Royal Road
Springfield, VA 22161
(703) 487-4600

U.S. Department of Commerce
World Trade Statistics
Room 2036
Washington, D.C. 20230
(202) 377-4855
World import and export statistics.

FIGURE 9.3 (*Continued*)

U.S. Department of Education
National Center for Education Statistics
Mail Stop 1001
400 Maryland Ave., S.W.
Washington, D.C. 20202
(301) 436-7900
Education statistics.

U.S. Department of Energy
National Energy Information Center
1F048 Forrestal Building
1000 Independence Avenue, S.W.
Washington, D.C. 20585
(202) 252-8800
General references on all aspects of energy.

U.S. Department of Energy
Technical Information Center
P.O. Box 62
Oak Ridge, TN 37830
Research on all energy-related topics.

U.S. Department of Health and Human Services
Information
200 Independence Ave., S.W.
Room 118F
Washington, D.C. 20201

U.S. Department of Health and Human Services
National Center for Health Statistics
3700 East-West Hwy., Room 1-57
Hyattsville, MD 20782
(301) 436-8500
Health statistics.

U.S. Department of Housing and Urban Development
Program Information Center
451 7th St., S.W.
Washington, D.C. 20410
(202) 755-6420
Information on all aspects of housing.

U.S. Department of Justice
Uniform Crime Reporting Section, FBI
9th and Pennsylvania Ave., N.W.
Room 6212
Washington, D.C. 20535
(202) 324-5038
Crime statistics.

U.S. Department of Labor
Bureau of Labor Statistics
441 G St., N.W.
Washington, D.C. 20212
(202) 523-1239
Statistics on employment, prices, living conditions,
productivity, and occupational safety and health.

FIGURE 9.3 *(Continued)*

U.S. House of Representatives
Bill Status Office
House Annex #2, Room 696
Washington, D.C. 20515
(202) 255-1772
Specific legislation activity.

Participation in professional societies offers opportunity for informal contacts with members of other firms. Many societies sponsor meetings and seminars where information is exchanged. Some (American Management Associations, for example) maintain libraries where consulting on documents and MIS techniques is available.

Trade associations fill a similar role. Contacts with customers, suppliers, and distributors may be a valuable source of information about other firms, including your competitors. A number of starting points for finding data about the firm's competitors have been listed in figure 9.2.

Information for Sale

There are many consulting organizations that make available existing company or industry surveys at prices ranging from hundreds to thousands of dollars. Such firms will also develop new information as required on a consulting basis. This section will describe the offerings of a few representative organizations of this nature to give a flavor of what is available.

International Resources Development, Inc., is an independent consulting firm specializing in market research, product planning, and service planning. They analyze financial services and high technology industries and markets in the United States and abroad. They also publish market studies that represent major research efforts. These are said to include information available nowhere else. A complete list of all studies is available (*Catalog of Publications*).

Bernstein Cumulative Index abstracts the work of other companies. Bernstein maintains a staff of highly trained business analysts. To collect the required data, the analysts keep close contact with key executives in the industries and companies they follow, attend trade shows, talk to users, and read appropriate trade and professional publications. Most important, they digest the data and formulate conclusions.

Inside R & D is a series of weekly reports that cover not only important news from around the world in chemistry, electronics, materials, process technology, and instrumentation, but also news of techniques for managing research and development.

Schumer (1983) reports on a company that uses a combination of cable television, supermarket scanners, and computers to track every commercial that plays in the homes of its panelists and to record every purchase they make at the supermarket. This company can test a commercial for a new product and see how the audience responds at the store. Its clients include ten of the largest U.S. consumer-product companies.

Chase Econometrics, a subsidiary of Chase Manhattan Bank, was formed to supply a critical need for reliable, up-to-date economic information. They serve individual business clients by maintaining and constantly updating multiple data bases covering all major sectors of the U.S. economy as well as the other leading economies around the world. More than half of the "Fortune 500" companies call on Chase Econometrics for data and for assistance in their strategic planning programs. A monthly business planning service, *Chase Econometrics Letter,* provides reporting, analysis, and interpretation of economic, demographic, and social trends for other companies.

Another decision-support service is described in the *Index of Industry Studies.* The company, Predicasts, provides current awareness, forecasting tools, and expert research and analytical services to its clients. It helps pinpoint specific information requirements, then assists in designing and building a customized business intelligence system. Many industry and company reports are available.

Another descriptive index, *Findex,* lists market research reports, studies, and surveys. The company, Find/SVP, also publishes an information catalog that lists a selection of currently available industry, market, and company studies as well as industry-related research tools provided by a variety of research, publishing, consulting, and investment firms. Find/SVP has global data gathering capabilities. They access two hundred fifty computer data banks and have a comprehensive business library. Their Quick Information Service will develop answers to specific questions, while their Research Projects Service provides in-depth research and written reports.

Protected Information

In the two previous classes of data, knowledge is available for the asking, with a range of costs. Another class of data is actively protected by its owner. The most common example, of course, is data pertaining to a firm's competitors. This category is sufficiently important so that it has been given the next section. Another important topic is the ethics of how competitive data may be collected, and this is discussed in the second section following.

We have already suggested that internal sources are valuable for collecting data. Even in the case of competitive intelligence, most useful information comes from public, not secret, sources. Organization and correlation of the various bits of data are therefore particularly critical. Certainly in industries where sensitive information is important, a firm must establish an intelligence office to organize the collection of data and to maintain its security after it is obtained. It is not hard to visualize a situation where the mere fact that your firm is collecting data on a particular competitor or subject would be of intense interest to that competitor or to another competitor.

We have mentioned the need for analyzing the credibility and reliability of information, and this becomes particularly important in the case of protected data. Some simple evaluation system can be devised to collect and relate the opinions of the collector and the users of information on these points. It is not too far fetched to imagine that a firm might issue false reports to throw its competitors off the track, and in fact, instances of this have been reported.

Finally, your firm may also have data that it wishes to protect. Such protection can be another function of the intelligence office. The security system, probably patterned after the military, should include at least limited counterintelligence abilities and classification of data, so that some is available to any of the firm's employees while other data is available only on a need-to-know basis.

COMPETITIVE INFORMATION

A senior business strategist must answer the question, What can I do to gain competitive advantage in my industry? A specialist in planning MIS might ask, How can I help my firm benefit the most from competitive intelligence? In today's intense economic competition for products, markets, and technologies, the information a firm can acquire and its ability to protect its own information can determine its success or failure.

In spite of the fact that most competitive information is openly available, there is also an active world of subterfuge. Dallos (1983) has summarized some of the espionage and counterespionage activities that corporations employ in efforts to get or protect sensitive information. The use of code names, closed circuit TV, clandestine meetings, bugging of offices, and secret agents to track spies is common. As already pointed out, some of the secrets being concealed in themselves seem insignificant. An example would be the planned transfer of an executive. But put together with other facts, important conclusions can result. Other data is of more obvious importance—a major change in dividend rate or a takeover agreement between two large corporations. The leaking of confidential material can cause a company to lose millions of dollars if its trade secrets, customer lists, or pricing structures are compromised. Stock traders can illegally enrich themselves by transactions made on the basis of private information. Even corporate telephone directories may contain sensitive information. One company surreptitiously acquires such directories and sells copies for up to $60 (Smith 1983).

At least one company specializes in commercial intelligence. This company publishes a newsletter, *Intelligence Update,* and offers services at three levels for their clients: literature search, fact-finding review, and document retrieval; (2) a research interview program to get information not available in print; and (3) a full-service market research and survey program. Their clients can make inquiries via electronic mail, using computer terminals at the client's location. As we will explore further in the next section, this company points out that commercial intelligence is not a dirty word.

ETHICS

The study of business policy and of management in general leads to many fuzzy situations. The question of ethics is even more fuzzy. What is ethical to one individual might be repugnant to another, though in a different situation the two individuals might reverse their positions. Ethics also has a strong cultural and national bias. These remarks on ethics apply to all information but have particular pertinence for protected and competitive data.

Many companies publish a code of ethics, which typically promises to conduct business according to the highest ethical principles. Such a promise may be hard to quantify. Over the years, each company will develop a list of examples of what type of conduct is tolerated and what type is not. All we can recommend here is to choose a middle ground. No ethical firm would wish to skate too close to the fuzzy border between ethics and legality. Similarly, no profit-oriented firm would arbitrarily turn away from all information about its competitor.

We conclude this section with a few examples and rhetorical questions. It is illegal (and therefore unethical) to burglarize a competitor's office to obtain his data files. It is entirely ethical to use information about a competitor when it appears in the *Wall Street Journal.* Is what is illegal always unethical?

It is illegal to bug a competitor's office, but many believe it is quite acceptable to buy his employee a few beers and, in the course of the conversation, to pry out invaluable information, even though you do not announce to the employee that you are his competitor. What is the essential difference?

We have seen in previous sections that there are many companies selling competitive information. How far must the purchaser go to assure himself that the information was obtained by ethical means? Or does he tell himself that this is not his problem?

Aerial photographs are an easy, safe, and cheap way of watching your competitor's movements. Through the number of cars parked in the competitor's car lot, you can learn roughly the number of employees. Of course, you immediately know of changes in plant facilities. Some might feel that this is an invasion of privacy, but oil companies in particular have for years used aerial photos to observe competitors. What is the essential difference between this and bugging an office or visiting a plant pretending to be a supplier instead of a competitor?

It is up to each CEO to establish what his company considers to be the borderline between ethical and nonethical behavior and to be sufficiently precise to give employees useful guidelines.

MANAGEMENT INFORMATION SYSTEMS

Most companies go about the task of assessing and collecting environmental information that is critical to their strategic planning and decision making. Often, however, the mechanisms for acquiring such information are largely ad hoc and informal. Key decision makers typically rely on contacts, on the services of various news media and other intelligence agencies, or on the advice of staff groups whose main expertise may not include the gathering of strategic information. Decision makers may expect they will be informed if some critical incident or development takes place, but in an informal system this may not take place.

Managerial decision making is increasingly complex and challenging due to a rapidly changing business environment and to the occurrence of interrelated factors that impinge upon a particular decision. It is now more difficult and more important for management to estimate accurately the impact of alternative decision choices. A key to overcoming this problem is a computer-based management information system (MIS) that

- has access to, and organizes data from information systems into a form that facillitates analysis
- represents (or models) relationships and objectives existing within the sphere of management decision making.

- calculates the best answers to management's "what if" planning questions in light of corporate objectives
- provides answers in a convenient, understandable, efficient, and cost-effective manner

The MIS places the analytic power and speed of the computer at management's disposal in addressing critical planning questions. Firms that have made a commitment to MIS are realizing substantial benefits from their use. Maximum benefits, however, are to be realized only when the MIS is designed in close coordination with the managers whose decisions it will support. This cooperative effort assures that the system is well suited to and custom tailored for corporate needs.

Introduction of MIS may change the management style of top executives, as reported by Bralove (1983). MIS may allow the CEO to bypass the usual intelligence channels and discover for himself what is going on. The ability to control what and how far the CEO sees is often regarded as power. If the CEO has direct access to information, staff groups fear their influence will diminish, and operating heads fear a loss of autonomy. Naturally, such political factors must be considered when installing an MIS.

In order to evaluate the MIS concept in general or a proposed system in particular, managers must be knowledgeable about the structure, requirements, capabilities, and limitations of such computer-based management tools. Many consultants are available, including Elam (1983) of the University of Texas, and Herrick (1982) of Margann Associates.

Many canned systems are available. Mapper (1983) allows the user to follow his natural thought process, to explore, to investigate options, to browse among vast information resources, and finally to develop customized reports. Another system called *Selecting and Evaluating a Decision Support System* gives a capability for financial planning and resource modeling. It is totally interactive and uses English commands to enable the user to construct planning models and information systems quickly and efficiently. The firm makes available advanced systems design, extensive training, documentation, and continuing support from a large staff.

We have already noted that there are hundreds of data bases commercially available that can be accessed and made a part of a particular firm's MIS. These are usually available for a monthly fee plus a telephone connect-time charge. The services of one of the better known of these, *Dow Jones News Retrieval*, have been listed in figure 9.4. Some of the information is updated as often as every ninety seconds, and some of the information goes back as far as 1978. Holloway and Meadows (1981) have discussed searching the business literature by computer.

FIGURE 9.4   Dow Jones News Retrieval

Economic News
   Dow Jones News
   Wall Street Journal highlights online
   Weekly economic update
   Text search
Dow Jones Quotes
   Current
   Historical
   Dow Jones averages
Financial and Investment Services
   Corporate information
   Corporate earnings estimator
   Media general
   Money market services
General News
   Master menu
   Encyclopedia
   World and national news
   Sports report
   Weather report
   Movie reviews
   Wall Street Week

EXERCISE 9

This and every exercise is intended to form the basis for a part of the term project: Prepare a strategic plan for an organization of your choice. Present a typed, one-page report, showing the directions your analysis will take for each exercise.

For this exercise, outline what your company will need in the various information categories: competitive intelligence, technical, the environment, and other.

In addition to the material of this chapter, the following references are pertinent: King and Cleland (1978), chapters 10 and 11; Steiner (1969), chapter 16.

INFORMATION SOURCES

Bernstein Cumulative Index. Sanford C. Bernstein & Co., Inc., 767 Fifth Avenue, New York, N.Y. 10153.

Catalog of Publications. International Resource Development, Inc., 30 High Street, Norwalk, Conn., 06851.

Chase Econometrics Letter. Chase Econometrics, Bala Cynwyd, Penn. 19004.

Dow Jones News Retrieval. Dow Jones & Co., P.O. Box 300, Princeton, N.J. 08540.

Encyclopedia of Associations. Gale Research, Detroit, Mich.

Findex. Find/SVP, 500 Fifth Ave., New York, N.Y. 10110.

Growth Pace Setters in American Industry. U.S. Department of Commerce.

Index of Industry Studies. Predicasts, 11001 Cedar Ave., Cleveland, Ohio 44106.

Industry Surveys. Standard and Poor's Corp., New York, N.Y.

Information U.S.A. Washington Researchers, 918 Sixteenth Street Northwest, Washington, D.C. 20006, 1982.

Inside R&D. Technical Insights, Inc., 158 Linwood Plaza, P.O. Box 1304, Fort Lee, N.J. 07024.

Intelligence Update. Information Data Search, Inc., 1218 Massachusetts Ave., Cambridge, Mass. 02138.

Investors Management Sciences, Inc. (subsidiary of Standard & Poor's). 1221 Avenue of the Americas, New York, N.Y. 10020.

Kiplinger Washington Newsletters. 1729 H Street Northwest, Washington, D.C. 20006.

Mapper. Sperry Univac, Department 100, P.O. Box 500, Blue Bell, Penn. 19424.

Selecting and Evaluating a Decision Support System. EPS, Inc., 1786 Technology Drive, San Jose, California 95110.

A Technological Assessment Methodology, vols. 1–7. Prepared by MITRE Corp. and distributed by the National Technical Information Service, U.S. Dept. of Commerce, 1971.

U.S. Census of Manufacturers. U.S. Department of Commerce.

U.S. Industrial Outlook. U.S. Department of Commerce.

U.S. News Washington Letter. 2300 N. Street Northwest, Washington, D.C. 20037.

References

Adams, Walter, ed. *The Structure of American Industry.* 5th ed. New York: Macmillan, 1977.

Bralove, Mary. "Direct Data." *Wall Street Journal,* Jan. 12, 1983.

Brownstone, D. M., and Carruth, G. *Where to Find Business Information.* Somerset, N.J.: Wiley, 1982.

Dallos, Robert E. "No Secret Is Safe." *The State* (Columbia, S.C.), July 10, 1983.

Elam, Joyce J. "Decision Support Systems Seminar." Arlington, Va.: Institute for Professional Education, 1983.

Herrick, Margaret A. "Data Base Concepts and Design Seminar." Cambridge, Mass.: Margann Associates, 1982.

Holloway, Clark, and Meadows, Nolan R. "Searching the Business Literature by Computer." *Business and Economic Review* (Dec. 1981), pp. 31–38.

King, William R., and Cleland, David I. *Strategic Planning and Policy.* New York: Van Nostrand Reinhold, 1978.

Schumer, Fern. "The New Magicians of Market Research." *Fortune* (July 25, 1983).

Smith, Randall. "For Sale: Corporate Phone Books." *Wall Street Journal,* July 14, 1983.

Steiner, G. A. *Top Management Planning.* New York: Macmillan, 1969.

Chapter 10

Relating Economic Strategy and Personal Values

The consideration of personal values has been implicit throughout many of the preceding chapters. In the following sections we will discuss a number of these important ideas explicitly. First, it must be emphasized that organizations do not have objectives, only people have objectives (Ansoff, 1965). The objectives of a firm are a negotiated consensus of the objectives of the influential participants. This negotiation may or may not take place in an atmosphere of conflict. The negotiation process is sometimes looked at as political maneuvering. Politics have somehow acquired undesirable connotations. For example, among other dictionary phrases, we find: "competition between interest groups for power and leadership", and "activities characterized by artful and often dishonest practices". We believe that office politics are normal, honest parts of corporate life and would prefer the dictionary definition that says politics are "the total complex of relations between people in society".

Values are often considered to be identical with ethics; that is, what behavior will the firm tolerate? There is also the aspect of considering what is more important; the old question of efficiency versus effectiveness. We must not be guilty of continuing to polish the brass after the ship has struck an iceberg. These questions must be given consideration.

Finally, as we look at the roles and activities of a variety of managers, we can identify three main aspects of leadership. These are: to originate, defend, and implement a strategy. Figure 10.1 shows the interrelationships among these elements and some of the internal stakeholders. For the sake of completeness, we list stockholders and employees, although they have direct input to strategy matters in only a very few firms. As discussed in more

FIGURE 10.1   Molding and Using Strategy

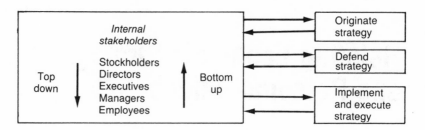

detail elsewhere, the organization may handle its strategy either by the top down, or by the bottom up approach. Particular attention is called to the feedback used when exploring the three elements. Having originated strategy, it is discussed and possibly refined or modified, and the discussion may or may not involve added levels of management.

ORGANIZATIONAL VERSUS EXECUTIVE OBJECTIVES

We intend this discussion to cover the entire hierarchy of strategic planning. This is the formation of mission, objectives, goals, and strategy, so that when we speak of one of the elements, we intend that the same remarks should apply also to the others. Let us illustrate the thrust of this section by an admittedly rather extreme example. Suppose we have a charity, staffed by volunteers, that is working for the elimination of a particular disease. No group, and particularly not the volunteers, would expect any personal benefit from the charity. It is possible for a pressure group to infiltrate the charity, however, and to begin demanding and receiving personal benefits. In this example, the infiltration is probably censorable, but in another example it might be praiseworthy. We have chosen this extreme example to make the point that the objectives of any organization are chosen by those who have the power to do so.

Strategic choice is a difficult and risky procedure. There is no way to insulate the most sensible economic strategy for a firm from the personal strategy of those who make the choices. In addition to considering what their company might do and can do, executives are strongly influenced by what they personally want to do. This should be a desirable rather than an offensive idea, in the same sense that it long has been accepted that the personal needs of the hourly worker must be at least partially satisfied. The executive will have to decide how bold he is willing to be, in the sense of having to suffer the consequences of wrong judgements, in terms of both the firm's posture and his own career.

The executive's attitude toward a proposed strategy is influenced by his personal attitudes and by his ambitions (the word *ambition* on the personal level equates closely with the word *objective* on the corporate level). A number of examples of such ambitions and other influencing factors can be given:

- The executive may want to go down in history as the shaper of the company.
- He may wish to differentiate his regime from that of his predecessor.
- He may be influenced by his previous functional background.
- The financial community or other external forces may shape his attitude toward risk.
- Short-run necessities may force tempering of strategic desiderata.
- He may modify his objectives to make a collective decision possible.

The interactive forces at play are suggested by figure 10.2. For simplicity, the figure shows only three participants. In real life every director, executive, and manager who participates in the formulation of strategy should be represented. By a process involving both dictation and negotiation, the corporate position evolves out of the personal wishes and beliefs of the participants. Note that the shaded area representing the corporate position is not necessarily the exact intersection of the participants' areas. The CEO, for example, may prevail to a greater extent than one of the vice presidents.

Sometimes the negotiations can take place on the basis of logic and reason. At other times conflict may arise. People may have secret motives they will not reveal. Jealousy and other motives may be present. For these and other reasons the firm is sometimes forced to accept strategies that are not optimum. Even in such undesirable situations, it is better to have a strategic plan than to not have one.

POLITICS

Strategic planners, particularly if strategic planning has only recently been introduced to the firm, should spend the majority of their time and effort in selling the idea of strategic planning. The most elaborate planning system is useless if the people who will have to supply the data and who must cooperate if the objectives are to be attained are not properly motivated. This requires the courage to use politics. Planning staffs may spend too much time on the technical and formal aspects of planning and on the establishment of elaborate planning systems and not enough time on the politics

FIGURE 10.2   Development of Organizational Objectives

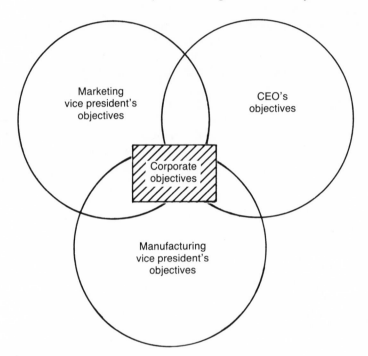

of planning or on human relations and on selling strategic planning throughout the corporation.

Corporations are to a large extent political, frequently in a negative
sense. There is game playing, dishonesty, and lack of frankness. The corporate planner must also play politics, but in a positive sense. He must be scru-
pulously honest, play no games, and be trustworthy. If he is not trusted by
people down the line, he cannot continue to operate. He has to know and
understand the games being played but not play them himself. Let us list
some of the types of factors to be considered in playing politics construc-
tively:

- Learn your organization, how it works, and what the power structure
  is.
- Get to know the people: have drinks with them; have lunch with
  them.
- Know who is secure; who is insecure; what a person's ambition is;
  who hates whom; who is honest; who has guts; what concerns the
  person; what the person's fears and problems are.

- Have sympathy and empathy, particularly when you as a planner look at the line manager. Understand what his day is like.
- Have in your mind a concept of planning and the planning system you are driving toward, but bend it when necessary to make it fit the real world.
- Use the line manager's language rather than your own jargon. Keep your system invisible and simple.
- Stress results. If you can solve one problem for the CEO, then no matter how imperfect your system, he has gotten something out of planning. To him, planning will have utility.
- Retain and develop your judgment in applying all of the above precepts. In each situation you must decide how much to change and how far to compromise the planning.

Ideally, the corporate planner should have matured within the organization and should have had a wide and varied experience within it. He should be the neutral person who can explain the CEO's motives, can engineer compromises, can smooth ruffled feathers and bruised egos, and can be a catalyst to promote other people's ideas. This is a large job. It requires both passion and compassion, and a realistic approach to problems. It calls for maturity, a deep understanding, and a liking for people. If at all possible, it is desirable to have the ability to walk on water.

The politics of planning can be considered in at least four areas.

Corporate Planning Politics

Strategic planning (SP) is apt to be a relatively new department, probably created by and for the benefit of the CEO. The first person likely to feel threatened by SP is the chief financial officer—let us call him the vice president of finance (VPF). Prior to the advent of SP, the CEO probably relied on him for financial planning and forecasting. Quite understandably, he may feel that SP is infringing on his territory. A threatened VPF is not likely to be cooperative in providing SP with the mass of historical and current data it requires for the success of planning. Such conflicts are not unusual in large corporations, and the CEO is the only person who can reduce problems of this type. If the CEO is truly committed to planning, he will find it easy to sit down with the VPF and end the conflict. If the CEO is less committed, an aggressive VPF can quickly undermine the credibility of the planning function. The vice president for SP usually reports directly to the CEO. With adequate political support it is possible to create a culture conducive to effective strategic planning.

Functional Area Politics

The VPF, discussed above, is unfortunately only one of the numerous functional heads who may become involved with political conflict with SP. Where computer-based planning models are to be created and used, we may find functional rivalry between management science (MS) and data processing (DP). Strategic planning models are often created, manipulated, and run by an MS department. Frequently, MS expertise to do this work is found within the SP department. We regard this as a good arrangement, since primary responsibility for the design of such models should rest with the SP department. There are many political problems which can arise, two of which are at opposite poles. First, the firm's computer may be loaded with routine accounting work, so that MS is allotted little time and an impossible turnaround schedule. At the opposite pole, there may be ample computer time, but MS may need or prefer the configuration of an outside computer. The author has experienced both problems. The economic solution is to maintain adequate computing facilities, with MS permitted to experiment with outside computers. DP and MS should then work together to transfer the applications to the firm's machine.

Obviously, the heads of marketing, production, or other functions may each have strong feelings that their departments should control those data, models, and techniques that pertain to their departments. The cooperation from each of the functional areas of the cooperation is essential for the success of strategic planning. Politics must be played to ensure this, without letting the situation deteriorate to one of political infighting.

Organizational Politics

An extension of the functional political problems discussed above is found in the case of decentralized firms that maintain separate strategic planning departments in each of the divisions. Each division prepares its own strategic plan, followed by consolidation of the plans into a corporate strategic plan by a headquarters strategic planning department. We propose the following guidelines to answer the many questions which arise:

- The corporate planning department (CPD) should be responsible for specifying the planning structure and techniques to be used by the divisions.
- Wherever possible, the same structure and techniques should be used by all divisions.

- Division planning should not proceed, and divisional models should not be developed, independently of CPD.
- Each division should be responsible for maintaining its own data base.
- Each division should be encouraged to acquire and use computer-based models in its planning.
- The corporate staff should have the responsibility for developing divisional models, but with every effort made to enlist the help, knowledge, and experience of the divisional staff.
- Corporate management and SP should have access to divisional models, but not vice versa.

Geographic Politics

When corporate headquarters are in New York or Pittsburgh and operating headquarters are in Houston or London, an additional difficulty in integrating the elements of strategic planning can occur. Just as we have functional jealousies, so we may have geographic jealousies. Although this is perhaps surprising in view of the jet airplane and telecommunication technology, it has been known to happen.

Values versus Objectives

The difference between values and objectives is not always clearcut. A firm, for example, might state as an objective their desire to treat their customers fairly. In a service industry, this could be a valid statement, because customer treatment is a major component of profit. Another firm, however, would choose to put such a statement in their creed or list of ethical principles.

All planning, from the need to be proactive to the desire to exploit technology, carries heavy human burdens. Rational decision making is complex, but to this must be added a variety of human prerogatives and obligations beyond what is normally mentioned in the various planning systems that have been proposed. There are three topics to be considered: (1) factors in the environment and in planning techniques that complicate the planning process beyond what is typically appreciated; (2) human capabilities that are required if we are to plan effectively in light of these complications; and (3) how to insure that the planning process is humane and wise rather than a mechanized ritual.

Environment

Firms are receiving more and more data about what is happening to people and to the environment. The firm is being asked and required more and more to confront problems of who receive the benefits and who is to pay the costs of the firm's activities. These may range from the impact of a new plant to the effects of pollution.

Consumerism, the organized expression of dissatisfaction with the quality of a firm's products, will force (or already has forced) feedback into the planning process. The luxury of being able to select the focus of attention in planning may be a thing of the past.

Future studies is another area where human burdens in decision making are enlarged. Formerly, we let the future take care of itself or selected a direction more or less in the dark. Now, as we have described in previous chapters, planning is proposing alternate scenarios. Planning has the active intention of being proactive, that is, of changing the environment. Ethical questions must necessarily arise.

Required Human Capabilities

Over the past decade, the roles that used to distinguish rather clearly what was required of a person as an employee from the person's role requirements as a family member or as a citizen have become more and more blurred. Evidence of this is found in the increasing militancy of women and other minorities in corporations. It is found in the increasing insistence of scientists that the ethical and moral responsibilities they have as citizens apply on the job as well.

There are certain human qualities required for dealing with the uncomfortable situations just mentioned. In the past, an organization told its people who they were and how they were to fit in. It is going to take a great increase in an individual's ability to cope with role ambiguity—who he is, what his abilities are, and what is expected of him—in order to deal with the consequences of planning.

Environmental turbulence and the increased uncertainty in planning requires a large increase in our capacity to live with this uncertainty. Many times we cannot even pretend to be able to assign risk probabilities to circumstances. Being able to live with uncertainty requires unusual self-understanding and courage.

We are seeing higher levels of preoccupation and sophistication about ethical dilemmas and alternative ethical approaches. This pertains not only to our own clientele, but also to outsiders, who adventitiously gain the benefits or suffer the costs that result from our servicing our own clientele. The planner cannot pass these questions on to somebody else. Most people are uncomfortable in dealing with them, but personal characteristics to permit doing so must be developed.

Wise Planning

Earlier chapters have laid down a guide to systematic strategic planning. In the areas of ethics and values, discussed above, we know something about the problems, but we are far from having full solutions. The rhetorical questions posed in the previous section have perhaps suggested their own answers. We must accept that, in large part, planning is a learning procedure rather than an engineering technology. We must spend time and money to develop the answers to our rhetorical questions.

ORIGINATING STRATEGY

We now consider three phases of leadership where personal values and objectives (as opposed to those of the organization) are important. First, the general manager is the architect of strategy. The requirements of this role are analytic ability, creativity, self-awareness, and sensitivity to society's expectations regarding a businessman's broader social responsibilities. The policy-making executive must be an innovator to find strategic choices that are not routine and reactive, and to determine a proactive strategy that is uniquely adapted to external opportunity and internal strengths. In addition to powers of analysis and innovation, the strategist must have a sense of personal purpose and of personal needs.

The strategy belongs to the general manager, but recall the cascade system displayed in figure 1.6. There is feedback up and down the line as well as to and from staff groups. The organization's strategy is thus a blend of many opinions and many inputs, even though the CEO takes a key role in spearheading the process with enthusiasm and vigor. Recall also figure 10.1, which illustrates again multilayered participation and the need for feedback.

DEFENDING STRATEGY

The manager is a defender of strategy, the one who supplies organizational leadership. Successful implementation of strategy requires the organization leader to promote and defend strategy against the conflicting interests that inevitably arise around it. The tendency of an organization is to veer off course in response to circumstances, special interests, and sudden opportunity. This means that the general manager must defend the planning strategy. Like administrators at other levels, the CEO finds himself in the roles of mediator and integrator. He must deal with conflict among special interests and among organizational tendencies leading in different directions. The general manager cannot effectively lead an organized advance toward chosen goals unless he is aware that his organization has certain needs that are not fulfilled by the pursuit of strategy itself. Individuals and departments demand recognition of the validity of their personal and organizational subgoals.

IMPLEMENTING STRATEGY

Finally, the general manager is charged with implementing strategy. Here again, feedback and the participation of all levels of management is essential. The most important characteristics of a favorable climate for successful implementation of strategy appear to be:

- Absence of political maneuvering for position, with penalties for unfair personal competition and petty conspiracies.
- Rejection of a program on grounds other than objective evaluation. Specifically, consideration of family relationships, friendships, and persons having similar ethnic, educational, or social backgrounds is not held to be objective.
- High standards for work, explicit both in work instruction and in work evaluation; expectations of continuous improvement in competence with increasing experience; and disciplined attention to meeting detailed commitments.
- High value assigned to interpersonal amity and tolerance of individual differences.
- Willingness to take risks (with acceptance of the inevitability of occasional failure) in delegating responsibility to the relatively inexperienced worker.
- Acceptance and encouragement of innovation with consequent freedom to act upon ideas. Disapproval in cases of failure must be attached to results and causes rather than to mere departure from conventional practice.
- High standards of moral integrity, including rejection of expediency, even at the cost of windfall profits.

The patient establishment and stubborn defense of these values are practicable undertakings for the leader of an organization. No other duties of his office, except perhaps decisions about objectives and strategy (and these are similar and related), are as important.

EXERCISE 10

This and every exercise is intended to form the basis for a part of the term project: Prepare a strategic plan for an organization of your choice. For each exercise, present a typed, one-page report, showing directions your analysis will take.

For this exercise, outline some of the potential areas of concern with respect to politics and personal values in your company and suggest possible ways of handling these areas.

In addition to the material of this chapter, the following references are pertinent: Andrews (1971), chapter 4; Argenti (1974), chapters 1 and 3; Naylor (1979), chapter 10.

REFERENCES

Andrews, K. R. *The Concept of Corporate Strategy.* Homewood, Ill.: Dow Jones-Irwin, 1971.

Ansoff, H. Igor. *Corporate Strategy.* New York, McGraw-Hill, 1965.

Argenti, John. *Systematic Corporate Planning.* New York: Wiley, 1974.

Naylor, Thomas H. *Corporate Planning Models.* Reading, Mass.: Addison-Wesley, 1979.

Uyterhoeven, H. E. R.; Ackerman, R. W.; and Rosenblum, J. W. *Strategy and Organization.* Homewood, Ill.: Irwin, 1977.

Chapter 11

Interrelating Planning and Control

A more or less smooth continuum leads from genuine creativity on the one side of the scale to planning, action, and measurement of the ultimate effectiveness of the management process through operational controls at the other side of the scale. There is no room for creativity in business without an objective of tangible results that can be put to the service of others, and there is no room for business activity that is not painstakingly measured in terms of what it has set out to achieve. Plans and controls are two sides of the same coin. Both planning and control should be an integral part of the daily thinking and acting of each manager. We must therefore understand how these fundamental activities interrelate.

Three types of controls will be considered in this chapter. The first is how to control the planning process itself each year. The second is to determine the results of planning over the immediate past year. The third is how we can both control and insure good results from planning over the planning horizon. We have already discussed (in conjunction with figure 2.3) the difficulty of determining how closely the objective of a multiyear plan has been reached, because each year a new plan is introduced that modifies the previous objective, even assuming that only a single quantitative measure is used.

MANAGEMENT

Managing means to make decisions. Decisions imply initiation of action. The initiation of action follows an assessment of a given situation based on experience, knowledge, and skill. It entails the application of the best available information to the development of strategic plans. This is one side of the management process. On the other side, controls are essential to see things through to accomplishment and to evaluate whether results are in line with the set targets.

Strategic planning involves primarily specific tasks: the accumulation and the integration of information in line with established objectives; the assessment of available and future resources; and realistic identification of major risks, uncertainties, and potential problems. What concerns us here is the critical endpoint after these planning tasks have been accomplished—the link to action, to execution, and to operations. It is left to management controls to evaluate the action required to see intentions materialize in line with set objectives.

As planning techniques have matured, a growing new concern has become evident. Are your plans not only sound and realistic but also effective? Do they represent not only an interesting assessment of the future but also firm guideposts for actually achieving objectives? Are proper yardsticks set? Are controls in place? Today, we find widespread recognition by almost any management that it must plan. We find that serious concern is given as to how such planning can be accomplished. Where plans fail, however, we find this is less often due to their poor quality or lack of leadership support, than to an absence of controls or an understanding of their need in order to see plans through to results.

Management must insure that all plans are integrated in the proper fashion and that plans result in appropriate current action. When planning is done on an annual cycle, there is a tendency for divisions to extrapolate from plans of the previous year to get the plan for the year added. If the CEO does not guard against extrapolation, it will take place as an easy way to respond to central headquarter's request for medium-range programs. This can affect plans that are made centrally as well as those prepared in the divisions. One of the reasons for dissatisfaction with strategic planning is the failure of managers to distinguish between commitments and plans. A commitment is a decision to act. It must not be confused with planning or the development of plans. Managers must constantly rethink the future. For formalized planning this means once-a-year revisions in the divisions, while management in the meantime reevaluates existing plans. If plans are set for five or six years ahead and blindly followed, the results may be disastrous.

The CEO must determine the degree of interrelationship between strategic plans and medium-range programs, and between medium-range programs and short-range plans. There is no formula that gives the proper balance over the planning time horizon between precise detail and close interrelationships, and between broad estimates and loose interrelationships.

Management must insist that plans are translated into concrete terms for current actions. When plans are prepared for current action, they must be capable of being implemented. Furthermore, top managers must review the performance of lower-level managers in terms that will stimulate better planning and adherence to plans. If the general manager of a division is measured principally upon the basis of the current return on investment of his division, he will seek to optimize that measure without much reference to the future.

Most people have a resistance to change. Strategic planning is designed to bring about change, often very great change. One major integrating force which stems from strategic planing is creating an adaptability to and an acceptance of change in an organization. This is a major responsibility of the CEO. Strategic planning has been described as being both the means of discovering what major changes should take place, and the means by which people come more readily to accept the results of the change.

Steiner (1969) has listed the following guides to the acceptance of change. Change is more acceptable when:

- it is understood.
- it does not threaten security.
- those affected have helped to create it.
- it results from an application of previously established impersonal principles.
- it follows a series of successful changes.
- it is inaugurated after prior change has been assimilated.
- it has been planned.
- people are new on the job.
- people share in the benefits of change.
- the organization has been trained to plan for improvement.

CONTROL OF THE PLANNING PROCESS

Each organization is advised to prepare a checklist of the elements it wishes to include in each year's strategic planning effort. Because of the diversity of companies and industries, we do not present a sample here. Source material has been given in chapters 4, 7, and 13:

Figure 4.2 Alternatives Spread Sheet
Figure 7.1 Outline of a Strategic Plan
Figure 7.2 Organization Chart for Planning

The simple process of reviewing last year's plans before beginning a new planning cycle can be enlightening and can lead to improvements in planning. For example, in figure 11.1 a, a firm prepared a five-year plan in 1985. The firm thoughtfully and realistically determined to raise its profit over this period. However, at the end of the planning horizon in 1990 (figure 11.1 b) when actual results are added to the plot, it is found that the general trend of profit has been downward. Perhaps there is no better way to demonstrate the need for continuous planning evaluation and control than to see such a graph. If a firm makes plots of this type each year, corrective action on the planning process can be taken before the disastrous situation of figure 11.1 b is reached.

CONTROL OF THE PLANNING OUTPUTS

We will not concern ourselves with how companies are controlled in the sense of ownership or worker participation or how they are controlled by society through laws, regulations, or market forces. At stake here is the perhaps more trivial but different question, How do we as managers control what we want to actually achieve—what our plans have promised to do?

Planning is not inherently good. Poor planning may be worse than no planning at all simply because no planning means only an absence of organized planning activities. In a no-planning environment, planning is done in a decentralized and uncoordinated way. This may be superior to organized planning that is done badly. It is difficult to distinguish between good plans and poor plans at first glance. It is only upon careful perusal and after time has elapsed that quality definitively can be assessed.

Plans suggest that all major issues, from first steps to optimum results, have been probed, show how all of these factors interrelate, and let the many participants in the decision process share in the total information thus generated. Controls mean the setting of standards of performance before action is taken. Later results are measured against these standards. Variances between standards and results are evaluated. A final result will be the identification of possible improvements as a consequence of the evaluation, no matter how good or bad the variances turned out to be. Note again that planning does not include decisions about plan implementation. Similarly, controls do not include the initiation of corrective action. They do, however, include responsibility for feedback to the units controlled as well as to the CEO as

FIGURE 11.1 Results Compared with Plans

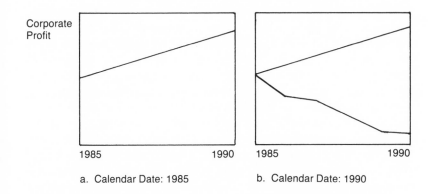

a. Calendar Date: 1985   b. Calendar Date: 1990

the focal point of action. This is the vital distinction between controlling and managing.

Planning is the concern for future years; in contrast, controls highlight what is to be done today and during the current period in order to safeguard achievement of those results on which the next plans at the beginning of future years will be built. In this sense, management controls are not established to see that the planning work itself is done appropriately, rather, it ensures that the planning objectives are actually realized in performance today. In a more general sense controls are thus the means by which

1. performance is ensured in coherence with the plan, and
2. delegation by those responsible for operating management becomes possible, while ultimate responsibility remains with the originator of delegation and control.

Planning, organization, and control are thus closely interlinked. Controls in themselves do not reflect any particular degree of centralization or decentralization, a common misconception.

PLANNING, BUDGETING, REPORTING—
THE LINKS TO FINANCIAL CONTROLS

In a business organization, results are ultimately expressed as return on resources employed. Standards, measurements, variances, and improvement proposals ultimately are expressed in financial terms. The chain from plans to financial controls is, therefore, our first concern. Strategic plans are established to reflect company objectives, ways of achieving them, and resources to be spent over an extended time span. They are flexible ''flight plans'' that are adjusted as changes occur in the environment, in our intentions, or in the available resources. Where strategic plans are taken seriously, we find no difficulty in seeing them firmly interlocked with company budgets, but this can be a major problem in start-up situations. In contrast to plans, budgets are yardsticks of performance. They are the measure by which operating results in the short run are assessed in financial terms. To the degree that company objectives are also expressed in financial terms, this measurement remains an ultimate evaluation of company success.

Information about the measurement itself is therefore also to be done in financial terms. Such measurements are based on individual business centers and accounts. Reporting from these base points has to include corresponding short-term forecasts, together with an evaluation of how firm or ''hard'' they can be considered to be. It is necessary also to include exposures omitted from forecasts, those ''soft-spots,'' that have a good probability of materializing. This process of financial reporting and measuring against preset budgets that are interlocked with long-term strategic plans is so useful that it justifies large staff efforts. It is essential for effective financial controls that this detailed information be generated at each major operating center, but under the central guidance of the comptroller and finance executive who report directly to the company's chief executive.

Financial controls remain a focal point for a business venture, but they cover only one specific aspect of those controls that are becoming increasingly critical for today's management in a rapidly changing business environment. Our concern is much broader in scope. Plans reflect the goals of a living organism; they are an expression primarily, even if indirectly, about people—their intentions, how they work individually and together, and how their organization finds ultimate fulfillment. Plans are primarily operational and thus in a wider sense management oriented. They have their own requirements and links with controls.

THE MANAGEMENT CONTROL GAP

With the above understanding of the management, planning, and control tasks in mind, we can now investigate more specifically how management controls work. How do we ensure in practice, in our day-to-day work, that results of performance are commensurate with the intentions expressed in the plan, particularly if we wish to go beyond the short-term financial statements in budgets and reporting? This is the pivotal question in management controls directed at interlinking distinctly different systems, the planning of operational standards and performance, and the planning of budgeting and measuring in financial terms. Overall controls must connect all of these items and provide the critical bridge to relate overall knowledge and insight to action.

While management has achieved widespread sophistication in planning, it has surprisingly neglected this other side of the coin. We have often not recognized that controls are to a large extent not financial in nature. Controls must also be directed towards the reality of the business world, where factors involving human interactions cannot be measured in financial terms. Instead, we usually satisfy ourselves with operational and budgetary controls, both mostly short-term in nature. We achieve sophistication in forecasting in units of sales, in production scheduling, in units of inflow and outflow, in inventory control for raw materials or processed goods, in manpower and compensation control, and so on. We are used to distinguishing such guideposts from overall, long-term oriented businesses planning. But our controls are rarely in place to pursue, measure, and evaluate the operational impact of today's performance on true progress toward the overall strategic company objectives. This is perhaps because these objectives often will be fully achieved only in the distant future.

This field is so wide that an entirely new management discipline has opened up. Few techniques for determining, establishing, and monitoring such controls have as yet been developed, beyond isolated approaches by some leading companies—a marked contrast to the rapid developments in planning during the last decade. This emphasizes the truism that plans without controls are merely wishful thinking.

ELEMENTS OF MANAGEMENT CONTROL

A number of elements of effective management controls can be identified. It will be helpful to first reduce a plan to its essential building blocks. In most simple terms, a plan responds to seven fundamental questions:

1. Where are you—your business, your environment, your prospects?
2. Where do you want to be? What are your intentions and objectives?
3. How and when do you want to get there? What are your strategies, targets, and framework of time?
4. What resources have you available—men; money; machines and facilities; and materials? What are the risks and alternatives you are willing to consider?
5. Who is going to do what, and when? What are your specific goals, projects, programs, and assigned responsibilities within overall completion dates?
6. What results are considered satisfactory? What are your standards of achievement, that is, goals above the critical minimum but open

to extraordinary accomplishments based on initiative and expertise?

7. What rewards may be expected—from personal fulfillment to material advantages and to status or other forms of recognition?

For the business as a whole and each of its segments, these main plan elements must be clearly identified in order to arrive at a sound conclusion of what controls should aim for. In this process, key prerequisites of control need to be taken into account:

- Has responsibility been properly delegated in line with the planned targets?
- Is two-way communication effective?
- Are standards of performance known, and will results be fully accepted at these performance levels?
- Is a balanced effort being organized and undertaken to reach established goals?
- Is it clear on which bases results will be reviewed?
- Do these reviews stimulate self-appraisal?
- Is leadership in place? Are attitudes sound? Are good human relationships fostering a positive and creative atmosphere of cooperation?

Management control provides the crucial link between the planning and the management processes. It does not, however, cover all aspects of company management itself; for example, the way decisions are made at the top or whether leadership actually comes through are not general concerns of manager control exercised from within the company organization. Such matters would have to be the subjects of an outside management audit. However, shortcomings in the management system will usually manifest themselves in one way or another. Bad leadership, for example, will result in poor delegation and communication. A bad decision-making process will often leave standards of performance inadequately determined. The real control problem starts where multitudes of products, technologies, company locations, country environments, and so on bring new problems of optimum interaction and new pitfalls where this integration does not take place. The critical importance of such management controls, as distinguished from financial or operational controls, becomes increasingly evident in multinational corporations, widely diversified companies, or multiproduct, multi-industry conglomerate enterprises. Needs for management controls mount with an accelerated rate of change in the environment for any large-size multiplant operation. They are critical for companies in a state of rapid expansion or for volatile businesses where success depends on fast reappraisal in light of new developments.

INFORMATION SYSTEMS: PREREQUISITES
OF MANAGEMENT CONTROLS

Information is a critical prerequisite of controls. The particular difficulty of achieving an integrated information flow useful for control purposes lies in the fact that strategic information is mostly imprecise. It reflects a high degree of uncertainty. This is in sharp contrast to the accuracy of the mostly historical or short-term forecast data in the financial information system. As techniques improve, more activities become susceptible to controls, in line with the trend toward an increasingly more scientific base for management.

As established earlier, management entails review, judgment, and action. Management reviews are based on a company's information system, which includes the financial reporting system that provides to its separate organization channels the building blocks for the critical ultimate measuring of financial results. But the financial system is increasingly overshadowed, in terms of importance to a business enterprise as a live organism, by the formal and informal management reports of a wide variety that in turn are interlinked with a whole span of information, from operating data to special project, product, and market reports to the overall strategic plans. To penetrate and understand such information in its relation to the company's overall objectives and to its human organization is precisely the job of management controls.

The information system embraces two elements: the collection of data the way they originate and the selection, integration, and upgrading of data as required for the issues submitted for management review. Selection, integration, and particularly upgrading require judgment, so first the aim of the management information system is to objectively crystallize the most essential facts and trends. These will enable the company management to start at the very core of the matter, without going through secondary details or issues. Second, the information system must be ready to repeat the process of data collection, selection, integration, and upgrading in as many different directions as there are different needs in order to cover alternative or new issues in the course of the management review.

Management controls must include both the objectivity and depth applied in the information process to prepare the management review. They must apply also to the validity of the critical data and the evaluation of progress as these were planned during the period of plan implementation, the period of action. Both planning and control are involved not only in the management review process but also in its achievement of aims. The contribution of planning is the assessment of decisions taken with regard to the assumptions provided and the understanding of the aims pursued. The contributions by management control are to ensure that operational plans and schedules safeguard in an optimum way the achievement of the aims of the first plan period and to actually measure these achievements against the plan as time moves on and progress is being made.

ACTION AS THE FOCUS OF MANAGEMENT CONTROLS

A wide arsenal of tools reflect the CEO's concern and provide the bridge from control information to corrective action. These fall basically into two categories: those that initiate action where the management process identifies a need for it (for example, almost invariably where any performance is off established targets) and those used to follow through to actual achievement once action has been initiated. In going briefly through some of the practical tools in the management controls, we could use as an example a hypothetical worldwide company headquartered in New York with operations in Europe. On one side, strong financial controls have long been the backbone of goal consciousness and thus success in financial performance. On the other side, management controls in many different forms are a frequent and everyday way of life. Organizationally, nonfinancial controls appear aligned with various functions, such as product line management. Further examples would be powerful operations staffs functioning in New York headquarters or with the planning department in Europe as the integrated counterpart. Control through action initiation is based on a far-reaching information process that intersects at the planning department. While financial information is further disseminated through finance or comptroller's channels, nonfinancial reports are also monitored here. Such reports include in particular the large number of so-called monthly manager's letters from the heads of all operations in Europe addressed to the president-Europe but reaching (through the planning department) directly all product line and functional departments in world headquarters as well. They follow a ten-point agenda from major exposures and accomplishments to an assessment of operating data, competition, and business development. Such management information includes all progress reports prepared along similar lines by the heads of the international product lines or functions reporting to the president. Added to these are many special reports expanding on major subjects that are covered in more detail where this is required. Such information is then analyzed by the planning department in its management control responsibility. This information is integrated primarily for what are called red flag items, accounts of any major financial or operational performance short of established targets. The planning department then reconciles information sources and considers the large number of major national operating companies or international groups at the level of their own relative impact on Europe-wide results. The analysis continues further into a summary of major orders received, competitive developments, and outlook in the economic environment. These are then combined, with a brief assessment of "soft spots" and highlights, by finance into an open, no-facts-hidden report for the president-Europe, and to the U.S. based parent corporation, with copies reaching all major operating and staff units throughout the large, diversified organization. This provides a fruitful open-management communication process. It is such total information, coordinated through an impartial and uninvolved management controls function, that is the first step in prompting operating heads, international product-line managers, and staff experts to deepen their own analysis. It is in their self-interest to follow through with action appropriate to their particular perspective.

There is also an extensive dissemination process of informal information. Frequent and broad-based management meetings include the heads of operations, functions, and international product lines from both sides of the ocean in addition to the required staff specialists. Quite often these meetings involve over one hundred participants. The control section of the planning function is responsible for the meeting process, including monitoring participation and processing agendas. The central section is then held accountable for defining and following through most action points originating in such meetings, identifying those responsible for assigned tasks monitoring their completion of the tasks.

With this example we have already turned from our focus on action initiation in management controls to the second focus—followthrough on initiated action. A key tool applied at this point is the identification of specific management action programs and their individual significant milestones as a part of the planning process. Such programs embrace those actions of unusual nature the CEO of any local or international operation has to carry out in the forthcoming first plan year. They relate to major issues in business expansion, adaptation of facilities, product development, cost reduction, reorganization, and the like. The selection and formulation of such programs involve judgment, and they require close cooperation with the companies and groups concerned. These major programs are identified by each manager as a focal point in his business plan summary. They are analyzed and compared with the total intentions documented in the plan, with both the planning and management controls aspects in mind. They are finalized after plans have been put to bed and budgets established in the manager's first monthly letter in January of the new year. They are then incorporated in worldwide computer programs through the U.S. based operations staffs function. They thus provide a new link in the management information system and are monitored monthly through the management controls function at the planning department in Europe, based on telex reporting from all department heads against the established critical milestones.

One other major example of action followthrough of the management controls function concerns monitoring contingency plans. Contingency plans are selectively established where, as part of the review of completed business plans, specific internal or external risks have been identified. These include some of the following: (1) economic downturns in any country or industry; (2) competitive moves or possible failures to create required new product developments to counter competition; (3) important orders that may thus not materialize; (4) quality problems causing high reject rates or necessary reworking; (5) production bottlenecks known to exist or likely to occur that cannot be overcome as quickly as called for in the plans; (6) unmet cost projections or offsetting price increases that cannot be fully imposed on the customers.

Such contingency plans should follow a set procedure and be submitted at the beginning of the current year. Their preparation is the responsibility of the business planning function; but the followthrough during a current year passes to the management controls function. The followthrough entails keeping contingency plans up to date; monitoring month by month or even week by week as required by indicated risks. Risks include identified economic indicators, reassessment of order prospects, production volumes achieved or reject rates incurred, and the outlook for higher costs or lower prices as the months go by.

When such danger spots materialize, followthrough on the implementation of contingency plans is a key activity in management controls. Costs must be reduced to lower levels that correspond to a lower level of business. Aggressive counterattack programs, as spelled out in the contingency plans, must be triggered. Of a similar nature is the development and critical scrutiny of an "early warning system." This could closely monitor the order pattern as compared to expectations and past experience; follow lead indicators in industries of importance; identify those product and market characteristics to which business results are particularly sensitive; and establish an overall account of major problems and opportunities identified in the manager's business plan and monthly reports. To crystallize management information and to achieve the determination and initiation of commensurate action programs long before adverse events strike is the ultimate goal of management controls.

One last, important area must be mentioned. In large, complex, multi-product or multinational operations, the most critical activity in management controls lies in the coordination of the diverse planning activities themselves. While business plans are all-encompassing, planning at the more specialized functional, product line, and operational levels is usually carried on within their own, often independent, framework. Product plans, for example, monitored through the marketing department, will have to line up with product line plans that form part of the overall business plans. A difficulty exists because their review cycle is often different. They certainly differ in scope, focusing first on development, pilot production, and market introduction. They differ also in the span of the product's life cycle of maybe a year or two in fashion-oriented consumer goods or twenty and thirty years for basic commodities or long-life systems such as telecommunication cables.

In similar fashion, technical development projects have their own targets, problems, and setbacks, with their own milestones, cost objectives, and aims to meet required specifications. Parallel to this but usually broader in scope are major capital investments, often serving multiproduct facilities or equipment, automation required to reach broad new economies, or common service facilities such as office buildings or warehouses. To bring these vital activities fully in step with one another is a difficult process indeed. Typically, these activities overlap in complex operations. The management process is not schematic. As an ongoing vital human process, it will often generate repetitive information, unclear focus for action, and moves that do not fully complement each other or that may even contradict each other. The management controls function has here an integrating responsibility of increasing significance. As management controls reach full maturity, this synthesis will also have to encompass required coordination among related management activities that are organized independently, such as project management established for particular undertakings across divisional or functional lines and across country borders or task force management as it is applied particularly in large conglomerate or multinational corporations to provide effective trouble-shooting in a multitude of different operating environments.

EXERCISE 11

This and every exercise is intended to form the basis for a part of the term project: Prepare a strategic plan for an organization of your choice. For each exercise, present a typed, one-page report, showing directions your analysis will take.

For this exercise show how your company will control its planning activities and how it will insure that plans are translated into action. Show checklists.

In addition to the material of this chapter, the following references are pertinent: King and Cleland (1978), chapter 15; Steiner (1969), chapter 11.

REFERENCES

Anthony, R. N.; Dearden, J.; and Vancil, R. F. *Management Control Systems: Text, Cases and Readings*. Homewood, Ill.: Irwin, 1972. P. 8.

King, William R., and Cleland, David I., *Strategic Planning and Policy*. New York: Van Nostrand Reinhold, 1978.

Steiner, George A. *Top Management Planning*. New York: Macmillan 1969.

Chapter 12

Strategic Planning and Management Science

To some extent, management science has joined the ranks of art or of pornography; we know it when we see it, but we cannot define it. The subjects covered are too many to help. In recent issues of *Management Science,* we find articles on advertising, finance, inventory, and production scheduling. Topics are not necessarily quantitative. We find references to consumer behavior, leadership, learning, organization design, and planning horizons. Techniques proposed are not new. We find linear programming, dynamic programming, simulation, Markov analysis, cost benefit analysis, and input-output models discussed year after year. To a large extent, management science and operations research are synonymous. Perhaps an acceptable definition would be: Management science is the application of analytical or mathematical tools to the solution of management problems; it is often supported by the computer.

The essential factor in business is profit. No company can improve the environment, provide social uplift, and give its employees security if it is bankrupt. A firm can survive only if it carefully plans each step for the future.

Developing plans and strategy that are consistent, meaningful, and daring—yet not foolhardy—is no easy task. With business becoming increasingly complex, with governmental and social demands increasing, and with time available for decision making decreasing, the executive's only hope is to take advantage of the computer-based management science aids now available.

No one will deny that some of the best planning has been done with soft pencils and yellow pads. Particularly as companies grow larger, there are many helpful things that can be achieved better on a computer. There are some things that can be done only on a computer.

However, the formalization of a detailed planning process must be done with great care. In those situations where thoughts and ideas are more important than figures and blueprints, an overcomputerized planning process may lead to excessive delegation and to stereotyped planning documents devoid of inspiration, innovation, or intuition. As shown in figure 12.1, management science cannot create something out of nothing. The dotted feedback line suggests, however, that when planning inputs are poor, management science may offer routes for improving them.

The sophisticated executive must know how to use mathematical models to supplement and augment his managerial abilities. In the following sections, after providing ideas on how management science must fit into an organization, we give several detailed examples of management science applications. Naturally, these are only illustrative. The field of management science is too broad even to hint at all of its potential directions. Management science is also heavily represented in chapter 8, economic forecasting; chapter 9, information systems; and chapter 13, functional planning.

ORGANIZATIONAL CONSIDERATIONS

Mintzberg (1976) has pointed out that managers and management scientists think differently. The explanation may be physiological; the left hemisphere of the brain handles logical thinking (management science) and the right handles emotion (management). Some brilliant management scientists have no ability to handle organizational politics, while other, politically adept individuals cannot understand the simplest elements of management science. The situation is summarized by the well-known personality typology of Jung, as displayed in figure 12.2. People tend to fall into either a thinking or feeling category and into either a sensing or intuition category. This results in the four quadrants of the figure.

The stereotype of a management scientist is a person who prefers thinking to feeling or emotion. He avoids intuition in favor of things that can be sensed. This places him in the upper left-hand quadrant of the figure. In contrast, the executive stereotype relies on intuition and feeling, so that the remaining three quadrants are his domain. Mitroff (1974) notes that a management composed solely of sensation types may be too limited and bound by current facts; it has a short planning horizon. On the other hand, a management composed solely of intuition types tends to live in the future and fails to pay proper attention to the present. He emphasizes that there is no one best personality type.

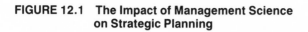

**FIGURE 12.1   The Impact of Management Science
on Strategic Planning**

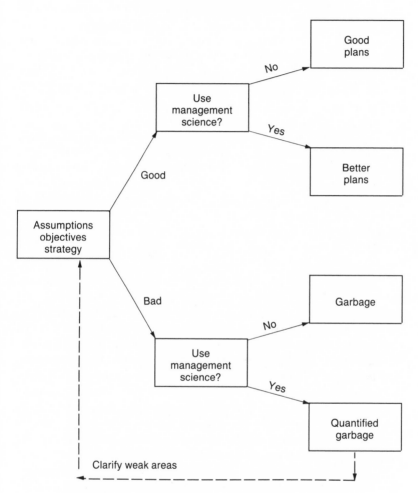

No individual exists entirely with one quadrant. In order to acquire a balanced strategic planning capability, management scientists should expand their interests and techniques into all quandrants. The chief executive officer (CEO) who bears ultimate responsibility for all aspects of his organization must develop an appreciation for the tools of management science if that appreciation is lacking.

Figure 1.5 in chapter 1 has given us the basic organizational chart for

FIGURE 12.2   The Jungian Typology Applied to Strategic Planning

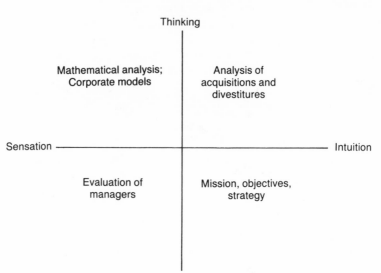

planning. Creating a balanced planning organization requires the same insights needed to create any balanced organization. The astute CEO should select his number-two man to provide abilities that he lacks. Similarly, he must ensure that the chief planner and the assistant chief planner not only balance him (the CEO) but also each other with regard to the cold logic of management science versus the abilities of intuition and feeling.

STRATEGIC PLANNING MODEL DESIDERATA

The use of computer models in strategic planning has followed the growth of the systematic and quantitative five-year and eight-year plans. Models make the implications of strategic assumptions easy to explore. Models deal with complex interactions and masses of data. They show how local decisions affect the whole, thus facilitating coordination. They give meaning to the risk and timing consequences of alternative actions. Using models allows one to understand corporate sensitivities to internal and external variables.

On the other side of the coin, this relatively new tool has demonstrated certain drawbacks. Models are expensive. Many have taken excessive time to develop. Data requirements are sometimes extensive and unrealistic. Models do not always represent business realities properly. Often, models are inflexible. As a result, many models are cut and simplified from their original format, many are used in a different context from that intended, many are used infrequently, and many are discarded before any profitable use has been gained from them.

There are a number of guidelines which will help develop a successful strategic model. While these points apply to any model, tactical or strategic, it is well to review them each time a model is proposed. One should verify that there are no undesirable elements that would tend to place the particular strategic model at a disadvantage. There is much literature devoted to such desiderata (Hammond, 1974; Harrison, 1976; Holloway and Jones, 1975; Jones, 1970; Kotler, 1970; Meyer, 1976; Naylor, 1973; and Russel et al., 1967). The guidelines are:

- Get the involvement and active participation of both the people experienced in model development and the people intimately familiar with the application areas. It is a great help to have a powerful advocate.
- Use a stepwise approach. Divide the overall project into discrete segments that can be used individually as stand-alone units.
- The system should be simple. Building in the flexibility to solve every problem requires a long developmental period and it creates a tool that is costly to run, difficult to maintain, and vulnerable to error.
- Calculations should be done in preprocessor and postprocessor programs. The model itself should not be used as an accounting tool.
- Educate users of the system. Each should understand the function of the system, how his individual department's activities are represented in it, and how the description and data from his department are used.
- Establish a scheduled data maintenance procedure. Select individuals to be responsible for its implementation on a routine basis.
- Permit rapid exploration and evaluation of planning strategies by using a fully integrated computer system, but allow manual override at any desired points.
- Minimize manual data-input effort. The input data format should be simple, easy to understand, and to use. It should be applications oriented. Data tables should differ only slightly, if at all, from those normally familiar to departmental personnel.
- The system should permit and encourage innovation. The model should be tractable and easy to expand, change, or contract.
- Consider whether a model should be interactive. Boulden and Buffa (1970), for example, say that a manager will be eager to use a com-

puter in decision making if it is fast, economical, and easy to work with. We have difficulty visualizing a CEO sitting at a computer terminal, but let us broaden the definition of interactive. We know of cases where management groups have asked a question of a linear programming model and have gotten the answer from the model during a morning meeting. In this sense we agree that an interactive capability is essential.

- Have the ability to work backward to determine input requirements to fit a desired goal, as discussed by Power (1975).
- Work with the social side of decisions. Be able to delay problem definition and avoid freezing goals till the last minute. Allow policy changes. In short, keep flexible (Jones, 1970).

These guidelines may be summarized into an easily remembered acronym, which we call the SEE principle.

The SEE Principle

*S*tart simple / *E*xpand stepwise / *E*nd development

Start Simple. John Little (1970) says, "The manager carries responsibility for outcomes. . . . We should not be surprised if he prefers simple analysis that he can grasp . . . to a complex model whose assumptions may be partially hidden. . . ."

Activities in model building fall naturally into four classes. All are best kept as simple as possible, and a project may be killed by undue complexity in any class.

1. Recognition that problem definition, data collection, and model development are interdependent.
2. Insistence on an "optimum" solution instead of accepting the best solution that is administratively feasible may be unwise.
3. In the validation phase, the model builder must rigorously attempt to destroy the model. Naturally, a complex model will be less apt to survive.
4. Subordination of all other aspects of a model to successful implementation.

Obviously, extreme simplicity would contribute nothing. What is desired is a model giving the broad picture seen from the top of the company. Later, more detail can be added stepwise, hopefully by management request. By using this approach, a working model is always available.

Most managers regularly work with pro forma sheets. A simple model can be an automated pro forma generator, easy for managers to understand, enormously useful for decision making, and highly likely to pay off.

Expand Stepwise. John Little also says, ''The best approach is to lead the potential user through a sequence of models of increasing scope and complexity. . . . Often, a user, having learned a simple model, will start to ask for just the additional considerations found in the advanced models.''

It is always good practice to get a simple model up and running quickly. Use it to skim off the cream of benefits and to permit management familiarization. After managers like what they are getting and understand that it was developed at low cost, then and only then consider expanding into the next step of complexity. Avoid the tendency to err in the direction of too much machinery and too minute detail.

End Development. The law of diminishing returns (the Pareto principle) tells us that additional development steps become harder and harder to justify. At some point a judgment must be made and the model frozen for usage over a significant period of time—say a year or two. This is not to say that the model cannot continue to reflect the changing conditions of the real world. The capability to represent acquisitions, disinvestments, and other business manipulations must be included in the flexibility of the model in all of its forms.

LINEAR PROGRAMMING

This section will explore the present place of linear programming in strategic planning and will show what that role could potentially become. The general feeling to date is that linear programming has at best a limited application; it is regarded as an operational and not a strategic tool (Naylor, 1973). Yet there is some evidence to the contrary. We do not regard linear programming as a cure-all or as a technique that should be forced into every problem.

A few ground rules should be laid out. First, we limit the discussion to the ordinary garden variety of linear programming (LP). While mathematical programming includes many variants such as quadratic programming, integer programming, mixed integer programming, and fractional programming (for example, Glover 1975; Schnaible, 1976; and Steuer, 1976), these are neither necessary or desirable as components of a strategic planning system. LP is well understood. It is supported by highly efficient computer packages; data is easily inserted into the model; output reports are readily generated in management formats; and FORTRAN can be used without difficulty to interface intermediate or special programs.

Our second ground rule would restrict the use of the word *model* to the case of a corporate model, where interrelated operations and decisions are under consideration. Examples would be the simulation model described by Gershefski (1969), "probably the largest and most complex corporate model yet developed" (as of 1969), or the LP model described by Newby (1969). It is impossible to calculate such models by a team of men manually within any realistic time (i.e., years). In precomputer days, it required the author and an assistant two weeks to solve manually a set of twenty simultaneous equations, and solution time increases faster than the square of the number of equations. Current models can easily include one thousand equations. Techniques for prediction (Chesshire and Surrey 1975) or calculative programs that one should "check manually to understand" (Zettergren 1975) are thus ruled out of our use of the word *model*. There is no restriction, however, on what algorithms are allowable (Gols 1976; Grinyer and Wooller 1975).

From this overview there appears to be no justification for avoiding the use of LP in strategic planning, indeed, the reverse may be the case. We next explore why LP may have gotten its bad name, and we examine some of the particular criticisms of LP.

Why Is LP Not Regarded as a Strategic Tool?

There are a number of reasons why linear programming has been stereotyped as an operating or tactical tool.

One school of thought is reluctant to concede that any model is useful and dwells on past failures (Allio and Randall 1976; Hayes and Nolan 1974; Naylor 1973). The most spectacular failure (Gershefski 1968, 1969) was not a LP model. However, LP models are thought of as big models therefore, "watch out!"

LP is generally conceded to be useful in operations or tactics. It is therefore doubted if it can be good in strategic planning. This stereotype (Naylor 1973) is based on the descriptions of successful tactical models (Aarvik and Randolph 1975; Newby 1969; and others). Some say the same model can be used both in strategy and tactics (Harrison 1976), while others say it cannot (Newby 1969).

Even when linear programming is presented as a corporate or long-range model (Naylor 1976; Naylor and Mansfield 1976; Naylor and Schauland 1976a, 1976b; Vandorffy 1973), it may be apparent to the informed reader that it is used in an operating context. The implication is that LP is misapplied.

It is apparent from some of the reports that LP applications have strategic implications: capital investment allocations (Mellen 1970), optimum plant location (Stobaugh 1969), and decay of advertising effectiveness over time (Thomas 1971).

LP is not fully understood. In spite of excellent early expositions of LP (Rapoport and Drews 1962, for example), we still find naive and elementary explanations of the technique in the literature (Culhan et al. 1975).

Frequently Cited Objections to LP

1. In linear programming, an objective function must be chosen. Wood (1970) says, "We rejected the use of mathematical programming techniques because of the difficulty of establishing meaningful objective functions. The attempt to find a precise mathematical optimum for a problem whose objectives are very ill defined has not seemed particularly useful." Others also find the choice of fixed objectives distasteful (Jones 1970). Goal programming also encounters the same objection.

On the positive side, it has been suggested (Edge 1970; Holloway 1974; Holloway and Jones 1975) that the major reason for using LP is less to attain optimization than to permit precise control of all quantities and interrelationships, to allow study of changing and easing restraints, and to use other incidental information. It is useful, for instance, to carry a number of objective functions simultaneously in a model. One must be specified as the primary objective function for a particular run, but the value of all the others is calculated and the results can be studied by the planner.

2. There is an "illusion of optimality" (Jones 1970) in LP. Most of the comment for 1 applies here also.

3. The user is forced to understand raw LP output reports. Unfortunately, this attitude is fostered even by some proponents of LP (Allen 1974). It is not necessary for any manager to see any input or output report in any style other than the normal report format traditionally used in his company.

4. LP is costly. This is not true. On one occasion we had two models that did the same job. One was simulation and one was LP. Either could use the same output report writer. Simulation was marginally cheaper for running one or two cases, but LP cost less when a longer list of cases had to be explored.

5. Contrary to some opinion, the flexibility of an LP model is greater than that of a simulation model, particularly when a matrix generator is used. The matrix generator permits rapid changes in matrix structure and permits the planner to control the matrix structure without the time-consuming step of computer programming. The generator should be data oriented, that is, the presence of data controls whether the matrix structure is generated.

6. Another criticism is that LP is too complicated. The critics have possibly been frightened before looking at the facts. Simulation models can be very complicated (Gershefski 1968, 1969), but much effort has been expended to make LP user oriented (Holloway 1974, 1976).

7. There is time lag in obtaining LP results. We have already cited the return of LP results within a morning management meeting. Although we have heard of an LP system being controlled and interrogated from a computer terminal on an interactive basis, we do not recommend this approach. For an LP model and a simulation model of the same size, doing the same job, there should be no difference in time response.

8. The real world is not linear. True, but one of the most nonlinear systems imaginable, gasoline blending, including tetraethyl lead octane number response, is regularly modelled by LP. There are any number of ways of getting around nonlinearities when they are significant. As it turns out, they usually are not (Holloway and Bonnell 1945).

9. Data handling is said to be an impossible task in LP. It is formidable but not impossible, and the planner must gear up to do the job (Holloway and Jones 1975). If one is using certain data, the same handling effort will be required regardless of the model algorithm used. One should not compare a simple simulation model with a sophisticated LP model.

A Proposed Strategic Planning System

We now speak of system instead of model in order to include the desirable adjuncts to the LP model to be described. The strategic requirements in particular are: flexibility, ability to develop and evaluate alternate plans and insights, and an ability to balance competing objectives, address related issues, and set priorities. Recent papers have outlined the elements of such systems (Hamilton and Moses 1975; Holloway and Pearce 1982). Some desirable features are:

- One or more preprocessors, with a threefold objective:
1. Accept field data and provide facilities for transforming the data as desired, including the insertion of missing points by interpolation or extrapolation.
2. Provide a printed report of such things as averaged prices, expenses and margins, so that personnel can provide and check the credibility of large quantities of forecasted data without an army of clerical assistants.
3. Provide consolidated data for other parts of the planning system in machine-readable format.
- Automatic matrix generation has become a must for work in linear

programming. In the planning situation, where changes are always required and planners must be able to react quickly to reflect changing conditions, ease of generating a new matrix or of revising an existing matrix is imperative.

- Calculated plans should be saved on disk files together with input data as a basis for printing output reports. The report writer accesses these files and generates planning reports in the format desired by management.
- Provide for graphics or special plots to enhance the planning presentation, as appropriate (Shostak and Eddy 1971). It might be useful, for example, to generate maps on the line printer to illustrate shifting product-demand patterns.
- Different models in addition to the LP model can be allowed to access the data base, with obvious advantages in economy and consistency. Risk analysis could thus be carried out using both the input data and the data generated by the LP model. (See Hamilton and Moses 1975; Holloway and Jones 1975).

PORTFOLIO ANALYSIS

Here, again, we couch our discussion in business terms. An innovative manager in government or other nonprofit organizations, however, might well be able to find applications for portfolio analysis in a nonbusiness environment.

Particularly for diversified firms and for multiproduct firms, portfolio analysis is probably the most common method of analysis of strategy. For less diversified firms, it can be used to analyze areas for the firm to enter so as to become more diversified. The approach is based on developing a two-dimensional matrix to permit the comparison and ranking of different businesses. Any two variables can be used. The most common list of variables is relative market share, sales growth rate, industry attractiveness, stage of product or market evolution, and relative competitive position. A third or even a fourth variable can be indicated on the two-way matrix.

The best known portfolio matrix is the one put forth by the Boston Consulting Group (BCG) and shown in figure 12.3. A detailed discussion has been given by Hedley (1976). Each of the corporation's businesses or divisions is put in the proper position on the matrix according to its relative market share and its growth rate. A third variable can be suggested since the size of each circle in the figure is made to be proportional to the sales revenue for that particular division.

**FIGURE 12.3   The Four-Cell Boston Consulting Group
Portfolio Matrix**

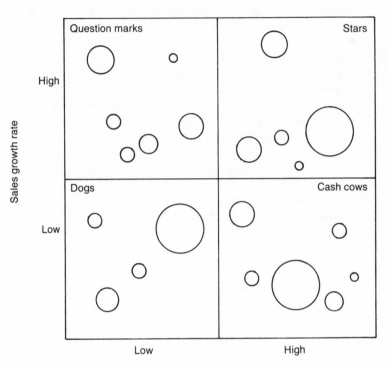

The four quadrants of this portfolio matrix have been christened by the
Boston Consulting Group (1969) as follows:
1. Star divisions have the largest market share in their industry and the
    industry is expected to grow rapidly.
2. Cash cow divisions have the largest market share of a dying or stag-
    nant industry. Most of the effective industrial management science
    projects have been done on cash cows, who have stability, adequate
    data, and market leadership to implement the results.
3. Dog divisions have low market share in a dying or stagnant indus-
    try.
4. Question marks have a low market share in an industry that is fore-
    casted to grow rapidly. Enormous cash flow will be needed to sus-
    tain the growth and at the same time to buy market share.

Classification of a company's divisions is only half of the story. The most important step is for the CEO to decide what strategy to follow, based on the portfolio analysis. An indication of recommended strategies for each of the four quadrants is given in figure 12.4. Considerable discussion is given by Thompson and Strickland (1981).

While the BCG business portfolio matrix has considerable appeal as a strategic tool, there are several shortcomings:

1. A four-cell matrix based on the two-way classifications does not account for the many businesses that are in intermediate positions. All businesses cannot be neatly classified as stars, dogs, cash cows, or question marks.
2. There are other relevant strategic factors besides growth rate and market share. Some of these have already been listed.
3. The variables of growth rate and market share do not always appropriately express the attractiveness of a business. Companies with a low market share sometimes outperform larger rivals.
4. The BCG matrix leaves certain questions unanswered. For example, is every "star" better than a "cash cow"? How should one "question mark" be compared to another?

In an attempt to overcome these difficulties, various extensions have been proposed. Thompson and Strickland (1981) discuss a nine-cell portfolio matrix based on long-term product-market attractiveness, business strength, and competitive position. In this matrix, the area of the circles is proportional to the size of the industry, and the pie slices within the circle reflect the business's market share, thus, four variables are being represented. To identify a developing winner type of business. Hofer and Schendel (1978) propose a fifteen-cell matrix in which businesses are plotted as stage of product to market evolution versus competition position. Again, the circles can represent the sizes of the industries involved and pie wedges can denote the business's market share. Points listed in the stage of evolution are: development, growth, shake-out, maturity, saturation, and decline.

The portfolio matrix technique is a tool that may be useful to selected companies. There is no right procedure; several types with various sets of variables can be constructed to gain insights from different perspectives. The important thing is not to follow rigorous methodological procedures but rather to gain insight in describing the firm's current portfolio position.

EXPERIENCE CURVES

The Boston Consulting Group (1969) have also developed the experience curve concept (Dhalla et al. 1976). When product price is plotted

**FIGURE 12.4   Strategic Alternatives to Fit a Company's Portfolio
Analysis (in approximate order of attractiveness)**

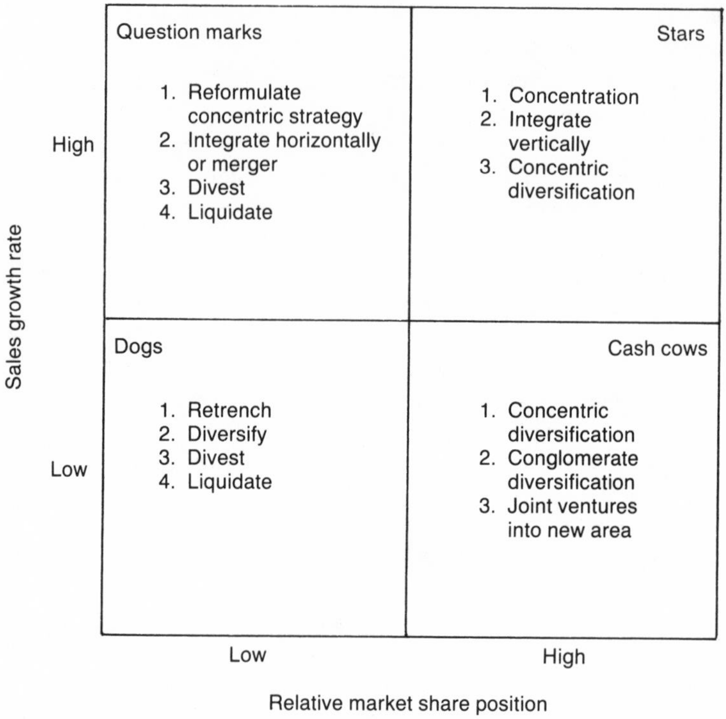

	Question marks	Stars
High	1. Reformulate concentric strategy 2. Integrate horizontally or merger 3. Divest 4. Liquidate	1. Concentration 2. Integrate vertically 3. Concentric diversification
	Dogs	Cash cows
Low	1. Retrench 2. Diversify 3. Divest 4. Liquidate	1. Concentric diversification 2. Conglomerate diversification 3. Joint ventures into new area

(Sales growth rate — vertical axis: High / Low)

Low   High

Relative market share position

against industry accumulated product production, both on logarithmic scales, a straight line results. It appears that over a considerable range of industries, prices decrease by 15 to 20 percent (adjusted for inflation) with each doubling of industry cumulative output. Two examples of such curves are given in figure 12.5.

The simplest hypothesis is that all competitors move down the same experience curve. The firm with the largest market share will thus move down the experience curve faster than a competitor with a smaller market share. It will therefore achieve a higher margin per sale and, hence, a higher return on investment. This hypothesis is supported by two empirical studies on the relationship between ROI and market share (Shepherd 1972; and Buzzell et al. 1975). Various other econometric studies attest to the value of experience curves, for example, see Rapping (1965), Arrow (1961), and Barkai and Levhari (1973).

Again, the experience curve technique is not a cookbook approach, but requires study and sophisticated analysis. There are several caveats. First, before deciding to buy market share on the basis of an extrapolated experience curve, we need to appreciate risk. Second, when plotting an actual experience curve, we discover that unit cost versus cumulative production is

FIGURE 12.5 Two Examples of Experience Curves

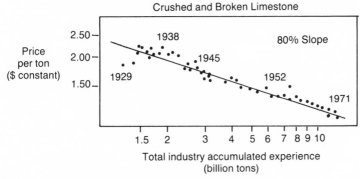

Source: U.S. Bureau of Mines

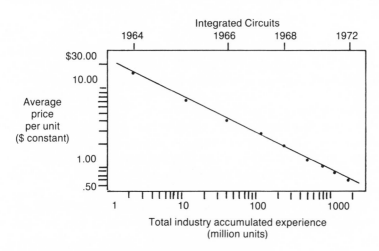

Source: Published Data of Electronics Industry Association.

rarely the straight line that theory predicts. One explanation is that some early production has been omitted. Another explanation is that a product is made and sold in a series of processes, each of which has its own experience curve, and the cost is therefore the sum of a point from each curve. In the case of gasoline, there is an experience curve for exploration, with experience stated in discovered barrels of crude. A second curve relates to production, with experience given as the number of fields produced. A tanker curve is expressed in ton-miles. Refining curves will be in barrels of crude, and in barrels of gasoline produced. Marketing curves deal in gasoline barrel-miles distributed, and in number of automobiles handled at service stations.

Some of the applications for experience-curve analysis are:
- studies relative to buying market share
- studies relative to internal development of market share
- analysis of competitor's costs
- diffusion of know-how among divisions
- control, for example, to compare actual against theoretical costs
- to predict costs and therefore rates of customer acceptance
- studies on the probability of overtaking a competitor

TIMING

At first thought, timing in the sense of being a management-science tool might seem out of place. Mature and intuitive businessmen have a feel or a flair for timing, but none find it easy to communicate about timing. This implies that timing is difficult to delegate. There are three pertinent timing topics: timing within the organization, uncontrollable time, and competitive timing.

Organizational Time

The first aspect of organizational time relates to office politics. Effort may be made to ensure that an item appears early on an agenda, or that it appears late, or that it is tabled for later consideration. The strategic planner usually lacks direct authority, so that favorable consideration of a management-science project may depend on his ability to manipulate these timing factors.

The second aspect concerns investment timing. Andrew Carnegie, when asked the secret of his success, reportedly said, "Buy low and sell high." Efficient market theory (Fama 1970) teaches that this is impossible.

If current information indicated that the current price were too low or too high compared with what it will become, then people would buy or sell in their search for higher than normal profits. By seeking these profits, people affect the price and bring it into line.

Acquisition analysis is an important task of strategic planners. Efficient market theory predicts that stockholders of acquiring corporations do *not* gain. Two studies confirm this conclusion: Mandelker (1974) and Mason and Goudzwaard (1976).

Uncontrollable Time

We cannot predict when the market will go up or down, but purchasing information that competitors do not have may give us some advantages. An ''efficient'' market is defined as a market where important current information is freely available to all participants. Since information is rarely free, a planner must judge how much to buy. One way of buying information is to engage in economic forecasting, as discussed in chapter 8. As always, the strategic planner must keep the big picture in mind. He must forecast things that are of importance. These may be technological, demographic, or perhaps even something as plebeian as the quantity of government regulation over the coming decade.

Competitive Timing

The management-science tool that comes to mind in this connection is game theory, but we are not aware of any examples where a practicing manager has used this technique. Every manager is aware of the type of questions that fall within this topic:

- The market is now too small to support a new plant. Whoever builds first will gain the dominant market share. How long can we wait and still precede our competitor?
- Which competitor will innovate first? Mansfield (1963) gives evidence that in most cases the largest firm innovates first, but under certain conditions innovation may come from a small competitor.
- Takeover of another firm in our industry will cause the federal government to intervene, unless we are the first to make such a takeover.
- If we are to be the pacesetter, do we have the necessary budget and organizational power?
- If we are not to be the pacesetter, do we have monitoring skills and the ability to react quickly?

EXERCISE 12

This and every exercise is intended to form the basis for a part of the term project: Prepare a strategic plan for an organization of your choice. For each exercise, present a typed, one-page report showing the directions your analysis will take in your final strategic plan.

For this exercise discuss the role of the computer and of management science in strategic planning in your company. Prepare an up-to-date list of ten to twelve good references on the subject.

In addition to the material of this chapter, the following reference is pertinent: Naylor (1979).

REFERENCES

Aarvik and Randolph. "Application of Linear Programming to the Determination of Transmission Fees in Electrical Power Network." *Interfaces* (Nov. 1975), p. 47.

Allen, D. H. "Linear Programming Techniques in R&D Project Planning." *Long Range Planning* (Feb. 1974), p. 61.

Allio, R. J., and Randall, Robert. "Planner at the Helm." *Long Range Planning* (July 1976), p. 1.

Arrow, Kenneth. "The Economic Implications of Learning by Doing." *Review of Economics Studies* (1969), pp. 155–73.

Barkai, Haim, and Levhari, David. "The Impact of Experience on Kibbutz Farming." *Review of Economics and Statistics* (Feb. 1973), pp. 56–63.

Boulden, J. B., and Buffa, E. S. "Corporate Models: On-Line, Real-Time Systems." *Harvard Business Review* (July 1970), p. 65.

Buzzell, Robert, et al. "Market Share—A Key to Profitability." *Harvard Business Review* (Jan.–Feb. 1975), p. 97.

Chesshire, J. H., and Surrey, A. J. "World Energy Resources and Limitations on Computer Models." *Long Range Planning* (June 1975), p. 55.

Culhan, R. H.; Stern, L. W.; Drayer, W.; and Seabury, S. "Linear Programming: What It Is: A Case Study." *Long Range Planning* (Sept. 1975), p. 21.

Dhalla, Nariman, and Yuspch, Sonia. "Forget the Product Life Cycle Concept." *Harvard Business Review* (Jan.–Feb. 1976), pp. 102–12.

Edge, C. G. "Financial Models." In Kendall, M. G., ed., *Mathematical Model Building in Economics and Industry*. 2d series. London: Charles Griffin, 1970.

Fama, E. F. "Efficient Capital Markets: A Review of Theory and Empirical Work." *Journal of Finance* (May 1970), p. 383.

Gershefski, G. W. "Building a Corporate Financial Model." *Harvard Business Review* (July 1969), p. 61.

Gershefski, G. W. "The Development and Application of a Corporate Financial Model." *Planning Executives Institute Bulletin* (1968).

Glover, F. "Improved Linear Integer Programming Formulations of Nonlinear Integer Problems." *Management Science* (Dec. 1975), p. 455.

Gols, A. G. "Use of Input-Output in Industrial Planning." *Long Range Planning* (Mar. 1976), p. 17.

Grinyer, P. H., and Wooller, J. "Computer Models for Long Range Planning." *Long Range Planning* (Feb. 1975), p. 14.

Hamilton, W. F., and Moses, M. A. "A Computer-Based Corporate Planning System." *Management Science* (Oct. 1975), p. 148.

Hammond, J. S. "Dos and Don'ts of Computer Models for Planning." *Harvard Business Review* (Mar. 1974), p. 110.

Harrison, F. L. "Corporate Planning Responds to Uncertainty." *Long Range Planning* (Apr. 1976), p. 88.

Hayes, R. H., and Nolan, R. L. "What Kind of Corporate Modeling Is Best?" *Harvard Business Review* (May 1974), p. 102.

Hedley, Barry. "A Fundamental Approach to Strategy Development." *Long Range Planning* (Dec. 1976), p. 2.

Hofer, Charles W., and Schendel, Dan. *Strategy Formulation: Analytical Concepts.* St. Paul, Minn.: West Pub. Co., 1978.

Holloway, Clark. "Developing Planning Models." *Long Range Planning* (Feb. 1974), p. 52.

Holloway, Clark. "Using the Computer in Planning." *Planning Review* (July 1976), p. 9.

Holloway, Clark, and Jones, G. T. "Planning at Gulf—A Case Study." *Long Range Planning* (Apr. 1975), p. 27.

Holloway, Clark, and Pearce, J. A. "Computer Assisted Strategic Planning." *Long Range Planning* (Aug. 1982), p. 56.

Jones, C. H., "Real Computer Power for Decision Makers." *Harvard Business Review* (Sept. 1970), p. 75.

Kotler, P. "Corporate Models: Better Marketing Plans." *Harvard Business Review* (July 1970), p. 135.

Little, John D. C. "Models and Managers: The Concept of a Decision Calculus." *Management Science,* 16, 8 (April 1970).

Mandelker, Gershon, "Risk and Return: The Case of Merging Firms." *Journal of Financial Economics* (Dec. 1974), pp. 304–35.

Mansfield, Edward. "The Speed of Response of Firms to New Techniques." *Quarterly Journal of Economics,* 77 (1963), pp. 290–311.

Mason, R. Hal, and Goudzwaard, M. B. "Performance of Conglomerate

Firms: A Portfolio Approach." *Journal of Finance,* 31, 1 (Mar. 1976), pp. 39–48.

Mellen, E. F. "Capital Investment Decision Models for Public Utilities." In Kendall, ed., *Mathematical Model Building,* P. 59.

Meyer, R. J. "The Triple Track to Successful Modeling and Model Implementation." *Long Range Planning* (Jan. 1976), p. 20.

Mintzberg, Henry. "Planning on the Left Side and Managing on the Right." *Harvard Business Review,* 54, 4 (July–Aug. 1976), pp. 49–58.

Mitroff, Ian I. *The Subjective Side of Science.* New York: Elsevier, 1974.

Naylor, T. H. "The Case for Simulation Models." *Planning Review* (Aug. 1974), p. 15.

Naylor, T. H. "State of the Art of Planning Models." *Long Range Planning* (Nov. 1976), p. 22.

Naylor, T. H. *Corporate Planning Models.* Reading, Mass.: Addison-Wesley, 1979.

Naylor, T. H., and Mansfield, M. J. "Corporate Planning Models: A Survey." *Long Range Planning* (May 1976), p. 8.

Naylor, T. H., and Schauland, H. "Experience with Corporate Simulation Models." *Long Range Planning* (April 1976), p. 94.

Naylor, T. H., and Schauland, H. "Survey of Users of Corporate Planning Models." *Management Science* (May 1976), p. 927.

Newby, W. J. "An Integrated Model of an Oil Company." In Kendall, M. G., ed., *Mathematical Model Building in Economics and Industry.* 1st series. London: Charles Griffin, 1969. P. 61.

Perspectives on Experience. Boston, Mass.: The Boston Consulting Group, 1969.

Power, P. D. "Computers and Financial Planning." *Long Range Planning* (Dec. 1975), p. 53.

Rapoport, A., and Drews, W. P. "Mathematical Approach to Long Range Planning. *Harvard Business Review* (May 1962).

Rapping, Leonard. "Learning and World War II Production Functions." *Review of Economic and Statistics* (Feb. 1965), pp. 81–86.

Russell, J. R.; Stobaugh, R. B.; and Whitmeyer, F. W. "Simulation for Production." *Harvard Business Review* (Sept. 1967), p. 162.

Schnaible, S. "Fractional Programming." *Management Science* (Apr. 1976), p. 858.

Shepard, William. "The Elements of Market Structure." *Review of Economics and Statistics* (Feb. 1972), pp. 25–37.

Shostak, K., and Eddy, C. "Computer Graphics." *Harvard Business Review* (Nov. 1971), p. 52.

Steuer, R. E. "Multiple Objective Linear Programming with Interval Criterion Weights." *Management Science* (Nov. 1976), p. 305.

Stobaugh, R. B. "Where Should We Put That Plant?" *Harvard Business Review* (Jan. 1969), p. 129.

Thomas, J. "Linear Programming Models for Production Advertising Decisions." *Management Science* (Apr. 1971), p. B474.

Thompson, A. A., and Strickland, A. J. *Strategy and Policy: Concepts and Cases.* Plano, Tex.: Business Pubns., 1981.

Vandorffy, J. "Mathematical Models in National Planning." *Long Range Planning* (Mar. 1973), p. 42.

Wood. M. K. "Sequential Economic Programming." In Kendall, ed., *Mathematical Model Building,* 2d series. P. 41.

Zettergren, L. "Financial Issues in Strategic Planning." *Long Range Planning* (June 1975), p. 23.

Chapter 13

Operational and Functional Planning

Strategic Planning is the glamorous sector of planning. Global strategies are laid out, the environment is analyzed and fended off or taken advantage of, and the course of the corporation is shaped for future years. In contrast, *tactical planning* has to do with stating how plans are to be implemented, with the day-to-day operating details, and how immediate goals are to be achieved. We regard operational planning and tactical planning as synonymous. There is not *a* corporate tactical plan in the same sense that there is a corporate strategic plan. At the level of tactics, plans are issued by divisions or functional departments. Because of the substantial detail involved, the various tactical plans are never formally collected or issued as *the* corporate tactical plan.

As the name suggests, *functional planning* is done by marketing, production, engineering, or other corporate functions. Functional planning can be strategic or it can be tactical. Most functions within a corporation would be expected to perform both types of planning. Bradway et al. (1982), Brandt (1982), and Sherman (1982) have given suggestions for conducting functional strategic planning.

Figure 13.1 gives an example of the interrelationships. Because of corporate preferences or industry differences, it must be emphasized that this is an example only. The figure shows that at the corporate level, a historical year and the current year are reported as a base point and that the strategic plan extends five years into the future. The tactical plan is considered to be the first one or two of these future years. Essentially the same situation applies at the functional level. Remember that the corporate and the functional plans are consistent and in agreement, having been developed by use of the

FIGURE 13.1   Strategic, Functional, and Tactical Plans

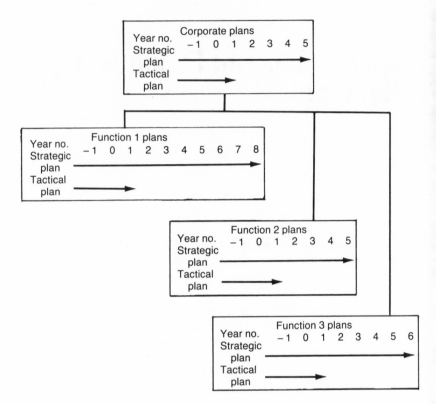

cascade and feedback methods. Notice that all functional plans do not have to extend over the same number of years. In a forest products company, for example, the tree planting division might be interested in a twenty-year plan, while its marketing division could adhere to a conventional five-year plan.

TACTICAL PLANNING

Tactics are plans that extend for no more than two years, usually for a year or less. They tend to be functionally specialized and are found at the lower level of the hierarchy of planning processes. Tactical planning can never be the starting point for strategic planning. To appreciate this, recall the old aphorism: "If you don't know where you are going, any road will get your there.'' Strategic planning explores and settles what the organization's objectives are to be, that is, where the organization wants to go. The immediate period of the strategic plan is then taken and expanded into a tactical plan that asks the question, How can the strategic plan be made to work? The process is displayed in figure 13.2, and, as always, the feedback principle is imperative. Each function (or division, as the case may be) conceives of its own strategic plan. All of the functional plans are examined at the corporate level, and fed back as necessary to the functions for changes or modifications, according to the cascade principle. In the course of preparing its strategic plan, each function will examine the associated tactical plans, to insure the feasibility of the proposed strategic plan. It is not meant to imply that there is a formal, stylized recycling schedule, with all functions presenting their plans for approval on fixed calendar dates. Rather, the procedure will be informal, with partial recycling and communication as necessary during the planning period. There will, of course, be a fixed calendar date when the final plans resulting from the informal recycle procedure are due.

We have already noted that there is no explicit corporate tactical plan, which is the reason for the quotation marks in figure 13.2. The implicit corporate tactical plan is the summation of all of the functional (or divisional) tactical plans. There may also be, in addition, tactics at the corporate level, such as short-range plans for immediate action, for example, plans for the purpose of thwarting a competitor's move.

A further factor, which makes the overall process easier than might at first be thought, is that the process is annually repetitive. In an ongoing cor-

FIGURE 13.2   Tactical Cascade Planning

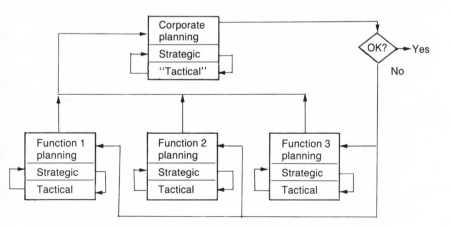

poration, the new tactical plans must be in agreement with, and closely related to, the tactical plans made for the previous year. Just as the strategic plans for a series of years must trace a smooth pattern, so too must the tactical plans.

Steiner (1969) has discussed the differences along various dimensions between tactical and strategic planning. These differences are summarized in table 13.1. Both conceptually and operationally, the lines of separation are fuzzy. Exceptions can be found from industry to industry, from company to company, or even from department to department within a given company.

FINANCIAL PLANNING

Profitability is the primary goal of every business operation. Management seeks a fair rate of return on investment while maintaining a competitive posture to assure continued growth and profitability. Financial planning is the means for achieving these objectives.

In the past, financial figures, for the most part, were used only for control purposes. Today, this function fills a major role in such important aspects of strategic planning as:

- Determining the total amount of funds the corporation will employ.
- Efficiently allocating these funds to various departments.
- Obtaining the best mix of financing.

Computer-based models are extremely useful in this area, and many off-the-shelf systems are available, for example, Financial Planning Simulator (1983). Such models, representations of the firm's physical and financial processes, have evolved to assist management make realistic plans and arrive at effective and timely decisions. Such a tool provides the ability to monitor plans in progress, to view many alternative plans, and to evaluate the consequences of changes in internal or external factors.

Problems to be solved are related to three major areas: investment decisions, financing decisions, and dividend decisions. Each of these must be considered in relation to the objectives of the corporation as expressed in its strategic plan. Clearly, financial planning is strategic in nature.

Capital budgeting, a major aspect of investment decisions, is the allocation of capital to investment proposals whose benefits, of course, are to be realized in the future. It is therefore one of the most important areas of decision making within a firm, because by these decisions the profit-making ability of the firm is protected and increased. A major assumption is the formulation of a strategy in the functional plan, which should be supported by the allocation of resources and the determination of the required rate of re-

TABLE 13.1 Tactical versus Strategic Planning

Characteristic	Tactical	Strategic
Level of management	Lower	Highest
Regularity	Periodic cycle	Both continuous and irregular
Managerial values	Objective	Objective and subjective
Range of alternatives	Limited	Great
Uncertainty	Limited	Great
Problem type	Structured; repetitive	Unstructured; one of a kind
Information needs	Internal; historical	External; future
Time horizon	Short—one year	Long—five years
Completeness	Discrete	Global
Reference	Supportive	Original; innovative
Detail	Many details	Few details
Evaluation	Straightforward	Results evident only in future
Target	Goals	Mission; objectives
Point of view	Functional	Corporate

turn to at least cover the cost of capital. This relates investment decisions to decisions about the capital structure of the firm, which determines the debt: equity ratio. The dividend policy must also be evaluated in light of one of the objectives of the firm, to choose a policy that will maximize the value of the company to its stockholders. The value of a dividend to investors must be balanced against the opportunity cost on the retained earnings so paid, as a loss towards equity financing.

The use of computer models in strategic financial planning leads toward a more integrated view. This is especially true for investment decisions, where it is important to evaluate the impact of an investment proposal on the balance sheets in future years, on profit and loss projections, and on the cash flow projection. From a corporate point of view, this is important because it takes into account the impact of a proposed alternative on all of the company's financial statements.

MANPOWER PLANNING

The statement is often heard that ''people are our most important asset.'' Yet, with regard to manpower planning, the behavior in some companies does not seem to support the statement (Muczyk, 1981). There are three tests for determining the status of a function in an organization:

* To whom does the function manager or executive report?
* What is the salary of the function executive?
* How much strategic planning takes place within, or on behalf of, the function?

In many and it is believed in an increasing number of companies, the first two criteria are satisfactory with respect to the personnel department. The executive in charge holds the title of vice president, reports to the CEO, and receives compensation in line with that of other senior executives.

It is the purpose of this section to explore what can and should be done in the area of strategic planning for the personnel function. Many companies have well developed strategic personnel plans. One such company is concerned with plans for nine thousand middle and upper managers. It makes detailed plans concerning jobs and candidates to fill them for periods of up to fifteen years, the average time required to develop a promising new-hire into a manager. It is clearly not acceptable for an organization to start looking for personnel after the need manifests itself—after someone resigns, transfers, retires, or is promoted, or after an increased work load can no longer be performed by the existing work force.

Figure 13.2 has shown how each separate function relates to the other functions and to the corporate level. Particularly in the case of personnel, interaction with all other functions is most important. Knowledge of proposed operations is a prerequisite for predicting the needed manpower. Personnel can be one of the functions shown in the figure, and there may well be personnel activities within other functions.

Strategic manpower planning seeks to insure that the right number and types of people will be available at the proper places and at the proper times, to make possible the attainment of the organization's objectives over the strategic planning horizon. The situation is further clarified by figure 13.3. Sales forecasts have impacts on each function, as shown by the dotted lines. Various environmental factors also impact each function, as shown by the solid lines. After considering all of these influences, the total manpower required by function and by type can be deduced. After estimating changes in and out due to retirements, transfers, promotions, and other causes, the calculation of net needed manpower is straightforward. This process should be carried out for each year of the strategic plan.

In addition to the recruitment and placement function just described, the personnel department often has other assignments. Where this is the case, additional types of strategic planning are required. Conceivably, the

personnel (or industrial relations) department might have to include the following elements in its strategic plan:
- Communications, including company magazine
- Wage and salary administration
- Employee benefits—insurance, pensions, savings plans, credit plans
- Management development programs
- Labor relations and union negotiations
- Special services—medical, safety, recreation, cafeteria, counseling

To be effective, strategic manpower planning requires a set of data bases, as does any planning endeavor. We have already discussed the need for business plans, sales forecasts, and environmental forecasts in connection with figures 13.2 and 13.3. These elements should include productivity standards in order that required manpower can be estimated from statements of units to be produced and sold.

The organization must also have a personnel inventory, sometimes called a skills inventory, which records facts about its present human resources. Frequently, this will be computerized for convenient and rapid access and maintenance. The following classes of data should be included:
- Personal data: age, sex, race, marital status, benefit plans, retirement year, seniority
- Skills: education, special training, experience
- Special qualifications: professional memberships, patents, honors
- Job history: jobs held, employers, salary increases
- Performance appraisals
- Promotion potential: health, test scores, probable next job (confidential)
- Career preference: desired job, location

Such a data base is invaluable, not only for evaluating the company's present resources but for identifying training and development needs. It will also show where new recruits are needed and what their qualifications should be.

MARKETING PLANNING

Strategic marketing planning will help the firm discover performance guidelines to:
- Profitable marketing, in both good and bad economic times
- Conducting market research as the basis for better decision making
- Developing a profitable aggressive position for a product or service
- Using pricing to offset the effects of inflation
- Readjusting sales activities to meet major market shifts and trends

FIGURE 13.3   The Manpower Planning Process
(executed each planning cycle)

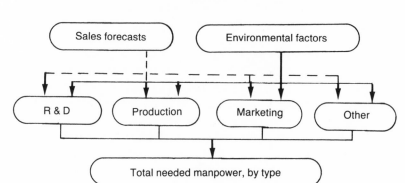

- Boosting sales in the trade and with customers
- Organizing an advertising program, from budget through copy and layout evaluation

All of this is accomplished by the strategic planning techniques already outlined and discussed—select objectives, evaluate the environment, propose and study alternatives, and use feedback to reconcile viewpoints at all levels. We do not take time here to discuss the obvious: define marketing; show the importance of marketing; illustrate the marketing concept; or point out that your firm should be market oriented. These factors are accepted as knowns.

The observations of the previous chapters are relevant. There is no universal way to make a strategic plan. The planning process is simple conceptually but not in practise, and this applies to strategic marketing planning too. Marketing must be considered as a behavioral, rather than a mechanistic, system. Marketing is a complex process in which consideration of human behavior and motivation are dominant. Marketing seeks to motivate buyers—from the ultimate consumer all the way back to the raw-materials buyer and the seller. This complexity provides great opportunity for strategic marketing planners to make more and better use of new methods of analysis, quantitative as well as behavioral.

The contents of a strategic marketing plan are shown in figure 13.4.

FIGURE 13.4   Contents of a Marketing Plan

Data Bases (perhaps five historical and ten forecast years)
  Environmental factors
  Company data
    Markets by product
    Market characteristics
    Expected volume and market share by product
    Strengths and weaknesses by product
  Competitive analysis
    Markets by product
    Expected volume and market share by product
    Strengths and weaknesses by product
  Analysis of future changes in strategic factors, by product and market
  Analysis of problems and opportunities for other functions in the firm to support marketing
  Suggestions for new and important opportunities or problems, based on study of the internal and external environment
Targets
  Mission
  Objectives
  Goals
Strategies
  New products
  Distribution
  Pricing
  Promotion
  Profitability
  Market share
Strategic Plans
Tactical Plans
Financial Summary

The major differences between this and the outline given in earlier chapters is the specific reference to markets by products, to the characteristics of specific markets, and to considerations of competitors. Parts or all of the marketing plan must be kept confidential. And to reiterate, the plan must integrate thouroughly into the corporate plan and must advance the corporate objectives.

Strategic marketing planning is a major responsibility of top management. By the time planning takes place, organizational decisions such as the functions of a marketing manager, the distribution of authority in the marketing organization, and the authority relationships among staff and line managers have been made. One of these decisions is which of the three fundamental ways of organizing marketing is to be used: by function, by product, or by market. As Chandler (1962) has pointed out, strategy preceeds structure. It may sometimes be necessary to change an organization's structure to better carry out a desired strategy.

Market research, sometimes called the marketing audit, is any inquiry that adds to the overall knowledge about the marketing system and the practices, policies, philosophy, organization, and management of a company. It is one of the basic inputs to strategic planning. Any aspect of products, sales, promotions, distribution, channels, pricing, or competition can be covered. Special areas for market research are sales potential, competition, and general environmental trends. Decisions must be made about who will conduct market research—create a special staff, request studies from functions outside of marketing (say engineering or accounting), or purchase the service from an outside company.

PRODUCT PLANNING

This effort of product planning might well be set up as part of the marketing function, particularly since ideas for new products most often originate in this department. Depending on the company or on the industry, product planning might also be conceived as a part of R & D or of production, or as an independent department. Some companies make an effort to stimulate new ideas; others only promote new ideas when they happen to occur. Depending on these factors and on the preferences of management, the firm could recruit a task force to promote and develop each new product, or it could establish a new products department as a permanent facility.

In any case, it is important to have a clear picture throughout the development process of what specifically the customer will be asked to buy. The illustration used by a cosmetics company is apt; the purchaser is buying dreams, not a lipstick.

As always, the usual strategic planning procedures and precepts must be followed. A list of guidelines are useful in addition in the case of product planning:

- The probability that any new idea will result in a successful product is very low, perhaps only 0.01. Factors contributing to failure are:

  poor market analysis   product defects
  costs above forecast   poor timing
  competition   poor marketing effort
  weak sales force   weak distribution

- Each proposal should have an advocate who is responsible for its success. Often, and desirably, the advocate is the originator of the proposal.
- Coordination of different functions—research, sales, finance, and manufacturing—can be achieved by a product committee.
- In addition to the overall advocate, responsibility for each major

phase of development should be assigned to a particular individual.
- A written plan for the development should be prepared. This may contain the equivalent of a PERT chart.
- All procedures in the plan should be detailed, with lists of things to be done and questions to ask.
- Each product is individual, and each may require stylized instructions.
- Communication and a reporting system are essential to keep all staff informed as the product passes through different stages, since certain staff may be involved only in particular phases.
- Finally, the advocate must ensure that the product is actively pursued and does not become the victim of inaction, inconclusive studies, or dormant ideas.

DIVERSIFICATION PLANNING

Most authors show close agreement on the various types of diversification, on why organizations diversify, and on the good points, bad points, and dangers of each diversification type. When a firm extends its goods or services toward the ultimate consumer, it is following "forward integration." If the firm extends itself toward the source of raw materials, that is called "backward integration." The use of forward or backward integration, together or separately, is called "vertical diversification." A well-known example is a petroleum refiner that acquires marketing facilities, oil producing facilities, or both.

"Horizontal diversification" is shown when a company broadens the goods or services it supplies to its existing customers. This would be exemplified by an office copier manufacturer beginning to produce computers.

In "concentric diversification," both new customers and new products are sought; but the new customers have some similarity to the old, and the new products have some similarity to the old products. For an oil company, concentric diversification could include the production of chemicals or entry into the nuclear power field.

"Conglomerate diversification" is entry into a new business area that apparently has no relationship with any of the firm's existing businesses. The only synergy would be that of management skills or other expertise that could be applied to the new business. Some companies, such as Textron and ITT, have consciously followed a diversification strategy. One might suspect that others have become conglomerates without realizing what they are doing, that is, without having a strategy.

Argenti (1974), Steiner (1969), and others have suggested numerous reasons why firms wish to diversify and have also answered the questions about the good and bad points of each diversification type. Our interest here is to present some thoughts on how diversification planning should be integrated into the strategic planning process. Recall the remarks of the previous section, since new product development is a specific form of diversification and could fall under any of the four major types. Note also that acquisitions and mergers may represent diversification, but do not necessarily do so. If, for example, a firm buys a competitor firm that has been supplying the same products to the same markets, it has not diversified.

There are three approaches to diversification: the spur of the moment, the planned, and some blend of the first two. There can be little question that the planned program is more likely to be successful, although examples of a spontaneous approach that has worked out can be given.

We illustrate the diversification planning process by figure 13.5., which is a modification of our figure 1.4. First, in planning year 0, the concept, desirability, and possibility of diversification is a gleam in the eye of the CEO. In planning year 1, the idea is made more specific and more quantitative, and particular goals are added. Perhaps the type and form of diversification are selected here. Finally, in planning year 2, various alternatives are explored, and the one appearing to be the best is selected.

Research and Development Planning

Research often suggests pure research, where a search for knowledge is carried out without specific ideas about how it can be applied. Of course, a firm would carry out its research in fields where there is some hope of application in the firm's interests. The word *development* connotes taking the results of pure research and turning them into a profitable product or service.

Research is done on both products and processes, and the list of relevant topics for a particular firm can become quite large. A petroleum company might maintain a research staff of hundreds or even thousands. The sale of insecticides can lead to the maintenance of an entomology laboratory. The production of agricultural material requires the study of chemistry and catalysts, as does the production of high octane or other specialty fuels. On the process side, there may be the study of special reactor materials or designs or the study of physics as required in the development of seismographic or other exploration techniques.

The amount of R & D done by an organization varies, of course, with the industry and with the firm. A high technology company would be expected to be very active, whereas another company might be low in technol-

FIGURE 13.5   Planning for Diversification

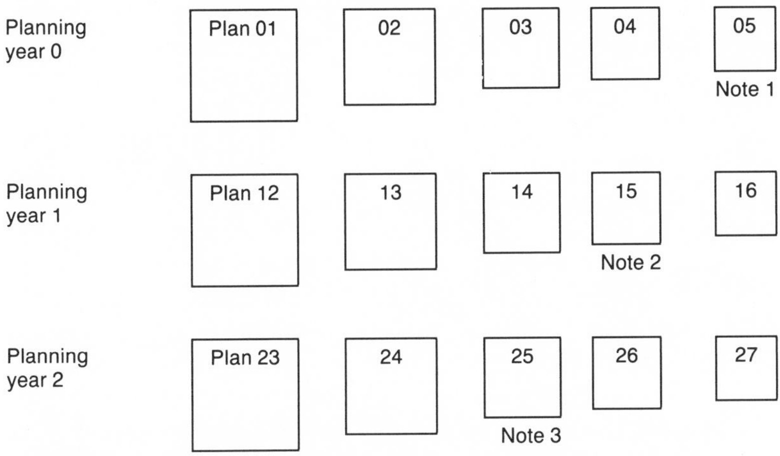

| Planning year 0 | Plan 01 | 02 | 03 | 04 | 05 Note 1 |

| Planning year 1 | Plan 12 | 13 | 14 | 15 Note 2 | 16 |

| Planning year 2 | Plan 23 | 24 | 25 Note 3 | 26 | 27 |

1. The CEO conceives the idea that diversification might be desirable.
2. Quantification is begun; objectives are stated.
3. Alternatives are explored; the best is selected.

ogy and do rather little research. Organizing the R & D effort is a major planning problem for a firm needing to do a significant amount of R & D. Forecasting consumer wants and the needed technology is extremely important. Even the basic step of selecting research projects is complex. The administration of scientists and engineers and the provision of necessary communications throughout the firm requires organizational planning.

The R & D process, displayed in figure 13.6, has many similarities to the planning process. The list of R & D areas shown is only illustrative; there may be others, and some of the terms may be used differently by different people. In general, terms in the top of the box refer to efforts aimed rather far in the future. In this sense, R & D would resemble strategic planning. Moving downward in the box brings one closer to developments of immediate interest, suggesting tactical planning. New ideas can be introduced to the process either in the research or in the development area. At the right of the diagram, we see feedback loops. Both in R & D and in the planning process, near-term results can suggest revisions for future work. It is important that research work is able to stand up under testing and scrutiny. Finally, at the bottom of the figure, the R & D process has resulted in the appearance of an acceptable commercial product. The planning parallel would have resulted in an acceptable strategic plan.

FIGURE 13.6   The Research and Development Process

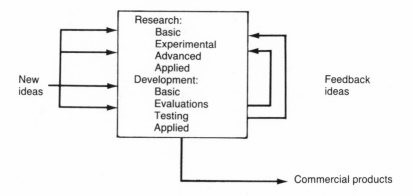

We have left the most difficult question for last: How is the R & D budget to be set? There is no good, clearcut answer. Perhaps each company can derive its guidelines by blending items from the following list:

- Use the industry average.
- Match the firm's competitors.
- Establish the budget at an arbitrary percentage of sales.
- Use the firm's historical budget, with a growth rate set to match the desired sales growth.
- Cost estimate the budget amount needed to achieve specific research objectives.
- Give the R & D department what it asks for and can justify.

As already noted, it will require a mixture of these factors and possibly others to develop a meaningful R & D buget. It should be apparant that the budget must be stable from year to year to permit retention of personnel and to avoid stops and starts in conducting research programs.

International Planning

A company with international operations could also be represented by figure 13.2. The block labelled "Function 2," for example, could represent an overseas marketing division, or it could be an integrated company consisting of marketing, production, and other activities. In any case, we would expect the tactical planning and operations of Function 2 to be more independent of corporate headquarters since they are overseas. Strategic planning must continue to interact fully with the rest of the corporation, but the Function 2 strategic plans transmitted to the headquarters may tend to become financially oriented and to omit product volumes. This is not necessarily so; in the case of a petroleum company, for example, the transfer of crude oil and oil products across international boundaries may be very important.

Planning for entering a new country requires serious study of the environmental differences. The legal system, politics, traditions, education, language, attitudes of people, moral values, social conditions, economic conditions, and so on may offer serious planning and operational difficulties. Often a government may have a national plan with which the firm may have to conform, and there are often laws regarding importing versus local manufacture.

If a firm is considering a move overseas, it must include in its strategic plan a statement of how this is to be carried out. There are numerous alternatives: licensing agreements of some kind; finance and build facilities; acquisition of an existing company; or setting up a joint venture with another company are a few examples.

Finally, the manpower supply must be planned for. Frequently, a company will transfer managerial and technical personnel from the home country on a semipermanent basis. When this is done, we have the expenses of family relocation, moving household goods, home leaves, overseas hardship pay, and other items. The company usually plans for gradual transfer of these managerial and technical positions to local personnel. From the start, recruiting must be done in the local areas for labor and semitechnical people.

There are many other functional areas that might be discussed—manufacturing, public relations, accounting, purchasing, and traffic to name a few. It is hoped, however, that the preceding sections have emphasized that there are no fixed rules in functional planning, and that there are similarities from function to function. Therefore, it is well to pick ideas from all. In our presentation, we isolated product planning as an example, but it could equally well be considered as a type of diversification planning.

In summary, the functional planner must innovate in his planning as well as in his function.

Exercise 13

This and every exercise is intended to form the basis for a part of the term project: Prepare a strategic plan for an organization of your choice. For each exercise, present a typed, one-page report, showing directions your analysis will take.

For this exercise, discuss where and how the split is made between tactical and strategic planning in your company and state the role of functional planning.

In addition to the material of this chapter, the following reference is pertinent: Steiner (1969), chapters 2, 18–23.

References

Argenti, John. *Systematic Corporate Planning.* New York: 1974.

Bradway, Bruce M.; Pritchard, Robert E.; and Frenzel, Mary Anne. *Strategic Marketing.* Reading, Mass.: Addison-Wesley, 1982.

Brandt, Steven C. *Strategic Planning in Emerging Companies.* Reading, Mass.: Addison-Wesley, 1982.

Chandler, Alfred D. J. *Strategy and Structure.* Cambridge, Mass.: M.I.T. Press, 1962.

Financial Planning Simulator El Sequndo, Calif.: Computer Sciences Corp., 1983.

Muczyk, Jan P. ''Comprehensive Manpower Planning.'' *Managerial Planning* (Nov. 1981).

Sherman, Phillip M. *Strategic Planning for Technology Industries.* Reading, Mass.: Addison-Wesley, 1982.

Steiner, George A. *Top Management Planning.* New York: Macmillan, 1969.

Chapter 14

Strategic Planning in Nonprofit Organizations

Throughout our earlier chapters we have apologized for using the words *company* and *firm* instead of the more general but longer and more cumbersome word *organization*. By implication we were saying that strategic planning is good for nonprofit as well as profit organizations; we now make that explicit. In this chapter we hope to make clear some of the planning differences and similarities between the two types of organizations.

It has been many decades since the Kremlin issued the first of the Soviet's studies each entitled "Five Year Plan." These were in no sense strategic plans. There was no feedback and no examination of alternatives. The word *plan* was used in a different sense, that of an assignment for each block of workers, without consideration of the laws of supply and demand. These thoughts have recently been documented ("The Stalled Soviet Economy," 1981).

Even now, only a few of our own states have begun to look at strategic planning. When the incoming governor of Texas in 1979 asked to see the state's long-range plan, he was told there was none. Since then, some progress has been made, but it may be difficult to sell a multiyear approach when there is an election coming up in the short term (Carlson 1982). A useful approach that could be used by a forceful governor would have planning started and pushed soon after inauguration for there to be time to get a program under way.

Other types of organizations have been more receptive to strategic planning. Hospitals, for example, continue to be threatened by a variety of environmental forces, including government regulations, growth of medical technology, health manpower specialization, financial limitations, public demands, court rulings, and competition from other providers of health care. Strategic planning has become an important management tool for adapting the hospital to the changing environment and for directing decision making (Ford, 1980).

Pekar (1982) has suggested some reasons why the growth of planning may be slow in nonprofit groups:

1. In the early stages of development, the organization is single-goal oriented, resulting in little emphasis on planning.
2. Unlike industry, a strong common thread is found in most associations. Thus, most members of the American Bar Association are lawyers. There may be a reluctance to accept outsiders; the organization is regarded as a private club.
3. Some functions are often performed by part-time or volunteer personnel. Salaries may be lower than in industry.
4. It is difficult for staff to take the initiative for planning if the organization is dependent on members, volunteers, and a board for funding. In a nonprofit organization, the one who holds the purse strings also dictates objectives and strategy.

ORGANIZATIONAL CONSIDERATIONS

By far, the bulk of the strategic planning literature is devoted to business organizations, although there are also many articles on the nonprofit sector. The planner for such an organization would be well advised to search the literature for articles on groups similar to his in order to obtain a preview of what differences or difficulties he might expect.

While it is usually straightforward to state the mission, objectives, and goals for a corporation, it is often difficult to do this clearly and precisely for the nonprofit organization (NPO). There is a wide range of types of NPOs. Some resemble corporate organizations quite closely. Others show essentially no similarities. The American Red Cross, for example, fits the corporate mold. There are executives, managers, and employees, all of whom are paid salaries, in addition to the volunteer workers. Some church denominations fit the opposite extreme, with no hierarchy at all. Each member of the congregation, including the minister, has an equal voice in temporal affairs. In this circumstance, the feedback and cascade principles are missing. In the absence of a leader it may be very difficult to ennunciate and agree on mission and objectives. Perhaps strategic planning is not applicable in this situation. We are not commenting on the spiritual side, where the minister is, in fact, the acknowledged leader. Many churches do have a hierarchy, which permits strategic planning. There are numerous articles in the literature discussing planning in churches (King 1982; Wasdell 1980; Hussey 1974).

We now discuss three examples of nonprofit strategic planning; in two of these the author served as a consultant. Although presented as a series of case histories, they should also be read as a series of recommendations.

STRATEGIC PLANNING FOR A PRIVATE SCHOOL

The Heathwood Hall Episcopal School was founded in 1951 and offers all grades from kindergarten through high school. Only recently did the school begin using strategic planning. Figure 14.1 shows the Mission Statement and a list of objectives taken from a recent plan. The statements seem straightforward and without need for comment. As is always the case with mission and objectives, the statements are a guide to long-term, continuing action. Although not shown here, each objective is supported by a list of five or six goals, which give near-term targets as stepping stones in moving toward the objective. This is a good situation, because, as you may recall from previous chapters, setting the mission and objectives is perhaps the single most important part of strategic planning.

One individual under the headmaster is charged with the process of planning. He collects subplans from fourteen planning areas as the basis for the overall plan. This is the starting point for discussion, according to our feedback and cascade principles. One feature of the near-term planning effort is the preparation of a detailed PERT-type chart, showing the interrelationships of all activities that must occur over the immediate eighteen-month period.

STRATEGIC PLANNING FOR A CHURCH

The forerunner of Trinity Cathedral was founded in 1812, in downtown Columbia, South Carolina. The main body of the present Trinity Cathedral building, with its twin towers and pointed arches, was erected in 1846. It was modeled after the Cathedral of St. Peter at York, England. In 1865, Columbia was invaded by the Union Army. When the city was set on fire, the rectory, the parish house, and all parish records were destroyed, but the church itself was spared.

In 1980 the church decided to undertake a formal strategic planning effort. This section will describe the administrative and technical steps taken. The planning process must be regarded as having been successful, because, by 1983, architects had completed their work on a $2.25 million building

**FIGURE 14.1   Mission and Objectives for
a Private School**

Mission

Heathwood Hall Episcopal School exists to provide an atmosphere of care, concern, and tolerance in which each individual will develop to his fullest potential.

Heathwood Hall Episcopal School is an independent school that exists to prepare its students for the highest quality experience which their abilities will allow.

Objectives

A. Given the different types of private, educational institutions—parochial, alternative, and independent—Heathwood Hall will endeavor to be a quality independent Episcopal school along the line of other such schools throughout the country. (That is, small class size and highly trained and qualified faculty dedicated to the philosophy written above.) The school will continue to maintain the most favorable teacher/student ratio possible within budgetary restraints. The school will continue to deliver an education designed to train ethical, dedicated leaders.

B. The school should continue to attract quality students from diverse backgrounds regardless of race, creed, color, or national origin. The school should continue to be affordable for middle-income families, and a sound scholarship program should be maintained.

C. The school will attract faculty regardless of race, creed, color, or national origin and will retain high quality faculty through fair compensation and continued development. The faculty, being the most direct contact with the student body, must agree with the broad consensus of the philosophy, mission, and goals of the school.

D. The school will continue to define the curriculum and maintain an ongoing and continuous review of the extracurricular programs.

E. The school will maintain attractive and appropriate facilities as required for a strong educational program.

F. By setting tuitions and by continuing development work, the school will operate on a sound financial basis.

G. The board of trustees will adopt an aggressive total development program in order to continue to provide appropriate attractive facilities, to provide an ongoing scholarship program, and to support faculty salaries and benefits, as well as special program needs of the school.

H. Continue the long-range planning process with an ad hoc long-range planning committee.

---

program, and essentially all of the necessary funding had been arranged.

The church's first steps were to form a long-range planning committee and to retain a planning consultant. One of the consultant's first activities was to recommend the writing down of a mission statement. Following this, the consultant developed with the committee a plan for planning. This resulted in a statement of the objectives of the committee, shown in Figure 14.2. The title deserves a word of explanation. It illustrates our comment in

FIGURE 14.2   Objectives of the Program and Property Development Committee

The Program and Property Development Committee, a continuing arm of the vestry, shall affirm at least annually for vestry consideration and approval:

1. that the statement of the mission of Trinity Cathedral is current and applicable;
2. that an organizational plan for the cathedral is current and includes, but is not limited to, job descriptions, lines of authority and responsibilities, committee designations and purposes, and their organizational alignment to puruse that mission;
3. that a method and procedure exists for obtaining a five-year plan for program development consistent with that mission by each Trinity committee, board, commission, and organization.

Furthermore, the Program and Property Development Committee, again with vestry advice and approval, shall:

4. spearhead and schedule planning activities within all committees and organizations of Trinity so that annual reviews and revisions of plans are conducted, with the objective of always having a five-year plan for Trinity Cathedral so that it can accomplish its mission;
5. as a part of the above item, cause the appropriate committees to maintain an orderly development plan for the Trinity block, including a plan for better utilization of existing facilities consistent with the five-year program objectives of the Trinity organizations;
6. help to establish the priorities for the accomplishment of objectives both within and among committees.

---

earlier chapters that an organization's objectives are the objectives of its members. It appeared to the consultant that the committee members had a strong and preconceived opinion that the committee's major functions were to promote and to organize a building program. By overwhelming vote, the name of the committee was chosen to be Program and Property Development rather than the perhaps more appropriate name, Strategic Planning Committee. Notice that this is not a critical comment. Such matters are indeed the prerogatives of an organization's members.

Another part of the "plan for planning" phase was the presentation to the planning and program development committee (PPDC) by the consultant of several lectures on the basic ideas and techniques of strategic planning. To accompany the lectures, a planning packet was prepared and distributed to the PPDC. The contents, titled "Planning Packet" and "Steps in the Planning Process for each Operating Committee," are presented in the next two subsections.

Planning Packet

The name strategic planning is felt to be preferred over its many competitors: long-range planning, total planning, overall planning, and comprehensive planning. *Strategic planning is the process of positioning an organization so that it can prosper in the future.*

There are several implications that flow from this definition. First, it is about decision making. It does not deal with future decisions but with the futurity of present decisions. Next, there are long-range connotations. Third, strategic planning deals with important topics. Next, it has to do with the inevitable obsolescence of existing products or processes and the provision for new ones to take their places. Finally, it deals with choices related to the organization itself as opposed to personal choices.

The time span of strategic planning varies according to the purposes of the organization. For some things, like forestry culture, thirty years is not too long. For others, such as dress designing, one year may be appropriate. For many organizations, including the church, a five-year planning span is about right.

The substance of planning is the choices that are made through a planning process. These choice elements of planning were described in table 1.1 (see chapter 1). Not all of those terms are used in the same way by all planners, but we believe them to represent a concensus of best contemporary usage. These decision elements by no means exhaust all of the synonyms and near-synonyms that are found. We group terms like "purpose," "basic socio-economic purposes," and "values of managers" into the term "mission." Policy is a slippery concept that sometimes means strategy, objectives, or mission, and sometimes it means all three.

The degree of permanence of the table 1.1 entries increases with their generality. The mission of an organization may not change in decades, but one must always be alert to the desirability of making a change. At the other end of the scale, projects could come and go in a matter of a few months.

Planning is cyclic. As we come to the end of each year, a new future year is added to maintain a five-year horizon, and the planning process is repeated. Plans for the four old years are reviewed and may be modified. Once an initial effort (now in progress at Trinity) is completed, continuing work is not great.

Plan for Planning. This is the work (now largely completed) undertaken by the Program and Property Development Committee (PPDC). In future years, PPDC will request plans from operating committees, consolidate such plans, modify the plan for planning if necessary, and remain alert to broader issues such as organizational planning or the mission statement.

Planning is interactive. This is illustrated by one of the charts prepared by PPDC, "Plan for Planning." Plans made in one time period influence plans in another time period. Plans made by one committee influence plans made by another committee. Mission and strategic plans may reciprocally influence each other.

Who Does Planning? It is a basic precept that planning must be done by line managers, not by staff personnel. In the church, planning must be done by the operating committees, for only they have full appreciation of the strengths and weaknesses of the organization as applied to their specialties, and only they fully appreciate the external threats and opportunities that impact on their respective areas.

Steps in the Planning Process for each Operating Committee

1. Mission statement. The dean, with the advice of PPDC and others, has prepared a mission statement.

> The mission (purpose) of Trinity Cathedral is to encounter, proclaim, and witness to the message of the gospel of Jesus Christ to Columbia, the diocese, and to the world. To accomplish this we will continue to develop our community of faith through worship, nurture, and fellowship, in order to enable and support us as we exercise our individual and corporate ministry of reconciliation and love.

Any committee work must be in agreement with this statement and must tend to support and further the mission of the cathedral.

2. Background information. A considerable amount of work has been done by the PPDC in assembling apparent strengths and weaknesses, threats and opportunities, and other information relevant to the areas of interest of each of the operating committees. This material is advisory only, and it is now up to each operating committee to begin its planning process, in the course of which it will review, accept, reject, or extend the background material. A summary of the information for each committee is given on a sheet entitled "Committee Information."

3. Committee objectives. This is a "blue sky" procedure. Individually and collectively, the committee must identify its long-run direction and what results need to be achieved. In the course of this work, a number of issues should be considered:

    a. Answer these questions:

        1) What Business Have We Been In?

        2) What Business Do We Want To Be In?

b. Identify major problems and opportunities.

c. Identify major strengths and weaknesses.

This work should result in a written committee objective (or possibly several objectives) of, at most, one-half page in length.

4. Committee goals. The objectives will lead to one or more goals. These are specific and time based. The planning checklist has been prepared to assist in this work. Detailed work and thinking about goals may suggest the need for a revision in committee objectives (planning is interactive).

5. Planning documents. The assemblage of all committee objectives statements become the statement of objectives for Trinity Cathedral. The assemblage of all committee goals, together with the listed resources and requirements and the calendar of target dates suggested in the planning checklist, become the detailed five-year plan for Trinity Cathedral. This is the document which is the starting point for consideration by a planning architect, and for other implementation phases.

6. Implementation. As suggested in the planning checklist, short-term action may begin as each such activity is identified. After the five-year plan is assembled and approved, each committee is encouraged and authorized to carry out its plan.

7. Review and evaluation. In future years, this should be an early part of the planning cycle. Ask: Did we achieve our goals? What went right? What went wrong? Are we moving toward our objective?

Planning Checklist for Each Committee

1. Name a specific goal. (The committee may have several goals. Use a separate sheet for each one.)

2. List strengths and resources (S&R) pertaining to this goal.

3. What immediate action can be taken using these S&R to show at least partial results within sixty to ninety days?

4. For the longer term, list what resources are needed (human, money, space, equipment) to accomplish this goal.

5. Against each of the required resources, indicate how it is to be obtained.

6. Provide a calendar of target dates, showing stepwise progression towards the goal.

Summary

The PPDC met monthly with the consultant, and representatives of each standing church committee met more often to prepare the objectives of the respective operating committees. The PPDC developed much more planning information than has been noted here. For example, a detailed church organizational chart, including all of the operating committees, was made, discussed, and revised. Job descriptions of each incumbent on the chart, including the dean, were prepared and discussed.

At the end of the planning year, a final report was prepared, including, along with the usual topics, a consolidated list of the committee objectives, each with a priority ranking. At this time, the consultant felt that need for his or similar services in the next year should be very much reduced. He resigned but left the following recommendations:

1. Implementation of the proposals in the final report should proceed after necessary vestry approvals.
2. The PPDC should be set up as a permanent organization, with appropriate rotating membership.
3. As a basis for the next year's work, a planning manual should be prepared. This had not yet been done for two reasons: planning was a new effort, and heavy emphasis on a building program had distorted normal planning procedures.

STRATEGIC PLANNING FOR AN AMERICAN RED CROSS CHAPTER

In May 1978, the national American Red Cross president gave a mandate for each of the chapters to engage in strategic planning:

> As we all know, planning has been and will continue to be a way of life for the American Red Cross. However, as we are faced on a daily basis with an ever-accelerating pace of change both inside and outside our organization, it is now necessary to approach our planning responsibilities as a total organization. The corporate planning system has been under way since October 1977, and we now have the corporate goals for 1979–1985 approved by the Board of Governors. . . . For the corporate goals to become a reality each segment of the Red Cross must establish objectives that will move us forward together. Therefore, I am requesting that each of you begin the process of developing unit objectives.

This document continued by stating the corporate ARC aims and objectives ranked by priority, and gave a statement of forecasted environmental trends as they might affect each department (disaster services, blood services, youth services, etc.).

Several other useful documents were also available from the national ARC. An eighty-eight page document, "Corporate Planning: Corporate Objectives for the American Red Cross" (January 1979), listed the corporate ARC objectives and goals in detail, together with measurement indexes for each, and names of the accountable and collaborating units. The purpose of this report was to illustrate objectives and goals and to encourage each unit to restate local-level objectives and goals. It permitted each unit to determine tasks, events, and the budget necessary to achieve the corporate objectives. Another pamphlet was "Comprehensive Chapter Planning: Introduction and Guidelines" (November 1979), a nineteen-page bulletin giving an introductory guide to strategic planning. It covered, among other things, the feedback concept, the overall process of planning, and a recommended series of action steps. The manual also related corporate to chapter objectives. A third publication was the "Chapter Performance Review" (February 1980), a twenty-nine page set of blank action-plan worksheets. It too gave a checklist of planning questions by department, with space for noting off priority ratings.

A long range planning committee (LRPC) was formed in the Columbia, South Carolina, chapter of the ARC, with membership drawn from each of the operating committees and from the chapter administration. It consisted of both volunteer and paid workers. The first activity was to set up the planning timetable shown in table 14.1. This drew heavily on the ARC guidelines already described and required the LRPC members to go back to their operating committees for considerable detailed work and information collecting.

The LRPC met monthly throughout the year. Its continuing strategy was to outline the needed detail in the planning work to be done by the various operating committees. Throughout the planning year, the committee was given enthusiastic support and encouragement from the chapter general manager. At the end of the planning year, a five-year strategic plan was issued as a ninety-three page report. The table of contents for this is shown in figure 14.3.

The introduction to the strategic planning document, given in figure 14.4, carries the important message that the plan is intended to be an active guideline to chapter operations over the period of the plan.

**TABLE 14.1   Tentative Timetable, American Red Cross, Central
South Carolina Chapter, Long-Range Planning Committee**

Target Completion Date	*Goals*

February 6, 1980	I. Set Up Timetable
	  A. Discuss tentative timetable
	  B. Adopt final timetable
	  C. Issue work assignments

February 7, 1980	D. Board approval
March 1980	II. Study ARC Aims and Corporate Goals—June 30, 1978

May 1980	III. Study Existing Chapter Planning
	  A. Present chapter aims and goals
	  B. Present chapter planning process
	    1. Use planning tool A (National ARC)
	    2. Use other planning evaluation tools

October 1980	IV. Collect Information Needed for Planning
	  A. Internal information
	    1. Strengths and weaknesses
	      a. *Chapter performance review*
	    2. Five years of annual reports
	    3. Desirable chapter future as seen by volunteers and staff
	  B. External information
	    1. Demographic analysis
	    2. Project future social issues and trends
	      a. Use *A Data Base for Planning*
	      b. Examine local trends
	    3. Community leader opinions
	    4. Service recipient opinions

January 1981	V. Write a Summary of All Above Steps
	  A. Add tentative ideas on implications
	  B. Full discussion of ideas in at least one meeting
	    1. Summarize at end of meeting
	    2. Distribute written summary for study after meeting

March 1981	VI. Meet Again to Formulate Tentative Long-Range Chapter Goals in Priority

May 1981	VII. Test Tentative Goals with Others
	  A. Internal to ARC
	  B. External to ARC

July 1981	VIII. Final Long-Range Chapter Goals
	  A. Revise tentative goals
	  B. Finalize

July 1981	IX. Formal Board Approval

FIGURE 14.3   Strategic Plan Contents

Introduction
Mission statement
Chapter strengths and weaknesses
Broad corporate goals
National service goals
Chapter goals
Organization chart
Statement of public support and revenue
Summary statement of total expenditures and revenue
Summary statement of expense program and support services
Space requirements
   Present utilization
   Space requirements
Equipment requirements
Vehicle utilization
Present job descriptions in chapter
Proposed job descriptions in chapter (1982–1986)
   Chapter director, Office Personnel
   Secretary, Nursing and Health and Public Relations
   Office clerk, Safety and Disaster Services
   Assistant chapter manager
   Assistant director, Public Relations
   Secretary, OVP–CVS
   Secretary to director of Personnel
   Assistant director, Nursing and Health
   Caseworker, SAF
   Night worker, SAF
   Secretary, SAF
   Assistant director, Safety and Disaster
   Chapter director, Office of Volunteer Services
   Junior accountant
   Chapter director, Community Volunteer Services
Statements of departments
   Management
   Accounting
   Public Relations
   Service to Armed Forces
   Office of Volunteers
   Nursing and Health
   Safety and Disaster Services
   Youth Services

FIGURE 14.4   Strategic Plan Report Introduction

This is the first strategic plan prepared by the Central South Carolina Chapter of the American Red Cross. It covers the five years 1982–1986. It is the intention to repeat this work each year, adding a new year and dropping off the oldest year.

It is not deemed necessary to develop a planning manual, since this document, by example, can be used as a model in future years. We have utilized the American Red Cross bulletin, "Comprehensive Chapter Planning—Introduction and Guidelines," and this bulletin should be reviewed by each year's planning committee.

After formal board approval, this document will be used by the chapter as a day-by-day basis for guiding its operations and implementing new facilities and procedures.

Exercise 14

This and every exercise is intended to form the basis for a part of the term project: Prepare a strategic plan for an organization of your choice. For each exercise, present a typed, one-page report showing directions your analysis will take.

For this exercise, analyze which of your planning difficulties would be easier (harder) if your organization were nonprofit (profit).

References

Borst, Diane, and Montana, Patrick J.,eds. *Managing Nonprofit Organizations*. AMACOM, 1977.

Carlson, Eugene. "Texas and Some Other States Try Out Long-term Planning." *Wall Street Journal*, July 6, 1982.

Flexner, William A.; Berkowitz, Eric N.; and Brown, Montague. *Strategic Planning in Health Care Management*. Rockville, Md.: Aspen Systems Corp.,1981.

Ford, W. R. C. "Business Not As Usual in Hospitals." *Hospitals* (Apr.1980).

Hussey, David E. "Corporate Planning for a Church." *Long Range Planning*(Apr.1974),pp.61–64.

King, Malcolm. "Planning the Deployment of Clergy." *Long Range Planning* (Apr. 1982),pp. 104–11.

Pekar, Peter P. "Setting Goals in the Non-Profit Environment." *Managerial Planning*, 30, 5 (1982).

"The Stalled Soviet Economy—Bogged Down by Planning." *Business Week* (Oct.19, 1981), p. 72.

Steiner, George A. *Strategic Planning*. New York: Free Press, 1979.

Wasdell, David. "Long Range Planning and the Church." *Long Range Planning* (June 1980), pp. 99–108.

Chapter 15

Training the Strategic Planner

In this chapter we discuss training for the activity of strategic planning, whether it will be applied in the role of a corporate planning official or in the role of the CEO. As we have brought out consistently, both take active parts in strategic planning. Most sections of this chapter will interest both executives, but some topics will apply more to one than to the other. Because of the differences among industries and because of differences existing from company to company even within the same industry, we leave the dividing lines to be determined by the individual managers.

Strategic planning is more amorphous than many professions—accounting, for example. To the author's knowledge, there is no college degree in strategic planning, and there is no accrediting agency for workers in the field. To some extent, the strategic planner resembles Gilbert and Sullivan's office boy, who polished up the brass handle of the big front door so assiduously that he got to be the "ruler of the queen's navee." Here again, there are traditions within various industries. In the petroleum industry it is common for many CEOs and other executives to hold degrees in chemical engineering. The author knows of one firm where this is true. In particular, the CEO, the vice president for planning, and the head of European planning are all chemical engineers.

One might have an interest in this chapter from either of the two opposing viewpoints. First, the individual could be interested in how he should train himself, and second, the personnel department or the strategic planning department of a company might like to develop a training program for its employees, either as a one-time or as a continuing effort. We discuss four approaches: academic training, off-site seminars and short courses, on-site seminars and short courses, and do-it-yourself training.

Academic Training

Many people are active in business with college degrees in English, French, or history, or with no college degree at all. Here, we talk briefly about the courses in a business administration program that would be useful to the planner. At the junior level, students usually are exposed to management, with the text often containing a chapter or two on strategic planning. In the senior year, business policy is studied, and there are topics on strategic management with emphasis on recognizing and solving difficult issues—those that arise in business, that must be planned for, and that must be solved. At some point in the four-year course, students will encounter courses in managerial economics, quantitative methods, and the computer. The latter are invaluable for understanding, and perhaps creating, planning models. It is the rare student who assumes an executive or a staff-planning job directly upon graduation, but the courses described will allow him to mature quicker and do a better job when he does reach that level.

Increasingly, we find that entrants into business possess a master of business administration degree. Some MBAs are preceded by undergraduate work in business, some by work in other fields. Typically, the MBA program will include an advanced course in business policy and one in strategic planning, covering material such as that presented in this volume. The MBA will probably not move directly into an executive position, but it is fairly common to hire an MBA for a staff-planning position.

It is not unheard of for a Ph.D. to be either a practising corporate planner or a practising CEO. We know of examples of both situations in a large multinational corporation. Usually, the strategic planning activities of a holder of the Ph.D. degree are in teaching, research, and consulting. The academic curriculum at this level consists of courses, seminars, and research in policy, strategy, planning, model building, and the other matters with which strategic planning is concerned.

Off-Site Seminars and Short Courses

Many organizations offer one- to ten-day seminars on subjects pertinent to strategic planning. Tables 15.1 through 15.4 list the titles, time duration, and cost of some representative ones, together with the names and addresses of the sponsoring organizations. In addition, current conferences are listed in the journal *Managerial Planning*. We have repeatedly stressed

TABLE 15.1 Seminars Sponsored by Universities

Title of Seminar	Time and Cost	Sponsoring Institution
Strategic Asset Management	One day, $890	Boston University Metropolitan College 755 Commonwealth Ave. Boston, MA 02215
Business Strategy	Two weeks, $2250	Graduate School of Business Columbia University New York, NY 10027
The Future of Corporate Planning and Modeling Software Systems	Two days, $325	Duke University P.O. Box 10050 Duke Station Durham, NC 27706
The Future of Optimization Models for Strategic Planning	Two days, $400	Duke University The Fuqua School of Business Durham, NC 27706
Strategic Management in the Sunbelt	One day, $45	Georgia State University University Plaza Atlanta, GA 30303
Resource Management: A New Approach to Corporate Planning	Five Days, $1000	Massachusetts Institute of Technology Cambridge, MA 02139
Industry and Competitive Analysis	Three days, $630	Graduate School of Business Administration The University of Michigan 1735 Washtenaw Avenue Ann Arbor, MI 48109
Long Range Planning through Financial and Market Analysis	Three days, $525	
Strategy: Formulation & Implementation	Three Days, $695	
Strategic Marketing Planning	Three Days, $720	
Strategic Planning in the 1980s: Issues and Options	Five days, $1375	Office of Executive Education The Wharton School University of Pennsylvania Philadelphia, PA 19104
Strategic Issue Management	One day, $300	Graduate School of Business 1416 Cathedral of Learning University of Pittsburgh Pittsburgh, PA 15260
Business Policy and Planning Research: The State of the Art	Three days, $350	

TABLE 15.1 *(continued)*

Title of Seminar	Time and Cost	Sponsoring Institution
Futures Research Techniques for Planners and Managers	Four days, $595	Graduate School of Business Administration University of Southern California Los Angeles, CA 90089-1421
Simulation Modeling and Analysis	Four days, $650	University Associates P.O. Box 541 Princeton, NJ 08540
Strategic Planning for the High-Tech Companies	One day, $775	Worcester Polytechnic Institute
Developing the Corporate Strategic Response Plan	One day, $875	Worcester, MA 01609
Making Corporate Planning Effective	Three days, $375	University of Bradford Management Center Heaton Mount Keighley Road West Yorkshire, BD9 4JU, England
International Seminar on Corporate Planning	Ten days, $2500	Center for Education in International Management 4 Chemin de Conches 1231 Conches-Geneva Switzerland
Strategy and Structure of European Enterprises	Three days, $300	INSEAD Institut Europeen d'Administration des Affaires Boulevard de Constance 77305 Fontainebleau Cedex, France
Strategic Management for Recovery	Five days, $3000	International Management Institute, Geneva 4, Chemin de Conches CH-1231 Conches-Geneva Switzerland
Corporate Planning in Practice	Six days, $600	The Management College
Practical Approaches to Strategic Management: Making Strategic Planning Work	Four days, $200	Greenlands Henley-on-Thames Oxon RG9 3AU
Strategic Planning for Growth & Innovation	Four days, $450	

TABLE 15.1 *(continued)*

Title of Seminar	Time and Cost	Sponsoring Institution
Exploring the Strategy-Making Process	Two days, $295	McGill University Faculty of Management 1001 Sherbrooke Street West Montreal, Quebec, Canada H3A 1G5

the need for feedback and interaction among the various people at various levels who are involved in an organization's planning. Sometimes, seminars present a ''canned'' analysis rather than a sense of the needed interaction in strategic planning.

One remedy is attendance by several members of the same firm at the selected seminar. Perhaps an even better solution is to conduct internal company seminars, thus providing the needed factual information and, at the same time, encouraging discussion among the participants: the CEO or his representative, staff planners, and the various divisions and functions. Many of the sponsors listed in tables 15.1–15.4 will present their seminars at private locations, provided a certain minimum attendance, often ten, is paid for. We discuss on-site seminars in the next section.

Naturally, the content of the seminars listed in the tables varies with the title of the subject to be covered. The advertising brochures describing each seminar quite commonly cover the same topics:

- Title page: name, dates, sponsor
- The need for the seminar and an overview of what will be covered
- Who should attend—a guide to discourage inappropriate attendance
- Structure; what pedagogical methods will be used
- Concepts and issues; overview of the reason for the subject matter
- Workshop leaders—biographical information
- Registration form—blanks for the registrant to fill out and return; statement of date and time; information on local hotels and vehicle parking; other detailed information
- Expanded program of topics to be covered

To give body to the above ideas, figure 15.1 gives the content of a brochure prepared by the author and J. Carl Clamp, distinguished lecturer at the University of South Carolina, in the format used by that institution's Daniel Management Center. Sections on workshop leaders and on registration have been omitted. This would be a three-day seminar.

TABLE 15.2   Seminars Sponsored by Professional Societies

Name of Seminar	Time and Cost	Address of Sponsor
Strategic Planning Advanced Practices in International Strategic Planning Strategic Planning of Corporate Research & Development	Four days, $860 Two days, $665 Three days, $665	American Management Associations 135 West 50th Street New York, NY 10020
Corporate Growth in a Deregulated Environment	Four days, $495	Association for Corporate Growth, Inc. 5940 W. Touhy Avenue, Suite 300 Chicago, IL 60648
Strategic Planning Conference for Senior Bank Management	Three days, $825	Bank Administration Institute 60 Gould Center Rolling Meadows, IL 60008
Recharging the Planner's Batteries Creativity in the Planning Unit, Reinforcing Strategic Direction	Two days, $350 Two days, $550	The Conference Board, Inc. 845 Third Avenue New York, NY 10022
Strategic Reorganization for the 1990s	Two days, $650	The Conference Board, Inc. P.O. Box 4026 Church Street Station New York, NY 10249
Effective Strategic Planning for Your Enterprise Decision Support Systems for Corporate Planners Annual Conference	Three days, $620 Three days, $465 Three days, $660	North American Society for Corporate Planning 1406 Third National Building Dayton, OH 45402
Planning for Global Interdependence	Four days, $250	Planning Executives Institute (PEI) P.O. Box 70 Oxford, OH 45056
Strategic Management: Planning for Profit and Growth in Unpredictable Times	Two days, $895	The Presidents Association 135 West 50th Street New York, NY 10020
Making Strategy Work	Four days, $375	Strategic Management Society Krannert Graduate School of Management Purdue University West Lafayette, IN 47907

TABLE 15.2 *(continued)*

Name of Seminar	Time and Cost	Address of Sponsor
Strategic Forecasting	Two days, $400	World Future Society 4916 St. Elmo Avenue Bethesda, MD 20814-5089
Strategic Planning for Multinationals in the Developing Countries	Three Days, $725	The World Trade Institute One World Trade Center 55W New York, NY 10048
Planning for Productivity	One day, $180	Society for Long-Range Planning 15 Belgrave Square London SW1
Manpower Planning	One day, $180	
Planning for Success	One day, $180	
An Introduction to Corporate Planning	One day, $120	
Strategic Planning for the Retailing Industry	One day, $155	
Financial Analysis for Strategic Decisions	Three days, $530	

ON-SITE SEMINARS AND SHORT COURSES

If an organization is about to engage in a formal strategic planning program for the first time or wishes to establish major improvements or a change of direction in an existing program, it might well consider setting up one or more on-site seminars. It may or may not be necessary to restructure the company; perhaps adding a staff planner will be sufficient. In a small business, the staff-planning function might be a part-time effort by one of the line managers. Certainly the importance of the strategic planning principles covered in our earlier chapters will have to be brought to the attention of those who will be implementing the planning. Perhaps the most effective way to do this is to hold a briefing meeting for these managers after the basic groundwork has been started. At such a meeting, the CEO would explain what is to be accomplished. The staff planner would define strategic planning, what is to be achieved, and the required steps in the process. This would include an explanation of what part each manager is expected to play over the planning cycle. It is well to allow time for general discussion (the feedback principle), either to give more specific instructions or to allow the managers opportunity to have their uncertainties cleared up.

It is not inconceivable that a firm might wish to repeat such a briefing session every year or two to update its strategic planning process, to review newly proposed techniques, or to maintain the enthusiasm of its managers.

TABLE 15.3   Seminars Sponsored by Consultants

Title of Seminar	Time and Cost	Sponsoring Institution
Competitor Intelligence: How to Get It . . . How to Use It	One day, $145	Information Data Search, Inc. The Corporate Intelligence Group Cambridge, MA
Simplified Strategic Business Planning	One-half day, $180	International Association of Strategic Planning Consultants P.O. Box 5198 Akron, OH 44313
Explore Your Options—Executive Issues for the 80s	One day, $450	National CSS, Inc. 187 Danbury Road Wilton, CT 06897
Stochastic Modeling and Prediction	Two days, $425	Prediction Systems, Inc. P.O. Box 276 Manasquan, NJ 08735
Decision and Risk Analysis	Three days, $975	SRI International 333 Ravenswood Avenue Menlo Park, CA 94025
Forecasting Corporate Opportunities and Risks	Three days, $750	U.S. Professional Development Institute 12611 Davan Drive Silver Spring, MD 20904
Gathering Company Intelligence	Two days, $525	Washington Researchers 918 16th Street, NW Washington, DC 20006

Depending on the wishes and needs of the CEO, the managers, and the staff planners, any of various additional seminars might be conducted. Sometimes a one-day appreciation course is useful to reinforce the briefing session. Mission, objectives, strengths, weaknesses, techniques, and other topics can be discussed. Longer courses may be appropriate—three days or one week, perhaps. These might be aimed at particular levels, either executive or staff planners. Even if the seminar were aimed at a particular group, other persons should not be excluded. If the seminar, for example, is for staff planners and is on a technical subject, the CEO or other executives should participate at selected points to provide interaction and feedback.

What is to be covered, as has been said many times, will depend on circumstances. Figure 15.1 gives a general guide to appropriate topics, as does the earlier contents of a strategic plan in figure 7.1. A company may wish to create its own seminar or seminars, or it may wish to use one described in the preceding section and have it presented by an outside sponsor.

TABLE 15.4   Seminars Sponsored by Publishers

Name of Seminar	Time and Cost	Address of Sponsor
Strategic Planning of the 80s: Evolution or Revolution?	Two days, $650	Business Week Executive Programs Suite 4049 1221 Avenue of the Americas New York, NY 10020
Strategic Planning for Information Systems	Two days, $695	The Datamation Institute 850 Boylston Street Suite 415 Chestnut Hill, MA 02167
Profit Strategies for the New Chemical Industry	Two days, $625	McGraw-Hill Conference Group
Strategic Planning and Management at the Corporate Level	Two days, $585	1221 Avenue of the Americas, Suite 3677 New York, NY 10020
Turning Uncertainty to Advantage	One day, $130	
Planning Strategically: The Key to Corporate Survival and Success	Two days, $550	
Strategy and the Management Matrix	Two days, $650	
Business Week's Fourth Annual European Corporate Planning Conference	Two days, $670	
Strategies for Surviving and Prospering	One day, $170	Palace Publishing Ltd 44 Conduit Street London W1R9FB England

DO-IT-YOURSELF TRAINING

There is no reason why an ambitious person should not become a competent strategic planner by a program of home study. There are a great number of books available (this, of course, is one). Other titles are included in the bibliography. After a person has read several general works, he may wish to select specialties in which he is interested—financial planning, computer models, or manpower planning, for example—and study some of the many books on that subject.

There are also home study courses for the planner. Some of those prepared by the American Management Associations are listed in table 15.5. Continuing Education Unit credits (CEUs) are given for each course satisfactorily completed. The AMA is also beginning to issue courses on one-

FIGURE 15.1 Sample Seminar Brochure

Title Page

Strategic Planning
A Workshop for Executives and Managers

May xx-xx, 19xx

Daniel Management Center
University of South Carolina

Why This Workshop

In today's volatile environment, where external and internal factors change rapidly and dramatically, how should a company go about the difficult task of devising a strategy in the eighties? For every organization that grows 15 percent annually in the next five years, another will decline 15 percent. Strategic planning is a practical, straightforward, and flexible approach to assist top management in implementing the strategic planning process in their organization. In case after case, what makes many businesses successful in their superior planning?

The twelve sessions of this STRATEGIC PLANNING workshop show you:

1. What a strategic plan is and why an organization needs one.
2. How to develop the strategic plan—scheduling the planning process.
3. What strategy is and how to apply it.
4. The tools of planning.
5. How to conduct an appropriate situational analysis.
6. How to develop meaningful strategic goals.
7. How to create action and contingency plans.
8. The human side of planning: selection and organization for strategic planning.
9. How to implement and control the planning process.
10. How to monitor actual performance against the plan—a management control device—and the planning document as a communications device.
11. When to make moves and decisions: TIMING is critical.
12. Actual planning experiences.

Who Should Attend

- Chief executive officers, vice presidents, division heads, key functional managers, owner/managers who are or should be involved in strategic planning.
- Senior strategic planners, financial executives and functional planners.
- Team attendance is recommended in order to assure a common perspective of the planning process.

Structure

The workshop will be practical and down to earth, featuring lectures to introduce concepts and tools, exercises for hands-on exposure, small group discussions to permit an exchange with others who attend, and case studies to demonstrate actual experiences.

Concepts and Issues

The workshop will emphasize practical methods of strategic planning. It will offer a proven process to help key decision makers seize opportunities, anticipate threats, and avoid surprises. Throughout the workshop, strategic planning concepts that have been found successful by forward-thinking companies will be presented.

Session 1   *What a Strategic Plan Is and Why an Organization Needs One*

Survey the experiences in planning during the 1970s and look ahead at new techniques and approaches for the 1980s.

The benefits of planning: establish direction; focus action; monitor performance; in-

256

Figure 15.1 (continued)

crease motivation; reduce costs by reducing risks; heighten communication; foster creativity. Organizations that plan significantly outperform those who do not plan.

A practical approach to strategic planning includes:
- Identification of strategic needs
- Evaluation of the competitive market
- Analysis of alternative solutions
- Development of appropriate systems; planning models and the computer
- Organizational aspects

Session 2 *How to Develop the Strategic Plan—Scheduling the Planning Process*
- Starting the planning process
- Planning for the plan and the situation analysis
- Implementing the strategic planning process
- Creativity in the planning unit
- The plan itself
- The planning function should be appraised frequently

Session 3 *What Is Strategy and How to Apply It*
Strategic alternatives; not overlooking divestiture; etc.

Session 4 *The Tools of Planning*
- Technological time scales
- How to assess a company's strategic position
- Role of computers in strategic planning
- Optimization models
- Basic financial concepts
- Planning is information intensive
- Portfolio analysis
- Scenario planning
- Reducing uncertainty about the future

Session 5 *How to Conduct an Appropriate Situation Analysis*
- The importance of determining a company's strengths and weaknesses; internal analysis of the firm; assessing the external environment.
- Identifying opportunities and threats.
- Gap analysis.
- How to appraise the various external environments: economic, social, political, ecological, and competitive.

Session 6 *How to Develop Meaningful Strategic Goals*

Session 7 *How to Create Action and Contingency Plans*
- Strategic plan title page
- Executive summary
- Product development plan
- Organization plan
- Contingency plans
- Plan approval
- Distribution of the strategic plan
- Table of contents
- Sales and marketing plan
- Operations plan
- Financial plan
- Annual objectives; operating strategies

Session 8 *The Human Side of Planning—Selection and Organization for Planning*
- Planning and organization
- The role of the CEO
- Computer support
- Coordination efforts
- Strategic planning in service organizations
- The planning department
- Information
- Statistical expertise
- Line managers

Figure 15.1 (*continued*)

Session 9   *How to Implement and Control the Planning Process*
- Why action is needed
- Evaluating results
- Reinforcing strategic direction
- Evaluation
- Communication
- Monitoring confidence
- Taking action
- Requirements of a control system
- Guidance from the corporate mission and objectives
- Feedback

Session 10   *How to Monitor Actual Performance against the Plan—A Management Control Device—The Planning Document as a Communication Device*
- The time frame
- What events should be monitored
- The problem of gathering data
- What to do when data are scarce
- The data-gathering continuum
- Planning as a continuing process
- Test the estimates
- Monitoring assumptions
- Testing assumptions for the future
- The costs of gathering data
- The use of estimated data and what it means to planning

Session 11   *When to Make Moves and Decision: TIMING Is Critical*

Session 12   *Actual Planning Experiences*

Reprinted by permission of the Daniel Management Center

TABLE 15.5   Home Study Courses

Long-Range Planning Strategic Marketing Planning Long-Range Planning for Marketing Organizations Planning and Control for Managers Financial Goals and Strategic Planning	$75 each; two CEUs for each	American Management Associations Extension Institute 135 West 50th Street New York, NY 10020

hour videotapes. Copies of an associated textbook are also provided. The videotape courses are aimed at small groups of, say, five persons.

The person seriously interested in strategic planning will undoubtedly wish to join one or more professional societies. These societies hold local monthly meetings at which speakers present an interesting planning topic. Members have the benefit of chatting informally with their peers, of discussing problems, and of seeing how others have arrived at solutions. There is also a status value in membership. Finally, each society holds national or regional meetings where prominent and expert planners conduct seminars and present state-of-the-art papers. A full directory of such societies is given in the appendix.

Whether or not a planner joins a society, he can subscribe to its publications or read them in his local library. The various articles keep one up to date. They may suggest new techniques or outlooks or answers to a troubling problem. Many of the journals also contain book reviews, news items, announcements about planning seminars, as well as advertisements for consultants or computer modeling services.

The new planner might also wish to enroll in an advanced college course on a part-time basis. This can be in pursuit of an advanced degree, say an MBA, or on a nondegree basis—just to obtain planning expertise from that specific course.

EXERCISE 15

This and every exercise is intended to form the basis for a part of the term project: Prepare a strategic plan for an organization of your choice. For each exercise, present a typed, one-page report, showing directions your analysis will take.

For this exercise, outline what the training program will be in your company for (1) staff planners, and (2) line managers.

In addition to the material of this chapter, the following reference is pertinent: Argenti (1974), chapter 16.

REFERENCE

Argenti, John. *Systematic Corporate Planning.* New York: Wiley, 1974.

Strategic Planning at South Carolina Electric and Gas Company

Robert D. Hazel, Dr. Ronald Wilder, and
J. H. Addison

Regulated public utilities operate in an external environment that is considerably different from that facing nonutilities companies. Because of this difference in environment, planners in public utilities must pay careful attention to strategic aspects of operating under regulation, in addition to the usual strategic considerations regarding the economic environment. In this chapter, the strategic planning process at South Carolina Electric & Gas Company will be discussed. Emphasis will be on those factors that cause differences in the strategic planning process between public utilities and nonutilities. The chapter will begin with a brief description of the company, its history, and its organization. Next, the evolution of the planning process at the company will be discussed and related to changes in the company's environment. The major section of the chapter will present elements of the current strategic planning process at South Carolina Electric & Gas Company and the relationship of the company's strategic plan with other management processes. The chapter will conclude by discussing prospects and outlooks for the future.

COMPANY HISTORY AND BACKGROUND

South Carolina Electric & Gas Company (hereafter referred to as SCE&G) is an integrated, investor-owned public utility providing electricity, natural gas, and bus transit services in service areas in a large part of the state of South Carolina (see figures 16.1 and 16.2). In 1982, SCE&G served 353,000 electric customers and 184,000 natural gas customers. It had 3,600 employees and a total asset base in excess of $2 billion. Key elements of the

Used by permission of the South Carolina Electric & Gas Company.

FIGURE 16.1 South Carolina Electric & Gas Company Electric Service Area

S Steam generation

H Hydro generation

N Nuclear generation

IC Internal combustion turbine generation

PS pumped storage hydro generation

FIGURE 16.2   South Carolina Electric & Gas Company Combined Natural Gas Service Area

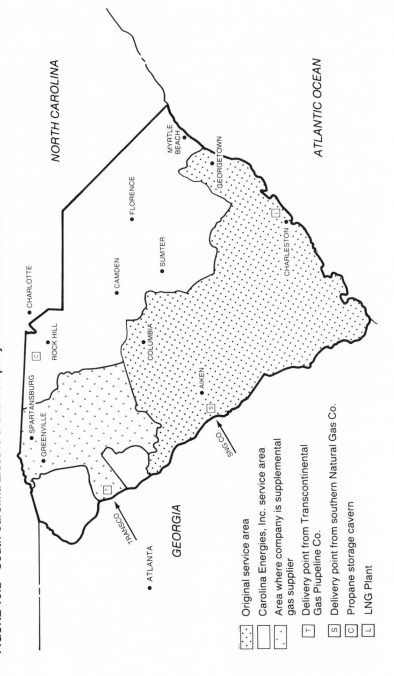

Original service area

Carolina Energies, Inc. service area

Area where company is supplemental gas supplier

T Delivery point from Transcontinental Gas Piupeline Co.

S Delivery point from southern Natural Gas Co.

C Propane storage cavern

L LNG Plant

company's customer base and operating characteristics are shown in table 16.1.

The present SCE&G company is a descendant of numerous ancestor companies, beginning as early as 1846 with the incorporation of the Charleston Gas Light Company. In 1894, another ancestor company, the Columbia Water Power Company, completed a power house, on the Columbia canal that produced electricity for the world's first electrically operated textile mill. In 1930, the Lexington Water Power Company, also a corporate ancestor, completed Saluda Dam, which was then the largest earthen dam for power production in the world.

Following the Public Utility Holding Company Act of the 1930s, a trend towards widescale holding companies in the electric utilities industry was reversed. The primary ancestor companies became independent utilities, culminating in the merger with South Carolina Power Company in 1950.

The most recent chapter in the corporate history was completed with the merger in April 1982 of Carolina Energies, Inc. Carolina Energies is an integrated natural gas company. Most of its activities are related to operating a natural gas pipeline and providing natural gas to residential, commercial, and large industrial users in South Carolina.

As a regulated public utility, SCE&G is required to provide electricity and natural gas service on demand to its customers at a reasonable price. At the retail level, SCE&G electricity and natural gas rates are regulated by the South Carolina Public Service Commission, a body of seven members elected by the South Carolina General Assembly. The Public Service Commission regulates many aspects of the company's operations, including rate base, price level, pricing structure, rate of return to stockholders, and level and quality of service.

SCE&G sells electricity at wholesale rates to electrical cooperatives and municipalities. The company also interchanges electric power with other utilities, including the South Carolina Public Service Authority. The wholesale sales and interchange transactions are regulated by the Federal Energy Regulatory Commission in a manner similar to state commission regulation. Sales at wholesale comprised 6.7 percent of total kilowatt hour sales in 1982.

The economy of the company's service area features important manufacturing, agricultural, and government sectors. The South Carolina climate results in peak electric demand occurring in the summer months and the peak natural gas demand occurring in the winter months. And, although South Carolina is a right-to-work state, some of the company's employees are unionized.

TABLE 16.1　Selected Descriptive Measures, South Carolina Electric & Gas Company, 1982

Electric Department			
Total electricity sales			
Kwh (Millions)			11,490
Thousands of dollars			590,044
Total electric customers			353,347
Generating capacity (1,000 kw)			3,359
Generating mix	Coal 89%	Hydro 8%	Other 3%

Natural Gas Department	
Total natural gas sales	
Thousands of therms	470,398
Thousands of dollars	266,389
Total natural gas customers	184,093
Miles of transmission pipeline	1,653

Total Corporation	
Total investment ($1,000s)	2,411,479
Total permanent employment	3,609

Source: Statistical Supplement to 1982 Annual Report.

In summary, SCE&G is a medium-sized electric and gas utility operating in a sun-belt state. As a public utility, its prices and profits are tightly controlled by state and federal regulations. Since it does not mine coal or produce natural gas, its primary function is as a transporter, converter, and distributor of energy.

PLANNING AT SCE&G BEFORE STRATEGIC PLANNING WAS FORMALIZED

Prior to 1981, SCE&G did not have a formal strategic planning process or a corporate planning department. This organizational fact does not mean that no planning was done prior to 1981; rather, the company's corporate planning before that date was less formal and involved less centralized coordination and control.

Electric utilities as a group were relatively late in formalizing the corporate planning process. The industry operated under extremely favorable economic conditions from the late 1940s through the late 1960s and early 1970s. Steady economic growth at the national level raised per capita incomes throughout this period. Higher incomes meant larger homes and a greater saturation of electrical appliances, assuring a steady growth in residential electric sales over the period. Industrial growth also meant steadily increasing industrial sales of electricity, given the close relationship in the 1950s and 1960s between energy consumption and industrial output.

The experience of the 1950s and 1960s produced a corporate planning environment in most electric utilities that was growth oriented. As a result, there was little apparent need for strategic thinking. The key element of corporate planning prior to the early 1970s was the demand forecast. Because the electric utility was required to meet the demand placed on its system, the planning process started with the demand forecast, which fed into construction planning, with both producing inputs into the rate needs of the company.

As electricity sales grew, favorable technological changes and relatively low interest rates allowed production costs to grow at a slower rate than output. SCE&G's average residential electricity price fell from 2.4 cents per kilowatt hour in 1955 to 1.9 cents in 1970. This decrease in the price of electricity further stimulated demand, and output grew to keep pace.

A similar trend occurred in the natural gas business, with residential natural gas prices in the SCE&G service area decreasing from 22 cents per therm in 1955 to about 13 cents in 1969. This fall in the real price of energy had a similar stimulative effect on the demand for natural gas, and the distribution network was continually expanded to feed the gas demand of new customers.

The planning process during the two decades ending in 1970 began with the corporate mission of providing electricity and natural gas service to meet the demands of the customer base. The generating capacity of the existing plant, in comparison with the peak-demand estimates produced by the demand forecasting process, determined the magnitude and timing of new plant construction over the ten to fifteen year planning horizon. Because of economies of scale and technological change, the electric utility industry was a decreasing cost industry during the 1950s and 1960s. That economic characteristic together with relative stability in fuel prices meant that average cost declined. Rates requests made to the regulatory commissions were for rate decreases rather than increases.

EVOLUTION OF A FORMAL
STRATEGIC PLANNING PROCESS

The orderly process of growth and construction came to a halt with the first energy crisis in 1973. SCE&G's total electricity sales, which had been growing at an annual rate of 7.7 percent in the 1960s, grew at an average rate of 10.2 percent over the period 1969–1973. With the crisis, sales decreased nearly 4 percent in 1974 and by more than 5 percent in 1975. At the same time that electricity sales were decreasing, construction costs and fuel costs increased sharply. The combination of reduced revenues and higher costs reduced profitability and caused cash-flow squeezes for all electric utilities, SCE&G included.

The regulated firm's expected reaction to a profitability shrinkage caused by factors beyond its control is to appeal to the regulators for increased prices. Because of regulatory lag, relief granted by rate increases in the 1970s had already been eroded by inflation. At the same time, however, the extensive construction programs required to meet the demand that had been forecasted based on the experience of the 1960s required continual infusions of new capital at higher interest rates.

For SCE&G, as for most electric utilities, the period between 1973 and 1980 was dark. SCE&G's common stock fell in price from the $33 range in 1968 to the $10 range in 1974. Return on common equity fell from the 14 percent range in 1968 to the 8 percent range in 1974, and SCE&G's corporate bonds were down-rated by the financial rating services.

Although the most adverse period was 1973–1974, difficulties persisted throughout the balance of the 1970s. Yet, there was a tendency for some industry observers and officials to view the drastic changes as temporary rather than permanent. As time passed and good times failed to return, the growing consensus in the industry and at SCE&G was that the basic philosophy of electric utility management would have to change to cope with the new reality.

The new reality represents a change in environment rather than in corporate mission. The major changes in the external environment facing electric utilities include the following:

1. A higher degree of regulatory uncertainty. This uncertainty is related to the increasing politicization in the regulatory process and the increasing importance of consumer advocacy organizations.

2. Decreased predictability of the economic environment. Utilities generally depend on consulting firms and federal government agencies for forecasts of the national economy. Forecasters were less accurate than usual in the 1970s because of international energy price shocks. Energy-demand forecasts, which used the national forecasts as a starting point, are growing more sophisticated in an attempt to keep pace with the variable economic environment. Topics such as price elasticity and load management are increasingly important.

3. The maturing of the electric and natural gas utility industry. As the industry reaches the maturity stage of its life cycle, it faces gradual

erosion of its natural monopoly position. Conservation and the development of substitutes for electricity and natural gas threaten continued growth of sales.

4. Greater resource scarcity. Slower rates of revenue growth and reduced profitability place growing emphasis on the careful allocation of scarce resources.

In summary, traditional ways of planning could not cope with drastic changes in the external environment. Changes in the environment brought new problems as well as new opportunities. The new problems included rapid price inflation, increasing competition (territorial and from substitutes), and a higher degree of internal competition for funds. The new opportunities included the more aggressive pursuit of market share, the search for new end usages for electricity and natural gas, and the advantages of economies of scale and experience as sales continue to grow, although at a slower rate.

The evolution toward a formalized strategic planning system at SCE&G was also promoted by the availability of needed management tools including information resources, computerized data bases, and improved internal communication within the company. Additionally, the management of the company responded to an increasingly hostile environment by demonstrating a willingness to be aggressive in taking on a proactive rather than a reactive managerial philosophy.

ELEMENTS OF THE STRATEGIC PLANNING PROCESS AT SCE&G

In concept, strategic planning at SCE&G involves the systematic identification of threats and opportunities foreseen in the future. These, in combination with other information, provide a basis for making decisions that will allow the company to avoid the threats, exploit the opportunities, and accomplish its mission. The strategic plan at SCE&G is part of the broader planning system that also includes a set of forecasts, an operational plan, and the capital and operating budgets. The strategic plan provides broad statements of company purpose. The planning process forecasts the external environment, analyzes issues in order to identify threats and opportunities, reviews objectives, establishes specific goals related to achieving these objectives, and develops strategies that lead to specific management decisions. Good strategic planning means that the company is better able to identify its objectives and communicate them to its managers and employees, thereby better accomplish its mission.

The major elements of the SCE&G's strategic plan are the following:
1. Mission statement
2. Objectives
3. Environmental assessment
4. Issues
5. Goals
6. Strategies
7. Monitoring

The current mission statement of SCE&G reflects its function as an energy company and identifies its contingencies. The mission statement appearing in the 1983 strategic plan is as follows:

> The mission of South Carolina Electric and Gas Company is to meet the energy needs and energy related requirements of the people and businesses within its service area. To accomplish this, the Company must earn an adequate return on the capital invested in its facilities by charging a fair price for its services, coupled with a high degree of efficiency in its operations.
>
> The mission of the Company implies adequate compensation to the owners and investors for the use of their capital, recognition of an involvement in future energy technology, a leadership role in the economic and industrial development of its service area, and a willingness to accept its share of social responsibility.
>
> While carrying out its mission, the Company recognizes its responsibility in meeting the reasonable and appropriate needs of its employees, its customers, and its investors.

Objectives are considered to be declarations of purpose that express management's fundamental intentions toward pursuing and accomplishing its mission. Objectives are therefore the broad statement of the company's intentions which follow from the mission statement. For example, the objectives stated in the 1983 strategic plan include the following:

A. Financial —Achieve a stronger financial position for the company.

B. V. C. Summer Nuclear Plant —Operate the V. C. Summer Plant safely with a high degree of reliability and efficiency.

C. Customer Relations —Meet customer requirements at a fair price consistent with reasonable costs and an appropriate standard of service.

D. Human Resources	—Improve the utilization, effectiveness, and development of human resources within the Company through innovative approaches and better training.
E. Image	—Improve the Company's credibility; strengthen and clarify the true picture of the Company and its operations.
F. Marketing	—Achieve and implement a comprehensive marketing plan.
G. Innovation	—Establish an environment that encourages different and more effective approaches to Company matters.

The purpose of forecasting the external environment and preparing the environmental assessment is to identify threats and opportunities in order that current and future managerial decisions will be made that minimize the threats and exploit the opportunities. Topics included in the environmental assessment are economic outlook, government and regulatory environment, technological outlook, material resources, consumer and social environment, and human resources.

One of the major end products of the environment assessment process is the identification of issues. An issue is a threat, opportunity, or other future condition that is likely to have a significant impact on company operations. Issues change as the external environment changes and reflect those topics that management is most attentive to at a particular time. A partial list of the issues identified in the 1983 strategic plan is as follows:

1. Financial	—The continuing need for financial stability (earnings).
2. Nuclear	—Operation of the V. C. Summer Nuclear Plant.
3. Image	—The need for a satisfactory corporate image.
4. Regulatory	—Changing regulatory requirements, including environment concerns.
5. Diversification	—Diversification or holding-company opportunities.

6. Human Resources —The continuing needs of and for human
resources.
7. Pricing —The price of our products.
8. Efficiency —The continuing need for improvement in
efficiency and productivity.

A set of corporate goals is the next component of the strategic plan. A goal is a more specific statement of intent, with an emphasis on measurability. Goals are steps along the way toward accomplishment of objectives. Conceptually, a goal is a measurable result attainable at some specific date through planned action. In SCE&G's 1983 strategic plan, goals were established in the following areas: financial, V. C. Summer Nuclear Plant, customer relations, human resources, image, marketing, and innovation.

The nature of the goals is best illustrated by example. Consider the following goals stated in the 1983 corporate plan:

1. Earn a firm A bond rating, a fixed charge coverage of 3.5 times, and a capital structure equity component equal to 40 percent by 1985.
2. Adopt marketing plans designed to manage the annual electric system peak territorial load growth rate at or below 3 percent annually, while improving the system load factor.

The final and most specific aspect of the strategic plan at SCE&G is the set of strategies. A strategy is viewed as the determination and evaluation of alternative plans to an already established mission or objective and, eventually, a choice from among these alternatives. Although they are closely tied to stated objectives and goals, strategies represent more specific statements of intent and method. Because strategies frequently cross organizational boundaries, a matrix management process is used to develop them. The strategy manager prepares the strategy in coordination with the functional area managers, who commit resources and handle the implementation of the plan.

The strategies incorporated in the 1983 SCE&G strategic plan are as follows:

1. The customer relations strategy: To develop a company-wide awareness that ensures proper utilization of employees, facilities, and equipment to meet customer requirements through desired standards of services.
2. The efficiency and productivity strategy: To improve effi-

ciency and productivity at SCE&G through a defined, coordinated effort supported by strong communications, educational resources, and enhanced reporting systems.

3. The Summer Nuclear Station strategy: To identify and effectively utilize resources to operate the V. C. Summer Nuclear Station in a safe, reliable, and efficient manner.

4. The innovation strategy: To develop, through a participatory process, an atmosphere that encourages, recognizes, and rewards that innovation that enhances the company's mission.

5. The image strategy: To establish an issues management system for present and future perceptions of the company through programs of total corporate involvement.

6. The human resource strategy: To develop SCE&G's human resources to assure effective staffing for present and future business activities by matching company needs and employee skills.

7. The marketing strategy: To develop marketing plans tailored to the various market segments served.

8. The rates strategy: To develop mini-strategies for each of the major areas of operations that will procure the revenues necessary to recover the cost of the company's products and services in a fair, equitable, and reasonable manner.

The presentation of the strategies in the strategic plan includes a detailed description of the strategy, a discussion of resources required to implement the strategy, an analysis of the strategy effect, and the identification of contingencies pertinent to the strategy.

Progress in the implementation of the strategies is monitored through a series of quarterly reports. The quarterly reports are prepared by the strategy managers and are expected to emphasize measurable progress in implementing the strategies.

ORGANIZATION FOR STRATEGIC PLANNING AT SCE&G

The initial involvement of SCE&G in formal strategic planning occurred because of a keen interest on the part of the chief executive officer (CEO). This initial interest of the CEO resulted in a strategic planning process that involves direct participation by all members of senior management. At the same time, however, the corporate planning process is based on the concept of "bottom-up" rather than "top-down" planning. The strategic planning process at SCE&G thus incorporates two fundamental principles: first, the CEO and senior management are actively involved in planning, and second, front-line and middle managers are also actively involved.

The organizational composition for strategic planning at SCE&G is summarized in table 16.2. The corporate planning department acts as a coordinating agency and source of documentation for the strategic planning process, but most of the planning activity is done by company managers who are not specialists in strategic planning. The planning staff is also responsible for planning research and for training and promotion activities relative to the planning process.

The logical information flow inherent in the strategic planning process is shown in figure 16.3. Based on information regarding new developments received from a large number of scanners, the planning support team prepares papers on potential issues. These papers are then forwarded to the planning team, which is comprised of eight to fifteen managers at the senior level. The planning team recommends issue priorities, objectives, and topics in strategy areas. These go to the CEO for approval. The CEO assigns strategy managers, who then prepare proposed strategies to be submitted to the planning team.

The final product of the strategic planning process is the strategic plan, which is published annually under the direct supervision of the strategic planning manager in the Corporate Planning Department. After being coordinated with those managers involved in the planning process, the strategic plan is presented to the Board of Directors for final approval.

The Corporate Planning Department at SCE&G is a relatively small staff unit. Reporting to the vice president for corporate planning and management services, the department is headed by the assistant vice president for corporate planning. Within the planning department are managers for strategic planning and financial forecasting, an associate manager of operational planning, and a supervisor of economic research and performance analysis.

STRATEGIC PLANNING IN THE OVERALL PLANNING PROCESS

The strategic planning cycle begins in November of each year with the gathering of environmental information and issue topics. The various iterations of the strategic planning process, as described above, culminate in the publication of the strategic plan in late spring of the following year.

TABLE 16.2   Participants in Strategic Planning at SCE&G

Group Name	Membership	Function
Scanners	Fifty middle management persons	To review articles from assigned publications and report to strategic planning any articles or contacts meeting with criteria set (new developments, shifts in trends, some breakthroughs, public-attitude changes, employee trends and projections).
Planning support team	Ten to twelve middle and upper management persons	To receive categorized information on, classify, and prepare papers on potential issues. Suggest objectives, goals, or changes therein.
Planning team	Eight to fifteen top management persons	To receive information and to identify and recommend priorities of issues, goals, objectives, and strategy topics; to receive and discuss proposed strategies from strategy managers.
Planning staff	Three management persons	Under the principal direction of the manager, strategic and operational planning, to administer the planning process; to gather, analyze, summarize, condense, categorize, and report information; to set the planning stage and calendar; to monitor, coordinate activities, and stimulate the planning process; to publish the strategic plan for the corporation.
Strategy manager	As assigned	To receive issues, goals, and objectives, and develop strategy in the assigned area for the corporation; to identify resources, to evaluate and prepare alternates for contingencies, to obtain approvals, and to manage approved strategies.

The operational plan and manpower plan are driven by the strategic plan (see figure 16.3). Those managers responsible for functional areas of the company initiate the operational plan by preparing executive guidelines. These managers allocate the resources required to accomplish the objectives and goals set forth in the strategic plan and determine the activities necessary to carry out current operations as well as additional programs and projects.

The economic forecast is prepared at midyear and updated quarterly. The economic forecast drives the forecasts for energy sales, electric demand, and gas sales, which, in turn, feed into the expansion and supply forecast and fuel forecast. The final elements of the planning process are the

FIGURE 16.3   SCE&G Planning Cycle

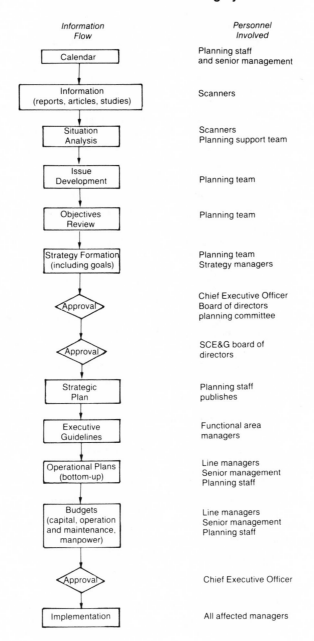

Information Flow	Personnel Involved
Calendar	Planning staff and senior management
Information (reports, articles, studies)	Scanners
Situation Analysis	Scanners Planning support team
Issue Development	Planning team
Objectives Review	Planning team
Strategy Formation (including goals)	Planning team Strategy managers
Approval	Chief Executive Officer Board of directors planning committee
Approval	SCE&G board of directors
Strategic Plan	Planning staff publishes
Executive Guidelines	Functional area managers
Operational Plans (bottom-up)	Line managers Senior management Planning staff
Budgets (capital, operation and maintenance, manpower)	Line managers Senior management Planning staff
Approval	Chief Executive Officer
Implementation	All affected managers

275

capital budget and the operation and maintenance expense budget, which comprise SCE&G's financial plan.

Financial planning activities, which include balancing the capital structure for the appropriate mix of debt and equity and securing funds for construction and operating needs, are under the direction of the financial department. The operating departments are responsible for electric and gas-system facilities planning and marketing planning.

PROSPECTS FOR THE FUTURE

The strategic planning process as described in this chapter has evolved from several years of discussion and experimentation. Additional modifications and enhancements will likely occur in the future to make the process more responsive to the requirements of the organization. The issues and strategies included in the planning process will also change to keep pace with changes in the external environment. Likely issue topics for the future include changing energy demands, deregulation, and acid rain.

CONCLUSIONS

During the last decade, the strategic planning process at SCE&G has evolved from a relatively informal process, based on steady growth in demand and the plant construction needed to fulfill that demand, to a formal strategic planning process designed to cope with a rapidly changing external environment. Among the payoffs perceived by the company as resulting from the strategic planning process are the following:

1. The development of a published document making explicit statements about mission, objectives, goals, and strategies.
2. Greater sensitivity to changes in the external environment.
3. Improved communication among all levels of management.
4. An increased awareness by company employees of current issues and problems facing the firm.
5. Important contributions to management development.

The major contribution of the strategic planning process is that it encourages management to think strategically. By viewing the world in terms of threats and opportunities rather than as a static world with no change, the manager is much better equipped to cope with a highly uncertain environment.

The reader interested in planning in regulated industries is urged to consult the current planning literature. See, for example, Ben-Yaacov 1978,

Boriamrene et al. 1980, Johnson 1978, Lackman 1980, Lere 1981, Norden 1978, Roper 1978, Tyson and Cochrane 1981, and Wood 1981.

EXERCISE 16

This and every exercise is intended to form the basis for a part of the term project: Prepare a strategic plan for an organization of your choice. For each exercise, present a typed, one-page report, showing the directions your analysis will take.

For this exercise, indicate the differences and why planning would be harder (or easier) if your organization were a regulated (nonregulated) firm.

REFERENCES

Ben-Yaacov, G. Z. "A Computer-Based Modelling System for Electric Utility Planning." *Long Range Planning* (Dec. 1978), p. 30.

Boriamrene, M. A., and Flarell, R. "Airline Corporate Planning—A Conceptual Framework." *Long Range Planning* (Feb. 1980), p. 62.

Johnson, Herbert E. "Comprehensive Corporate Planning for Commercial Banks." *Magazine of Bank Administration* (Jan. 1978), p. 20.

Lackman, Conway L. "Dialing F-U-T-U-R-E at the Phone Company." *Planning Review* (May 1980), p. 26.

Lere, John C. "Planning for Electricity Demand." *Managerial Planning* (Nov. 1981), p. 21.

Norden, R. F. "The Norwegian State Railways—Profit Motivated Enterprise or a Community Service?" *Long Range Planning* (Apr. 1978), p. 13.

Roger, D. A. "Planning Developments in British Nuclear Fuels, Ltd." *Long Range Planning* (Oct. 1978), p. 32.

Tyson, W. J., and Cochrane, R. C. D. "Corporate Planning and Project Evaluation in Urban Transport." *Long Range Planning* (Oct. 1981), p. 62.

Wood, D. Robley, Jr. "Comprehensive Planning at a Multi-National Bank." *Planning Review* (Jan. 1981), p. 27.

Chapter 17

Planning Philosophy in Gulf Oil Corporation

William C. King, Vice President, Corporate Planning, Gulf Oil Corporation

One of the first topics that must be considered in the area of strategic planning is how to *reduce* uncertainty. Frankly, we do not know how to reduce uncertainty. Crystal balls don't help, and any effective methods are either illegal or politically oppressive. What we can do is address, at considerable length, how to *deal with* uncertainty.

Most of the uncertainties facing us cannot be reduced by analytical effort, no matter how sophisticated and intense that effort might be. Some uncertainties are resolved over time, but others of equal or greater importance take their place. We have to learn to live with uncertainty. This is not as bad as it may seem. Uncertainty means change, and change presents opportunities. And there are a variety of tools we can use to help us take advantage of these opportunities and to cope with uncertainty.

Before delving into what these tools are, we need some historical background. During the 1950s and 1960s, oil industry planners produced long-range forecasts and constructed plans to fit them. Of course, there were surprises, but, all in all, it was a satisfactory approach. It worked because the basic trends and relationships in our external world were fairly stable over those two decades. In short, our basic assumptions remained valid; they did not change.

Early in the 1970s, this stability changed—dramatically. The increase in crude prices changed the basic economic factors underlying our industry. Trends and relationships that had been familiar became unknown. Today, these are still very much in question. Numerous press articles cite contro-

---

versies on energy conservation, on petroleum demand elasticities, on costs of finding oil, and on the size of the resource base, not to mention just the price of oil in the immediate future.

The interrelationships among economics, government policy, technology, and competitive forces have become more complex and dynamic. You cannot safely extrapolate a single trend anymore. Too many factors impinge. As a result, the half-life of our planning assumptions is now measured in weeks, instead of years.

One solution to this uncertainty is to throw up our hands. We cannot forecast, so why plan? We believe just the opposite—we cannot forecast, so we must plan. But we must have clear and achievable goals for planning under uncertainty.

PLANNING OBJECTIVES

At Gulf we have three basic goals for our planning process. First, we try to develop core strategies that can survive a wide range of possible future conditions and be successful in many of them. Second, we try to maintain flexible implementation of our strategies, so that we will be able to adapt our plans as circumstances change. Third, we want our planning systems to be an important source of competitive advantage.

We use the word *core* to describe a strategy that can survive a wide range of possible future conditions. The strategy must be simple enough to be clearly and firmly stated, and it must be frequently reaffirmed both by words and by consistent actions.

We want to pursue our core strategies consistently, but not by rigidly implementing plans that, no matter how well conceived, make less sense as conditions change. We want to adapt plan implementation flexibly as circumstances change—as they always will.

The purpose of our planning efforts is to give our company a competitive edge. Planning systems—the way we make decisions and follow through on them—can be an important source of competitive advantage, especially in today's fast-moving environment.

THE GULF PLANNING PROCESS

At Gulf, our planning process used to be a cumbersome annual effort. We gathered extensive, detailed data. Then we consolidated, refined, and reviewed this data and presented the final plan at the annual strategy review meeting. By that time, the basic assumptions were frequently out of date, and little could be done to modify the plan. Our operating people saw the planning process as a burden rather than a help, and the corporate executive was provided with few real options.

We have now gone to a more flexible process—with the help of computers. For a planning process to be effective, the development and modification of plans have to be fast, readily manageable, and able to generate plans of consistent quality. Given this capability, operating people are much more likely to get involved both in developing and in using the plan. Participation of operating people in planning is essential. As the one who must implement the plan, they are in the best position to recognize when plan assumptions no longer match environmental conditions.

PLANNING TOOLS AT GULF

I would now like to turn to some of the specific planning tools we use in achieving these goals. Although developed by a central planning group, these tools must be designed so operating people can use them readily.

There are three major planning tools that we use to help corporate management construct our core strategies:
- Scenarios
- Plan options
- Issues analysis

There are also three other major tools that aid flexible plan implementation:
- Contingency planning
- Environmental monitoring
- Plan updating

Each of these needs a brief description.

Scenarios

Creating scenarios is very different from forecasting. Forecasting is based on assumed certainties—trends and conditions presumed to be known. A forecaster concentrates on answering questions, How much? and When? What is going to happen? is not much in dispute.

Scenarios, on the other hand, are based on uncertainties—trends and relationships that are unknown and unknowable. The key question is, What?

Scenarios are alternative views of the different ways the major unknowns could logically combine and dynamically interact to create our future. Each scenario is internally consistent and is distinct from other scenarios. The various scenarios encompass a reasonably wide range of uncertainty.

Another characteristic of scenarios is that they should be custom tailored to the user's business and to the user's current decisions. The scenarios we created in 1980, when synthetic fuels development was a major decision facing Gulf, were quite different from those we use today, because today's conditions are very different. As it turned out, one of those 1980 scenarios accurately anticipated the current trend in crude prices.

That's the value of scenarios. They force you to stretch your thinking about what could happen. Then, should it happen, it is possible to recognize it sooner and respond to it more quickly.

We pick one scenario as the basis for our plans and options. We then use the alternative scenarios to test what would happen if the world turns out differently. This gives us a sense of how the various actions we could take might turn out under different assumptions. The payoff comes from this linking of the scenarios to our decision-making process.

Plan Options

The second tool we use at Gulf is plan options. Early in the year we identify specific options for specific businesses, in addition to their current plans. These options suggest different ways to run the business and reasons why these should be considered. They come from a wide variety of ongoing strategic analyses and may originate from either corporate or operating management. After they are reviewed and discussed, several are selected to be developed along with the business plans.

This options aspect of our process has been very successful in reinforcing the corporate executives' involvement in planning. Before our use of options, the executive received fully defined plans and could only approve or make rough modifications. I say "rough" because, while the executives could cut or add, they could only guess at the impact of their actions. With options, the executives can make real choices with clear implications. They can personally decide how each individual business should contribute to the overall corporate strategy.

Issues Analysis

The third tool we use to construct our core strategies is issues analysis. While scenarios examine the dynamic relationships among many uncertainties, there are often single critical issues—for instance, natural gas price regulations—that deserve special attention. The impact of these specific issues can be lost in the complexity of a scenario. Issue analysis is too narrow to examine the dynamics of our environment, and scenario analysis is too broad to examine the implications of key individual issues. So we do both. Our experience is that issue analysis complements and enriches scenario analysis.

Contingency Planning

In addition to the three tools we use to construct our core strategies, we use three tools to support flexible implementation of our plans. The first is contingency planning. When plans are tested against scenarios, we see what would happen to a given set of actions under alternative sets of assumptions. The result is not another plan, because it would not be implemented. Clearly, we would change our actions if major assumptions changed. But scenario analysis does help us identify key exposures and opportunities, which we can follow up with contingency planning, an effort to prethink what we would do differently if certain possibilities not assumed in our plan were to occur. Scenario analysis allows us to focus contingency planning efforts selectively on those few areas where the payoff would be quite high.

Environmental Monitoring

The second implementation tool, environmental monitoring, is a companion to contingency planning. Environmental monitoring is directed at determining if our key plan assumptions are still valid.

There is a natural human tendency to treat assumptions as facts and to interpret subsequent events to fit those assumptions. When effectively carried out, environmental scanning raises warning flags when business plan assumptions become shaky. Contingency plans provide a way to quickly and accurately adjust operations and plans to more effectively carry out our strategy.

Plan Updating

The third implementation tool is plan updating. It is essential that the planning process be both fast and easy to use by operating people in the running of their businesses. The use of computers with good data bases and top-down business models helps accomplish this.

We can make major changes in basic plan assumptions and generate the resulting financial and operating performance in a few days. This means that management can consider a number of "what if" alternatives and determine the plan they believe will be best in the future. This approach also makes it practical to revise the plan as conditions change, and it is essential in dealing effectively with uncertainty.

All of these planning tools are useful in and of themselves. But it is their combined use that results in a planning process that provides a competitive edge.

MANAGEMENT PLANS, PLANNERS FACILITATE

Dealing with uncertainty requires core strategies with a high degree of consistency and plan implementation with a high degree of flexibility. Together, these provide the resiliency needed in today's environment. Increasingly, corporate and operating division executives must work closely together to ensure that strategies and plans have these attributes, and they must mutually support each other. The planning process and the planning tools mentioned can help, but only if they are seen by operating management as being practical and useful. This is a major caution for professional planners. We frequently become overzealous in developing planning tools to the neglect of the practical.

In the eyes of management, planning can too easily become overly academic and esoteric. If we fully applied all of our tools in all of their possible uses, the planning effort could consume enormous resources without yielding much in the way of useful results. It is possible to get 80 percent of the value for 20 percent of the effort, and I believe we must. (See the Pareto principle, discussed in chapter 8.) Oversophistication in planning only defeats itself. It wastes resources and pretends a level of accuracy we know is not possible. As planners, we need to worry about directions, not decimal points. (Note the SEE principle, discussed in chapter 7.)

Another guideline for planners is: You don't have to do everything in each planning cycle. If you focus selectively and develop new capabilities in an evolutionary way over several cycles, you are likely to progress further in the long run.

The key to successful planning is to involve operating management. Develop a planning system that provides practical help in managing the business. Give operating management a major say in the focus of the planning process—the scenarios, the options, the issues. Many times I've heard that operating management is the client for the planning process. But that isn't good enough. Operating management must be a major participant in the planning process if they are to implement the plan effectively. Otherwise, planning won't help your company deal with uncertainty in a way that helps you beat the competition.

Exercise 17

This and every exercise is intended to form the basis for a part of the term project: Prepare a strategic plan for an organization of your choice. For each exercise, present a typed, one-page report showing directions your analysis will take.

For this exercise, consider your work on your organization thus far, and determine what planning philosophy issues have arisen. Compare or contrast them with the Gulf issues.

Chapter 18

Planning Models in Gulf Eastern

This chapter traces the historical development of planning models in Gulf Eastern, the eastern hemisphere branch of the Gulf Oil Corporation. The objective of the chapter, of course, is to aid the thinking of others who may be in the position of introducing a similar planning function. It is sometimes felt that planning is difficult to introduce, that it may meet resistance from executive levels of the company. This was not our experience. We used a stepwise procedure, getting one phase operating and displaying benefits before moving on to the next operation. We observed a consistent reaction of enthusiasm and interest in statements such as, "This is the best thing that ever happened to Gulf in London."

It should be noted that Gulf world headquarters planning has now led to the withdrawal of the corporation from European operations and from other geographical areas. This in no way negates the following narrative as an example of an excellent "plan for planning" that was carried into planning itself and into execution of those plans.

ORGANIZATION FOR PLANNING

The Gulf Oil Corporation maintains a planning and economics staff at its world headquarters in Pittsburgh. This chapter describes the activities of a similar staff maintained at the London regional headquarters to control planning activities for Europe and other Eastern Hemisphere facilities. All

Adapted from Clark Holloway and G. T. Jones, "Planning at Gulf—A Case Study," *Long Range Planning*, 8 (Apr. 1975). Used by permission of Pergamon Press, Ltd.

such regions (Asia, South America) report to world headquarters. The Eastern Hemisphere is further divided into geographical profit center areas. One of these, for example, is Scandinavia. A planning council made up of area representatives and headquarters experts in refining, marketing, exploration, and other functional departments is active in preparing planning studies. This chapter describes the experiences of the Eastern Hemisphere region in designing and implementing an integrated computer system for corporate planning.

The earliest planning effort was the manual creation of an actual long-range forecast. Because of manpower limitations, only with extreme effort could more than a single such forecast be produced each year. Planning only occurs when many alternate forecasts can be developed and studied for the purpose of optimizing operations. Over the years there was a gradual acquisition of automatic techniques to permit the company to generate a large number of plans for each planning period, perhaps as many as a dozen or more.

OBJECTIVES FOR PLANNING MODELS

In the application of computer models to solve planning problems, certain abilities are required: to consider many problems rapidly; to ensure good data documentation; to allow choice of best alternatives; to provide flexibility for many varied studies; and to consider the operation of all departments simultaneously. The same tools are also extremely valuable for solving operational problems.

Any system developed, therefore, must ideally meet the following criteria. It must:

- permit rapid evaluation of planning strategies using a fully integrated computer system but allow manual override at any desired point
- operate on an inhouse computer, perhaps with expanded versions (requiring a larger computer) available
- minimize manual data-input effort
- maximize usage of existing linear programming and simulation models
- avoid disturbing the on-going operation of these existing models
- provide consistency and interchangeability among new and existing packages
- be flexible in representing changing conditions or in altered reporting requirements

System Design Principles

Underlying all aspects of the system must be a number of fundamental concepts established by analyzing the successful and unsuccessful efforts in many companies.

1. Get the involvement and active participation of the people experienced in model development and the people intimately familiar with the application areas.
2. Use a stepwise approach. Divide the overall project into discrete segments that can be used on their own as stand-alone units.
3. The system should be simple. Building in the flexibility to solve every problem requires a long development period and creates a tool that is costly to run, difficult to maintain, and vulnerable to error.
4. Calculations should be done in preprocessor and postprocessor programs. The model itself should *not* be used as an accounting tool.
5. Educate users of the system. Planning council members should understand the function of the system, how their individual departments' activities are represented, and how to identify and use data from their departments.
6. Establish a scheduled data maintenance procedure and select individuals to be responsible for its implementation on a routine basis.

An attractive ideal from the point of view of many companies would be the availability of a generalized computer-based planning package that would fit their own particular situation or that could be constructed by selection from a number of basic routines. Computer software companies and the computer manufacturers themselves are obviously aware of this need, and some progress has been made toward the development of such systems. A study was carried out by IBM (Wagle et al. 1970) to "investigate the feasibility of a generalized computer system to aid the corporate planning process and to define the direction and emphasis that further research and development should take in that area" concluded that there was a need for two types of corporate planing systems:

1. A simple system, designed for managers to build their own financial models, that uses a specially developed flexible planning language. The system would have simple data entry and have available a range of graphical output facilities that could be selected by the user who is mostly concerned with financial reports.
2. A sophisticated package covering in-depth various areas where computer aids are possible. It would be largely for the use of specialists reporting to management and would cover not only financial

functions but also forecasting and strategy evaluation. The basis of the system would be a new powerful planning language that would provide a link between planning techniques as well as a range of useful industry macros.

A number of companies that have the required resources have gone ahead with the development of their own planning systems, designed specifically to meet their particular needs. But while these companies have worked essentially independently, a great deal of commonality of approach exists as the survey part of the IBM study showed. Certain techniques that lend themselves to planning applications have been used by a number of companies, often to overcome similar problems. Other companies have expressed the desire to use these techniques, given the resources and skills necessary to do so. This chapter describes Gulf Eastern's approach to the problems of integrated planning systems and the experience they gained.

Techniques in Planning

Among the most widely used techniques in a planning context are simulation and linear programming. Each of these has different characteristics and therefore is suited more to some planning applications than to others. For instance, many major companies, particularly oil companies, traditionally have used linear programming to solve problems in the supply and distribution area because this technique is well suited to finding an optimum feasible solution (in terms of, say, minimum cost) for a complex distribution system operating under a large number of constraints. The use of linear programming in this medium-term operations planning area is common.

Simulation, on the other hand, has been used widely in such areas as risk analysis (in the context of project appraisal) and in operations planning, for such things as the "sizing" of production, storage, and transportation facilities for balanced operations. One of the major strengths of simulation lies in its ability to deal with uncertainty. It is possible to work with probability ranges of data rather than with fixed, single-values estimates. It is thus more flexible in some ways and lends itself readily to long-range planning where a great deal of uncertainty exists. For instance, if we are estimating possible market size for ten years hence, it is more realistic to express this in terms of a range built up from estimates of minimum, maximum, and most likely figures. It would be overambitious and hazardous to attempt a single-point estimate.

It could be argued, then, that company models fall into two broad types: (1) optimization models and (2) simulation models. The optimizing family of company models, as the name suggests, attempts to optimize some well-defined objective function of the company, while taking into account the constraints under which the company operates. For example, the objective may be to optimize the overall discounted rate of return over a given period under constraints governing overall market-growth rates of products, raw materials availability, and financing and dividend policies.

Simulation models include not only stochastic but also descriptive models. These simulate progress of the company over a given period of time and provide projections of balance sheets, profit and loss accounts, cash flows, and so forth. The corporate simulation model can be understood more easily by senior and corporate management, but its greatest asset is the speed with which it can answer a whole range of "What if" questions. For example, what is the effect on the company's financial position if the corporate tax rate changes to 45 percent, or if we increased dividend payments from 8 percent to 10 percent, or if prices are increased by 5 percent.

One of the limitations of the simulation approach is, of course, the lack of optimization. Because of this limitation, one must operate the model on a case-study basis.

COMBINATION OF TECHNIQUES

Given the desire for an integrated corporate planning system, a useful step would be to combine two or more techniques into a more comprehensive system for planning. Such a system would attempt to combine the strengths of the component techniques to produce a more comprehensive and flexible approach.

Although it may be an enormously difficult task to build up a really detailed general planning system, it should be possible to go some of the way to a partially integrated system. This may increase the company's planning capabilities considerably, while, at the same time, involving fewer technical problems. Since simulation and linear programming are two of the most established and widely used techniques in the planning field, an obvious first stage is the combination of the attributes of these two techniques. The aim, of course, would be to combine the flexibility and sensitivity analysis procedures of simulation with the optimizational power of linear programming.

THE COORDINATION PROBLEM

The major reason for using linear programming for long-range planning is less to obtain optimization than it is to guarantee internal balances and to permit precise pinpoint control of all quantities of interrelationships.

A sensitivity model can easily be adapted to generate results that indicate the probability of certain events happening, that is, to carry out risk analysis. If, however, a linear programming model is regarded as an authoritative reference point, one is immediately faced with the rather large problem of ensuring the agreement of the sensitivity model with, or approximately with, the linear programming model.

An early attempt to combine LP and simulation involved writing two linear programming subroutines for inclusion in the sensitivity model. These subroutines were to optimize crude oil refinery and delivery of the product to markets. The first covers constraints in transportation and the refining capabilities of the refineries, while the second contains the lower limit constraints of market demands. They are used within the sensitivity model and go some way to ensure the feasibility of solutions reached in the cases considered with this model. There is, of course, the distinct danger of suboptimization, particularly as the two subroutines are not interlinked within the model. This approach also goes only a small part of the way toward the system required.

A development of this approach is described schematically in figure 18.1. The corporate plan is developed in broad outline using the simulation (sensitivity) model. The objectives of the company, perhaps in terms of market volumes or gross income, are translated into departmental targets (this process is, of course, outside the model). The sensitivity model is used to carry out a balancing operation for a period of, say, ten years hence. Refining capabilities, market volumes for each product group, transportation requirements, and so on are calculated for each year. To some extent, the model has the capability to "buy in" resources, raw materials, or products to meet shortfalls. If this need is shown as consistent over a simulated period of a number of years, a need for capital investment is identified. Expansions of, say, refining capacity or shipping fleet will then be included and the model will recycle to insert the necessary capital expenditure in an earlier year to take account of construction time. In this way the outline corporate plan is developed.

If an increment of refining capacity is established as being necessary in a particular year, then an LP model could be used to identify the optimum location of the new plant. This calculation could be carried out using a modified form of the full company LP model or, perhaps more conveniently, using a special-purpose LP submodel, which may be a lot less detailed than the full model. The sensitivity model could then be run again, with the proposed investment included in its optimum location in the base case (as if the expansion actually took place in that year) and the full effect studied.

This approach has certainly been shown to have great possibilities. The main limitation is that the transition from sensitivity model to LP model and

FIGURE 18.1   The Second Stage in Combining the Techniques

```
                ┌──────────────┐
                │  Objectives  │
                └──────┬───────┘
                       │
                       ▼
        ┌─────► ┌──────────────┐ ◄──────────────► ┌──────────────┐
        │       │   Targets    │                  │  Simulation  │
        │       └──────┬───────┘                  └──────────────┘
        │              │
        │              ▼
        │       ┌──────────────┐
        │       │  Forecasts   │
        │       └──────┬───────┘
        │              │
        │              └──────► ┌──────────────┐ ◄──────
        │                       │   Balance    │
        │                       └──────┬───────┘
        │                              │
        │                              ▼
        │                       ┌──────────────┐
        │                       │Corporate plan│
        │                       │  (outline)   │
        │                       └──────┬───────┘
        │                              │
   ┌────┴─────────┐            ┌────────▼──────────┐
   │ Side studies │ ◄──────────│Proposed investments│
   │ LP sub-models│            └────────┬──────────┘
   └──────────────┘                     │
                                        ▼
                                ┌──────────────┐
                                │Corporate plan│
                                │   (final)    │
                                └──────┬───────┘
                                       │        ┌──────────────────┐
                                       │ ┌─────►│Financial documents│
                                       ▼ │      │     Budgets      │
                            ┌───────────────┐   └──────────────────┘
                            │Short-term detailed│
                            │operations. LP full-model│
                            └───────────────┘
```

back again is manual. This slows down the process, and the data transactions involved are tedious. The special LP submodels can be written so that problems of compatibility are minimized.

The Research Approach

Some problems arise if the full LP and sensitivity models are used in experiments on combination of models. These are large models, and since several runs of each may be required within any given experiment, a great deal of computer time can be used (in addition to elapsed time). Both models use a large amount of data, so the manual intervention between runs to transfer data is time and cost consuming.

Consequently, small experimental versions of these models were developed that could be used more conveniently to study the principles involved. We were conscious of the fact that these are "models of models" and as such are subject to the danger of wandering far from the truth. The main models are themselves only representations, and therefore approximations, of the company. These minimodels take us a step still further from reality although care was taken to represent accurately the features of the main models. There are mitigating factors: the principles of the problem are fairly clearly defined and the data interface problems very much the same. Information gained in these areas from experiments with the small models was of some significance with respect to the real situation.

Conclusions—The Problems Encountered

The above experiments certainly showed the desirability of integrating available planning systems and also that under certain controlled conditions such integration was technically feasible. We were drawn, nevertheless, to the conclusion that the actual direct integration of Gulf's two major models would be extremely difficult and that the effort involved would not be justified. This is mainly due to wide difference of basis of the two models and the consequent interface problems.

This problem is not confined to Gulf. It is a common problem experienced by many companies, particularly those established in the operations research area. The models and packages they have developed for various purposes are frequently on totally different bases (different geographical regions, different product groupings, and so on), and, therefore, they are not immediately compatible. This means that since each model may use different data, data transactions between models are difficult, if not impossible. One cannot use output from one model as input to another without manual intervention. Reports coming from the models may look quite different. Because they are on different bases, comparisons cannot be made without first carrying out various corrections. The general result is that any attempt to bring together such models into an integrated system is difficult. From the point of view of management, the result may well be more confusing than instructive.

The reasons why models are generally developed on different bases are many. The advent of the computer has brought with it the opportunity to develop sophisticated packages using techniques that must be computer based because of the large volume of computational work involved. These techniques have been developed at different times. Their use in industry for planning applications also dates from different times. Moreover, the thinking within companies as well as the organizational structure may have changed since the models were designed.

The reasons for building models and the purposes they were originally designed to meet may have been very specific. For this reason, integrating them into a newly conceived overall system may be taking them beyond the limits of their feasibility. Furthermore, and perhaps most important of all, models are frequently designed and built as a result of the enthusiasm and skill of an individual, or group of individuals, within the company. Particularly in the large multidivisional company such persons may work with only a limited knowledge of other related activities that may have gone on or be going on.

Gulf has had its fair share of those problems. For these and other reasons the company decided to adopt a totally new approach to integrated planning aids, one which did not involve the direct integration of the main models.

Analysis of their mutual advantages suggested the retention of separate simulation and LP models in the system to be developed. The optimization model would cover only that part of the problem where flexibility of a model is useful, meaningful, and practical in realistic terms. Other calculations would be made in auxiliary programs comprising the simulation model and united with the optimization model. The simulation model would be used in three ways: to give initial appraisal of possible planning cases, to assist in determining proper timing for capital investment, and to provide risk analysis studies on a limited number of attractive planning cases.

There were already in operation a number of useful components. Among these were refinery models representing most of the company's European refineries. In addition to their other uses, they prepared data for corporate long-range plans. It would be greatly advantageous to permit all models to receive input data from the same data bank and to permit all models to supply calculated data to this data bank.

COMPONENTS OF THE SYSTEM

Matrix generation. An LP matrix generation and maintenance system developed by the company had many strong points. The system was composed of an optimization model coupled with auxiliary calculation programs. It had a simple input data format that was easy to understand and to use, since it offered a data organization concept that was application oriented. Its data tables differed only slightly from those normally familiar to departmental personnel. This data organization also helped avoid errors in data handling; it checked for consistency and simplified data modification. Its structure was such that an effective data maintenance procedure could be built around the data tables. It was easy for anyone with a knowledge of LP model formulation to learn and use. It is important that a system that is to be used over a long period of time be easily learned, since there may be future developmental stages for extensions and prime responsibility for running the system may well change hands. It was an efficient and economical system for running large-scale LP models and had the required flexibility and capacity for change that is needed for a planning application. The user could expand, revise, or reduce the data table, which effectively produced a different model without any changes required in the model generation statements.

Data base. Storage files that contain all data necessary for generation of the integrated planning model and reports for solution analysis are the data base. The tabular format makes a data element easy to identify. It is the key to the success of the data maintenance procedures. The input data requirements for the data base by department were known from previous models.

Preprocessor programs. The input data available from each department must be transfered into model matrix coefficients. The preprocessor programs place input data into the data base after performing any necessary arithmetical calculations.

The combination of the above packages (preprocessor/data-base matrix generator) accomplishes the following: It provides data documentation through a data base rather than through the LP matrix. It also reduces computation cost by reducing matrix size. This is done through techniques that eliminate the redundant model constraints usually present for report generation. This is possible due to the existence of a separate data base. Data storage in a tabular format permits more rapid identification compared to a matrix coefficient format and is the base for the data maintenance procedure.

Report writers. The problem solution must be transformed into reports suitable for analysis by the planning council. Report generation involves access to both the data base and the problem solution file, appropriate arithmetic calculations to prepare the desired information, and output of the information in a format acceptable to the appropriate department. An extensive set of output reports had been available for a previous LP model. Since additions to this model did not change the basic naming structure, these reports all continued to be operable. In addition to the volumetrics, new reports include financial information of the following types:

1. Area summary of products by area
2. Market reports by country
3. Refinery operating plans
4. Processees operating plans
5. Processors operating plans
6. Exchange agreement reports
7. Product detail reports
8. Product movement reports
9. Crude oil reports

In addition, a new generalized report writer was developed. A user can call for any desired information without computer programming assistance.

The above components of the linear programming part of the system are displayed in figure 18.2. The linear programming model itself has been named GEM, (Gulf Eastern Model). For simplicity of understanding the data base, it has been divided on figure 18.2, into two parts, a REVISE file and a SOLUTION file.

The REVISE file is created both by manual key-punched cards and by automatically generated cards from other programs, as indicated in the top part of the figure. In addition, extrapolation and interpolation procedures are used. The matrix generation proceeds from a different set of data tables, which are used both to control the type of matrix generated and to introduce typical or default data. The data from the REVISE file is introduced into the matrix by standard procedures, and optimal solutions are obtained. All years are combined to form a SOLUTION file, which is the second part of the data base. The entire data base is then available for the production of all output reports.

INPUT DATA

For the simulation model, much of the input data is prepared in the form of probability distributions. This allows the value of a factor to be stated in terms of a most probable value, lowest and highest values, and a range in intervening values. Thus management is not forced to commit itself to a fixed estimate of the market for a given product ten years hence but is able to express its uncertainty of this figure in terms of range of values. Specific values are then chosen automatically on a random basis by the model from within this range.

The actual data distribution can be arrived at from the estimates of relevant experts within the field. Empirical distributions are then built up from these estimates by the analyst. Alternatively, if it is felt that the shape of the

FIGURE 18.2   The LP System

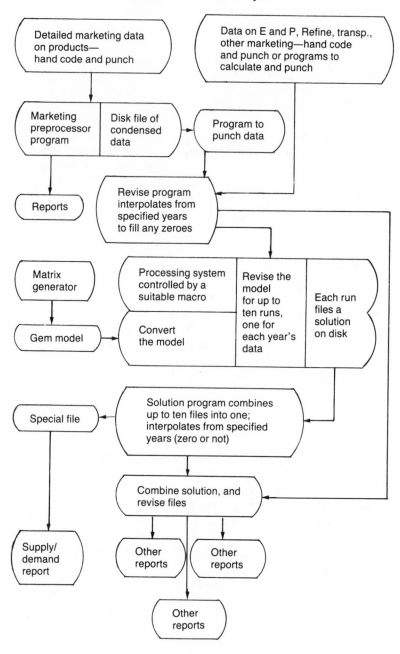

data distribution will approximate a standard normal mathematical distribution, the equation for the appropriate curve can be used within the model.

Because of the obvious uncertainties in the data fed into the model, numerical answers require proper interpretation. The model would not be used as a forecasting tool to predict profits accurately in a certain year, for example. The numerical answers will give only a good indication of financial and operating data under a given set of conditions. The relative magnitude of the change in the answers resulting from a different set of assumptions is of value in planning, however.

Data required by LP are highly detailed and are described in the following sections.

Marketing Data

Sales volumes are required for each product grade by country. The model shows a breakdown of demand levels into categories such as:
- Regular marketing
- International marine bunker
- International aviation
- Power plants
- Petrochemical requirements
- Contract sales
- Company use and loss

Sales volumes are inserted into the model at the national demand level. The model does not deal with demands by terminal. Transportation and distribution factors within national boundaries are therefore not included.

Refinery Data

Refinery operations are represented by yield patterns. These yield patterns can show the effect of different crudes or different objectives, for example, to maximize gasoline yield or to maximize distillate yield. One alternative to using yield patterns would be to include the refinery models themselves, but this immediately implies a prohibitively large model.

Another possible approach would be to include mini models. Each refinery would then be represented by forty to sixty equations instead of about four hundred for a complete refinery representation. This approach is not recommended. It does not have the accuracy of either the yield patterns or the full refinery representation. It merely adds complexity.

Product Supply Data

Details of volumes of products given and received at each location under international exchange agreements is required. Charge and yield statements are required for processing agreements. Details of inventory levels at refineries and marketing terminals are required. This may be given in the form of fixed levels at the beginning and end of the period or as a range between the maximum and minimum. Tank capacity details are also required.

The representation of product movements is restricted in that movements are not allowed from all refineries to all countries. To do so would unnecessarily increase the size of the model, resulting in an increased requirement for computer time and in limiting the amount of space available for incorporating new features and developments. An updated list of allowable movements by product is inserted into the model on a continuing basis.

The model deals with demands on a national rather than a terminal level. The Worldscale 100 rates that are inserted into the model as indications of relative freight rates are averages of the rates to specified import terminals. Special measures, however, have been taken to represent the movements by coaster vessels.

Additional costs have been added to the model to represent the import taxes incurred by movements into EEC countries and any other tariff barrier that may from time to time exist.

Data Updates

Development of the model involved the participation of virtually every department, and the maintenance and updating of the model requires similar cooperation. Data for the model was originally collected with the cooperation of staff at different locations and within different functional areas. If any data errors are noted by these staff upon their seeing reports from the model, revisions coded in the same format as the original data can be made.

In addition, each study made on behalf of a particular department requires critical review from that department regarding its area of specialization. This approach involves groups of specialists, each member contributing to the project in his field of competence. Membership is fluid depending on the type of project.

When operating a multitime period model, inventory levels are automatically adjusted to minimize external purchases. This is achieved by allowing inventories to vary between maximum and minimum desirable levels, these levels being part of the specified input data. When seasonality is an important factor in a study, as when four quarterly periods are being reviewed, the model will cover a deficit of products by external purchases. This is done for the period when those purchases are forecast to be at the lowest cost within the constraints of the maximum inventory carryover. Some tolerance can be allowed on inventory levels in the single-time period model in order to minimize external purchases, but such variations do not take account of purchases or cargo sales in adjacent time periods.

THE SIMULATION MODEL

The simulation model represents an entirely different concept from linear programming. It is intended as an aid to management decisions and for the development of broad strategies. The answers are aimed at the company level and are general in nature. The model has served to evaluate the effect of changes in major company strategies and changes in the environment. Specific problems below the country level could not be analyzed properly with this model, but variations of it (minimodels) could be easily developed for such investigations, if circumstances justified this.

General Characteristics

The main purpose of this type of model is to generate strategic guidelines for adaptation to growth and change. It will provide the means to study the sensitivity of plans to assumptions and changes in operations and in costs, and it will assist in scheduling the desirable order of development consistent with least cost, discounted to present value. One of the most useful applications of a computerized cash-flow business model is to estimate relative variations in profitability due to changes in the business environment. The simulation model would typically study problems such as these:

- If we allow the debt/equity ratio to go up by 5 percent, how much shall we save on our cost of capital? Are there significant consequences on cash flows?
- By how much could the tax rate of country A be increased before our operations in that country become unprofitable?
- What would be the effects of different pricing strategies, of pricing light versus heavy products, or of considering variations between country and profit-center areas?
- In view of the effect of continually increasing crude oil royalties in the various producing countries, what are the ways in which these increases could be offset?

A useful feature of this model is its ability to "cycle back" on investments. If the model discovers a consistent shortfall from the marketing estimates in refining capacity in a particular geographical area, it can suggest investment to meet this shortfall. Because major extensions in refining capacity would take about three years from approval to start up, the model automatically cycles back to put the investment into the appropriate year. The model also shows relationships between factors such as investment and through-put to allow estimates of scale of investment to be made.

Investment is included under conditions to give an accurate estimate of the use of imputed investment on an average cost basis. To estimate cash requirements the model assumes construction of facilities over a realistic period of years. It also considers excess capacity of new plants and facilities where economies of scale are critical, and it allows for nondepreciable investments, such as working capital (inventories and customer accounts).

A depreciation routine is incorporated into the model to permit calculation of income taxes. The calculation of the income tax liability includes local European taxes plus any excess U.S. income tax.

Asset depreciation can be calculated by any of the following methods:

1. Straight line
2. Sum of the year's digits
3. Double declining balance
4. 150 percent declining balance
5. Single declining balance

At the end of the time span, the following assets treatment can be selected:

1. Book value of assets in the last year of problem.
2. Ignore the book value of assets in the last year of the problem.
3. All assets fully depreciated by the end of the last year through accelerated depreciation of assets acquired when the number of years remaining in the problem is less than the depreciable life of the new asset.

The cardinal principle should be to resist overdeveloping the sensitivity model. Its primary purpose is to permit rapid runs for long-term planning alternatives in order to test various strategies and their effects on possible future events. For this purpose, excessive detail is a deterrent. Where more precise control of intermediate variables is required, the linear programming model should be used. It should function from the same data base as the sensitivity model, rather than forcing the sensitivity model into unsuitable areas. Although it is commonly thought that simulation is a more flexible tool, a simulation model is not necessarily flexible at every phase of its use. The user has, of course, the freedom to model a situation as he wishes and to a level of detail that he considers appropriate. If a sophisticated model is an overall description of a company, it is not always simple to include modifications for updating. It may be laborious to check whether new instructions will upset the logic of another part of a program, whether some variable names will conflict with the names previously used, whether the validity of programming loops has been maintained, what the implications for input and output statements are, and so on. At the very least, it may require that the people who developed the model, managers as well as analysts, are still available. It must be emphasized, however, that a simulation model can more easily handle logical and dynamic relationships across several time periods. It is partly for this reason that it has a role to play in longer term, "broad brush" planning. A simplified flowchart of the model logic is shown in figure 18.3.

Output from the Model

Output from the GOC-EH model is controlled by the data input. Error listings and reports showing all the input data are produced for each run. In a "base case" run, all reports are printed. In an "alternate" run, only reports affected by data changes are printed. Only that data to be changed from the base case needs to be entered. A "sensitivity" run is an alternate run where data are entered as percentages of the base data.

Statement of input data. The first section of the output shows all the input data, including statements of all options requested. This allows a clear identification of each case run. Among those listed would be:

1. Statistical information
2. Crude operation data
3. Transportation data
4. Product supply data
5. Refining data
6. Marketing data

Crude and products movements projected by base case. This section is primarily concerned with operating data. It identifies the projected timing and size of expansions of existing processing facilities and the location, timing, and capacity of new facilities. Factors included are optimum allocation of new capacity in terms of crude availability and refined products demand, location of the demand, transportation costs, minimum economic size of facilities, and the cost of excess capacity versus the incremental cost of third-party processing of Gulf's crude oil.

This section of the output also has a yearly summary of crude oil movements from each crude source to each refinery. It summarizes product movements from each refinery to each country where the products are marketed. Finally, there is a yearly summary of projected excess refining capac-

FIGURE 18.3   Simulation Model Block Diagram

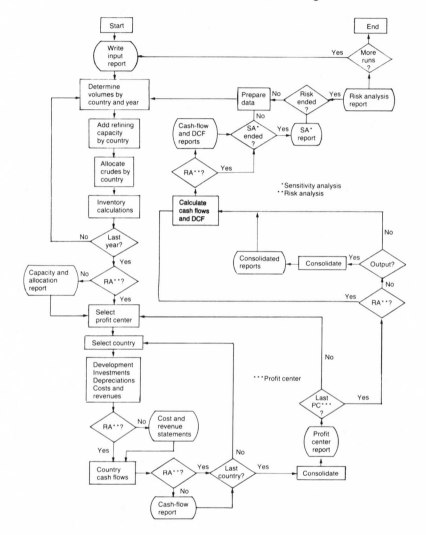

ity whether due to new facilities being built in sizes larger than required because of economies of scale or due to changes in the market or the sale of
marketing outlets. There is also an annual summary of projected product
deficiencies by type of product and by country.

Calculated results by country.   This section gives operating information and a cash-flow analysis separately for each country. In addition, it gives a cost and revenue analysis for marketing activities by type of product (light or heavy) in each country. This section would help to identify potential high-profit and problem areas in each functional activity and within each country that might result from management decisions or from changes in the business environment. This could be the most important output of this model in terms of planning for the future.

Calculated results by profit center. The fourth section of the output presents volumetric operating data and cash-flow statements for each profit center. A profit center is defined by the user of the model as a country or group of countries indicated in the input. This permits studies of corporate organization and profit responsibility allocation within the GOC-EH system. The performance of this type of analysis requires that input data be given separately for each country.

Calculated Results by Functional Area. This section contains consolidated data for GOC-EH but is broken down by the functional areas, that is, crude operations, transportation, refining, product supply, and marketing. The information contained in this section consists of operating data plus a statement of cash flow for each functional activity. This type of information indicates the degree of balance in the GOC-EH operation, and the cash-flow requirements by functional activity.

Calculated Results—Consolidated GOC-EH Summary. This section of the output includes consolidated GOC-EH volumetric operating data on exploration, crude oil, LPG and natural gas production, product supply, refining, and marketing for each year of the analysis. It also includes a consolidated statement of cash flow on a yearly basis and the discounted cash-flow analysis results.

Financial Summary. The last section of the output is essentially a yearly financial summary by country. It indicates the cash position, cash requirements, cumulative gross investment, annual return on invested capital, and other data that might be of help to management in evaluations and decisions.

The model requires a great deal of flexibility to accomplish the various types of studies. A number of options are available to the user so that many variations of a particular case can be tested without having to modify the program itself.

THE LINEAR PROGRAMMING MODEL

The development of a supply and distribution linear programming model for Gulf Eastern Hemisphere operations began in 1966. The model has continued to be used each year for the development of product supply and demand balances for eighteen-month forecasts and for revision of the profit plan budget. The model produces a product supply and demand balance for Western Europe. Imbalances in the supply position are removed by the use of external purchases or cargo sales.

The model represents Gulf's operations for a single time period. Data for alternative time periods are carried within the model, but only one time period can be used in a single computer run. Generating a larger model to include successive time periods is done by automatic copying of the central part of the model and attaching proper time-dependent data. In the work that has been done up to the present time, the link between time periods is product inventory. The results are particularly important and interesting when a number of quarterly periods are tied together. In the longer term planning work that we visualize, the link between periods would be capital requirements, since the facilities required must be anticipated by several years.

Demand requirements are met by moving available products from the supply points to produce the lowest transportation costs. The transportation rates used in the model are periodically revised to reflect the latest worldscale rates. No attempt is made to adopt actual transportation costs, because the relative rates alone suffice to determine the distribution pattern.

Automatic techniques allow the number of products to be reduced from the seventeen in the "basic" matrix to any smaller number. This permits subtotaling to suit the requirements of particular studies, with the advantage of working with a smaller matrix. The reduced list of products handled is usually naphtha, gasoline, distillate, low sulphur fuel oil, high sulphur fuel oil, asphalt, and LPG.

Use of the LP Model—Philosophy

Figure 18.4 gives an outline of the overall structure of the model, and table 18.1 gives an estimate of model size required to represent current operations by department for a single time period. The overall objectives of management in developing this model were:

- To provide a fast, systematic, and powerful method of analysis of the overall business.
- To evaluate alternatives and plans in the short term as well as in the time span of corporate planning.
- To assist in the exploration of feasible policies and objectives.
- To provide a basis for imposing controls over the execution of plans.

As we have seen, the model has been used primarily for determining an

FIGURE 18.4 Linear Programming Structure

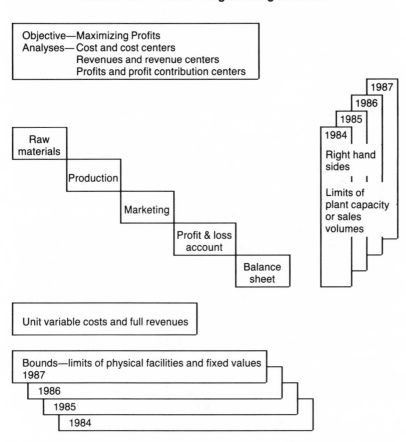

Objective—Maximizing Profits
Analyses— Cost and cost centers
Revenues and revenue centers
Profits and profit contribution centers

Raw materials

Production

Marketing

Profit & loss account

Balance sheet

1987
1986
1985
1984
Right hand sides

Limits of plant capacity or sales volumes

Unit variable costs and full revenues

Bounds—limits of physical facilities and fixed values
1987
1986
1985
1984

TABLE 18.1   Estimate of Model Size Required

	Rows (relationships)	Columns (variables)	Bounds
Crude oil	75	300	30
Transportation	75	750	—
Refining	200	750	75
Product supply	100	450	400
Marketing	200	750	750
Total	650	3000	1255

307

operational plan for supply and demand distribution. However, it is also used for postoptimal analyses or sensitivity analysis.

Other types of questions that might be answered by using the model are: How much does it cost to deviate from linear programming solutions for political or other reasons? What are the costs involved in deviating from the optimal solution in order to provide funds for activities such as exploration?

Objective Functions

The pursuit of different business objectives will normally lead to somewhat differing operating strategies. The minimization of cost is not equivalent to maximization of profits. Within the LP model, a number of different objective functions can be carried, and although only one can be used as an objective function in a single computer run, the value of each function is calculated automatically in each run.

Management may wish to study the impact of pursuing different objectives and examine their mutual compatibility. To illustrate, possible objective functions and their interrelationships are shown in figure 18.5.

Report Writers

Since linear programming is run using a generalized package, the reports produced will not be specifically designed for management use. They will not be appropriate for perusal by management because they will be too technical in nature. To overcome this problem, a number of computer programs exist that automatically develop a series of relevant management reports. Choices are available within any particular run as to which of these reports should be generated. Some of the reports are:

1. Area summary of product movements
2. Marketing report
3. Refinery operating plans
4. Processees operating plans
5. Processors operating plans
6. Exchange agreements reports

SYSTEM DEVELOPMENT, IMPLEMENTATION, AND MAINTENANCE

Successful development, implementation, and maintenance of a planning system require the commitment and active participation of operating

FIGURE 18.5 Alternative Objective Functions

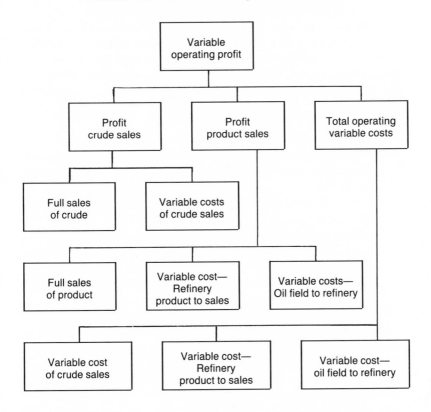

departments (via the planning council). During implementation, a planning analyst was introduced into the organization. The complexity of the system necessitated an individual responsible for its use and maintenance, one who could translate the ideas and planning alternatives generated by the planning council into computer statements of the problems and could solve the problems. This person had to communicate the solution results back to the planning council, aid in analysis of the solutions, and file maintenance and minor system modifications.

To assume these responsibilities, this individual should possess a thorough understanding of the following:

- Linear programming formulation techniques, solution procedures, and solution analysis
- The capabilities and limitations of the existing system

- The system components and their relative roles
- The various economic criteria that may be used as model objective functions to evaluate planning alternatives
- Departmental operations in sufficient detail to thoroughly define planning studies in cooperation with the departments themselves

This knowledge permits the planning analyst to maintain the communications network established during the development and implementation phases in order to achieve effective data maintenance and system modifications that will reflect current and future operations.

System development proceeds approximately as follows:

1. Develop preprocessor programs to obtain tabular data for the data base from various sources by direct transfer and arithmetic calculations.
2. Formulate the LP extensions in detail. Develop the matrix generation program to represent departmental operations. For each department, specify every variable and relationship. Define the objective functions.
3. Define comprehensive data-table structures for the data base with the department that ultimately will be responsible for maintenance of these data.
4. For each department, establish procedures for transfering available data from the source into the data base in the required tabular format defined above. The procedure may be performed either manually or by a preprocessor program.
5. Collect additional data necessary to meet the data base requirements for expanded applications in order to generate a model to represent current operations.
6. Validate the preprocessor programs, the data base structure and content, and matrix generation programs through partial and complete model generation. Define detailed validation procedures for the LP model and the entire system.
7. Modify existing postprocessor programs to prepare reports for solution analysis with specific content and structure defined by each department and the planning council.
8. Validate the system and document the detailed implementation and maintenance procedures.

The system is documented through a user's manual. The objective is to ensure that planning council representatives understand the system capabilities and limitations sufficiently to derive maximum benefit through its utilization. It is well to control development work by charts similar to the one in figure 18.6.

FIGURE 18.6   Development Time Table

Week No. 1 2 3 4 5 6 7 8 9 10 11 12 13 14 15 16 17 18 19 20 21 22 23 24 25 26 27 28 29 30 31 32 33 34 35

System Completion ⟶

Note: Completed work is shown as solid bars, future work as unshaded bars.

Refinery Models		Opening Status
Matrix Generator Development		Operating
Corporate LP Model	Supply/demand Version	Operating
	Economics Version	
	Single point Version	Operating
Sensitivity Version	Sensitivity Version	Operating
	Risk analysis Version	
Data Bank	All of the above will receive input data and will supply calculated data	
Preprocessors	Marketing	
	Transportation	
	Refining	
	Exploration and production	
Reports Package	Operate from data bank, rather than a particular model	Operating within models

Data Maintenance

Since the validity of the information derived is a direct function of the validity of the data present in the model, a reliable data maintenance procedure is an essential component of the system. If routine data maintenance is not performed, the model data base is unlikely to be updated until a specific study is requested. Between studies, the model data base may rest undisturbed on a magnetic tape or disc pack for long periods. Usually little time is provided for the case study, and no time is allocated for updating the model data base.

The recommended data maintenance procedure emphasizes a formal routine for the communication of data modifications from each departmental representative to the planning analyst. The planning council, through the planning analyst and its designated departmental representatives, assumes the responsibility for the success of its operation. An inherent discipline comes from this data maintenance procedure. It delegates responsibility, establishes a formal regular schedule, provides formal lines of communication, and authorizes one individual to supervise its operation.

CONCLUSIONS

From the previous discussion, we see that the company has in operation an extremely powerful and hard-hitting computer-based system for conducting long-range planning studies. The system is divided into two self-contained parts. The first of these parts is the sensitivity model that requires its own style of input and produces reports integrated with calculations of the model. The second part of the system is the linear programming system that consists of a rather large number of independent but interrelated computer programs. The existing components can be consolidated, integrated, and operated as a single package. The consolidation of packages into a single automated system is displayed in figure 18.7.

When conducting risk analysis, since the major planning tool is the linear programming system, it is necessary either to guarantee that the simulation model (which is used directly for risk analysis) is in exact agreement with the linear programming system or to develop a separate model by automatic generation from the linear programming matrix and data that would be capable of conducting risk analysis. Direct usage of linear programming in risk analysis is, of course, impossible because of computer time requirements.

The planning process is much more complicated than might be appreciated. Data must be received and coordinated from each of five profit-center

FIGURE 18.7   Running Procedure

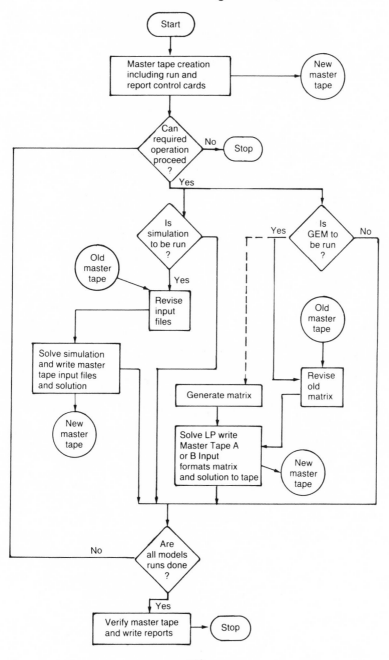

areas. Many alternate long-range plans must be considered, perhaps several dozen. Parts of the base-case plan or other plans must be extracted and used in other alternatives. Each year a deadline for submission to world headquarters must be met. In order to manage a complex project of this nature, it is often desirable to set up a suitable system for controlling and coordinating the creation of long-range plans based on critical path scheduling.

Exercise 18

This and every exercise is intended to form the basis for a part of the term project: Prepare a strategic plan for an organization of your choice. For each exercise, present a typed, one-page report, showing the directions your analysis will take.

For this exercise, write a critique of the systems reported here. Suggest mistakes that may have been made or strong points that were achieved. Compare the Gulf system with a proposed system for your company.

In addition to the material in this chapter, any of the references previously given may be pertinent.

References

Holloway, Clark, and Jones, G. T. "Planning at Gulf—A Case Study." *Long Range Planning* (Apr. 1975), p.27.

Wagle, B. V.; Goat, R. C.; Boot, P.; Jones, G. T.; Longbottom, D. A.; and Jenkins, P. M. *The Development of a General System to Aid the Corporate Planning Process—A Feasibility Study.* IBM (U.K.) Report, 1970.

Chapter 19

Introducing Strategic Planning in a Medium-Size Company

Paul N. Finlay

Within an organization pursuing a participative style of management, the organizational effort required to implement a strategic planning process, as against a corporate plan, is not generally recognized. This chapter describes the strategic planning approach that was taken by a medium-sized United Kingdom (U.K.) company engaged in the production and marketing of consumer goods. The description of the approach falls naturally into four parts:

1. A review of the state of planning in the company prior to the large planning effort made during 1976–1977.
2. A description of the planning activities carried out during this period.
3. A critique of this planning.
4. A description of developments since then.

STRATEGIC PLANNING PRIOR TO 1976

The company is one of many within a multinational group. Its operations were controlled by a supervisory board located at group head office, which had overall strategic authority. It had a conventional, formal organi-

Adapted from Paul N. Finlay, "Introducing Corporate Planning in a Medium-Size Company: A Case History," *Long Range Planning* (Apr. 1982). Used by permission of Pergamon Press, Ltd.

zation, with departments of production, marketing, personnel, accounting and finance, and management services.

In order to plan for the activities of all the companies in the group, the planners within the supervisory board set guidelines for the company in which their expectations for the company were spelled out. These guidelines arrived in January of each year. In April the supervisory board then received from the company a preliminary briefing document setting forth a draft plan for the company covering the following three years.

After reviewing the preliminary briefing document, any necessary modifications would be incorporated into the company plan that was presented to the supervisory board in September. This fitted the company's financial year, which ran from 1 October to 31 September.

In the years prior to 1976–1977, the main work of producing strategic plans had rested with the management accountants, (although naturally the responsibility for the final plan and its ultimate transmission to group head office lay with the board). In this work the accountants were abetted by the management services department, which had produced computer models to aid in planning. Three models were in use by 1976:

1. A Company Summary Model for forecasting profit and loss accounts, balance sheets and cash flows. This model was constructed along the traditional lines of purely financial planning models.
2. A Materials Model to forecast raw material purchases and associated variable costs for classes of product. This model was an extremely simple input-output model.
3. A Marketing Model that allowed marketing area contribution to be calculated. This model was simply a financial planning model constructed around the region/area/territory structure of the marketing department.

Although considered valid by the accountants and by the management services department, these models, and the use to which they were put, were not widely accepted in the company. Indeed, the planning process itself was viewed by some departments as being far too financially oriented and controlled by financial personnel.

While this rudimentary strategic planning was being developed, the company had been moving towards a positive commitment at board level to the acceptance of a participative style of management. This trend, coupled with the dissatisfaction expressed by nonfinancial management about their lack of involvement in the planning process, led to the initiation of a new and forceful direction to strategic planning. This occurred in mid-1976.

THE DEVELOPMENTS IN STRATEGIC PLANNING DURING 1976–1977

Organizational Changes

To carry out the required planning, an organization different from the departmental organization was required. The first step in its construction was the identification of interests that were a key to the survival and well-being of the company. The core interests so defined were:

1. Marketing
2. Profitability
3. Productivity
4. Employee relations
5. Employee development
6. External relations

The board realised that it would not be able to devote sufficient time to the large task of creating the mechanism needed for the participative planning envisaged or for the detailed control required. A team, called the coordinating team, was set up to take over responsibility for creating and operating the mechanisms by which the quantitative side of the plans would be computed. It would be responsible for identifying, publicizing, and achieving resolution of any inconsistencies between the mechanisms and for defining and monitoring the progress of plan formulation and reporting it to the board.

A team was brought together to be responsible for the planning associated with each core interest. The leader of each core interest group was normally the director most closely concerned with the area (for example, the marketing director would head the marketing core interest group). The membership of a core interest group lay between four and eight and contained a member of the coordinating team.

Acting at one level below the core interest groups were departmental planning teams. The responsibilities of the teams were defined by the departmental director concerned, although each department would be picking up objectives, policies, and so forth defined during the strategic planning phase. Although composition of these teams varied considerably from department to department, members of the coordinating team were naturally included in their departmental team.

The relations between planning groups and the overlaps of membership that occurred are summarized in figure 19.1. (For the sake of clarity, only

FIGURE 19.1   Membership Overlap of Planning Groups

one core interest group and its associated departmental planning team are depicted.

Formal Plans and Documents

The tangible end-product of a phase of planning was the production of a plan. During the yearly planning cycle, five formal plans were produced. These were:

1. Skeletal plan—a broad statement of the company's intentions broken down by core interest. It was produced in March with a time horizon of three and a half years (year one beginning in October). Its scope was wider than that of the preliminary briefing document to allow stronger links to departmental planning.

2. Preliminary briefing document—a document based on the skeletal plan that satisfied the requirements of the supervisory board for its broad planning purposes.

3. Company plan—a document covering the same ground as the skeletal plan but based on more detailed departmental planning. In its first year it was a summary of the more detailed budget.

4. Budget—a detailed financial picture of a financial year, with expected income and expenditure defined to the levels required for subsequent control.

5. Company action plan—an extract from the company plan listing the objectives to be attained during the current year. It constituted the basis for on-going control of progress toward those significant objectives not explicitly controlled by quantitative review against budget (for example, control of the progress toward one negotiating period for all the unions represented in the company).

Two more formal documents were produced.

1. Guidelines—a document issued by the board to the core interest groups and the coordination team giving a company scenario and setting out its expectations by core interest and the constraints within which each core interest group would operate to formulate its contribution to the skeletal and company plans.

2. Planning manual—in which all relevant features of the planning process were documented, for example, the definition of all terms used in planning and the composition of core interest groups.

The link between these formal documents is shown in figure 19.2.

Two major phases occurred in the planning cycle, one ending with the production of the skeletal plan (the preliminary briefing document merely consisting of extracts from it), and one ending with the production of the company plan. This second phase followed rather traditional lines and will not be discussed further.

The Development of Planning Mechanisms

After defining core interests and the organization to go with them, it was necessary to develop mechanisms to aid both the planning activities and the control of these activities. In particular it was necessary to have:

1. A means of defining and controlling the sequence of activities necessary for the planning process

2. An appropriate means of eliciting expert knowledge and data from the relevant core interest groups

3. A means of processing these data into comprehensive financial and physical pictures of the company and of the areas of activity within it and of exploring the sensitivity of the solutions to differing assumptions

4. A means of drawing together the qualitative and quantitative responses from all relevant groups.

FIGURE 19.2 The Link between Formal Documents and Timings

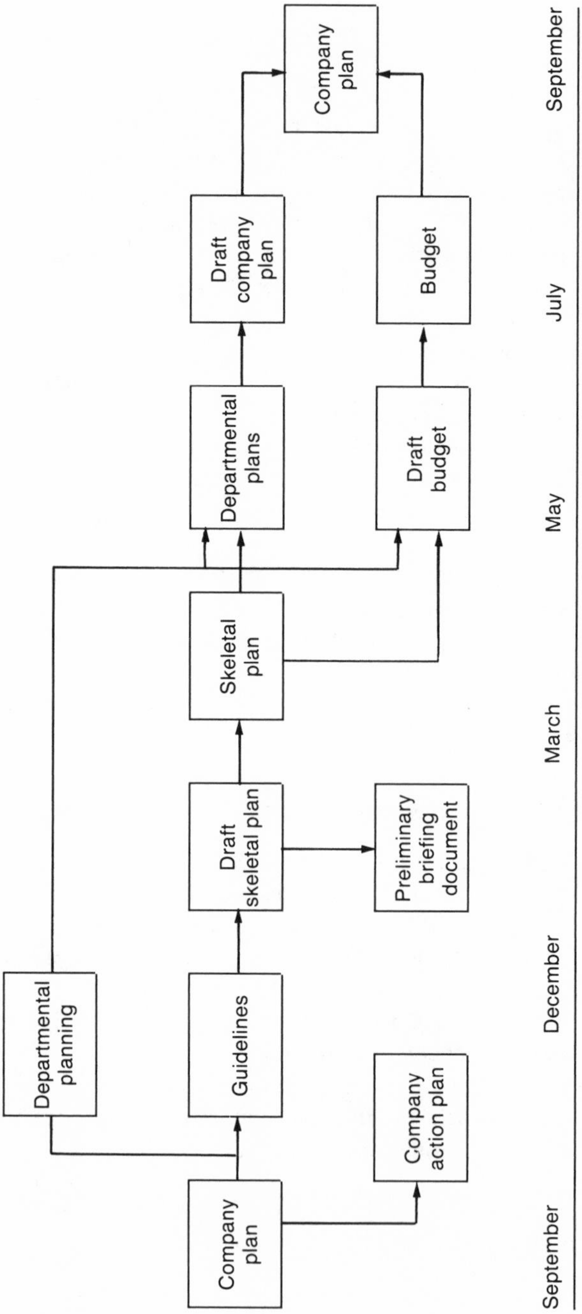

The Mechanisms

The guidelines issued by the board in December set the framework within which the skeletal plan was to be constructed. The aim of the guidelines was to allow all relevant expert knowledge and opinion within the company to be tapped and used in the planning process, while at the same time eliciting the small amount of data necessary to calculate the significant physical and financial consequences of any proposals put forward. It was important that broad thinking would be encouraged positively and concentration on detail be suppressed.

This aim was achieved by constructing the guidelines in two parts. Part one was a scenario specifying company expectations and stating the assumptions and constraints within which those contributing to the plan should work. The second part consisted of a questionnaire in two parts to elicit views on policies and philosophies and to gather specific sets of data. The answers to part one of the questionnaire were used to produce the main "qualitative" part of the skeletal plan. Answers to part two were used mainly as input to the computer models, in order to enable the calculations of the physical and financial consequences associated with the "qualitative" part of the plan. This procedure is depicted in figure 19.3.

To structure the questionnaire it was important to identify for each core interest those issues where the policy adopted would be important to the performance of the company as a whole (rather than at departmental level or below). An example should make this clear. A very important issue for the company within the "productivity" core interest covered the purchase and storage of one type of raw material. By concentrating on strategic issues, four areas where policy statements would be needed were identified. These covered:

1. The duration of stock to be held
2. Average quantity of the material to be used in the finished product
3. Sources of the raw material
4. Expenditure on warehousing

On these issues, broad policy statements were required with little quantification.

For part two of the questionnaire, it was important only to ask for data that might affect strategic decisions and at a level of appropriate precision. The precision required was determined by the following logic.

It was known from a review of past projections of sales, that the standard deviation of estimating was around 5 percent. This meant that the spread in estimating the company profit was at least this size. The board were exposed to the argument that little would be lost if the overall precision

FIGURE 19.3   The Place of the Questionnaire

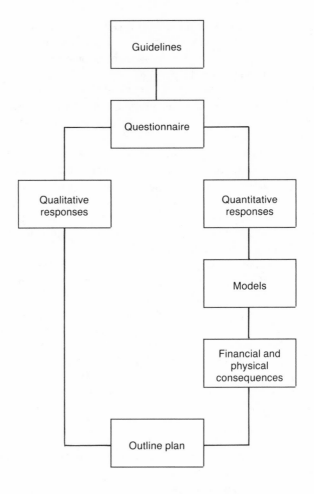

of the modeling process was such as to increase this uncertainty in profit estimation by 10 percent, that is, to 5.5 percent. On this basis it could be shown that "errors" of up to around 2 percent of turnover could be accepted.

Armed with the board's agreement to this and knowing the approximate size of each contributory factor to the company's turnover, the precision needed for each element in the corporate financial plan could be calculated. For the important raw material this imprecision came to about £250,000 per year. Knowing the amount and that the main areas were as shown above, further requirements of precision could be devised and allotted to these main areas. Thus, the second part of the questionnaire could be devised. The one for the important raw material is reproduced in figure 19.4.

The means of defining and controling the sequence of activities necessary to the planning process was through a rather traditional network analysis. The level of detail in the analysis can be judged from the fact that a total of 120 activities were individually identified.

Computer Models

The means of collating the data from questionnaires to form the financial picture of the company was through the use of four models. Three of these have already been referred to: the company summary model, the materials model, and the marketing model. These were modified slightly during the year and joined by a fourth model called the personnel model. The relationship between these models is depicted in figure 19.5.

The personnel cost model was of a significantly different type from the other three models in that it attempted a much more subtle modelling than their definitional modelling. For each department at each of the company's factories, a model was derived that related the size of groups of employees to the production volume of classes of product. In general, five groups of employees were identified in each department: managers, skilled employees, two types of unskilled employees, and employees whose wage depended on measured output. An equation relating the size of each group to output was constructed for each group within a department. Labor costs were then determined by multiplying these numbers by the average company cost for the group and summing over groups. Where company cost per employee was related to output, a similar but more complicated calculation was necessary. With these four models, the quantitive consequences of answers to the questionnaires could be quickly assessed and collated, and the consequences of "what if" questions could be explored.

Responsibility for checking on the consistency of the qualitative and quantitive responses from the core interest group lay with the coordinating team. The mechanism for such activity was very simple. The relevant core interest groups were notified if inconsistencies were shown up in the returns (for example, when assumptions made by the marketing core interest group failed to agree with those made by the productivity core interest group). As the time approached for submission to the supervisory board, this referral to a core interest group was cut out in favor of a direct approach from a member of the coordinating team to the most affected directly responsible company employee.

FIGURE 19.4 Questionnaire for Commodity X

Outline Plan: Questionnaire—Commodity X

In the COMPANY PLAN it was stated that _____
(Repeat here of statements concerning durations, inflation etc.) and in the CALCULA-
TION OF PURCHASE QUANTITIES etc. the FOLLOWING DATA WERE USED
(Statement of data for overall product characteristics).

Bearing in mind the COMPANY OBJECTIVES, would you state your intentions regarding changes in the FOLLOWING OVER the next three years, with ACCOMPANYING
EXPLANATION.

1. *Policy on durations held of commodity X.*
2. *Quantity of commodity X used per unit product.*
3. *Policy on proportions by source.*
4. *Storage expenditure.*

Would you please complete the table below:

	1976/1977	1977/1978	1978/1979	1979/1980
1. Average duration (to nearest 0.2 months)				
2. Cost inflation (to nearest 1%)				
3. Changes to basic recipes (to nearest 1%)				
4. Changes in storage expenses (to nearest £100,000 p.a. in 1976/1977 pounds)				

CRITIQUE OF THE PLANNING ACTIVITIES OF 1976–1977

The main points of the critique were directed to various general factors and to the models.

General Factors

1. Although the preliminary briefing document was meant to give a very broadly based view of the company's plans for the next few years, the planning associated with it and with the skeletal plan of which it was an extract were too detailed and polished. This took place in spite of the acceptance of the logic underlying the consistency of precision described earlier. This seemed to have been caused by those board members responsible for presenting the preliminary briefing document to their bosses (the supervisory board) not having gotten agreement on the level of precision re-

FIGURE 19.5   Relationship among the Company Models

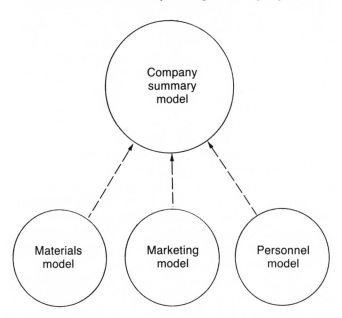

quired. Working under such uncertainty as to what was required by one's bosses, it was natural to become precise and detailed and also to amass a lot of even more detailed back-up information should the presentation of the plan become sticky.

2. The effort to form interdepartmental core interest groups was only partly successful. An interchange of ideas between departments did take place, but since the composition of these teams were heavily biased in favor of associated departments (for example, the production department provided many of the members of the productivity core interest group), the dominant department would generally work out a position prior to core interest group meetings, and that departmental view would prevail without much discussion. Thus the debate within the core interest group that could have been so educative to the other group members was rather limited.

3. The chairmen of the core interest groups did not seem to fully understand their responsibilities. This led to uncertainty as to the role of the core interest groups.

4. The structure of core interest groups tended to reflect a head office view, limiting and restricting the voice of the factories. This problem was identified by Currill (1977).

5. The pace of development of planning was too great for the company to absorb.

6. The management accountants, who had played the major role in producing company plans prior to 1976–1977, retained their view that it was the financial statements in the plan that were important and that the planning process was rather inconsequential. One reason for this attitude appeared to be that they wished to satisfy their functional "bosses." As the financial statements were all-important, they had to look right. This led the accountants who were responsible for these statements to reconcile the data received from other areas within the company. In a sense they were correct to do this, since incomplete or otherwise unacceptable returns were being made by the core interest teams. Frequently the relevant people were unobtainable, and the accountants themselves had a reasonable grasp of the company's activities. However, this reconciliation of the data was the very antithesis of planning, in which the intention is to allow a greater understanding of relationships by participants. Since, in general, the accountants did not have sufficient knowledge of markets or product trends, their adjustments could only have been interpolations or extrapolations.

7. The emphasis in the planning remained on the quantitative core interests: marketing, profitability, and productivity. The creation of the company action plan was an important step towards controlling those activities not directly quantifiable.

8. The link between operational data and that used in the planning models was tenuous. Although one can argue that if one is planning over a three-year time scale, the exact state of play at the time the planning is taking place is rather inconsequential, many hours were expended arguing and determining exact stock positions and so on, and taking the emphasis away from high level thinking.

The Models

1. The computer models had mixed fortunes. The marketing model was used by marketing managers to help in their planning and was judged a success. The company summary model was set up for the management accountants and financial director to use and satisfied their needs very well. The materials model was less successful. The main reasons for this were that the managers responsible for the purchase and storage of raw materials had been involved only peripherally in the creation of the model. They had never had what was to them a satisfactory explanation of its workings. The problem was exacerbated by the fact that a computerized tactical planning model (more detailed but of lesser scope than the materials model) was already in

existence and was used to help in determining purchases of the most important raw material during the subsequent year. Management had grown to know and rely upon this tactical model. When, not surprisingly, small discrepancies appeared between the expenditures forecast by the two models, the materials model was adjudged wrong and its results rejected. The problem of gaining acceptance for the materials model was compounded by the unwitting use of different assumtions and different data when a comparison of the materials model and the second model was made. Naturally enough, large discrepancies appeared, and time pressures prevented the reasons for the discrepencies being cleared up straight away. Naturally enough, management preferred to trust the model they were familiar with.

2. The personnel model was almost a complete disaster. It had been produced so that the manning levels and labor costs at the factories could be "flexed" to follow changes in marketing forecasts. Without the model, it was a time-consuming business to obtain a revision of the manning levels from the factories. The problem was that the objectives of the model were not sufficiently clear. Had the model been restricted to planning rather than attempting also to provide a budgetary control mechanism it would have succeeded. Its failure must rest primarily with the failure of the business analyst to identify the problems effectively and the failure to secure real commitment from all end users. Yet, given the time available and the organizational structure in the company, this was difficult to accomplish.

The basic problem with the personnel model was that the "judgmental modeling" used in it was far too sophisticated for practical use by the company. The other three models were basically "definitional models" in which all the rules were either widely accepted definitions or approximations to them. (Generally these models were restricted to dealing with financial and accounting definitions.) In the personnel model, however, an attempt was made to model a situation in which no one had thought in terms of explicit relationships. The idea of writing down an equation with symbols that would later have numbers attached was not understood and the implications to the company were not fully appreciated.

3. The use of questionnaires designed to elicit both wide-ranging thinking and the necessary detailed data was a successful innovation. It struck a balance between extrapolative and visionary planning, thus overcoming the problem cited in Currill (1977) and mitigating the problems of data collection given in Hayes and Nolan (1974).

4. The link-up of questionnaires and models was not close enough and the models not easy enough to use to allow quick feedback of the results of proposals from the core interest groups. Consequently, few iterations in the planning process were possible.

DEVELOPMENT AFTER THE 1976-1977 PLANNING CYCLE

Given the nature of the large planning effort made in 1976-1977, it was felt worthwhile to seek an independent view of the planning activities. To this end, an outside consultant was employed to review the situation. He concluded that the planning mechanisms were good and suggested, *inter alia*, that the company should appoint a full-time planning coordinator.

The company's momentum towards increased participation was continued by the appointment of a manager to assist in the development of company and departmental roles in planning. At the same time as the 1976-1977 planning was being undertaken, a separate team within the company was working totally independently on a project that was scheduled to come on stream in 1978. It would call for a production and marketing effort comparable to that currently being undertaken by the entire company. While this project team reported to the managing director, the supervisory board was closely involved, since the company itself would not have been able to support the cost of investment. Over a period of several months, there was discussion of how to treat this proposed activity. Should it be in or out of the formal company planning? How should costs be apportioned between current activities and those associated with the project? Finally, the project was (rather uneasily) incorporated within the operational planning framework about two years after it was begun.

Throughout 1977-1978, the company was preoccupied with the project, and all other planning activities were considered of minor concern. Large modifications to the company summary model were needed to incorporate this new activity. The company summary model was used extensively during this period. Interestingly, its ability to provide rapid analyses for management meant that a large amount of managerial time and effort was spent making minor adjustments to the figure rather than using the models to answer more fundamental "what if" questions. For a similar instance, see the new factory discussion below.

The personnel model was abandoned. The reversion to manual calculation of factory manning levels was not at all successful due to a near complete failure to coordinate head office and factory planning (the relevant core interest group—the productivity core interest group—in fact never met.) Manning levels were produced by each factory on inconsistent bases with little apparent regard for the planning assumptions.

A fundamental shift in process took place during 1977-1978. This was caused by the priorities given to other group activities and by substantial changes in key personnel associated with the planning activities. The accountants successfully exploited this situation to reassert their dominance over the planning process. They proposed drawing up the skeletal plan at a very detailed level, but still submitting the higher-level preliminary briefing document to the supervisory board. This proposal was accepted by the company's board, since it would enable board members to answer detailed questions and would reduce difficulties in reconciling the preliminary briefing document and company plan. The advantage of concentrating on broad thinking clearly had not been accepted or understood by many managers during the previous year.

The planning emphasis now reverted to "getting the figures right." The qualitative aspect of the questionnaire all but disappeared, and in some instances the questionnaires became computer input forms. Although planning was now effectively back under the control of accountants, there was less reconciling of the data due to the increased planning experience of the core interest teams. When illogical data were produced, the accountants now sought to influence change at the data source.

In 1977–1978, a planning coordinator was appointed, who reported to the managing director. However, the coordination team died through inaction, and the questionnaires and the core interest groups were quietly abandoned.

By the end of 1978, a potential shortfall in productive capacity was foreseen for the early 1980s. A project team was set up to examine the feasibility of setting up a completely new factory in the United Kingdom. The parallel with the 1978 project was close: the project team worked in almost total independence of what was left of the planning process and mechanisms. Soon after the project started, it was realized that a computer model was needed to provide a financial evaluation of the various proposed strategies.

The model proved invaluable in coordinating marketing, production, and financial assumptions. Once again, however, there was a preoccupation with detailed questions and little senior management direction regarding the basic methodology underlying capital investment decisions (inflated or real value results; NPV, IRR, or some other criterion: the treatment of internal company transfer payments). During 1979, the proposal to build a new factory was rejected because the supervisory board was sceptical about the projected sales growth and concerned about the magnitude of the investment. Subsequently, the company's financial position deteriorated sharply. To cope with this setback, the company decided to cut staff levels and move toward a more streamlined organization. As a result of the reorganization, the managerial posts that had responsibility for planning coordination and for company and departmental role development were abolished, and the management services department analyst responsible for the planning models moved to supporting lower level accounting systems. Control of the planning process now rested firmly in the hands of accountants. Budgeting had taken priority over planning. In another guise, Gresham's Law had triumphed once again.

CONCLUSIONS

The events described above took place over about four years. Within this time the company had gone through a complete cycle of planning activities and was almost back where it started—with emphasis on "getting the figures right" and on budgeting rather than planning. The broad reasons for the regression may be summarized as follows:

1. The intrusion of group projects running parallel with the main company planning process had damaging effects on the credibility of the planning.
2. Throughout there had been a tendency to underestimate substantially the resources needed to develop and maintain the planning process and its associated mechanisms.
3. As well as underestimating the resources required, the speed with which the organization could change its ways of thought was also grossly overestimated. Too much was attempted over too small a time scale.
4. The accountants, who were influential in the company, never understood the planning process. They did not understand the difference between data for planning purposes and data for operational control.
5. The problem of level of detail had never been solved. Even when senior management issued clear instructions to proceed at a certain level of detail, the same senior managers undermined the credibility of those instructions. When presented with results, they frequently asked questions that requested information at variance with their own instructions.
6. There was too great a reliance on key personnel. Too much depended on their abilities and their grasp of a complex planning process with which they were unfamiliar.

References

Curril, David L. "Introducing Corporate Planning—A Case Study." *Long Range Planning* 10 (1977), pp. 70–79.

Finlay, Paul N. "Introducing Corporate Planning in a Medium-Size Company: A Case History." *Long Range Planning* (Apr. 1982), p. 93.

Hayes, R. H., and Nolan, R. L. "What Kind of Corporate Modeling Functions Best?" *Harvard Business Review* 52, 3 (1974), pp. 102–12.

Appendixes

A. *Directory of Economic Forecasting and Related Services*

B. *Directory of Planning Societies*

C. *Glossary of Planning Terms*

D. *Careers in Planning*

Appendix A

Directory of Economic Forecasting and Related Services

This appendix is presented as a guide to those considering consultancy as a career and to those in the process of choosing a consultant for their organization.

Characteristics of a Good Consultant

There are a number of qualities that a good consultant will possess. No individual will have them all.

Intelligence. A consultant is not called into an organization to solve simple problems. Most of the issues he must face are complex, fuzzy, and full of interlocking, interrelated features. Out of this, he must develop coherence, integrated insights, and workable recommendations.

Knowledge. Even a genius can operate better if he or she has a solid background in the pertinent business fields, as well as experience and knowledge in strategic planning itself.

Organizational sensitivity. Even when the basic issues seem to relate to planning, economics, or marketing, the consultant must never overlook the factors of personal values, departmental jealousies, and other behavioral considerations.

Integrity. The consultant must be able to withstand pressures from areas of the organization where he may not be welcome, while at the same time securing information and participation from all departments, including those where he is unwelcome. Being able to operate in such an environment and to produce impartial, factual reports requires a great deal of personal integrity.

Drive and energy. A client usually wants the results of a study yesterday. The consultant must be able to work long hours at peak productivity and to sustain such a pace throughout his consulting career. Consulting is an entrepreneurship, requiring an orientation toward high achievement and the willingness to take personal risks.

Ability to communicate. Last but by no means least, the consultant must be able to tell the client what he has found out. At a minimum, ideas must be presented clearly and in good style, both orally and in written form. It is even better if the consultant can be forceful and inspirational.

The One-Time Problem

A number of situations exist where a consultant might be needed. The first that comes to mind is the one-time problem. Here, a new issue has arisen that is beyond the expertise of the organization. Either the issue, when solved, is not expected to occur again or hiring fulltime employees to handle the issue would be too time consuming. The consultant comes in, solves the problem, and, if it is expected to recur, perhaps helps to recruit and train permanent employees to handle it.

Start Up a New Effort

Suppose a new function, strategic planning, for example, is to be implemented. The consultant would advise on what needs to be done and what chronological steps need to be taken and, in general, would point the organization in the right direction. After one or at most two planning cycles had been completed, the effort could be carried on internally.

Continuing Consultancy

An organization may be faced with a continuing stream of new and varied problems. Sometimes an organization needs a research arm but is unable to afford a full-time department. Sometimes the CEO wishes a continuing and objective appraisal of what is being done. For these, or various other reasons, the firm may be able to justify the retention of a consultant on a more or less continuing basis.

What-If Sessions

Companies are eager to anticipate events and prepare for them. Rather than relying on executives or planners to come up with fortuitous ideas, it may be useful to the company for a consultant to prepare abstracts of the host of future-oriented articles in the firm's area. Periodically, say quarterly, the executives can spend a day with the consultant in a "brainstorming" session. Using the abstracts as a starting point, potential trends and associated profit opportunities can be explored.

In-House Seminars

The use of consultants to design and conduct in-house seminars was discussed in chapter 15.

Finding a Suitable Consultant

Determine the desirable characteristics for a consultant using the list above as a starting point and adding to it the particular requirements of the firm. Following is a directory of consultants. This can be expanded by reading advertisements in current journals. A set of promising consultants can be selected on the basis of geography, hearsay, or at random for particular investigations. Inquire about their background and expertise, and ask for a list of references of satisfied clients. The initial inquiry would include a broad statement of the firm's problem and what it wished to accomplish. Also, both the Association of Strategic Planning Consultants (ASPC) and the International Association of Strategic Planning Consultants (IASPC) in the directory offer free referral services to help a firm locate the right consultant for its particular situation. They also have directories of planning consultants that concisely list the credentials and specialities of each consultant.

STRATEGIC PLANNING CONSULTANTS

(NOTE: AN ASTERISK * INDICATES WORK ON COMPUTER SYSTEMS.)

ADP NETWORK SERVICES, INC.*
425 PARK AVE.
NEW YORK NY 10022

APPLIED DATA RESEARCH
ROUTE 206 CENTER, CN-8
PRINCETON NJ 08540

ASSOCIATION OF STRATEGIC PLANNING
CONSULTANTS (ASPC)
P.O. BOX 5198
FAIRLAWN OH 44313

BATTELLE*
COLUMBUS LABORATORIES
505 KING AVENUE
COLUMBUS OH 43201

BOEING COMPUTER SERVICES
P.O. BOX 24346, MS 6K-01
SEATTLE WA 98124

BUSINESS INTERNATIONAL CORP.
ONE DAG HAMMARSKJOLD PLAZA
NEW YORK NY 10017

CACI*
12011 SAN VINCENTE BLVD.
LOS ANGELES CA 90049

CAMBRIDGE PLANNING AND
ANALYTICS, INC.
P.O. BOX 276
CAMBRIDGE MA 02138

CAPITAL STRATEGY GROUP, INC.
20 NORTH WACKER DR.
CHICAGO IL 60606

COMSHARE
DECISION SUPPORT SYSTEMS
MARKETING
P.O. BOX 1588
ANN ARBOR MI 48106

CORPORATE PLANNING, INC.
ABOARD THE KAY V
2456 N.E. 26TH ST.
LIGHTHOUSE PT. FL 33064

EPS CONSULTANTS
35 SOHO SQUARE
LONDON, ENGLAND W1V 5DG

EPS, INC.*
ONE PENN PLAZA, SUITE 1540
NEW YORK NY 10119

EXECUCOM
P.O. BOX 9758
AUSTIN TX 78766

EXECUTIVE ENTERPRISES, INC.
33 WEST 60TH ST.
NEW YORK NY 10023

WILLIAM R. FOGLE & CO.
P.O. BOX 1152
ANN ARBOR, MI 48107

THE FUTURES GROUP
76 EASTERN BLVD.
GLASTONBURY CT 06033

INTERNATIONAL ASSOCIATION OF
STRATEGIC PLANNING
CONSULTANTS (IASPC)
P.O. BOX 5198
AKRON OH 44313

MDCR, INC.
760 HIGHWAY 18
EAST BRUNSWICK NJ 08816

NAYLOR GROUP*
P.O. BOX 3297
CHAPEL HILL NC 27514

PLANNING DYNAMICS, INC.
DEPT. D, 850 RIDGE AVE.
PITTSBURGH PA 15212

PRITSKER & ASSOCIATES, INC.
P.O. BOX 2413C
WEST LAFAYETTE IN 47906

RAND CORP.
PACIFIC COAST HIGHWAY
SANTA MONICA CA

RAPIDATA
20 NEW DUTCH LANE
P.O. BOX 1049
FAIRFIELD NJ 07006

SIMPLAN
300 EASTOWNE
CHAPEL HILL NC 27514

STANFORD RESEARCH INST.
333 RAVENSWOOD AVE.
MENLO PARK CA 94025

STRATEGIC ANALYSIS, INC.
2525 PROSPECT STREET
READING PA 19606

STRATEGIC PLANNING INSTITUTE
955 MASSACHUSETTS AVE.
CAMBRIDGE MA 02139

STRATEGIC PLANNING ASSOCIATES,
   INC.
600 NEW HAMPSHIRE AVE., N.W.
WATERGATE 600
WASHINGTON, D.C. 20037

STSC, INC.*
2115 EAST JEFFERSON ST.
ROCKVILLE MD 20852

TECHNOLOGY CONSULTING GROUP,
   INC.
ONE COMMERCIAL WHARF NORTH
BOSTON MA 02110

Appendix B

Directory of Planning Societies

The benefits to the individual of membership in one or more planning societies are discussed in chapter 15. Briefly, these are association in a society with one's peers in the planning world, a subscription to the journal of that society, and a certain element of status through the membership. Of course, the journal can be purchased without membership, but the cost of the journal plus membership is usually little more than the journal alone.

Not all countries support a planning society, as we found out by making a brief survey of a number of Central American and Middle East countries. Membership in the major societies of the United States and other countries is available to residents of such countries, so that a person can receive the journal and enjoy the status of membership, but would miss the benefits of attendance at local chapter meetings.

The following list gives the names, a contact address, and a brief amount of information about some of the better known societies. For some of the smaller groups, the only address available is that of an officer, and the officer may change from time to time, thus requiring a bit of detective work. Usually, the current address may be obtained through the International Affiliation of Planning Societies. Technically, some of the organizations listed are not planning societies, but all have a strong interest in the subject.

Asociacion Mexicana De Ejecutivos En Planeacion, A.C.
Parque Via No. 198 of 218
Col. Cuauhtemoc
Mexico 5, D.F.

Association Francaise pour la Planification d'Entreprise (AFPLANE)
President: Mr. Henry KLIPFEL, Thomson-CSF
32 avenue du Chateau
92190 Meudon Bellevue, France
Member IAPS, EPLAF

Associazione Italiana Planificazione Aziendale (AIPA)
President: Dr. Giorgia FANFANI, Montedison
Piazzale Morandi 2
20121 Milano, Italy
Member IAPS

CENADE—Centro Argentino de Estrategia
President: Ing. José María Romero Maletti
Address: Rodrí Peña 1180
1020 Buenos Aires—Argentina

College on Planning Institute of Management Sciences (TIMS)
290 Westminster St.
Providence RI 02903
> Journal: *Interfaces* (Jointly with Operations Research Society of
> America)
> *Management Science*

Consejo Profesional de Ciencias Económicas
de la Capital Federal
Comisión de Planeamiento y Control
President: Dr. Angel Toninelli
Address: Viamonte 1145
1053 Buenos Aires—Argentina

Corporate Planner's Association (CPA)
Ms. Laura J. Kent
703 Market Street, 251
San Francisco, Calif. 94103
Member IAPS
> The purpose of the Association is to achieve a better
> understanding and utilization of planning skills and their
> potential contribution to business, industry and government.

Corporate Planning Special Group
Operations Research Society of America (ORSA)
Mount Royal and Guilford Avenues
Baltimore MD 21202 USA
> Journal: *Interfaces* (Jointly with TIMS)
> *Operations Research*
> Benefits: Meetings, journals, newsletters, employment notes
Member IAPS

European Planning Federation (EPLAF)
Secretariat
15 Belgrave Square
London SWIX 8PU, England
> This is an umbrella organization which coordinates the
> efforts of European planning groups. The basic goal of the
> European Planning Federation is to further the principles,
> methods, and practices of long-term strategic and corporate
> planning without profit motive throughout its membership.
> The federation from time to time sponsors the World
> Planning Congress and the European Planning Congress.
> Newsletters, notices of meetings, and a Directory of Officers
> for all EPLAF member societies are held by individual
> secretariats in each country and are available at the current
> EPLAF secretariat office.

European Society of Corporate and Strategic Planners (ESCSP)
Rue Brederode 2
1000 Brussels, Belgium
>The purpose is to foster the evolution, development, promotion, and the application of planning (strategic and long term) in the economic and social environment in a ''European'' framework.

Gesellshaft fur Planning (AGPLAN)
Dr. Aloys Galweiler
Brown Boveri and Co.
Kafertaler Strasse 258
6800 Manheim, West Germany
Member IAPS, EPLAF

Hawaii Society of Corporate Planners (HSCP)
President: Mr. Hollis E. Wright
P.O. Box 3391
Honolulu, Hawaii 96801
>Journal: *Quarterly Journal, Newsletter*
>Benefits: Monthly meetings, biennial seminars.
Member IAPS
>The purpose of the Society is to promote a better understanding of planning skills, and to further the effective utilization of those skills within members' organizations (and others).

International Affiliation of Planning Societies (IAPS)
Mr. Philip C. Preston, President
Alexander Grant & Co.
2300 Gas Light Tower
Atlanta GA 30043
>This is an unbrella organization that coordinates the efforts of all the major corporate planning groups in the free world and provides a forum for communication among these groups.

The Institute for Strategic Health Care Planning (ISHCP)
Narberth
PA 19072

Japan Society for Corporate Planning (JSCP)
President: Dr. Ei-ichi FURAKAWA
Kyodo Building
Shimbashi, 2–4–10 Higashi-Shimbashi, Minato–Ku
Tokyo, Japan
Member IAPS

Midwest Planning Association (MPA)
President: Mr. Henry Hufnagel
6 East Monroe, Room 800
Chicago IL 60603
Member IAPS

Objective is to provide a forum for the exchange of planning information leading toward greater success and professionalism for the planners of the area.

National Planning Assn.
1606 New Hampshire Ave., N.W.
Washington, D.C. 20009
    Journal: *Looking Ahead*

As a member of NPA, supporting NPA's current research programs, you will receive all of NPA's reports and studies and a subscription to *Looking Ahead.* NPA is expanding its membership by issuing invitations to join to individuals whose work and personal interests require them to be well informed on contemporary economic and social developments.

New Zealand Business Planning Society (NZBPS)
Mr. Ralph U. Penning, Administrator
P.O. Box 2347
Auckland, New Zealand
Member IAPS

Promotes the understanding and use of business planning, particularly medium- to long-term planning, in both the private and public sectors of the New Zealand economy. Fosters the training, education, and qualifications of persons practising or intending to practise the planning profession in New Zealand. Enhances the skills of planners by exchange and extension of information and by the provision of lectures, meetings, conferences, and publications, and promotion of research in planning.

New Zealand Society for Long Range Planning, Inc.
P.O. Box 12418
Penrose
Auckland, New Zealand

North American Society for Corporate Planning (NASCP)
300 Arcade Square
P.O. Box 1288
Dayton OH 45402
Member IAPS
    Journals: *Planning Review*
               Newsletter
               The Planner

Provides a forum for the interchange of ideas on planning in order to educate members and to improve their capabilities to plan and carry out planning activities.

Planners League
Mr. Brian Smolens, Membership Chairman
c/o STSC, Inc.
7316 Wisconsin Ave.
Bethesda MD 20014
>Sponsors workshops on a theme of current interest and need. Stimulates members to write papers, make presentations, and become active in relevant activities. Makes resources available to encourage research projects. Size is limited to around 100 members, with a balance among professional disciplines whose work interests can influence the application of planning concepts.

Planning Executives Institute
Mr. Jeff McDonald, President
P.O. Box 70
Oxford OH 45056
Member IAPS
>Journal: *Managerial Planning*
>The world's largest professional association for the corporate planner, PEI has become widely known for significant contributions to the development of planning process, education of its practitioners, and acceptance of the profession in the business community. Through continuing education, cross-communication, and practical information, thousands of planners are now utilizing PEI's extensive resources to advance and enhance their professional endeavors.

Society for College and University Planning
Joanne E. MacRae, Executive Secretary
2001 School of Education Bldg.
University of Michigan
Ann Arbor MI 48109
>Journal: *Planning for Higher Education*
>SCUP is the only professional association in higher education whose primary focus is the integration of academic, financial, administrative, and facilities planning.

Society for Strategic and Long Range Planning
15 Belgrave Square
London SW1X 8 PU, England
Member IAPS, EPLAF
>Journal: *Long Range Planning*
>Objectives are to awaken the need for, and understanding of, long-range planning in both the private and public sectors of the economy; to enhance the skills of long-range planners; to exchange and extend the information available to long-range planners; to bridge the gap between

long-range planners in industry, government, and the
academic world. A series of study groups are sponsored and
newsletters are distributed.

Southern California Corporate Planners (SCCP)
Marilyn Tullius, Vice President
Tullius and Associates
520 S. Sepulveda Blvd.
Suite 307
Los Angeles CA 90049
Member IAPS, NASCP
    Members: 140
        The purpose is to achieve a better understanding and
        utilization of planning skills and their potential contribution to
        business, industry, and government. Monthly dinner
        meetings and an annual seminar are held.

Strategic and Corporate Europlanners Society (SCEPS)
Count E de Villegas de Clercamp, Chairman of Executive Committee
Boite Postale No 17
Brussles 42
1040 Brussels
Belgium
Member IAPS, EPLAF
    Journal: *Newsletter*
        Eight luncheon conferences per year and three annual
        seminars are given.

Svenska Operations Analysforereningen (SORA)
Mr. H. Berg, Secretary
Garpg 5
S 72462 Vasteras
Stockholm, Sweden
Member EPLAF

Swedish Association of Future Studies
P.O. Box 5073
5-102-42
Stockholm, Sweden
Member IAPS, EPLAF

Vereniging voor Strategische Beleidsvorming (VSB)
W. Krijn, Secretary
Van Alkemadelaan 700
2597 Aw Den Haag
The Netherlands
Member IAPS, EPLAF
        The activities can be grouped as follows: two to three
        national conferences a year (mostly devoted to large strategic
        developments); four to six national so-called technical

meetings where a strategic subject is discussed in depth;
round-table discussions where a restricted number of both
planners and their decision makers meet in a one-day
discussion; seven regional branches, meeting about six times
a year; study groups and working groups;
seminars—workshops and short-term courses; and literature
research and the promotion of publications.

Appendix C

Glossary of Planning Terms

Accountability	The obligation to carry out duties and responsibilities and to exercise the authority of a position in conformance with understood and accepted standards.
Action plan	A plan that is intended to be completed within a definite period of time.
Adaptation	The process by which an individual attempts to influence the organization's goals.
Alternative futures	*See* Scenarios.
Authority	The sum of the powers and rights assigned to a position.
Brainstorming	Face-to-face interactive communication intended to stimulate creative and innovative proposals.
Budget	A plan in detail of the results expected from an approved program.
Budgetary control	Use of the budget as a road map to maintain the planned course.
Cascading	When parts of a plan are delegated, so that its essential requirements are translated into implementing plans at successively lower levels.
Cascade system	An organizational chart showing the hierarchical planning structure and including feedback loops.
Commitment analysis	The process of identifying and defining the overall categories to which continuing allocation of resources will be made.
Communicating	Creating understanding among the people involved.
Comprehensive planning	*See* Strategic planning.
Concentration growth strategies	When resources are used to expand one set of products or markets; can involve growth around a single product line with multiple markets or around a primary market with multiple products.
Consensus theory	Allocation of benefits as a result of agreement among the beneficiaries.
Constraint	Any fixed and inflexible barrier in planning.
Contingency plan	An alternative to the basic plan to be implemented if the anticipated future environment is not realized.
Control	The process of assessing and regulating work as it is being done and when it is completed.
Corporate planning	*See* Strategic planning.
Corporate simulation models	Models that attempt to portray a complex organization and its environmental interactions.

Critical few principle | In any given group of occurrences, a small number of causes tend to give rise to the largest proportion of results.

Cross-impact matrix | Device for assessing future environments used when several forecasts are believed to interact with one another.

Culture | *See* Planning climate

Decision making | Arriving at conclusions and judgments necessary for people to act.

Delegating | Assigning to others the work they must do and the right to make the necessary decisions; creating an obligation to do the work and make the decisions in terms of agreed-upon standards.

Delphi forecasting | A method of eliciting expert opinion about the future in a systematic manner, involving also clarification by a neutral observer and feedback to the experts.

Delphi technique | A method of probing expert minds in a series of interviews from which some consensus is sought.

Dialectic policy analysis | Policy Delphi applied in face-to-face communication rather than through a neutral observer.

Econometric forecasting model | A large-scale model that depicts the national economy in terms of hundreds of statistically estimated equations.

Effectiveness | Selecting the most appropriate task to carry out. *See also* Efficiency.

Efficiency | Carrying out a task in the best possible manner. *See also* Effectiveness.

Enterprise plan | The course of action to be followed by the enterprise as a whole in relation to the publics it must satisfy; also called corporate, strategic, or long-range plan.

Environmental scanning | Personal surveillance of environments by individual managers performed in a variety of ways ranging from methodically reading business journals to casually conversing with fellow managers at lunch.

Ethos | How an organization behaves towards its internal and external stakeholders.

Factors | Elements that affect the planning process. Uncontrollable factors have no direct, traceable cause. Controllable factors can be managed at least in part by the organization.

Gap analysis | Analysis that identifies the gap between long-range expectations and current actuality.

Goal	A specific, time-based point of measurement that the organization intends to meet in the pursuit of its broad objectives.
Groupthink	A mode of thinking that people engage in when they are deeply involved in a cohesive in-group, when members striving for unanimity override their motivation to appraise realistically alternative courses of action.
Growth plan	A plan that represents growth beyond the normal expansion of operations already in place.
Hierarchy	A structure of objectives, organization, or other elements in which the most important or global ones rank first, with the least important or provincial ones last.
Identification	The process by which an individual adopts the group's goals as his own.
Intermediate-range plans	Plans usually covering from three months to three years. *See also* Tactical plans.
Key objective	The overall results the organization as a whole will commit itself to use its resources to accomplish. It is the overall, primary, continuing objective that determines the purpose and nature of the enterprise.
Key standards	Standards that provide measures for success in meeting the key objective.
Key strategies	Strategies that define the general approach that will be followed to achieve the key objective and to meet the key standards.
Leading function	Influencing people to take effective action.
Line relationships	The command relationships of those persons and positions directly accountable for achieving objectives and therefore vested with the authority needed for that purpose.
Long-range plan	A plan that extends as far ahead as it is possible to specify the desired end results. *See also* Strategic plan.
Long-range planning	*See* Strategic planning.
Management action	Action that concentrates on correcting or improving the underlying plans; applies primarily to work that is intended to secure results through others.
Management by objectives (MBO)	A process in which members of complex organizations working in conjunction with one another identify common goals and coordinate their efforts toward achieving them.
Managerial values	Fundamental beliefs and ideas held by a manager that establish a standard by which important decisions are

made. They concern not only the ends but also the means for achieving those results.

Management functions	Planning, organizing, staffing, leading, directing, coordinating, reporting, and budgeting.
Management information system (MIS)	A planned system of gathering, processing, storing, and recovering information to permit effective management decisions.
Management leaders	Leaders who have learned to act in ways that will satisfy the needs of their followers. They concentrate on work that will enable them to get results through a group as a whole, working as a team.
Management work	The physical and mental effort exerted by individuals in leadership positions to receive results through the efforts of other people.
Marketing-management concept	The fundamental idea that the best way for an enterprise to accomplish overall objectives is by committing the enterprise and each of its components to persons who will manage their activities so as to satisfy the identified needs of internal and external customers or clients.
Means	How the organization proposes to carry out its purpose and ethos.
Medium-range programming	The process whereby specified functional plans are prepared and interrelated to display the details of how strategies are to be carried out to achieve long-range objectives, company missions, and purposes.
Metagame analysis	An extension and modification of game theory for business situations.
Mission	A statement of what any organization is, why it exists, and the unique contribution it can make; the WHY of planning. See *also* purpose
Motivating	Inspiring, encouraging, and impelling people to act.
Multidimensionality	An attribute of most modern corporations that usually have several objectives to achieve simultaneously— profits, sales, ROI, ROA, dividends, legal standards.
Natural leadership	Leadership characterized by centralized decision making; an organization built around strong personalities, one-way communication, and control by inspection rather than by exception.
Needs analysis	A mechanism for identifying and defining the critical few problems or opportunities that warrant broad and coordinated management action and set the stage for the long- and short-range action plans that will correct the situation.

Objective	A desired or needed result to be achieved in the long-run future; the WHAT of planning.
Organizational development	A term applied to a variety of behavioral methodologies for systematically attempting to bring about organizational change.
Organization structure	The work that must be done arranged in logical groups: the organization chart.
Organizing	Seeing that the organization's resources work together via planning.
Overall planning	*See* Strategic planning.
Pareto's law	*See* Critical few principle.
Performance evaluation	Determining how well work has been done and results achieved by comparing them with the standards established.
Performance standards	The criteria by which the work or results are measured.
PIMS	A statistical model (multiple regression) used to analyze data on business characteristics and performance that are submitted by U.S. firms to the Strategic Planning Institute.
Planning	The development of a program for reaching the organization's desired objectives and goals.
Planning climate	The environment within the organization in which planning takes place.
Planning premises	Planning assumptions about the total environment in which the plans are to operate.
Policy Delphi	Delphi applied to the comparison of alternative scenarios where no single optimal solution exists.
Point of control	The greatest potential for control tends to exist at the point where action takes place.
Policy	A standard decision that applies to repetitive problems and questions of overall importance. Policy is a slippery concept sometimes used to mean strategy, objective, or mission, and sometimes to mean all three.
Position	A set of related and continuing accountabilities in an organization that one suitably qualified person can maintain.
Position plan	A plan that covers that part of the total organization for which a manager is accountable.
Procedure	A standardized method of performing work that must be done in a uniform manner.

Product/service commitment	Committing resources to providing something of value to users, either internal or external.
Program	A time-shared action sequence used to guide and coordinate operations in the pursuit of a goal.
Programming	Determining the action steps necessary to achieve desired results.
Project	The implementation of a program or part of a program by identifiable activities and resources that leads toward the attainment of specific goals.
Purpose	The reason the organization was formed or why it exists. *See also* Mission.
Purpose commitment	The critical factor that provides overall guidance in committing available resources. *See also* Mission.
Resistance-to-change principle	The greater the departure of planned changes from accepted ways, the greater the potential resistance by the people involved.
Responsibility	The work assigned to a position.
Rules and regulations	The simplest and most detailed of all standing plans.
Scenario	An assumed sequence of future events, some controllable and some uncontrollable, together with the predicted outcomes.
Scheduling	Determining the time sequence for action steps.
Scope commitment	Concentrating resources within the most promising geographic or other limits to maximize success.
Sensitivity	Search for a strategy that performs well under a variety of scenarios.
Short-range plans	Plans usually covering between a day and a year. *See also* Tactical plans.
Single-use plans	Nonrecurring plans such as programs, budgets, and organizational plans.
Staff relationship	The relationship of those positions and components accountable for advice and service to those positions and components accountable for direct accomplishment of objectives.
Stakeholders	All of the external and internal interest groups of an organization.
Standard	A criterion that enables one to differentiate between good and poor work and results.
Standing plans	Plans that, once established, continue to apply until modified or abandoned.
Strategic data base	Concise statements of the most significant items related to stakeholders or environment.

Strategic planning	The process of deciding on objectives, on changes in those objectives, on the resources used to attain these objectives, and on the policies that are to govern the acquisition, use, and disposition of these resources. The process of positioning an organization so that it can prosper in the future.
Strategic plan	Plan made according to the strategic planning process.
Strategy	A set of decision rules and guidelines to assist orderly progression toward an organization's objectives, the How of planning. Strategy must precede structure.
Structure	*See* Organization structure.
System	An integrated whole made up of diverse but interdependent parts that work together in unison under the influence of an overall logic.
Systems dynamics	An extension of industrial dynamics used in environmental assessment and requiring a high level of analytic ability in problem definintion, influence diagram development, and equation structuring.
System simulation	Models depicting the world as a system and used to project the consequences of changes in interacting subsystems into the future.
Tactical action program	A plan for going between two milestones in the strategy: an action plan, with checkpoints every few weeks, working toward a milestone that may be many months ahead.
Tactical plans	The near-term part of the strategic plan amplified in detail to permit operational implementation.
Technical action	Action that is applied directly to resources by the people accountable for the work.
Technical work	The physical and mental effort exerted by individuals to secure results through their own efforts.
Total planning	*See* Strategic planning.
Trend extrapolation	A forecasting method in which historical observations are projected into the future either as a curve or as a straight line.
Trigger point	The clear and unequivocal environmental information that gives the signal to implement a contingency plan.
Value-based planning	Processes used in evaluating alternatives and investment opportunities in which the principal objective is maximizing the financial value of a firm's common stock.
Values of managers	Beliefs and ethics of managers that tend to shape mission and that must be consonant with mission.
Vunerability analysis	A method forcing the analyst to specify both the

magnitude of environmental impact and the probability of its occurrence.

Work classification

A logical arrangement according to recognized criteria of different kinds of work in groupings.

Zero-based budgeting

A process that requires each manager to justify his entire budget request anew each period and that shifts the burden of proof to each manager to justify why he should spend any money at all.

APPENDIX D

CAREERS IN PLANNING

Strategic planning is a top-level job that is being given increasing respect. Management literature is full of articles complaining about the lack of strategic planning in American corporations and the lack of attention to planning skills in typical business school curricula. Traditionally, most planners came from the finance area. Planners are now entering the field from academia, government service, marketing, engineering, and other areas (Ross 1983). As we have noted repeatedly, there is a strong contingency aspect, with planners in high-tech fields like electronics tending to have technical training and planners in petroleum tending to be chemical engineers.

Ross (1983) points out that planning is among the top twelve money-making careers, with the top third of corporate strategic planners drawing between $50,000 and $70,000. One recruiter offers $150,000 and a VP title; five years ago the same firm paid $60,000 without the title. More concerns give wider responsibilities to chief planners, who once worked on specific tasks. Many look at broad strategic problems and where their firm is heading. Most chief planners are high in the hierarchy, reporting directly to the CEO, with the associated status of that level. ("Corporate strategists expand. . ." 1980)

In order to indicate the type of candidates being sought by recruiters for planning jobs, we have analyzed 130 advertisements. These came from the *Wall Street Journal* and from employment bulletins issued by the North American Society for Corporate Planning. Advertisements searching for financial planners were omitted as these appear to be finance positions rather than planning positions. In the tables to be given, percentages will not add to 100 percent, because some ads omit the mention of certain factors, while other ads mention more than one aspect of a factor. It is hoped that the person considering a planning career will be able to use these tables both to identify the needed experience or knowledge to be acquired, and to identify items to be emphasized on his resume.

Type of Firm

Field	Percent
High technology	30
Health care	15
Energy, chemicals	10
Consumer products	9
Other	24

Degree Desired. Of the 20 percent who preferred an engineering or technical college degree, the desirability of following this with an MBA was often stated. Also as noted below, preference for a ''top business school'' was sometimes indicated.

Degree	Percent
MBA	72
Engineering, technical	20
BS/BA	7
MBA or PhD.	4
Graduate business degree	8
Top business school	11

Years of Experience. In a few cases, the requirement was stated in two phases, so many years in general business plus so many years in planning.

Years	Percent
0–5	42
6–10	25
Over 10	9

Area of Experience

Area	Percent
Planning	57
Finance	19
Marketing	13
Consumer products	12
Technical	10

Salary. It was unusual to find actual dollar values quoted in an advertisement.

Comment	Percent
Excellent	24
Competitive	21
From $46,000 to $60,000	6
Over $90,000	2

Advancement Potential. In 39 percent of the advertisements, phrases such as ''highly visible'' or ''exceptional career opportunity'' were included.

Job Titles. The words in this list appeared in various combinations, for example, senior planner or director of strategic planning.

Title	Percent
Strategic (or corporate) planner	48
Manager (or director)	46
Planner	28
Analyst	19
Business planner	15
Senior	9
Vice president	8

Skills Required.   This interesting category emphasizes again the precepts that every idea is worthless until it is put into practice and that in order to put an idea into practice, it is necessary to go through the step of communication.

Skill	*Percent*
Oral and written communication	45
Analysis	28
Ability to work at senior (or all) levels	27
Decisive, aggressive, assertive, high powered	24
Creative, innovative, bright	18
Quantitative	18
Interpersonal	16

References

''Corporate Strategists Expand Their Clout.'' *Wall Street Journal,* Aug. 26, 1980.

Ross, Steven S. *Business Week's Guide to Careers.* New York: McGraw-Hill, 1983.

Bibliography

Aarvik, O., and Randoph, P. "Application of Linear Programming to the Determination of Transmission Fees in Electrical Power Network." *Interfaces* (Nov. 1975), p. 47.

Abell, Derek F., and Hammond, John S. *Strategic Market Planning: Problems and Analytical Approaches*. Englewood Cliffs, N.J.: Prentice-Hall, 1979.

Ackoff, R. L. *A Concept of Corporate Planning*. New York: Wiley, 1970.

Ackoff, R. L. *Redesigning the Future*. New York: Wiley, 1975.

Ackoff, R. L. *Creating the Corporate Future: Plan or Be Planned For*. New York: Wiley, 1981.

Adams, Walter, ed. *The Structure of American Industry*. 5th ed. New York: Macmillan, 1977.

Allen, D. H. "Linear Programming Techniques in R & D Project Planning." *Long Range Planning* (Feb. 1974), p. 61.

Allen, L. A. *Making Managerial Planning More Effective*. New York: McGraw-Hill, 1982.

Allio, R. J., and Randall, Robert. "Planner at the Helm." *Planning Review* (July 1976), p.1.

Almon, C. *The American Economy to 1975: An Interindustry Forecast*. New York: Harper and Row, 1966.

Amara, Roy C., and Lipinski, Andrew J. *Business Planning for an Uncertain Future*. London: Pergamon Press, 1982.

Andrews, Kenneth R. *The Concept of Corporate Strategy*. Homewood, Ill: Irwin, 1971.

Ansoff, H. Igor. *Corporate Strategy*. New York: McGraw-Hill, 1965.

357

Ansoff, H. Igor. "The Changing Shape of the Strategic Problem." In Dan E. Schendel and Charles H. Hofer, eds., *Strategic Management: A New View of Business Policy and Planning*. Boston, Mass.: Little, Brown, 1969. P. 30.

Ansoff, H. Igor, and Leontiades, James C. "Strategic Portfolio Management." *Journal of General Management*, 4, 1 (Autumn 1976).

Ansoff, H. Igor, et al. "Does Planning Pay?" *Long Range Planning* (Dec. 1970).

Anthony, R. N.; Dearden, J.; and Vancil, R. F. *Management Control Systems: Text, Cases and Readings*. Homewood, Ill.: Irwin, 1972.

Argenti, John. *Systematic Corporate Planning*. New York: Wiley, 1974.

Armstrong, J. Scott. *Long Range Forecasting: From Crystal Ball to Computer*. New York: Ronald Press, 1978.

Armstrong, R. H. R., and Hobson, M. "The Use of Games in Planning." *Long Range Planning* (Mar. 1972), p. 62.

Arrow, Kenneth. "The Economic Implications of Learning by Doing." *Review of Economic Studies* 28 (1961), pp. 155–73.

Ayres, R., and Kneese, A. "Production, Consumption, and Externalities." *American Economic Review* 59, 3 (1969), pp. 282–95.

Baer, William. "Counterfactual Analysis—An Analytical Tool for Planners." *Journal of American Institute of Planners* 42, 3, (July 1976) pp. 243–52.

Bailey, Earl L., ed. *Product-Line Strategies*. New York: Conference Board, 1982.

Barkai, Haim, and Levhari, David. "The Impact of Experience on Kibbutz Farming." *Review of Economics and Statistics* 55 (Feb. 1973), pp. 56–63.

Barna, Tibor, ed. *Structural Interdependence and Economic Development. Proceedings of an International Conference on Input-Output Techniques*. New York: St. Martin's Press, 1963.

Ben-Yaacov, G. Z. "A Computer-Based Modeling System for Electric Utility Planning." *Long Range Planning* (Dec. 1978), p. 301.

Berg, Norman, and Pitts, Robert A. "Strategic Management: Multimission Business." In Schendel and Hofer, eds., *Strategic Management*, p. 339.

Bernstein Cumulative Index. New York: Sanford C. Bernstein and Co., 1983.

Boriamrene, M. A., and Flarell, R. "Airline Corporate Planning—A Conceptual Framework." *Long Range Planning* (Feb. 1980), p. 62.

Borst, Diane, and Montana, Patrick J., eds. *Managing Nonprofit Organizations*. New York: AMACOM, 1977.

Boston Consulting Group. *Perspectives on Experience.* Boston, Mass.: Boston Consulting Group, 1969.

Boulden, J. B., and Buffa, E. S. "Corporate Models: On-Line, Real-time Systems." *Harvard Business Review,* 48, 4 (July 1970), p. 65.

Boulding, K. E. "Reflections on Planning: The Value of Uncertainty." *Planning Review* 3 (March 1975), p. 11.

Bourque, P., and Cox, M. "An Inventory of Regional Input/Output Studies in the United States." University of Washington Graduate School of Business Administration, Occasional paper no. 22, 1970.

Bradway, Bruce M., Pritchard, Robert E., and Frenzel, Mary Anne. *Strategic Marketing.* Reading, Mass.: Addison-Wesley, 1982.

Bralove, Mary. "Direct Data." *Wall Street Journal,* Jan. 12, 1983.

Brandt, Steven C., *Strategic Planning in Emerging Companies.* Reading, Mass.: Addison-Wesley, 1982.

Brownstone, D. M., and Carruth, G. *Where to Find Business Information.* Somerset, N.J.: Wiley, 1982.

Bryant, James W., ed. *Financial Modeling in Corporate Managment.* New York: Wiley, 1982.

Buzzel, Robert, et al. "Market Share—A Key to Profitability." *Harvard Business Review* 53 (Jan.-Feb. 1975), p. 97.

Canning, Gordon. "A Strategic Framework for Analyzing Product Development." *Planning Review* 3 (Nov. 1975), p. 23.

Carlson, Eugene. "Texas and Some Other States Try Out Long-Term Planning." *Wall Street Journal,* July 6, 1982.

Carter, Anne P. "The Economics of Technological Change." *Scientific American* 214, 4 (April 1966), pp. 25–31.

Carter, Anne P. *Structural Change in the American Economy.* Cambridge, Mass.: Harvard Univ. Press, 1970.

Carter, Anne P., and Brody, A., eds. *Applications of Input/Output Analysis: Part III, Stability of Coefficients; Part IV, Forecasting Coefficients,* Amsterdam: North-Holland Pub., 1970.

Carter, H., and Ireri, D. "Linkage of California-Arizona Input/Output Models to Analyze Water Transfer Patterns." In A. P. Carter and A. Brody, eds. *Applications of Input/Output Analysis.*

Catalog of Publications. Norwalk, Conn.: International Resource Development, Inc., 1983.

Chandler, Alfred D., Jr. *Strategy and Structure,* Cambridge, Mass.: M.I.T. Press, 1962.

Channon, D. F. "Strategic Portfolio Planning Models: Practical Progress and Problems in Practice." In Schendel and Hofer, eds. *Strategic Management,* p. 122.

Chase Econometrics Letter. Bala Cynwyd, Pa.: Chase Econometrics.

Chenery, Hollis B., and Clark, Paul G. *Interindustry Economics.* New York: Wiley, 1959.

Chesshire, J. H., and Surrey, A. J. "World Energy Resources and Limitations of Computer Models." *Long Range Planning* (June 1975), p. 55.

Cohen, K. J., and Cyert, R. M. "Strategy: Formulation, Implementation, and Monitoring." *Journal of Business* (July 1973), p. 349.

Cooper, A. C. "Strategic Management: New Ventures and Small Businesses." In Schendel and Hofer, eds., *Strategic Management,* p. 316.

"Corporate Strategists Expand Their Clout." *Wall Street Journal,* Aug. 26, 1980.

Culhan, R. H.; Stern, L. W.; Drayer, W.; and Seabury, S. "Linear Programming—What It Is—A Case Example." *Planning Review* (September 1975), p. 21.

Curril, David L. "Introducing Corporate Planning—A Case Study." *Long Range Planning* (Aug. 1977).

Dallos, Robert E. "No Secret Is Safe." *The State* (Columbia, S.C.), July 10, 1983.

Daniells, Lorna M. *Business Intelligence and Strategic Planning.* Publications Office, Baker Library, Harvard Business School, Reference List No. 32, Boston, Mass., 1983.

Dhalla, Nariman, and Yuspch, Sonia. "Forget the Product Life Cycle Concept." *Harvard Business Review* (Jan.-Feb. 1976), pp. 102–12.

Dobbie, J. N. "Formal Approaches to Setting Long Range Goals." *Long Range Planning* (June 1974), p. 75.

Dobbie, J. N. "Strategic Planning in Big Firms—Some Guidelines." *Long Range Planning* (Feb. 1975), p. 81.

Dory, J. P., and Lord, R. J. "Does TF Really Work?" *Harvard Business Review* (Nov. 1970), p. 16.

Dow Jones News Retrieval. Princeton, N.J.: Down Jones & Co.

Drucker, Peter. *Management: Tasks, Responsibilities, Practices.* New York: Harper and Row, 1973.

Duncan, R. B. "Qualitative Methods in Policy Research." In Schendel and Hofer, eds., *Strategic Management,* p. 424.

Duncombe, H. L. "The Dangers of Centralized Economic Planning." *Long Range Planning* (June 1976), p. 16.

East, R. J. "Comparison of Strategic Planning in Large Corporations and Government." *Long Range Planning* (June, 1972), p. 2.

Edge, C. G. "Financial Models." In Kendall, M. G., ed., *Mathematical Model Building in Economics and Industry.* 2d series. London: Charles Griffin, 1970. P. 169.

Elam, Joyce J. "Decision Support Systems Seminar." Arlington, Va.: Institute for Professional Education, 1983.

Ellis, Darryl J., and Pekar, Peter P., Jr. *Planning for Nonplanners: Planning Basics for Managers.* New York: AMACOM, 1980.

Emshoff, James R. *Managerial Breakthroughs.* New York: AMACOM, 1980.

Encyclopedia of Associations, 18th ed. Detroit, Mich.: Gale Research, 1984.

Fama, E. F. "Efficient Capital Markets: A Review of Theory and Empirical Work." *Journal of Finance* (May 1970), p. 383.

Financial Planning Simulator. El Segundo, Calif.: Computer Sciences Corp., 1983.

Findex. New York: Find/SVP, 1983.

Finlay, Paul N. "Introducing Corporate Planning in a Medium-Size Company: A Case History." *Long Range Planning* (Apr. 1982), p. 93.

Flexner, William A.; Berkowitz, Eric N.; and Brown, Montague. *Strategic Planning in Health Care Management.* Rockville, Md.: Aspen Systems Corp., 1981.

Forbes, A. M. "Long Range Planning for the Small Firm." *Long Range Planning* (Apr. 1974), p. 43.

Ford, W. R. C. "Business Not as Usual in Hospitals." *Hospitals* 54, 7 (Apr. 1, 1980), p. 159–61.

Friedman, Milton F. *Capitalism and Freedom.* Chicago, Ill.: University of Chicago Press, 1962.

Friedman, Y., and Segev, E. "Horizons for Strategic Planning." *Long Range Planning (Oct. 1976), p. 84*

Galbraith, J. R., and Nathanson, D. A. *"Strategy Implementation: The Role of Organization Structure and Process."* In Schendel and Hofer, eds., *Strategic Management,* p. 249.

Gershefski, G. W. "The Development and Application of a Corporate Financial Model." *Planning Executives Institute Bulletin* (1968).

Gershefski, G. W. "Building a Corporate Financial Model." *Harvard Business Review* (July 1969), p. 61.

Gerstner, L. V. "Can Strategic Planning Pay Off? *Business Horizons* 15 (Dec. 1972), pp. 5–16.

Glover, F. "Improved Linear Integer Programming Formulations of Nonlinear Integer Problems." *Management Science* (Dec. 1975), p. 455.

Glueck, William F. *Business Policy and Strategic Management.* New York: McGraw-Hill, 1980.

Goldman, Morris R.; Marimont, Martin L.; and Vaccara, Beatrice N. "The Interindustry Structure of the United States: A Report on the

1958 Input-Output Study." *Survey of Current Business* 44, 11 (Nov. 1964), pp. 10–17.

Gols, A. G. "The Use of Input-Output in Industrial Planning." *Planning Review* (Mar. 1976), p. 17.

Goodman, D. A. "A Goal Programming Approach to Aggregate Planning of a Production and Work Force." *Management Science* (Aug. 1974), p. 1569.

Gordon, T. J. "The Current Methods of Futures Research." In A. Toffler, *The Futurists*. New York: Random House, 1972. Pp. 164–89.

Grant, J. H., and King, W. R. "Strategy Formulation: Analytical and Normative Models." In Schendel and Hofer, eds. *Strategic Management*, p. 104.

Grant, J. H., and King, W. R. *The Logic of Strategic Planning*. Boston: Little, Brown, 1982.

Grinyer, P. H., and Wooller, J. "Computer Models for Long Range Planning." *Long Range Planning* (Feb. 1975), p. 14.

Growth Pace Setters in American Industry 1958–1968. Washington, D.C.: Bureau of Industrial Economics, 1968.

Gup, B. E. "Portfolio Theory—A Planning Tool." *Long Range Planning* (June 1977), p. 10.

Hamilton, W. F., and Moses, M. A. "A Computer-Based Corporate Planning System." *Management Science* (Oct. 1974), p. 148.

Hammond, J. S. "Dos and Don'ts of Computer Models for Planning." *Harvard Business Review* (Mar. 1974), p. 110.

Hardy, James M. *Corporate Planning for Nonprofit Organizations*. New York: Association Press, 1972.

Harrison, F. L. "How Corporate Planning Responds to Uncertainty." *Long Range Planning* (Apr. 1976), p. 88.

Hatten, K. J. "Business Policy Research: The Quantitative Way, Circa 1977." In Schendel and Hofer, eds., *Strategic Management*, p. 448.

Hayes, R. L., and Radosevich, R. "Designing Information Systems for Strategic Decisions." *Long Range Planning* (Aug. 1974), p. 45.

Hayes, R. H., and Nolan, R. L. "What Kind of Corporate Modeling Functions Best?" *Harvard Business Review* 52, 3 (1974), pp. 102–12.

Hedley, Barry. "A Fundamental Approach to Strategy Development." *Long Range Planning* (Dec. 1976), p. 2.

Henderson, Bruce D. *Henderson on Corporate Strategy*. Cambridge, Mass.: Abt Books, 1979.

Herrick, Margaret A. "Data Base Concepts and Design Seminar." Cambridge, Mass.: Margann Associates, 1982.

Higgins, James M. *Organizational Policy and Strategic Management.* Chicago, Ill.: Dryden Press, 1983.

Hobbs, J. M., and Heany, D. F. "Coupling Strategy to Operating Plans." *Harvard Business Review* (May 1977), p. 119.

Hofer, Charles W., and Schendel, Dan. *Strategy Formulation: Analytical Concepts.* St. Paul, Minn.: West Pub. Co., 1978.

Holloway, Clark. "A Systematic Method of Finding Defining Contrasts." *Journal of American Statistical Association* (Mar. 1957), pp. 46–52.

Holloway, Clark. "Developing Planning Models." *Long Range Planning* (Feb. 1974), pp. 52–57.

Holloway, Clark. "Strategy for Costing Computer Projects." Paper presented at TIMS XXI, Puerto Rico, Oct. 1974.

Holloway, Clark. "The Significance of Planning." Paper presented at TIMS XXII, Japan, July 1975.

Holloway, Clark. "Using the Computer in Planning." *Planning Review* (Jul. 1976), pp. 9–10, 22–24.

Holloway, Clark. "Does Futures Research Have a Corporate Role?" *Long Range Planning* (Oct. 1978), pp. 17–24.

Holloway, Clark. "A Leading Indicator for Forecasting Petroleum Product Prices." Paper presented at ORSA-TIMS, Houston, Texas, Nov. 1981.

Holloway, Clark. "Strategic Management and Artificial Intelligence." *Long Range Planning* (Nov. 1983), pp. 89–93.

Holloway, Clark. "The Administration of Management Science." Paper presented at the National Meeting of ORSA/TIMS, Orlando, Fla., Nov. 1983.

Holloway, Clark. "Mechanization of Policy Decisions." Paper presented at the Southern Management Assn., meeting, Atlanta, Ga., Nov. 1983.

Holloway, Clark, and Balint, F. J. "Computer to Computer Communications." *Oil and Gas Journal* (Nov. 30, 1964), pp. 70–73.

Holloway, Clark, and Bonnell, W. S. "Octane Number and Lead Susceptibility of Gasoline." *Ind. Eng. Chem.* (Nov. 1945), pp. 1089–91.

Holloway, Clark, and Cattley, J. M. "Computerized Search Strategy for Documents." *Petro/Chem Engineer* (Dec. 1965), pp. 35–36.

Holloway, Clark, and Clamp, J. Carl. "Planning Is More Than Forecasting." *Wall Street Journal* (Oct. 17, 1983), p. 31.

Holloway, Clark. and Jones, G. T. "Planning at Gulf—A Case Study." *Long Range Planning* (Apr. 1975), pp. 27–45.

Holloway, Clark, and King, William R. "Evaluating Alternative Approaches to Strategic Planning." *Long Range Planning* (Aug. 1979), pp. 74–78.

Holloway, Clark, and Meadows, Nolan R. "Searching the Business Literature by Computer." *Business and Economic Review* (Dec. 1981), pp. 31–38.

Holloway, Clark, and Pearce, J. A. "Computer Assisted Strategic Planning." *Long Range Planning* (Aug. 1982), pp. 56–63.

Holmberg, S. R. "Monitoring Long Range Plans." *Long Range Planning* (June 1974), p. 63.

Hopkins, David S. *The Marketing Plan.* New York: Conference Board, 1981.

Hosner, LaRue T. *Strategic Management.* Englewood Cliffs, N.J.: Prentice-Hall, 1982.

Hrebiniak, L. G., and Joyce, W. F. *Implementing Strategy.* New York: Macmillan, 1984.

Humphries, G. E. "Technologies Assessment and a New Imperative for Corporate Planning." *Planning Review* (Mar. 1976), p. 6.

Hussey, D. E. "Corporate Planning for a Church." *Long Range Planning* (Apr. 1974), pp. 61–64.

Hussey, D. E. *Corporate Planning Theory and Practice.* Oxford: Pergamon Press, 1974.

Hussey, D. E., ed. *The Corporate Planners' Yearbook.* Oxford: Pergamon Press, 1978.

Hussey, D. E., and Langham, M. J. *Corporate Planning: The Human Factor.* Oxford: Pergamon Press, 1979.

Index of Industry Studies. Cleveland, Ohio: Predicasts.

Industry Surveys. New York: Standard and Poor.

Inside R&D. Fort Lee, N.J.: Technical Insights.

Intelligence Update. Cambridge, Mass.: Information Data Search.

Isard, W. "On the Linkage of Socio-economic and Ecologic Systems." *Papers of the Regional Science Association* 21 (1968), pp. 79–99.

Isard, W., and Langford, T. "Impact of Vietnam War Expenditures on the Philadelphia Economy: Some Initial Exeriments with the Inverse of the Philadelphia Input/Output Table." *Regional Science Association Papers* 23 (1969), pp. 217–65.

Johnson, Herbert E. "Comprehensive Corporate Planning for Commercial Banks." *Magazine of Bank Administration* (Jan. 1978), p. 20.

Jones, C. H. "Real Computer Power for Decision-Makers." *Harvard Business Review* (Sept. 1970), p. 75.

Kahalas, Harvey. "Planning for R&D—The Impact on Society." *Long Range Planning* (Dec. 1975), p. 37.

Kahalas, H., and Bjorklund, R. L. "An Enviromental Decision Model for Dynamic Planning." *Long Range Planning* (Feb. 1976), p.81.

Kahn, H., and Weiner, A. J. *The Year 2000.* New York: Macmillan, 1967.

Kami, M. J. "Revamping Planning for This Era of Discontinuity." *Planning Review* (Mar. 1976), p. 1.

Kaye, Doris. "Astrology: A Tool for Planning." *Planning Review* (May 1975), p. 1.

Khalhaturov, T. S., ed. *Methods of Long Term Planning and Forecasting.* London: Macmillan, 1976.

King, Malcolm. "Planning the Deployment of Clergy." *Long Range Planning* (Apr. 1982), pp. 104–11.

King, William R., and Cleland, David I. "Environmental Information Systems for Strategic Marketing Planning." *Journal of Marketing* (Oct. 1974), p. 35.

King, William R., and Cleland, David I. *Strategic Planning and Policy.* New York: Van Nostrand Reinhold, 1978.

Koontz, Harold. "Making Strategic Planning Work." *Business Horizons* (Apr. 1976), p. 37.

Kotler, P. "Corporate Models: Better Marketing Plans." *Harvard Business Review* (July 1970), p. 135.

Lackman, Conway L. "Dialing F-U-T-U-R-E at the Phone Company." *Planning Review* (May 1980), p. 26.

LaLonde, B. J., and Zinszer, P. H. "Managing in Uncertain Times: The Case for Planning." *Long Range Planning* (Oct. 1975), p. 18.

Lanford, H. W., and Imundo, L. V. "Approaches to Technological Forecasting as a Planning Tool." *Long Range Planning* (Aug. 1974), p. 49.

Lee, D. R., and Orr, D. "Further Results on Planning Horizons in the Production Smoothing Problem." *Management Science* (Jan. 1977), p. 490.

Leontiades, M., and Tezel, A. "Planning Perceptions and Planning Results." *Strategic Management Journal* (1980), p. 65–76.

Leontief, Wassily W. *Input/Output Economics.* Oxford: Oxford University Press, 1966.

Leontief, Wassily W. "Input-Output Economics." *Scientific American* 185, 4 (Oct. 1951), pp. 15–21.

Leontief, Wassily W. "The Structure of the U.S. Economy." *Scientific American* 209, 3 (Sept. 1963), pp. 148–66.

Leontief, Wassily, W. "The Structure of the U.S. Economy." *Scientific American* 212, 4 (Apr. 1965), pp. 25–35.

Leontief, Wassily, W. "The Dynamic Inverse," In Carter and Brody, eds., *Contributions to Input/Output Analysis.*

Leontief, Wassily W., and Hoffenberg, Marvin. "The Economic Effects of Disarmament." *Scientific American.* 204, 4 (Apr. 1961), pp. 47–55.

Lere, John C. "Planning for Electricity Demand." *Managerial Planning* (Nov. 1981), p. 21.

Lesko, Matthew. *Information U.S.A.* Washington, D.C.: Washington Researchers, 1982.

Lesko, M. J. "How to Tap Big Brother for Information." *Planning Review* (Jan. 1977), p. 25.

Levin, Dick. *The Executive's Illustrated Primer of Long-Range Planning.* Englewood Cliffs, N.J.: Prentice-Hall, 1981.

Leyshon, A. M. "Marketing Planning and Corporate Planning." *Long Range Planning* (Feb. 1976), p. 29.

Linszone, H. A., and Turoff, M., eds. *The Delphi Method—Techniques and Applications.* Reading, Mass.: Addison-Wesley, 1975.

Litschert, R. J., and Nicholson, E. A. "Corporate Long Range Planning Groups—Some Different Approaches." *Long Range Planning* (Aug. 1974), p. 62.

Little, John D. C. "Models and Managers: The Concept of a Decision Calculus." *Management Science* 16, 8 (Apr. 1970), pp. 3466–85.

Locander, W. B. "A Planning Model for Multiple New-product Introductions." *Journal of Business Administration* (Spring 1976).

Lorange, Peter. "A Framework for Strategic Planning in Multinational Corporations." *Long Range Planning* (June 1976), p. 30.

Lorange, Peter, and Vancil, Richard F. *Strategic Planning Systems.* Englewood Cliffs, N.J.: Prentice-Hall, 1977.

Makridakis, Spyros, and Wheelwright, Steven C., eds. *The Handbook of Forecasting: A Manager's Guide.* New York: Wiley, 1982.

Mandelker, Gershon. "Risk and Return: The Case of Merging Firms." *Journal of Financial Economics* (Dec. 1974), pp. 304–35.

Mansfield, Edward. "The Speed of Response of Firms to New Techniques." *Quarterly Journal of Economics* 77 (1963), pp. 290–311.

"Mapper." Blue Bell, Penn.: Sperry Univac, 1983.

Martin, W. H., and Mason, S. "Leisure 1980 and Beyond." *Long Range Planning* (Apr. 1976), p. 58.

Mason, R. Hal, and Goudzwaard, M. B. "Performance of Conglomerate Firms: A Portfolio Approach." *Journal of Finance* 31, 1 (Mar. 1976), pp. 39–48.

Mason, Richard O., and Mitroff, Ian I. *Challenging Strategic Planning Assumptions.* New York: Wiley, 1981.

Massy, W. F. "A Dynamic Equilibrium Model for University Budget Planning." *Management Science* 23, 3 (March 1977), pp. 248–56.

McClain, and Thomas. "Horizon Effects in Aggregate Production Planning with Seasonal Demand." *Management Science* (Mar. 1977).

McHale, John. "The Changing Pattern of Futures Research in the USA." *Futures* (June 1973), p. 257.

McNamara, J. H. "A Linear Programming Model for Long-Range Capacity Planning in an Electric Utility. *Journal of Economics and Business* (Spring 1976), p. 227.

McNichols, Thomas J. *Policymaking and Executive Action.* New York: McGraw-Hill, 1983.

McNichols, Thomas J. *Executive Policy and Strategic Planning.* New York: McGraw-Hill, 1983.

Mellen, E. F. "Capital Investment Decision Models for Public Utilities." In Kendall, M. G., ed. *Mathematical Model Building in Economics and Industry,* 2d series. London: Charles Griffin, 1970.

Meltzer, Morton F. *Information: The Ultimate Management Resource.* American Management Assn., 1981. New York.

Meyer, Henry I. *Corporate Financial Planning Models.* New York: Wiley, 1977.

Meyer, R. J. "The Triple Track to Successful Modeling and Model Implementation." *Long Range Planning* (Jan. 1976), p. 20.

Michael S. R., and Carlisle, A. E. "National Planning in the United States." *Long Range Planning* (June 1976), p. 21.

Miernyk, W. "An Interindustry Forecasting Model with Water Quantity and Quality Constraints." *Proceedings of the Fourth Annual Symposium on Water Resources Research,* Ohio State University, 1970.

Mintzberg, Henry. "Planning on the Left Side and Managing on the Right." *Harvard Business Review* 54, 4 (July–Aug., 1976), pp. 49–58.

Mitroff, Ian I. *The Subjective Side of Science.* New York: Elsevier, 1974.

Mitroff, Ian I. and Featheringham, T. R. "On Systematic Problem Solving and the Error of the Third Kind." *Behavioral Science* 19, (1974) pp. 383–93.

Muczyk, Jan P. "Comprehensive Manpower Planning." *Managerial Planning* (Nov. 1981), pp. 36–41.

Murdick, R. G.: Moor, R. C.; Eckhouse, R. H.; and Zimmer, T. W. *Business Policy: A Framework for Analysis.* Columbus, Ohio: Grid Pub. Co., 1984.

Narayanan, V. K. "Role and Status of Futurism: An Empirical Study." Unpublished paper, 1977.

Naylor, T. H. "The Case for Simulation Models." *Planning Review* (Aug. 1973), p. 15.

Naylor, T. H. "The Politics of Corporate Model Building." *Planning Review* (Jan. 1975), p. 1.

Naylor, T. H. "State of the Art of Planning Models." *Long Range Planning* (Nov. 1976), p. 22.

Naylor, T. H. *Corporate Planning Models*. Reading, Mass.: Addison-Wesley, 1979.

Naylor, T. H. ed. *Strategic Planning Management*. Oxford, Ohio: Planning Executives Institute, 1980.

Naylor, T. H. ed. *Corporate Strategy: The Integration of Corporate Planning Models and Economics*. Amsterdam: North-Holland Pub. Co., 1982.

Naylor, T. H., and Mansfield, M. J. "Corporate Planning Models; a Survey." *Planning Review* (May 1976), p. 8.

Naylor, T. H., and Schauland, H. "Experience with Corporate Simulation Models." *Long Range Planning* (Apr. 1976), p. 94.

Naylor, T. H., and Schauland, H. "Survey of Users of Corporate Planning Models." *Management Science* (May 1976), p. 927.

Neubauer, F. F. "A Management Approach to Environmental Assessment." *Long Range Planning* (Apr. 1977), p. 13.

Newby, W. J. "An Integrated Model of an Oil Company." In Kendall, M. G., ed. *Mathematical Model Building in Economics and Industry*. London: Charles Griffin, 1969. P. 61.

Newman, W. H., and Logan, J. P. *Strategy, Policy and Central Management*. Cincinnati, Ohio: South-Western Pub. Co., 1971.

Noonan, F., and Giglio, R. J. "Planning Electric Power Generation: A Nonlinear Mixed Integer Model Employing Benders Decomposition." *Management Science* (May 1977), p. 946.

Norden, R. F. "The Norwegian State Railways—Profit Motivated Enterprise or a Community Service?" *Long Range Planning* (Apr. 1978), p. 13.

Nutt, A. B.; Lenz, R. C.; Lanford, H. W.; and Cleary, M. J. "Data Sources for Trend Extrapolation in Technoligical Forecasting." *Long Range Planning* (Feb. 1976), p. 72.

O'Connor, Rochelle. *The Corporate Planning Department: Responsibilities and Staffing, Report 806*. New York: Conference Board, 1981.

O'Connor, Rochelle. *Evaluating the Company Planning System and the Corporate Planner*. New York: Conference Board, 1982.

Odiorne, George S. *The Change Registers: How They Prevent Progress and What Managers Can Do About Them*. Englewood Cliffs, N.J.: Prentice-Hall, 1981.

Ohmae, Kenichi. *The Mind of the Strategist: The Art of Japanese Business*. New York: McGraw-Hill, 1982.

Orwell, George. *1984*. New York: Harcourt, Brace, 1949.

Oxenfeldt, Alfred R., and Schwartz, Jonathan E. *Competitive Analysis*. New York: Presidents Association, 1981.

Paine, Frank T., and Anderson, Carl R. *Strategic Management.* Chicago: Dryden Press, 1983.

Paine, Frank T. and Naumes, William. *Organizational Strategy and Policy.* Chicago: Dryden Press, 1982.

Pekar, Peter P. "A Typology for Identifying Risk." *Managerial Planning* (Sept. 1976), p. 13.

Pekar, Peter P. "Setting Goals in the Non-Profit Environment." *Managerial Planning* 30, 5 (Mar./Apr. 1982), pp. 43–46.

Pennington, M. W. "Why Has Planning Failed?" *Long Range Planning* (Mar. 1972), p. 2.

Pennington, M. W. "Why Has Planning Failed and What Can You Do About It?" *Planning Review* (Nov. 1975), p. 12.

Perry, P. T. "Organizational Implications for Long Range Planning." *Long Range Planning* (Feb. 1975), p. 26.

Peters, Thomas J., and Waterman, Robert W. *In Search of Excellance: Lessons From America's Best-Run Companies.* New York: Harper and Row, 1982.

Polenske, K. "Empirical Implementations of a Multiregional Input/Output Gravity Trade Model." In Carter and Brody, eds., *Contributions to Input/Output Analysis.*

Porter, Michael E. *Competitive Strategy.* New York: Free Press, 1980.

Power, P. D. "Computers and Financial Planning." *Long Range Planning* (Dec. 1975), p. 53.

Quantum Science Corp. *MAPTREK Economic Services.* New York: Quantrum Science Corp., 1968.

Rapoport, L. T., and Drews, W. P. "Mathematical Approach to Long Range Planning." *Harvard Business Review* 40, 3 (May 1962), pp. 75–87.

Rapping, Leonard. "Learning and World War II Production Functions." *Review of Economic and Statistics* (Feb. 1965), pp. 81–86.

Rasmusen, H. J. "Multilevel Planning with Conflicting Objectives." *Swedish Journal of Economics* (June 1974), p. 155.

Reich, Robert B. *The Next American Frontier.* New York: Times Books, 1983.

Rhenman, E. *Organization Theory for Long Range Planning.* New York: Wiley, 1972.

Rogers, Rolf E. *Corporate Strategy and Planning.* Columbus, Ohio: Grid Pub. Co., 1981.

Roper, D. A. "Planning Developments in British Nuclear Fuels, Ltd." *Long Range Planning* (Oct. 1978), p. 32.

Rosen, Stephen. "The Future from the Top: Presidential Perspective on

Planning." *Long Range Planning* (Apr. 1974), p. 2; (June 1974), p. 34; (Aug. 1974), p. 73.

Rosenkranz, F. *An Introduction to Corporate Modeling.* Durham, N.C.: Duke University Press, 1979.

Ross, Steven S. *Business Week's Guide to Careers.* New York: McGraw-Hill, 1983.

Rothschild, William E. *Putting It All Together: A Guide to Strategic Thinking* New York: AMACOM, 1976.

Rue, L. W. "Tools and Techniques of Long Range Planners." *Long Range Planning* (Oct. 1974), p. 61.

Russell, J. R.; Stobaugh, R. B.; and Whitmeyer, F. W. "Simulation for Production." *Harvard Business Review* 45 (Sept. 1967), pp. 162–70.

Saaty, T. L. "Measuring the Fuzziness of Sets," *Journal of Cybernetics* (1974), pp. 4, 53–61.

Saaty, T. L. "A Scaling Method for Priorities in Hierarchical Structures." *Journal of Mathematical Psychology* (1977), pp. 15, 234–81.

Saaty, T. L. "Exploring the Interfaces between Hierarchies, Multiple Objects, and Fuzzy Sets." In D. J. Dubois and H. Prade, eds., *Fuzzy Sets and Systems.* New York: Academic Press, 1980.

Sackman, H. *Delphi Critique-Expert Opinion, Forecasting and Group Process.* Farnborough: Lexington and Heath, 1975.

Sawyer, George C. *Corporate Planning as a Creative Process.* Oxford, Ohio: Planning Executives Institute, 1983.

Schellenberger, R. E., and Boseman, G. *Policy Formulation and Strategy Management.* New York: Wiley, 1982.

Schendel, Dan E., and Hofer. Chares W., eds. *Strategic Management: A New View of Business Policy and Planning.* Boston, Mass.: Little, Brown, 1979.

Schendel, Dan, et al. "Corporate Turnaround Strategies—A Study of Profit Decline and Recovery." *Journal of General Management* (Spring 1976), p. 3.

Scherer, C. R., and Joe, L. "Electric Power System Planning with Explicit Stochastic Reserves Constraints." *Management Science* (May 1977), p. 978.

Schlaifer, Robert. *Analysis of Decisions Under Uncertainty.* New York: McGraw-Hill, 1969.

Schnaible, S. "Fractional Programming." *Management Science* (April 1976), p. 858.

Schoeffler, Sidney. "COPE Team Tells How PIMS Academic-Business Search for Basic Principles Can Get Line Managers into Strategic Planning." *Marketing News* (July 16, 1976), p. 6.

Schumer, Fern. "The New Magicians of Market Research." *Fortune* (July 25, 1983), pp. 72–74.

Scobel, Donald N. *Creative Worklife*. Houston, Tex.: Gulf Pub. Co., 1981.

Selecting and Evaluating a Decision Support System. San Jose, Calif.: EPS, Inc. 1982.

Shepard, William. "The Elements of Market Structure." *Review of Economics and Statistics*. (Feb. 1972), pp. 25–37.

Sherman, Philip M. *Strategic Planning for Technology Industries*. Reading, Mass.: Addison–Wesley, 1982.

Shostak, R. and Eddy, C. "Computer Graphics." *Harvard Business Review* (Nov. 1971), p. 52.

Shuman, J. C. "Corporate Planning in Small Companies—A Survey." *Long Range Planning* (Oct. 1974), p. 81.

Simon, H. A. "The Architecture of Complexity." *Proceedings of the American Philosophical Society*. 106 (Dec. 1962), pp. 476–82.

Simon, H. A. "The Structure of Ill-structured Problems." *Artificial Intelligence* 4 (1973), pp. 181–201.

Smith, Randall. "For Sale: Corporate Phone Books." *Wall Street Journal*, July 14, 1983.

"The Stalled Soviet Economy—Bogged Down by Planning." *Business Week* (Oct. 19, 1981), p. 72.

Stander, A., and Rickards, T. "The Oracle That Failed." *Long Range Planning* (Oct. 1975), p. 13.

Steiner, George A. *Top Management Planning*. New York: Macmillan, 1969.

Steiner, George A. "Contingency Theories for Strategy." In Schendel and Hofer, eds., *Strategic Management*, p. 405.

Steiner, George A. *Strategic Planning*. New York: Free Press, 1979.

Steiner, George A., and Miner, John B. *Management Policy and Strategy*. 2d ed. New York: Macmillan, 1982.

Steuer, R. E. "Multiple Objective Linear Programming with Interval Criterion Weights." *Management Science* (Nov. 1976), p. 305.

Stevenson, H. H. "Defining Corporate Strengths and Weaknesses." *Sloan Management Review* (Spring 1976), p. 51.

Stobaugh, R. B. "Where Should We Put That Plant?" *Harvard Business Review* (Jan. 1969), p. 129.

Taylor, Bernard. "Strategies for Planning." *Long Range Planning* (Aug. 1975), p. 27.

Taylor, Bernard, and Hussey, David. *The Realities of Planning*. Oxford: Pergamon Press, 1982.

A Technological Assessment Methodology, vols. 1–7. National Technical Information Service, U.S. Dept. of Commerce, 1971.

Tersine, R. J. "Forecasting: Prelude to Managerial Planning." *Managerial Planning* (July 1975), p. 11.

Thomas, J. "Linear Programming Models for Production Advertising Decisions." *Management Science* (Apr. 1971), p. B474.

Thomas, P. S. "Environmental Analysis for Corporate Planning." *Business Horizons* (Oct. 1974), p. 27.

Thompson, A. A., and Strickland, A. J. *Strategy and Policy: Concepts and Cases.* Plano, Tex.: Business Pubns., 1981.

Thorelli, Hans B., ed., *Strategy + Structure = Performance, The Strategic Planning Imperative.* Bloomington: Indiana Univ. 1977.

Thune, S. S., and House, R. S. "Where Long Range Planning Pays Off." *Business Horizons* (Aug. 1976).

Thurston, P. H. "Make Technological Forecasting Serve Corporate Planning." *Harvard Business Review* (Sept. 1971), p. 98.

Tipgos, M. A. "Structuring a Management Information System for Strategic Planning." *Managerial Planning* (Jan. 1975), p. 10.

Toffler, Alvin. *The Futurists.* New York: Random House, 1972.

Tyson, W. J., and Cochrane, R. C. D. "Corporate Planning and Project Evaluation in Urban Transport." *Long Range Planning* (Oct. 1981), p. 62.

U.S. Department of Labor. Bureau of Labor Statistics. *Capital Flow Matrix.* BLS Bulletin No. 1601. Washington, D.C.: U.S. Government Printing Office, 1968.

Utterback, J. M. "Environmental Analysis and Forecasting." In Schendel and Hofer, eds., *Strategic Management,* p. 134.

Uyterhoeven, H. E. R.; Ackerman, R. W.; and Rosenblum, J. W. *Strategy and Organization.* Homewood, Ill.: Irwin, 1977.

Vancil, R. F., and Lorange, P. "Strategic Planning in Diversified Companies." *Harvard Business Review* (Jan. 1975), p. 81.

Van Dam, Andre. "Taxonomy." *Planning Review* (Nov. 1975), p. 20.

Vandorffy, J. "Mathematical Models in National Planning." *Long Range Planning* (Mar. 1973), p. 42.

Van Over, Raymond. "Altered States of Consciousness: Creative Alternatives in Decision Making." *Planning Review* (July 1975), p. 24.

Wacht, R. F. "A Long Range Financial Planning Technique for Non-Profit Organizations." *Atlanta Economic Review* (Sept. 1976), p. 22.

Waddel, R., et al. *Capacity Expansion Planning Factors.* Washington, D.C.: National Planning Association, 1966.

Wagle, B. V.; Goat, R. C.; Boot, P.; Jones, G. T.; Longbottom, D. A.; and

Jenkins, P. M. *The Development of a General System to Aid the Corporate Planning Process—A Feasibility Study.* IBM (U.K.) Report, 1970.

Waller, R. A. "Assessing the Impact of Technology on the Environment." *Long Range Planning* (Feb. 1975), p. 43.

Walters, A.; Mangold, J.; and Haran, E. G. P. "Comprehensive Planning Model for Long Range Academic Strategies." *Management Science* (Mar. 1976), p. 727.

Wasdell, David. "Long Range Planning and the Church." *Long Range Planning* (June, 1980), p. 99–108.

Watt, KEF *The Titanic Effect: Planning for the Unthinkable.* London: Freeman, 1974.

Weir, G. A. "Developing Strategies: A Practical Approach." *Long Range Planning* (Oct. 1974), p. 7.

Wilson, A. C. B. "Human and Organization Problems in Corporate Planning." *Long Range Planning* (Mar. 1972), p. 67.

Wood, D. Robley, Jr. "Comprehensive Planning at a Multi-National Bank." *Planning Review* (Jan. 1981), p. 27.

Wood, M. K. "Sequential Economic Programming." In Kendall, ed., *Mathematical Model Building.* 2d series. p. 41.

Wortman, M. S. "Strategic Management: Not-For-Profit Organizations." In Schendel and Hofer, eds. *Strategic Management,* p. 353.

Yavitz, Boris, and Newman, William. *Strategy in Action.* New York: Free Press, 1982.

Zentner, R. D. "Scenarios in Forecasting." *Chemical Engineering News* (Oct. 6, 1975), p. 22.

Zetterman, L. "Financial Issues in Strategic Planning." *Long Range Planning* (June 1975), p. 23.

Index

About the Author

Clark Holloway received the B.S. degree in chemical engineering from Purdue University in 1937, the M.S. degree from the University of Illinois in 1938, and, following thirty-six years in industry, the Ph.D. degree in business administration from the University of Pittsburgh in 1981. He joined the University of South Carolina Business Administration faculty in 1979 after teaching briefly at Point Park College and at the University of Pittsburgh.

Dr. Holloway is the author of many engineering and statistics publications. Currently his teaching and research interests are in the areas of strategic planning and business policy. He is the author or coauthor of a number of articles on planning: "Mechanization of Policy Decisions," 1983; "Strategic Management and Artificial Intelligence," 1983; "Computer Assisted Strategic Planning," 1982; "Evaluating Alternative Approaches to Strategic Planning," 1979; "Does Future Research Have a Corporate Role?" 1978; "Using the Computer in Planning," 1976; "The Significance of Planning," 1975; "Planning at Gulf—A Case Study," 1975; and "Developing Planning Models," 1974. He is a member of the North American Society for Corporate Planning, the Society for Long-Range Planning, the Business Policy and Planning Section of the Academy of Management, and of many other professional societies.

Dr. Holloway spent ten years with Gulf Oil in London as senior advisor on planning systems and member of Gulf's European Planning Council. He consulted and advised on management science, management information, and operations research problems throughout Europe. He was also member of a task force on increasing corporate profitability in Europe and was founder and manager of a management science department. While with Gulf Research and Development Company in Pittsburgh, he was manager of Gulf's major computer installation. Earlier, he was an engineering economist, conducting economic and statistical studies. Coal hydrogenation evaluations were made for the National Petroleum Council. Studies on octane number blending and on computer information retrieval were done for the American Petroleum Institute. Still earlier, he supervised about forty engineers and technicians in pilot plant research.